*Pitt Latin American Series*

# THE ECONOMICS OF
# CUBAN SUGAR

•

JORGE F. PÉREZ-LÓPEZ

UNIVERSITY OF PITTSBURGH PRESS

Published by the University of Pittsburgh Press, Pittsburgh, Pa., 15260
Copyright © 1991, University of Pittsburgh Press
All rights reserved
Baker & Taylor International, London
Manufactured in the United States of America

Library of Congress Cataloging-in-Publication Data

Pérez-López, Jorge F.
  The economics of Cuban sugar / Jorge F. Pérez-López.
    p.  cm. — (Pitt Latin American series)
  Includes bibliographical references and index.
  ISBN 0-8229-3663-1
  1. Sugar trade—Cuba.  2. Sugarcane industry—Cuba.  I. Title.
II. Series.
HD9114.C89P39  1991
338.1′7361′097291—dc20                         90-40875
                                                  CIP

*To Kathleen*

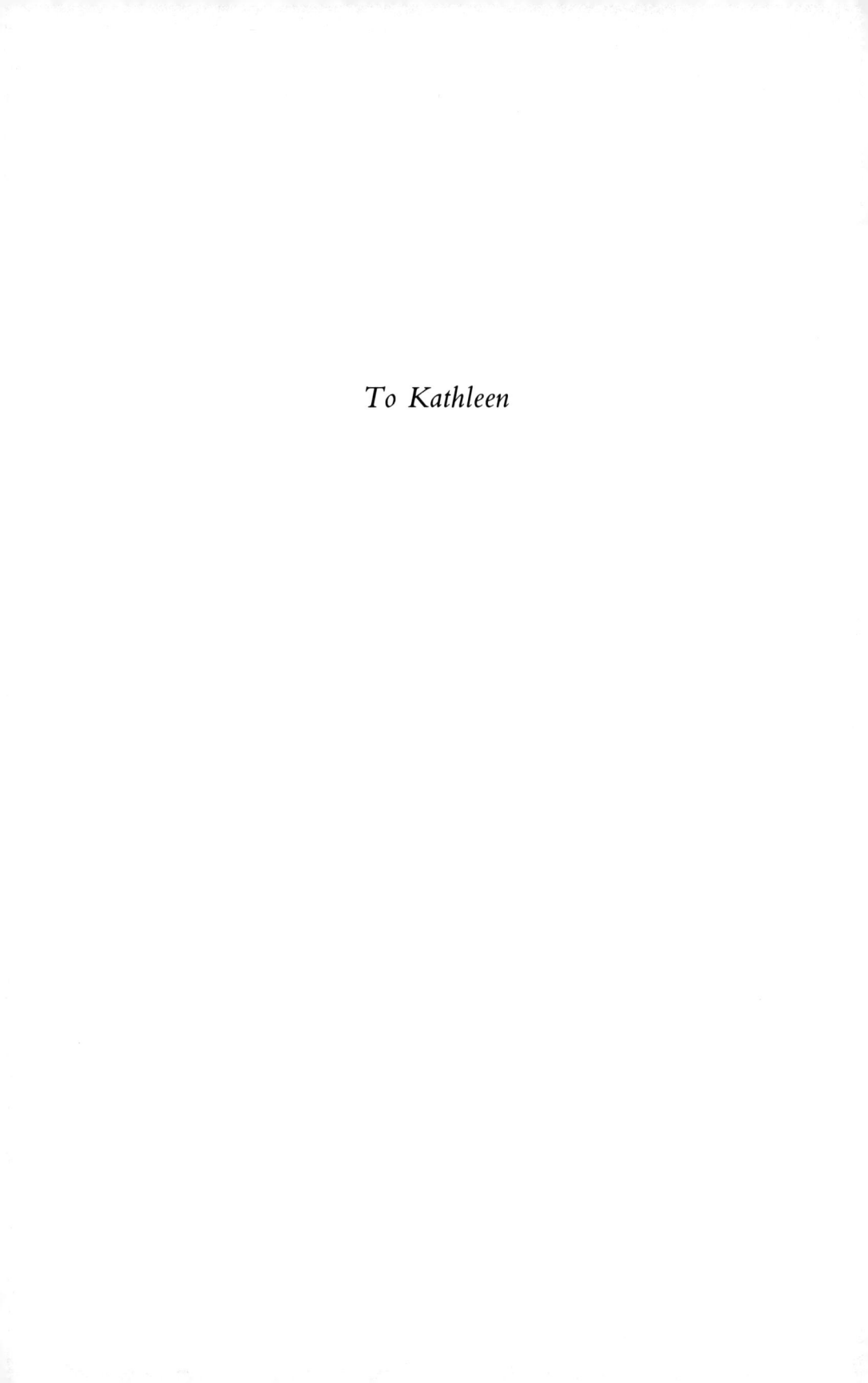

# CONTENTS

•

TABLES AND FIGURES ix

PREFACE xiii

| | | |
|---|---|---|
| 1 | Sugar and Development Strategies | 3 |
| 2 | Agriculture | 20 |
| 3 | Industry | 37 |
| 4 | Labor and Agricultural Mechanization | 56 |
| 5 | Energy and Transportation | 78 |
| 6 | Refined Sugar and Sugarcane Derivatives | 92 |
| 7 | Production Costs | 111 |
| 8 | Foreign Trade | 121 |
| 9 | Subsidies in Cuban-Soviet Sugar Trade | 157 |
| 10 | International Cooperation | 173 |
| 11 | Assistance to Third World Nations | 189 |
| 12 | Sugar and the Economy | 199 |

APPENDIXES 233

REFERENCES 275

INDEX 307

# TABLES AND FIGURES

•

## TABLES

| | |
|---|---|
| 1 | Agricultural Production Cooperatives, Total and Sugarcane, 1979–1987   24 |
| 2 | Sugarcane Production, 1952–1987   26 |
| 3 | Sugarcane Yields, 1952–1987   30 |
| 4 | Sugarcane Yields, State and Nonstate Sectors, by Province, 1977–1981, and 1986   32 |
| 5 | Gross Value of Output of Agriculture and of Sugarcane Production, 1962–1987   35 |
| 6 | Sugar Sector Investment Plan, 1965–1969   41 |
| 7 | Distribution of Investment by Branches of the Industrial Sector, 1975–1987   44 |
| 8 | Sugar Industry Performance, 1951–1987   49 |
| 9 | Distribution of Gross Industrial Output by Branches of the Industrial Sector, 1975–1987   54 |
| 10 | Cane Cutters Deployed in Selected *Zafras,* 1963–1985   60 |
| 11 | Selected Labor Indicators for Sugarcane Agriculture, 1980–1987   62 |
| 12 | Sugarcane Mechanization and Yields, 1962–1988   68 |
| 13 | Labor Savings Associated with Sugarcane Harvest Mechanization, 1958–1985   70 |

| | | |
|---|---|---|
| 14 | Employment in Sugar Industrial Operations, 1975–1987 | 75 |
| 15 | Bagasse in Domestic Energy Supply, 1959–1987 | 80 |
| 16 | Sugarcane Milled, Estimated Bagasse Production, and Bagasse for Industrial Use, 1972–1987 | 81 |
| 17 | Fuel Oil Consumption in Sugar Mills, 1965–1984 | 85 |
| 18 | Rolling Stock of the Railroad System, 1987 | 88 |
| 19 | Production of Refined Sugar, 1960–1987 | 95 |
| 20 | Selected Indicators of the Sugar Refining Industry, 1978–1987 | 96 |
| 21 | Domestic Consumption of Refined Sugar, 1965–1987 | 98 |
| 22 | Sugarcane Derivatives | 102 |
| 23 | Production of Selected Sugarcane Derivatives, 1970–1987 | 104 |
| 24 | Sugar Production Costs, 1939 and 1949 | 112 |
| 25 | World Sugar Production Costs, 1979/80 to 1982/83 | 119 |
| 26 | World Sugar Production and Trade, 1954–1987 | 123 |
| 27 | Size of the World Sugar Market | 124 |
| 28 | Prices in the World Sugar Market, 1950–1988 | 126 |
| 29 | Cuban Sugar Exports by Destination, 1954–1987 | 128 |
| 30 | Tariff Treatment of Cuban Sugar in the U.S. Market | 130 |
| 31 | Cuba-U.S. Sugar Trade, 1934–1960 | 136 |
| 32 | Prices in Cuban-Soviet Sugar Trade and in Other Markets | 140 |
| 33 | Cuban-Soviet Sugar Trade, 1965–1970 | 143 |
| 34 | Contract Price of Cuban Sugar Exports, 1971–1982 | 147 |

*Tables and Figures*    *xi*

35  Unit Values of Soviet Sugar Imports from Cuba and of Cuban Crude Oil Imports from the Soviet Union, 1971–1987    148

36  Cuban Participation in the World Sugar Market, 1971–1987    153

37  Sugar Production, Consumption, and Net Exports, 1950–1987    155

38  Unit Value of Soviet Sugar Imports from All Sources, 1971–1987    160

39  Estimates of Soviet Sugar Price Subsidies, 1960–1987    170

40  Sugar Production Restrictions, 1920–1958    175

41  Cuba and International Sugar Agreements, 1930–1984    178

42  Area under Sugarcane Cultivation    205

43  Area under Cultivation for Selected Crops    206

44  Food Imports, 1970–1987    207

45  Production and Imports of Food Products for Selected Periods, 1961–1987    209

46  Export Concentration Indexes    212

47  Sugar Export Shares Based on Total Exports and Nonfuel Exports, 1975–1987    213

48  Sugar Exports as a Share of Nonfuel Exports, 1962–1987    215

49  Instability Indexes in Monthly Market Prices for Selected Primary Commodities    219

50  Soviet Union and PRC Sugar Exports, 1960–1987    223

51  Commercial Raw Sugar Production, *Zafra* Compared to Calendar Year, 1971–1987    237

## FIGURES

1 Sugar World Market Prices  127
2 Cuban Sugar Exports by Destination  129
3 Prices in Cuban-Soviet Sugar Trade  151

# PREFACE

•

SINCE THE END of the sixteenth century, sugar and the Cuban economy have been linked. For generations the health of the economy could be gauged on the basis of the price of sugar in the world market. So critical was the behavior of world market prices of sugar to the standard of living of the average Cuban that terms related to those prices made their way into the popular language. When prices were up, it was *vacas gordas,* a time of relative prosperity; when they were down, it was *vacas flacas,* a time for belt-tightening. When they were extremely high, a rare occurrence, it was party time, for example, during the short-lived *danza de los millones* of 1920.

The historical context of the link between sugar and the Cuban economy has been enriched in the last twenty-five years by the publication of a number of important books, monographs, and articles. Three of these works stand out for their originality, thoroughness, and reliance on primary information.

Volume 1 of Moreno Fraginals's multivolume treatise (1978) tells the fascinating story of the development of the Cuban sugar sector using the sugar mill as the focal point. Volume 2 places Cuban sugar developments in an international context, while volume 3 contains, to my knowledge, the most complete set of historical statistics on Cuban sugar production and foreign trade. Marrero's monumental economic history of Cuba (1975– ), still in progress, traces the history of sugarcane cultivation since the crop was introduced into Cuba in the first half of the sixteenth century. It is clear from both of these works that, by the middle of the nineteenth century, sugar had firmly established its position as Cuba's premier export commodity and that the United States had become Cuba's primary sugar market.

A different but complementary contribution is Ely's (1963). The scope of his work is narrower, concentrating on the development of the Cuban sugar sector from 1833 to 1868 through the papers of sugar magnate Moses Taylor. The expansion of the Cuban sugar sector during the second half of the nineteenth century was undoubtedly the result of Cuba's status as a low-cost producer, a factor only partially attributable to slavery. It has been shown (Turu 1981) that in Cuba, unit labor costs of sugar production—which take into account compensation and productivity—were not significantly different for sugar produced by slaves or by free workers.

Several more recent works (L. Pérez 1978, 1980; Pollitt 1984; Scott 1985a; 1985b) explore class conflicts in Cuba in the nineteenth and twentieth centuries and the role played by sugar interests, while others trace the development of Cuban economic thought under the influence of a sugar export mentality (Alvarez Díaz et al. 1964, 279–300). Finally, a substantial body of literature has emerged that examines the implications for the Cuban economy of the development of a sugar industry heavily influenced by foreign capital (mainly from the United States) (Benítez 1970; 1977; López Segrera 1981; L. Pérez 1983; Pino Santos 1975; 1980).

Despite the importance of the sugar sector for the economy of contemporary Cuba—and for world sugar trade, as Cuba continues to be the world's largest raw sugar exporter—there is no current, comprehensive study on the economics of Cuban sugar. To be sure, over the last twenty-five years scholars inside and outside Cuba have written on specific aspects of sugar production and trade, but these contributions are partial and either out of date or not widely accessible to researchers and students. Among significant contributions by Cuban scholars and analysts are those of Charadán López (1982), Fernández Font (1986) and Silva León (1971). In addition, there is a plethora of information on microeconomic aspects of sugar production and trade scattered in Cuban journals and other publications. Examples of important contributions by scholars outside Cuba are works by Brunner (1977), Edquist (1985), Hagelberg (1979), and Roca (1976).

My objective in this volume is twofold: to survey the economics of Cuban sugar, including production, trade, and diplomacy; and to explore the influence of sugar on the Cuban economy and the extent to which this relationship might have changed over time. The emphasis is on contemporary Cuba, that is, roughly the last three decades, or the period during which the revolutionary regime has been in power. Relevant information regarding prerevolutionary Cuba is also presented, where appropriate, to place contemporary events and policies in historical perspective. The approach is quantitative but descriptive. The discussion relies on statistical information gathered from a variety of sources; these data are presented in tables in the text and in appendixes. Issues related to the availability and reliability of official Cuban statistics on the sugar sector are discussed in an appendix.

At the risk of stating the obvious, I must emphasize that what I have been able to discern, or have not been able to discern, about sugar and the Cuban economy is largely determined by my situation as an outside observer. There is no doubt that Cuban officials with responsibility for sugar production or export have access to statistics, memoranda, and internal studies that clarify many aspects that are ambiguous to those who have to rely on the open literature. My hope is that this book will stimulate additional research to fill some of the gaps in data and analysis, thereby enhancing the common understanding of the economics of sugar in contemporary Cuba.

The volume is divided into twelve chapters. Chapter 1 describes economic policies of the Cuban revolutionary government, with special emphasis on the role reserved within these policies for sugar production and trade. Chapters 2–5 deal systematically with the microeconomics of Cuban sugar production: agriculture (chapter 2), industry (chapter 3), labor and agricultural mechanization (chapter 4), and energy and transportation (chapter 5). Chapter 6 is devoted to refined sugar and sugarcane derivatives, two areas likely to become more important in the future as Cuba attempts to increase the range of products produced from sugarcane. The very sketchy information on costs of sugar production in Cuba is discussed in chapter 7.

While chapters 2–7 address primarily internal, microeconomic issues, the next four look into external relationships. Chapter 8 presents an overview of international sugar trade and of markets for Cuban sugar exports, including preferential markets. The issue of subsidies related to sugar trade between Cuba and the Soviet Union is discussed in considerable detail in chapter 9; several estimates of the magnitude of the subsidy are presented in that chapter. Chapters 10 and 11 deal with aspects of Cuba's sugar diplomacy. Cuba's sugar-related activities in multilateral fora, such as the negotiation of price stabilization agreements, are discussed in chapter 10. Bilateral relations, in the form of technical assistance to Third World nations in developing their sugar industries, are the subject of chapter 11.

Chapter 12 wrestles with the critical, and very difficult, question of structural change in the Cuban economy. To what extent have policies of the revolutionary government changed the fundamental monoculture that characterized the economy of prerevolutionary Cuba? Attempts to address this question using the economist's standard tools lead into a statistical maze. Using a variety of indicators, I conclude in chapter 12 that Cuba has been slow to restructure its economy away from sugar and that sugar production continues to occupy a prominent role in the economy.

The body of literature that deals with some aspect of the economics of Cuban sugar is voluminous. In addition to the works mentioned above, I relied heavily on the following Cuban journals as sources of information and data:

- *CubaAzúcar,* bimonthly publication of the Ministry of the Sugar Industry (Ministerio de la Industria Azucarera, MINAZ). Publication started in January 1966.
- *ATAC,* bimonthly publication of the Cuban Sugar Technicians' Association (Asociación de Técnicos Azucareros de Cuba). Publication (in the current format) began in 1962.
- *Sobre los Derivados de la Caña de Azúcar,* the organ of the Cuban Institute for Research on Sugarcane Derivatives (Instituto Cubano de Investigaciones de los Derivados de la Caña de Azúcar [ICIDCA]). Publication of the journal began in 1967; it is published three times per year.

Technical journals, such as *Boletín INICA,* published four times per year by the National Institute for Sugarcane Research (Instituto Nacional de Investigaciones de la Caña de Azúcar), were used as appropriate.

In addition, articles dealing with economic aspects of sugar production and trade appear frequently in the bimonthly journal *Economía y Desarrollo,* published since 1970 by the Economics Institute (Instituto de Economía) at Havana University. Several other journals, whose publication was terminated during the mid 1960s, also carried articles on sugar with significant economic content: *Cuba Socialista* (old series), *Nuestra Industria. Revista Económica,* and, to a lesser extent, *Comercio Exterior.* Journals of more recent vintage containing relevant materials include *Cuba Socialista* (new series), *Revista Estadística, Cuestiones de la Economía Planificada,* and *Temas de Economía Mundial.*

Though the bulk of the materials on which I have based my research originates in Cuba, I have also made extensive use of materials published elsewhere. The most coherent and comprehensive treatment of the economy of prerevolutionary Cuba, including sugar production and trade, is the massive volume produced in the early 1960s in the United States by the Cuban Economic Research Project

(Grupo Cubano 1963; CERP 1965b). On certain topics the literature produced outside Cuba is particularly rich. This is the case, for example, in the areas of sugarcane mechanization (Edquist 1985; Pollitt 1982a), sugar policies (Brunner 1977; Hagelberg 1979; Roca 1976), international sugar agreements (I. Smith 1983), and aspects of sugar trade with the Soviet Union (Domínguez 1989; Mesa-Lago and Gil 1989; Radell 1983; Zimbalist 1982). With regard to world sugar production and trade, I have relied heavily on analyses by international sugar experts (e.g., Brown 1987; Fry 1985) and on statistics published by the International Sugar Organization (ISO 1949–88).

As a student of the Cuban economy, I have had a long-term interest in the economics of Cuban sugar. The development of that general interest into this specific volume had its roots in an invitation by Jorge I. Domínguez in early 1986 that I participate in a panel dealing with the scholarly study of Cuba that he and Nelson P. Valdés were organizing for the Thirteenth International Congress of the Latin American Studies Association (LASA). The intent of the organizers was to bring together an interdisciplinary panel of researchers on Cuba each of whom would assess the state of scholarship in a given subfield within his or her discipline. As we discussed potential subfields that might be of interest to me, and to the LASA audience, the notion of surveying economic aspects of the sugar sector emerged as the choice.

At the Thirteenth International Congress of LASA in October 1986, I presented preliminary results of my work, focusing only on sugar trade with the Soviet Union and the issue of trade subsidies. Subsequently I expanded the survey to cover other areas, including the microeconomics of sugar production and sugar policies and their effects. In the fall of 1987 a preliminary version of the larger survey appeared under the title *Sugar and the Cuban Economy: An Assessment* as a working paper published by the Research Institute for Cuban Studies, Graduate School of International Studies, University of Miami. Early versions of my treatment of two specific topics in this book have appeared as journal articles: the discussion on sugar trade with the Soviet Union as "Cuban-Soviet Sugar Trade: Price and Subsidies Issues" in *Bulletin of Latin American Research* (1988); and on sugar policies and their effects as "Sugar and Structural Change in the Cuban Economy" in *World Development* (1989).

In researching this volume I have been fortunate to be able to draw on the excellent collection of Cuban materials at the Library of

Congress. Bruce Sherman, director of the Information Center, Radio Martí Program, United States Information Agency, and César Rodríguez, Yale University Library, helped me in obtaining some hard-to-get materials. I appreciate very much their assistance.

I am in debt to a number of dedicated colleagues who read parts of the manuscript and took the time to make detailed comments and constructive suggestions. First, I am grateful to Jorge I. Domínguez for urging me to work in this area, for his help in conceptualizing the study, and for his detailed comments on very early drafts. José F. Alonso, Carmelo Mesa-Lago, and Andrew Zimbalist reviewed and commented on parts of the study; James Fry and G. B. Hagelberg did the same from their vantage point as experts on international sugar issues. My heartfelt thanks to all for their generosity with their time and constructive criticisms and suggestions.

The research that underlies the discussion of Cuban assistance to sugar industries in the Third World (chapter 11) is part of a broader investigation of Cuban civilian internationalism that I have undertaken jointly with Sergio Díaz-Briquets, which is still in progress. I appreciate being able to use part of those materials in this volume. Finally, I am also grateful to Jaime Suchlicki of the University of Miami for providing me with encouragement to complete what appeared to be a never-ending project and for allowing me to use the working paper series of the Research Institute for Cuban Studies to circulate preliminary views.

# THE ECONOMICS OF
# CUBAN SUGAR

# CHAPTER 1

•

## Sugar and Development Strategies

THROUGH THE first half of the eighteenth century, sugar production in Cuba was relegated to small-scale enterprises and was secondary in importance to other economic activities such as tobacco growing, forestry, the raising of livestock, and shipbuilding (Marrero 1984, 10:135–272; Moreno Fraginals 1978, 1:15–102). In the second half of that century and the first half of the nineteenth century, however, growing demand for sugar from Europe, coupled with very limited growth in output from traditional sugar producers—primarily small Caribbean nations—made sugar production and export profitable and greatly stimulated the expansion of the Cuban industry.

By the middle of the nineteenth century, Cuba was already firmly established as a world-class sugar producer and exporter. In the 1860s, for example, the Cuban sugar industry turned out over one-quarter of world sugar output and one-third of sugar produced from sugarcane (Moreno Fraginals 1978, 3:37). Exports grew very rapidly—from about 5,000 tons in 1760 to about 500,000 tons in the 1860s (ibid. 3:43–44)—and established the sugar industry as the premier earner of foreign exchange. (Unless otherwise noted, all references are to metric tons of 1,000 kilograms.) Moreover, despite the colonial relationship, as early as the 1820s, Cuba's most important sugar market was the United States rather than Spain. In the 1860s, for example, Cuba exported ten times as much sugar to the United States as it did to Spain.

The phenomenal expansion of the Cuban sugar sector over the second half of the eighteenth and the first half of the nineteenth centuries had its roots in foreign demand. As the sugar industry expanded, so did its political clout in Cuba. A severe tension existed between those who supported the industry and its expansion and those who favored lessening the importance of sugar and diversifying the economy. This ongoing debate took on nationalistic overtones as the sugar industry—as an industry created to service foreign demand—was subject to the vagaries of foreign markets and to the whim of foreign purchasers.

Economic development strategies have shaped the role of the sugar industry in the Cuban economy. Typical of the love-hate relationship Cubans have traditionally enjoyed vis-à-vis sugar, the treatment of the industry in development policies has ranged from neglecting it to singling it out as the engine in an agriculture-led growth strategy.

This chapter briefly reviews economic development strategies pursued by Cuban governments in the twentieth century and highlights the role played by the sugar sector. While the emphasis is on the post-1959 period, an overview of development strategies in prerevolutionary Cuba is also presented to provide a historical context within which to analyze more contemporary developments. The rest of the book examines the effects of these overall strategies on specific aspects of the sugar sector.

## Prerevolutionary Cuba's Development Strategies

The first two decades of the Cuban republic saw a vigorous expansion of the sugar industry and an acceleration in the fusion between the Cuban and U.S. economies. The Reciprocity Agreement, signed in 1902, granted tariff preferences to Cuban sugar, tobacco, minerals, and other products in the U.S. market, but also improved the access of U.S. agricultural and manufactured products to the Cuban market. Foreign investment—primarily U.S. capital—flowed freely into the Cuban economy, principally into the sugar sector.

Sugar production expanded strongly. In 1903, Cuba produced slightly over 1 million tons of sugar, only the third time the domestic industry had reached that mark (previous such peaks occurred in 1892 and 1894). Annual production exceeded 2 million tons of sugar in 1913 and 3 million tons in 1916. In 1919–20, Cuba produced about 4 million tons per annum, a quadrupling of production in less than two decades. Production exceeded 5 million tons per annum in 1925 and 1926. Sugar exports to the United States grew from about 900,000 tons in 1903 to over 2.6 million tons in 1919–20 and to a record high 3.5 million tons in 1925.

This was also a period of economic prosperity in Cuba. Population doubled, monetary income quadrupled, and real per capita income grew from 176 pesos in 1903 to 293 pesos in 1924 (CERP 1965b, 290–91). Not only was the domestic labor force fully employed, but between 1902 and 1931 the country permanently absorbed over 1.2 million immigrant laborers from Spain, the United States, Haiti, Jamaica, the British Antilles, and China (Mesa-Lago 1972, 9–10). The income generated by exports—primarily sugar—greatly increased the capacity to import and gave rise to an economic boom.

The outbreak of World War I in 1914, and the threat the war posed to the European sugar industry, pushed world market prices to record levels and stimulated further expansions in Cuban sugar production capabilities. (Between 1921 and 1927, eleven new sugar mills were completed; sugar industrial capacity would not expand again for over fifty years.) With the recovery of the European industry after the end of the war, world market prices plunged, and chaos swept Cuba. National banking institutions, which had been created during the expansionary period—primarily to provide funds for the sugar industry—became insolvent when sugar enterprises could not meet their obligations. Foreign banks, backed by resources from abroad, took over bankrupt sugar enterprises and wound up controlling a substantial share of the island's productive resources.

Through the Tarafa Act of 1926, the Cuban government began its futile attempts to stabilize international sugar prices by reducing domestic production and exports. This policy of supply management (discussed in more detail in chapter 10) was largely unsuccessful because neither unilateral nor multilateral restrictions could effectively limit world sugar supply and strengthen prices, except during exceptional periods. Cuba's policies of limiting domestic sugar production—which were adopted by every Cuban government before the revolutionary government that took power in 1959—translated into severe underutilization of resources (agricultural land, industrial plant, human resources) and stagnation of the sugar sector.

The Import Tariff (Arancel de Aduana) of 1927 attempted to lessen sugar's dominance over the economy. It offered some tariff protection to agricultural and industrial producers and encouraged the establishment of new enterprises. This protection stimulated domestic production of agricultural products such as coffee, beef, and corn and of consumer goods such as vegetable oils, crackers, canned fruits and vegetables, dairy products, and beverages (Grupo Cubano 1963, 705–12). Coming on the heels of government actions to restrict sugar output, the 1927 tariff also signaled government intervention in favor of industrialization and economic diversification away from sugar.

An economic crisis—triggered by very low international sugar prices, further reductions in Cuba's sugar production and exports resulting from adherence to the Chadbourne plan, passage of the U.S. Smoot-Hawley Tariff Act, and the Great Depression—and severe political unrest were serious obstacles to the success of the economic diversification envisioned by the 1927 tariff. The significance of the Smoot-Hawley Act and the Chadbourne plan is discussed in chapter 10.

Despite international efforts to prop up world sugar prices (such as the so-called Chadbourne agreement, through which Cuba cut back further on sugar production and exports), world market prices reached abysmally low levels in 1932 and 1933, well below the cost of production. Cuban sugar production in 1931 was only 3.2 million tons, 34 percent lower than the 4.9 million tons produced in 1930; production in 1932–33 averaged under 2.4 million tons. Also having an adverse impact on the world sugar market was the 1930 Smoot-Hawley Tariff Act, which increased U.S. sugar import duties from 2.2 to 2.5 cents/pound; for Cuban sugar imports, which received preferential treatment in the U.S. market by virtue of the Reciprocity Agreement of 1902, the rate was increased from 1.76 to 2.00 cents/pound. While the Cuban economy was in crisis, political unrest ran rampant. In 1933 the unpopular Machado government was overthrown and replaced with successive governments that instituted important social and economic reforms. Significant legislation was passed in the areas of minimum wages, length of the work day, and the nationalization of employment (for example, a 1933 law that provided that at least 50 percent of employees in every business or industry had to be Cuban nationals, that at least 50 percent of total salaries and wages had to be paid to Cubans, and that gave preferential treatment to Cuban nationals in hirings and dismissals).

The 1934 Jones-Costigan Act, which changed the U.S. sugar import regime to one based on a system of quotas, had a favorable impact on Cuba's sugar export prices, but the industry continued to stagnate. Production averaged under 3 million tons per annum for 1934–41. Also in 1934, Cuba and the United States entered into a new bilateral agreement that reduced the tariff on Cuban sugar in the U.S. market. This agreement also granted tariff preferences to imports from the United States of products previously protected by the 1927 tariff. The 1934 pact was perceived by some (e.g., Le Riverend 1974, 635) as a step backward along the road toward industrial and agricultural diversification and political and economic independence from the United States.

The outbreak of World War II paralyzed European sugar production and allowed the Cuban sugar industry to recover some ground and produce at levels comparable to those of the 1920s. Sugar production climbed from 2.5 million tons in 1941 to 3.5 million tons in 1942, 4.4 million tons in 1944, 5.9 million tons in 1947, and 6.1 million tons in 1948.

The decline in international trade caused by war conditions increased Cuba's foreign exchange holdings and stimulated both the establishment of new industries and the expansion of others to meet the demand for products that had previously been imported. An additional incentive for the establishment of new industries was legislation passed in 1942 that exempted from import duties and taxes industries engaged in production in support of national defense or to meet domestic demand. In 1945 this statute was modified to exempt from duties and other charges all imported machinery, equipment, and raw materials used by "new" industries.

In the postwar period, government policies encouraged the expansion of the nonsugar industrial sector and the diversification of agricultural production. A host of government institutions was created to finance broad-based development and economic diversification, among them:

- Banco Nacional de Cuba (Cuban National Bank [BNC]), the first Cuban central bank, established in 1948, which began operations in 1950;
- Banco de Fomento Agrícola e Industrial de Cuba (Agricultural and Industrial Development Bank), created in 1951 to provide credit for the promotion of agricultural diversification and new industries;
- Fondo de Seguro de Crédito (Credit Insurance Fund), created in 1952 to promote the expansion of personal savings and to insure deposits against the risk of bankruptcy of commercial banks;
- Financiera Nacional de Cuba (National Finance Corporation), established in 1953 to finance self-liquidating public and quasi-public works and services projects;
- Banco Cubano del Comercio Exterior (Cuban Foreign Trade Bank), established in 1954 to coordinate and promote Cuban exports;
- Banco de Desarrollo Económico y Social (Economic and Social Development Bank), established in 1954 to provide credit for the promotion of social and economic development in general; and
- other institutions such as the Instituto Cubano de Investigaciones Tecnológicas (Cuban Institute for Technological Research) and the

Corporación de Fomento de Hipotecas Aseguradas (Mortgage Insurance Development Corporation).

The government further stimulated the creation of new industrial enterprises through the passage (in 1953) of a Law-Decree on Industrial Stimulation; pursuant to this law, fiscal and import tariff incentives were offered to investors who established new industries. Between 1953 and 1957, these incentives were instrumental in the establishment of 130 enterprises (CERP 1965c, 163) manufacturing a wide range of products including chemicals, herbicides, and aluminum and paper products.

The process of "Cubanization" of the economy, and in particular of the sugar industry, was accelerated during the 1940s and 1950s. In 1939, Cuban nationals owned 56 sugar mills (out of 174 in operation), producing 22.4 percent of total sugar output; in 1958 they owned 121 sugar mills (out of 161 in operation), producing 62.1 percent of total sugar output (AAC 1958, 87).

In the 1950s sugar production fluctuated severely, from an alltime high of nearly 7.3 million tons in 1952—when no production controls were in effect—to 4.6 million tons in 1954. Over the entire decade, production averaged over 5 million tons, the best sustained performance of the industry since the second half of the 1920s.

An empirical study of the growth of industrial activity from 1930 to 1958 (Pérez-López 1977) suggests that the Cuban industrial sector was not stagnant and, moreover, that some economic diversification away from sugar was occurring. According to estimates, overall Cuban industrial output grew at an average annual rate of 2.7 percent during 1930–58 and 4.7 percent in the postwar period (1946–58). Meanwhile, nonsugar industrial production grew at average annual rates of 4.9 and 5.7 percent, respectively, while sugar production stagnated (0.9 percent per annum growth rate) during 1930–58.

In 1949–58, a period for which fairly reliable national product statistics are available, the sugar sector generated on average 28–29 percent of gross national product (GNP); in 1957–58 sugar's contribution to GNP was around 25 percent, confirming that the nonsugar economy was expanding and the relative importance of sugar within the economy was declining (Mesa-Lago 1971, 278).

Nevertheless, the Cuban economy of the late 1950s faced a number of serious problems (Mesa-Lago 1971, 277): (1) relatively slow growth; (2) still excessive significance of sugar in the economy and in exports; (3) overwhelming dependence on the United States for capital inflows and trade; (4) high rates of unemployment and underemployment; and (5) wide differences in standards of living between urban and rural areas. These were the principal socioeconomic challenges the revolutionary government had to confront upon taking power on 1 January 1959.

## Revolutionary Cuba's Development Strategies

Prior to the revolutionary takeover, the Cuban economy was predominantly capitalistic. With some notable exceptions—for example, railroads—the means of production were owned by either domestic or foreign individuals or corporations. Soon after taking power, the revolutionary government issued a series of law-decrees that authorized confiscation of assets controlled by the deposed dictator, Batista, and his collaborators. Under these provisions, the state took control of several sugar mills, construction companies, agricultural enterprises, factories, hospitals, etcetera.

The first Agrarian Reform Law, promulgated on 17 May 1959, had as its objective the elimination of latifundia and the distribution of land to those who worked it. The law established an upper limit of 30 *caballerías* (about 400 hectares) on landholding by individuals, with some exceptions for sugar and rice plantations and cattle ranches with productivity well above the national average. Landholdings beyond the upper limit were to be expropriated with compensation, divided, and distributed to landless peasants. Some land redistribution took place during 1959–61; however, the bulk of the land that was expropriated was not divided up but was instead organized into state-controlled production cooperatives along the lines of the Soviet *kolkhozy*. Over 3.1 million hectares of sugar lands controlled by sugar mills were expropriated and distributed to small farmers and especially to production cooperatives.

In the second half of 1959, the government began to take control of numerous key industries, including those owned by foreign investors. Enterprises in the chemical, oil refining, textile, and metal products industries, among others, were nationalized. In June 1960 the Cuban government "intervened" subsidiaries of three foreign oil companies operating in Cuba, and, when the United States responded by virtually eliminating the Cuban sugar quota for 1960, Cuba retaliated by authorizing the nationalization of all American-owned property in Cuba. Pursuant to this law, the Cuban government seized the oil companies, 36 sugar mills, and the telephone and electricity companies. By August 1960 the state controlled 40 percent of the land, about 38 percent of the sugar industry, key public services, and a significant portion of the industrial sector, including about one-half of the enterprises with more than 500 workers.

In October 1960, Cuba nationalized remaining investments in Cuba owned by U.S. nationals, those owned by other foreign nationals, and key enterprises owned by Cuban citizens, virtually eliminating private enterprise. Pursuant to this legislation, the state took control of the banking system, insurance companies, and 382 large corporations, including 105 sugar mills, 89 manufacturing enterprises, 13 department stores, and 47 warehouses. By 1961, it has been estimated (Mesa-Lago 1970, 204), the government had complete control over wholesale and foreign trade, banking, and education and commanding control over the industrial, construction, and transportation sectors; only in the agricultural (37 percent) and retail trade (52 percent) sectors was state control less than overwhelming.

The so-called Second Agrarian Reform Law, of 3 October 1963, authorized the nationalization of landholdings exceeding 5 *caballerías* (about 67 hectares). Passage of this law resulted in almost a doubling of the state's share of the agricultural sector, from about 37 percent in 1961 to 70 percent in 1963. In December 1962 large- and medium-sized retail firms had been nationalized; in March 1968 the remaining small private businesses were taken over. Thus, by mid 1968, the state controlled all productive resources with the exception of those in agriculture. Over time, the state's share of the agricultural sector has risen as a result of the retirement of farmers and of government policies that encourage the incorporation of private farmers into production cooperatives.

In the early 1960s, Cuba experimented with a model of economic organization that emphasized highly centralized physical planning and a development strategy centered on rapid industrialization. Later it shifted to other organizational models, ranging from market socialism to very radical centralization, and concentrated on agriculture as the focal point of its development strategy. After 1970, Cuba adopted an organizational model based on centralization—but incorporating some market levers—and continued to single out agriculture as the key to its development strategy.

In the mid 1970s, Cuba began to implement a Soviet style Economic Management and Planning System (Sistema de Dirección y Planificación de la Economía [SDPE]) that attempted to improve efficiency in the allocation and utilization of capital and of human resources by means of such instruments as credit, interest, rational prices, budgets, monetary controls, and taxes (Mesa-Lago 1981, 14–30). The system was implemented progressively until 1986, when the "Rectification Process" signaled a return to the more centralized, moralistic model of the second half of the 1960s.

## THE INDUSTRIALIZATION DRIVE

The development strategy crafted during 1960 and 1961 by Cuban officials, with the technical assistance of experts from abroad, stressed agricultural diversification and rapid industrialization. These policies were popular not only because of the large national income and employment gains that were projected, but also because they played on the deeply ingrained sucrophobia of a large portion of the population, which had increasingly grown to associate the sugar industry with the ills of the economy: unemployment, monoculture, export instability, external dependence.

It has been suggested (Ritter 1974, 133–34) that another reason for turning away from sugar was the poor world market price and prospects; Cuba's 1961 bumper crop, coupled with high production in Western Europe, had driven down world market prices of sugar, a common outcome whenever Cuban production was high. Moreover, Fidel Castro (1965, 16) has argued retrospectively that the decision to harvest all available sugarcane lands in 1961—and subsequently turn some of them to other crops—was not motivated by a deliberate strategy to diminish the importance of the sugar industry but rather responded to the lack of export opportunities for Cuban sugar after the loss of the U.S. market.

In accordance with the agricultural diversification drive, large sugarcane estates were cleared and replanted with other crops—rice, fruits, vegetables (Boorstein 1968, 185, 201, 205). In 1961 alone, cooperatives diverted 13,000 *caballerías* (nearly 175,000 hectares) from sugarcane to the cultivation of beans, peanuts, rice, cotton, tubers, etcetera, and to pastureland (Aguirre 1961, 24). Although this trend was reversed beginning in 1962 (C. R. Rodríguez 1963, 21), nevertheless total area under sugarcane cultivation fell by 25 percent between 1958 and 1963 (Mesa-Lago 1971, 283). Between 1959 and 1962, 9 sugar mills, combining about 2.7 percent of grinding capacity, were dismantled (CERP 1965a, 89; AAC 1959, 91–3). Retrospectively, the Central Planning Board (Junta Central de Planificación [JUCEPLAN]) has indicated that investment in the sugar industrial sector (e.g., for maintenance and repairs of sugar mills) in the early 1960s fell well below acceptable levels (El desarrollo industrial 1966, 148).

Industrialization plans bordered on the idyllic. In August 1961, Minister of Industries Guevara (1961a, 427–32) spoke of plans to make Cuba the most highly industrialized country in Latin America relative to its population, diversify the economy, and reduce the dependence on sugar exports from the then current 80 percent of the value of exports to 60 percent, an optimistic goal also shared by Cuban technicians and foreign advisors (e.g., Boti 1961; Kalecki 1960). Earlier, Guevara (1961b, 39–40) had indicated that Cuba had short-term plans to develop a transportation equipment industry that would produce tractors, trucks, internal combustion engines, and so on; after 1965, according to Guevara, Cuba would produce passenger automobiles.

The shift of resources out of the sugar sector resulted in severe reductions in sugar output and exports. Whereas in 1961 output reached 6.8 million tons, in 1962 it was 4.8 million tons (a decline of 29 percent), and in 1963, 3.8 million tons (a further decline of 21 percent). The performance of the sugar industry in 1963 was the poorest since 1945, when output was 3.6 million tons. Similarly, sugar exports declined from 6.4 million tons in 1961 to 5.1 million tons in 1962 and 3.5 million tons in 1963, the last being the lowest level of exports in two decades. (See appendix 1 for a general discussion of the quality of Cuban sugar statistics and related issues involved in comparing sugar industry statistics for prerevolutionary and revolutionary Cuba.)

THE RETURN TO SUGAR

Overwhelmed by a balance of payments crisis and the abject failure of the agricultural diversification/industrialization drive, the Cuban government in 1963 shifted gears and redefined its development strategy to give agriculture—and specifically sugar—a central role. Under this new strategy agriculture was tapped as the leading sector of the economy and sugar as the engine of growth. The intention was to expand sugar production and exports in order to raise additional revenue to finance imports of capital goods; these, in turn, would be used domestically to produce a range of intermediate and final consumer goods theretofore imported (Brunner 1977, 38–39).

To deal with severe labor shortages in sugarcane harvesting, Cuba turned to mechanization. Domestically produced mechanical cutters were used extensively in the 1963 *zafra*, the first sugar harvest in which mechanization played an important role. Though the early mechanical cane cutters were crude and did not turn out to be entirely successful, their introduction set Cuba on a path to mechanize the sugar harvest that has continued over the years and has had implications for other sectors of the economy.

Consistent with sugar's assigned role as engine of growth, an ambitious plan for the sugar industry for the period 1965–70 was drawn up. This Prospective Plan for the Sugar Industry foresaw substantial expansion in the area devoted to sugarcane cultivation, planting of improved varieties, increases in the area under irrigation, mechanization of harvesting, modernization of mills, etcetera. The objective was to produce 10 million tons of sugar in 1970—compared to a historical high production of 7.2 million tons in 1952—and for annual production to remain at the 10 million ton level during 1971–75 and then to rise to about 12 million tons.

At the early stages of implementation of the Prospective Plan, several Cuban economists (Borrego Díaz 1965; Herrera 1965; Regalado 1965) publicly discussed potential bottlenecks in sugar agriculture and industry that could jeopardize the attainment of the 10 million ton target in 1970 and, more importantly, the ability to produce at that level of output in subsequent years. With regard to the impact of the sugar push on the rest of the economy, in 1966 a Cuban economist, Borrego Díaz (1966, 166), pointed out that almost 70 percent of total planned investment for 1965–70 was targeted on the sugar industry, draining the rest of the economy of investment resources.

The Prospective Plan turned out to be a monumental failure. Not only did the sugar sector fail to meet its quantitative targets in every year after 1965—especially the much publicized 10 million ton target set for 1970—but the nonsugar economy was also adversely affected by the single-minded pursuit of expansion of sugar output.

## DEEPENING RELIANCE ON SUGAR

In the aftermath of the 1970 *zafra* and the severe economic dislocations that occurred, government policies toward the sugar industry underwent significant change. The emphasis shifted from giant, barn-bursting *zafras* to stable and more efficient production, with gradual increases in output (Petushkov 1975, 32–34; Charadán López 1982, 143–248). Efforts were made to increase industrial yields, reduce fuel consumption by sugar mills, broaden the scope of mechanization in cutting and loading sugarcane, improve on the timeliness of export deliveries, and so on. Rationalization of the sugar industry probably was influenced by Cuba's formal accession into the Council for Mutual Economic Assistance (CMEA) in 1972. Since then, Cuba has been assigned the role of sugar supplier within the CMEA, a factor that has tended to work against diversification and may be a long-run obstacle to the country's industrialization (Brezinski 1986, 302).

During the five-year plan 1976–80, Cuba implemented a massive plan to modernize and expand sugar industrial capacity. More than 40 mills were overhauled, and two new mills were put in operation in 1980, the first new mills built in the country in over fifty years. Output rose steadily through 1979, when 7.8 million tons were produced—the second largest *zafra* on record—but fell sharply in 1980 when sugarcane was hard hit by an epidemic of *roya* (cane rust), which affected yields. Output in 1980 was about 6.8 million tons, well short of the goal of 8–8.5 million tons.

In July 1981, Cuba and its three primary markets within CMEA— the Soviet Union, Bulgaria, and the German Democratic Republic— signed the General Agreement on the Integral Development of Sugar Production (also known as the CMEA Sugar Program), which formalized Cuba's role as the primary supplier of sugar to CMEA (Contreras 1982, 19–20; Díaz-Vázquez 1985, 73–74; 1986, 12–13; Ferrer 1981, 2; M. T. Valdés 1984, 141). According to this program and other bilateral arrangements, Cuba receives preferential price treatment for sugar exports to CMEA markets and assistance (low interest credits, technical aid) for the development of its sugar industry. Reportedly, CMEA assistance to the Cuban sugar industry was projected at $635 million during 1981–85 and $540 million during 1986–90 (UNIDO 1986, 25; Ibáñez López 1983, 37). The sugar agreement with CMEA, and a similar pact dealing with citrus production, "consecrated" Cuba's role as a purveyor of agricultural commodities within the socialist division of labor (Ferrer 1981, 2).

During the 1981 *zafra,* Cuba converted four sugar mills and their neighboring agricultural lands into agro-industrial complexes. By bringing agricultural and industrial activities under a unified management structure, authorities hoped to eliminate bottlenecks in the delivery of sugarcane to the mills and improve the quantity and quality of output. Gradually, all sugar mills and associated sugar lands have been turned into agro-industrial complexes.

For 1981-85, Cuba's development plan called for the start-up of construction of at least 7 new sugar mills, expansion of 23, and renovation of 18 others; sugar output was expected to average about 20-25 percent above the 7.1 million tons per annum achieved during 1976-80 (Lineamientos 1980, 79-80). For 1985 output was projected at 8.2-8.5 million tons, roughly the same level projected earlier for 1980 but not achieved; actual production in 1985 was about 7.9 million tons, 4-7 percent below projections. In the first half of the 1980s, Cuba was not able to meet its sugar export targets and in fact turned to the world market to purchase significant volumes of sugar for reexport to socialist countries in order to fulfill supply commitments.

PLANS TO 2000

The 1986-90 plan again foresees heavy investments in the sugar industry, including completion of several mills already under construction and expansion and modernization of existing mills. The objective of the plan is to increase sugar output by 15 percent compared to the average production of 7.8 million tons per annum achieved during 1981-85 (Lineamientos 1986, 73-74); these increases in production are to be accomplished through an 11 percent increase in the volume of sugarcane processed and a 4 percent improvement in industrial yield (the ratio of sugar produced to sugarcane milled) (Herrera Machado 1986, 9). Production of white sugar—primarily refined sugar—is to increase by 48 percent compared to 1981-85 output (ibid. 11).

Whereas the emphasis in the first half of the 1980s appears to have been on increasing the sugar manufacturing capacity, a shift favoring improvements in sugarcane agriculture is noticeable in the second half of the 1980s. As Sugar Industry Minister Herrera Machado has put it (Lazo 1987, 52):

> If we are not able to reach the volume of sugarcane that the country needs, we will not be able to reach the objectives of the sugar plan, because all other objectives flow from sugarcane. This is why increasing the volume of sugarcane and the volume of sugarcane produced per *caballería* [1 *caballería*=13.42 hectares] are the tasks to which the Sugar Ministry is devoting most of its efforts.

Improvements in agricultural yields (sugarcane produced per hectare of land harvested) and stabilization of flows of cane to the mills are essential to the success of the 1986–90 plan. They are also critical to the longer-term plans for the industry: in 1990 sugar production is expected to reach 11 or 12 million tons per annum, rising to 13–14 million tons per annum by the year 2000 (Comparecencia 1981, 2; Torralbas González 1983, 97; Díaz-Vázquez 1986, 13).

While Cuba expands its sugar production, industry analysts have expressed concern about global oversupply and pessimism about the economic viability of sugar investments. According to Harris (1987, 127), the central problem of the world's sugar economy is "that the demand for sugar in the developed world has ceased to grow and in some cases is falling, whereas in the developing world there is a large unsatisfied demand because of the lack of resources to fill it. The consequence has been that the growth in the world's [sugar] production capacity in recent years has far outpaced the growth in consumption." Brown, in a study prepared for the World Bank (1987, 53), gives the following assessment of sugar industry investments:

> For the foreseeable future, border prices for sugar will remain below the production costs of all but the most efficient producers, and it is unlikely therefore that investments in new production capacity would prove economically viable. Domestic markets with significant natural protection, or the substitution of lower-cost direct consumption sugars may justify expansion, but in most cases the focus of strategy in the sugar sector should be on improved technical and economic efficiency within the context of *present or reduced production levels* (emphasis added).

In the face of worldwide oversupply and generally weak current and prospective international market prices, Cuba justifies the expansion of sugar production thus (Otra batalla 1979, 20):

> It may appear paradoxical that at a time [early 1979] when the price of raw sugar in the world market barely covers production costs, a country would build four new sugar mills. Severed from fluctuations

in the world market, Cuban sugar has guaranteed demand in the Soviet Union and all other socialist countries. Moreover, this industry which continues to be the most important in the nation, is also the most economical one. It is a noble industry which can generate even the electricity it consumes and from whose derivatives can be obtained paper, particleboard, alcohol, cattle feed, among others.

More recently, President Fidel Castro (1985a, 20) has stressed the special conditions in trade with the socialist nations that justify Cuba's expansion of its sugar industry:

> Cuba's situation is different because we have an enormous market in the socialist countries. All our sugar is already sold. The sugar we will produce in the next five-year period, as well as in the next fifteen years, has already been sold to the socialist countries. When the Cuban revolution triumphed, these countries had plans to increase their sugar output. They moderated their expansionary plans, directed investments to other areas of their economies, and reserved an important part of their markets for Cuban sugar exports. Cuba has already sold to the socialist countries all the sugar it can produce—above its world market quota—in the next fifteen years. Thus we are expanding sugar production and even building new sugar mills.

Marcelo Fernández Font (1986, 202), the former foreign trade minister, has argued that expansion of the sugar industry is the appropriate policy for the country to follow:

> Cuba is perhaps the only sugar-exporting developing country that can, and should, increase sugar production even in the current depressed conditions of the world sugar market in order to meet the growing needs of the socialist countries as well as to regain historical participation levels in the free market.

Indeed, sugar consumption in the socialist countries has been growing. In fact, sugar consumption has been declining in some developed countries because of the high levels of per capita consumption already reached—approaching satiation levels—and competition "from starch-based sweeteners, the adoption of more sedentary lifestyles and the continuing pressure to reduce sugar consumption from the health lobby" (Harris 1987,127; Fernández Font 1988). Growth of demand in the socialist countries has prevented world demand from actually dropping in absolute terms.

The most important markets for Cuban sugar among socialist countries (in terms of amount of sugar purchased) are the Soviet

Union, the German Democratic Republic, Bulgaria, and the People's Republic of China (PRC). The first three are of particular significance to Cuba because the amount of their sugar purchases is quite predictable from year to year, and they—particularly the Soviet Union—pay a preferential price for Cuban sugar (see chapters 8 and 9).

During 1982–87, Cuban sugar shipments to these four socialist nations averaged the following levels (see appendix 5):

| | |
|---|---|
| Soviet Union | 3,830,500 tons |
| German Democratic Republic | 267,480 tons |
| Bulgaria | 329,375 tons |
| People's Republic of China | 665,200 tons |

Combined exports were just over 5 million tons per annum; exports to all socialist nations averaged about 5.5 million tons per annum, or around 79 percent of total sugar exports, while world market sales amounted to about 1.5 million tons per annum or 21 percent of total exports. In 1987, Cuba's sugar exports to the Soviet Union were slightly over 3,860,000 tons; to the German Democratic Republic, 283,500 tons; to Bulgaria, 305,000 tons, and to the People's Republic of China, 611,830 tons. Taken together, sugar shipments to the four socialist nations were over 5.0 million tons; sugar exports to all socialist nations were around 5.5 million tons or 85 percent of total exports, while those to the world market were 950,000 tons or 15 percent of exports.

When the poor prospects for growth of world sugar demand in the nonsocialist countries—because of declining consumption in developed countries and lack of resources to acquire sugar in developing ones—are considered, is it reasonable to expect that demand in socialist countries will be able to grow to absorb the projected increases in sugar output and exports?

- During 1982–87, annual Cuban domestic sugar consumption ranged from 650,000 to 887,000 tons. It is not unreasonable to assume that domestic consumption may stabilize at about 1 million tons per annum through 2000.
- Given a 1 million ton per annum level of domestic consumption, achievement of the output goals envisioned by the government (11–12 million tons by 1990; 12–14 million tons by 2000) would generate 10–11 million tons of exportable sugar by 1990 and 11–13 million tons by 2000.
- Projecting some growth in the world market so that Cuban exports to that market would reach about 2 million tons per annum (Cuba last

shipped at this level in 1982 and shipped less than 1 million tons in 1987) would mean that the socialist countries would have to absorb 8–9 million tons of Cuban sugar by 1990 and 9–11 million tons by 2000. Projected import levels for 1990 would be 60–80 percent higher than actual imports in the first half of the 1980s, and for 2000 about 80–120 percent higher.

Questions about the ability of the Soviet Union to increase sugar imports from Cuba have been raised in the literature, for example, by Turits (1987, 177):

> Though the Soviets have not increased their domestic sugar production very significantly since the Cuban Revolution, and thus have become increasingly dependent on imports, it is unclear how much more sugar they can absorb. One analyst believes even that the Soviets are already witness to a large black market of moonshine produced from Cuban sugar. Yet the Cubans hope to increase production from eight to 12 million tons per year by 1990. . . . Given the surfeit of sugar in the world, and sugar's price on the free market below the cost of production, the heavy emphasis on sugar production which is implicit in Soviet subsidies may contribute to Cuba's dependence on the Soviet Union, and/or on an almost moribund world market for sugar.

Short of dismantlement of the domestic sugar industry of the Soviet Union, a move that would have severe short-term adjustment problems for that nation, the PRC, with the world's largest population and very low current levels of per capita sugar consumption (Harris 1987, 128), may be the only outlet for increases in Cuban sugar output of such magnitude.

# CHAPTER 2

•

## Agriculture

THE AGRICULTURAL CENSUS of 1946, the only such census taken in prerevolutionary Cuba, confirmed that cane cultivation dominated Cuban agriculture and affected land tenure patterns. As a result of the Agrarian Reform Laws of 1959 and 1963, the structure of landholding changed significantly, with the state taking control over the lion's share of agricultural land, including sugarcane lands. In sugarcane agriculture, private farmers (including those organized in production cooperatives) still operate alongside state enterprises. Sugarcane continues to be the single most important crop within the Cuban agricultural sector.

### STRUCTURE OF PRODUCTION

In 1945, 894 farms (0.5 percent of all farms) controlled nearly 3.3 million hectares (36.1 percent) of Cuban agricultural land. Most of these large estates were owned or operated by sugar enterprises. At the other extreme there was a minifundia complex, consisting of more than 80 percent of farms, comprising less than one-fifth of the agricultural land; 39 percent of these farms were smaller than ten hectares, and more than 70 percent were less than 25 hectares (World Bank 1951, 87–88; Bianchi 1964, 74–75).

The key actors in sugarcane production in prerevolutionary Cuba were the *colonos* (cane farmers), independent operators who produced sugarcane and sold it to the mill that offered the highest price. The *colono* system was strongly supported by Cuban economic thinkers in the nineteenth century, such as the Conde de Pozos Dulces, who saw it as preventing the establishment of a plantation type system that would perpetuate slavery (Martínez-Alier 1973, 4–5).

With the expansion of the Cuban sugar industry in the second half of the nineteenth century and the first quarter of the twentieth, sugar mills steadily increased their control over agricultural land.

After 1898, U.S. capital flowed increasingly into Cuba, much of it directed at the sugar industry; vast expanses of land, particularly in Camagüey and Oriente provinces, were taken over by U.S.-owned sugar mills (Pino-Santos 1984, 424–37). According to estimates, sugar mills controlled (through ownership or lease) 7.0 percent of agricultural land in 1860, 10.3 percent in 1912, 17.7 percent in 1925, 26.7 percent in 1939, and 24.3 percent in 1953 (U.S. Department of Commerce 1956, 32); in 1959 the corresponding percentage was 20.9 percent (Bianchi 1964, 76). The sugar companies seldom farmed their own or leased land, however, preferring to let *colonos* do so (Arredondo 1969, 93; Martínez-Alier 1973, 21). It has been estimated that in 1959, 35 percent of agricultural land was devoted to cultivation of sugarcane (Menéndez Cruz 1961, 34).

The relative decline in the sugar industry's control over agricultural lands after the mid 1930s is attributable to the Great Depression and to two legislative initiatives. First, the Sugar Coordination Act (Ley de Coordinación Azucarera) of 1937, which sought to limit domestic production of sugar in order to prop up international prices (see chapter 10), favored small *colonos* in the assignment of production quotas and granted them immunity against eviction from their land so long as production quotas were met (CERP 1965a, 97–98; 1965b, 339–45). Second, provisions in the Constitution of 1940 prescribed the maximum amount of land a person or entity could own, limited foreign ownership of land, and favored the return of land owned by foreigners to nationals (World Bank 1951, 92).

The sweeping Agrarian Reform Law (Ley de Reforma Agraria) of 1959, passed on 17 May 1959, proscribed latifundia and limited landholdings held by an individual or entity to 30 *caballerías* (402.6 hectares). An exception was made for extraordinarily productive land dedicated to sugarcane or rice production, for which holdings of up to 100 *caballerías* (1,342 hectares) would be permitted provided yields were higher—by 50 percent—than the national average. Also exempt from the limitation were large estates (e.g., sugar estates) that could be more efficiently operated as a single unit. These large estates were to be operated in the form of production cooperatives under the stewardship of the National Institute for Agrarian Reform (Instituto Nacional de Reforma Agraria [INRA]). The law (Article 12) also provided that, one year after enactment, sugarcane *colonias* could not be operated by individuals with financial interests in sugar mills. Another provision (Article 67) set forth that *colonos* owning over 5 *caballerías* would have the right to buy land they farmed up to the 30 *caballería* limit (de la Cuesta 1974, 475–95). Article 67 was never implemented, however (Martínez-Alier 1973, 23).

Implementation of the Agrarian Reform Law with respect to the sugar industry began in January 1960, after a tactical delay by the government aimed at minimizing opposition from mill owners, who were also among the largest landholders (MacEwan 1981, 44). As a result of the Agrarian Reform Law, the roughly 234,000 *caballerías* formerly controlled by sugar mills were distributed as follows: cooperatives, 80,000 *caballerías* (34 percent); small farmers, 79,846 *caballerías* (34 percent); and large farmers, 74,578 *caballerías* (32 percent) (Menéndez Cruz 1962a, 1–2).

In November 1961 there were 602 sugarcane cooperatives in operation (Aguirre 1961, 20–22; Menéndez Cruz 1961, 36). These units were not cooperatives in the sense of being self-administered units in which producers were remunerated by sharing the cooperatives' proceeds (MacEwan 1981, 49–50); instead, members were wage earners, managers of the cooperatives were appointed by INRA, which also prepared production plans, provided inputs, and purchased outputs (Bianchi 1964, 107–10; Mesa-Lago 1976, 276). In August 1962 sugarcane cooperatives were converted into state farms, a mere formalization of the way in which they had in fact been operating (Menéndez Cruz 1962b; Gutelman 1970, 65).

On 3 October 1963 the so-called Second Agrarian Reform Law was promulgated (de la Cuesta 1974, 495–98). Under authority provided in this legislation, the government nationalized landholdings exceeding five *caballerías* (about 67 hectares); as a result, the state's share of the agricultural sector almost doubled, from about 40 percent in 1961 to 70 percent in 1963 (Mesa-Lago 1970, 204). Around 1965 there were some 52,000 private farmers engaged in sugarcane production, controlling nearly 908,000 hectares of land, of which 358,000 hectares were devoted to cane cultivation (Regalado 1965, 37–38).

The First Congress of the Cuban Communist Party, held in December 1975, called for "superior forms of production" in the agricultural sector (Proyecto de directivas 1975, 35), where the "superior forms" are attained through integration of privately held land either into state farms or into agricultural production cooperatives (cooperativas de producción agropecuaria [CPAs]). The growth of CPAs has been impressive: from 125 CPAs controlling about 12,600 hectares in 1977 (Rojas Requena et al. 1985, 70) to 1,418 controlling just under 1 million hectares at the end of 1987 (AEC 1987, 306). Presumably, private farmers join CPAs voluntarily, turning over their land in return for wages and a share of the cooperatives' profits, access to credit and machinery, better housing, improved access to educational, public health, and recreational facilities, and the like (Ramírez Cruz 1984, 2–3).

However, there is a core of private farmers who refuse to give up their land to the state or to cooperatives for a number of ideological, economic, and personal reasons (Pérez Rojas 1987, 106–07). The state has ceded some land to CPAs to facilitate their formation, particularly in mountainous areas; for CPAs formed through the end of 1982, private farmers had contributed 88 percent of the land and the state 12 percent (Rojas Requena et al. 1985, 68).

Among CPAs those growing sugarcane play a dominant role: they are the most numerous, control the highest percentage of land, and tend to be larger in terms of both average size and number of members. In 1987, for example, sugarcane CPAs accounted for 30 percent of the total number of CPAs (432 out of 1,418) and controlled nearly 40 percent of the land; the average sugarcane CPA controlled about 900 hectares and had 69 members, compared to 690 hectares and 49 members for all CPAs taken together (table 1). In 1984 sugarcane CPAs had, on average, more than 5 wheeled tractors and 1 combine harvester as well as other types of farm machinery (Ghai et al. 1988, 73). Reportedly, cane cultivation is the most profitable activity in the cooperative sector (Ramírez Cruz 1984, 11).

In general, Cuba does not publish statistics on the distribution of agricultural land between the state and nonstate (including cooperative) sectors either globally or by crop. For the period 1968–87 only, statistics on land planted with sugarcane by the state and nonstate sectors are available, however. In 1968, the first year for which such information was published, the state sector already controlled about three-quarters (76.4 percent) of the land planted with sugarcane. Its share increased steadily through 1979, when it controlled nearly 86 percent. During 1979–87, plantings in the nonstate sector expanded—mostly as a result of the growth in sugarcane CPAs—while those in the state sector remained stagnant, resulting in a gradual increase in the share of cane plantings outside direct state control. In 1987, the state controlled 83 percent of sugarcane plantings (AEC 1987, 308).

The effect of the two agrarian reforms and other government policies on the structure of sugarcane land cultivation is also evident

TABLE 1
AGRICULTURAL PRODUCTION COOPERATIVES (CPAs): TOTAL AND SUGARCANE

|  | 1979 | 1980 | 1981 | 1982 | 1983 | 1984 | 1985 | 1986 | 1987 |
|---|---|---|---|---|---|---|---|---|---|
| ALL CPAs | 725 | 1,035 | 1,128 | 1,416 | 1,472 | 1,414 | 1,378 | 1,368 | 1,418 |
| Land controlled (000 hectares) | 104.3 | 212.9 | 383.4 | 690.5 | 938.2 | 988.3 | 1,008.8 | 1,011.5 | 977.0 |
| Number of members | 16,692 | 29,535 | 39,519 | 63,285 | 82,611 | 72,297 | 69,896 | 67,672 | 69,604 |
| Average size (hectares) | 143.9 | 205.7 | 339.9 | 487.7 | 637.4 | 698.9 | 732.1 | 739.4 | 689.0 |
| Average number of members | 23 | 29 | 35 | 45 | 56 | 51 | 51 | 49 | 49 |
| SUGARCANE CPAs | 218 | 314 | 348 | 431 | 441 | 433 | 422 | 428 | 432 |
| Land controlled (000 hectares) | 35.7 | 85.1 | 173.1 | 283.9 | 372.4 | 395.1 | 402.3 | 409.7 | 388.9 |
| Number of members | 4,607 | 9,685 | 14,892 | 23,546 | 32,597 | 31,449 | 30,959 | 30,480 | 29,910 |
| Average size (hectares) | 163.6 | 271.1 | 497.3 | 658.8 | 844.5 | 912.2 | 953.2 | 957.4 | 900.2 |
| Average number of members | 21 | 31 | 43 | 55 | 74 | 73 | 73 | 71 | 69 |

SOURCES: 1987—AEC 1987, 306; 1980–86—AEC 1986, 301; 1979—AEC, 1983, 193.
Note: Figures are given for December 31 of each year.

from data on sugarcane land harvested. Prior to 1959 all sugarcane lands were privately owned. By the 1962 *zafra,* after the first Agrarian Reform Law had taken effect, nearly 37 percent of sugarcane lands harvested were under the control of the state; the state's share rose to about 41 percent in 1963, 65 percent in 1964, and 69 percent in 1965, reflecting the implementation of the Second Agrarian Reform Law. In subsequent *zafras* the state's share of harvested land rose steadily, exceeding 80 percent in every *zafra* since 1971 and peaking at about 85 percent in 1980. Spurred by the growth in CPAs, the share of harvested cane land in the nonstate sector recovered somewhat in the 1980s.

## Sugarcane Production

A large sugar industry such as Cuba's requires prodigious volumes of cane as input into the industrial process. Assuming an industrial yield of 11 percent—roughly the average yield obtained in Cuba in the last three decades—the agricultural system must deliver 100 tons of sugarcane to sugar mills to produce 11 tons of raw sugar.

Table 2 presents official data on sugarcane production during each of the *zafras* 1952–87. The data suggest that there has been a gradual rise, except for some years when weather conditions or other phenomena (e.g., the giant 1970 sugar campaign) seriously affected output.

Average sugarcane production during the 1982–84 *zafras* (73.4 million tons) was roughly twice the corresponding production level twenty years earlier (34.6 million tons in 1962–64). This comparison tends to exaggerate increases in sugarcane production, however, since it takes as a base the three consecutive years with the lowest production levels in the last three decades. As can be seen from the raw data in table 2, production during the first three years of revolutionary government (1959–61) was quite high, especially in 1961. Not until the mid 1970s does output consistently exceed the 1961 production level. Sugarcane production fell sharply in 1985 and 1986; the lower output during these two *zafras* has been officially attributed to a hurricane and severe drought conditions.

Sugarcane production figures for the periods 1952–60 and 1961–87 are not strictly comparable. As early as 1926, through the Verdeja Act, the Cuban government intervened in the sugar industry to limit

# TABLE 2
## Sugarcane Production, 1952–1987
*(in millions of tons)*

| Zafra | Total | State | % | Nonstate | % |
|---|---|---|---|---|---|
| 1952 | 58.7 | | | | |
| 1953 | 40.2 | | | | |
| 1954 | 38.8 | | | | |
| 1955 | 34.3 | | | | |
| 1956 | 36.5 | | | | |
| 1957 | 44.1 | | | | |
| 1958 | 45.1 | | | | |
| 1959 | 47.4 | | | | |
| 1960 | 46.8 | | | | |
| 1961 | 53.6 | | | | |
| 1962 | 36.0 | 14.4 | 40.0 | 21.6 | 60.0 |
| 1963 | 31.1 | 13.4 | 43.1 | 17.7 | 59.6 |
| 1964 | 36.7 | 24.5 | 66.8 | 12.2 | 33.2 |
| 1965 | 50.4 | 35.0 | 69.4 | 15.4 | 30.6 |
| 1966 | 36.4 | 26.0 | 71.4 | 10.4 | 28.6 |
| 1967 | 50.5 | 37.3 | 73.9 | 13.2 | 26.1 |
| 1968 | 41.5 | 30.1 | 72.5 | 11.4 | 27.5 |
| 1969 | 41.7 | 30.4 | 72.9 | 11.3 | 27.1 |
| 1970 | 81.5 | 62.5 | 76.6 | 19.0 | 23.3 |
| 1971 | 52.2 | 41.0 | 78.5 | 11.2 | 21.5 |
| 1972 | 44.3 | 35.6 | 80.4 | 8.7 | 19.6 |
| 1973 | 48.2 | 39.3 | 81.5 | 8.9 | 18.5 |
| 1974 | 50.4 | 41.5 | 82.3 | 8.9 | 17.7 |
| 1975 | 52.4 | 42.8 | 81.7 | 9.6 | 18.3 |
| 1976 | 53.8 | 44.0 | 81.8 | 9.8 | 18.2 |
| 1977 | 60.4 | 48.4 | 80.1 | 12.0 | 19.9 |
| 1978 | 69.7 | 57.2 | 82.1 | 12.5 | 17.9 |
| 1979 | 77.3 | 63.8 | 82.5 | 13.5 | 17.5 |
| 1980 | 64.0 | 53.4 | 83.4 | 10.6 | 16.6 |
| 1981 | 66.6 | 54.5 | 81.8 | 12.1 | 18.2 |
| 1982 | 73.1 | 60.2 | 82.3 | 12.9 | 17.7 |
| 1983 | 69.7 | 54.9 | 78.8 | 14.8 | 21.2 |
| 1984 | 77.4 | 63.2 | 81.7 | 14.2 | 18.3 |
| 1985 | 67.4 | 55.0 | 81.6 | 12.4 | 18.4 |
| 1986 | 68.5 | 56.2 | 82.0 | 12.3 | 18.0 |
| 1987 | 70.8 | 58.2 | 82.2 | 12.6 | 17.8 |

SOURCES: 1987—AEC 1987, 309; 1985–86—AEC, 1986, 304; 1968–84—AEC 1984, 192; 1965–67—AEC 1980, 69; 1962–64—AEC 1978, 68; 1958–61—AAC 1961, 24; l952–57—AAC 1958, 115.

output in order to prop up international prices. The Verdeja Act ordered a reduction in overall sugar production and gave the Cuban president the authority to establish the date on which mills were to begin *zafra* operations and the amount of sugar each mill could produce (CERP 1965b, 241).

With a few exceptions—1929, 1930, 1957, and around the time of World War II and the Korean War—Cuban sugar output was controlled through a system of domestic production quotas (see chapter 10). For example, in 1952, a year when production controls were suspended, raw sugar output reached a prerevolutionary record of nearly 7.3 million tons; in that *zafra,* over 1.4 million hectares of sugarcane land and were harvested, yielding 58.7 million tons of cane, a production level not regularly matched until the mid 1970s.

Sugarcane land actually harvested during the 1952–58 *zafras* represented the following percentages of sugarcane land available for harvesting (AAC 1958, 125; 1961, 24; Herrera 1965, 4):

| | |
|---|---|
| 1952 | 99.8 percent |
| 1953 | 62.9 percent |
| 1954 | 62.1 percent |
| 1955 | 57.8 percent |
| 1956 | 74.0 percent |
| 1957 | 91.9 percent |
| 1958 | 80.3 percent |

That is to say, in prerevolutionary Cuba it was the level of demand for sugar—rather than the limitations imposed by sugarcane production—that determined the volume of sugar produced (Bianchi 1964, 86).

During the first few years of revolutionary government, agricultural diversification away from sugarcane took high priority. In the spring of 1961 acreage under cane cultivation was cut back in order to free up land for other crops. After the 1961 *zafra* was completed, thousands of hectares of sugarcane lands were plowed under and planted with beans, peanuts, rice, cotton, tubers, and other crops (Boorstein 1968, 185). In 1961 alone, sugarcane cooperatives diverted 13,000 *caballerías* (nearly 175,000 hectares) from sugarcane to other crops (Aguirre 1961, 24; F. Castro 1975, 17). One author reports that between 1960 and 1963, land under sugarcane cultivation fell by 19 percent (Boorstein 1968, 205), and another indicates that the decline was 25 percent from 1958 to 1963 (Mesa-Lago 1971, 283).

Revolutionary Cuba has not instituted explicit measures to limit sugar production, as was customary in prerevolutionary Cuba. Nevertheless, sugarcane land harvested after 1961 dropped considerably, as the revolutionary government undertook a policy of agricultural diversification and land devoted to sugarcane was reduced (Guevara 1964, 620). Sugar output also dropped significantly. Arguably, such a decline in sugar production need not have taken place for, as one analyst has noted, more intensive use of underutilized sugar lands could have ensured that agricultural diversification would not entail any significant opportunity costs (Bianchi 1964, 86).

Beginning with the 1962 *zafra,* data are available on sugarcane produced by the state and nonstate sectors. The nonstate (mostly private) sector provided about 60 percent of cane produced in 1962–63, and its share dropped steadily in subsequent years, settling at an average of about 18 percent in the late 1970s and early 1980s (table 2).

## Sugarcane Yields

Sugarcane yields are affected by several factors in addition to climatological ones. These include the quality of the soil, the variety of cane planted, and the intensity with which agricultural services—replanting, weeding, fertilizing, irrigation—are applied. Historically, Cuba's sugarcane yields have been low compared with other important sugar-producing areas such as Hawaii, Louisiana, Taiwan, Australia, and South Africa (Bianchi 1964, 91; Evenson 1976, 210–11). However, unlike at least some of these other locations, Cuban cane fields did not have to be replanted every year, with a given planting capable of being harvested four to eight times (Alienes Urosa 1950, 113). Thus the argument has been advanced that cumulative (i.e., over the productive life of the plant) production from Cuban sugarcane fields far exceeded production elsewhere (Arredondo 1969, 91–92).

It is clear from table 3 that dramatic gains have been made in Cuba in sugarcane produced per hectare of land harvested (agricultural yield) in comparison with yields obtained in the early 1960s and in the prerevolutionary period. Whereas sugarcane yields during 1952–58 averaged just under 40 tons/hectare, they averaged 45 tons/hectare in the first half of the 1970s, 52 tons/hectare in the second half of the 1970s, and 56 tons/hectare during 1981–84. (These national averages mask very significant differences across the nation; for example, it has been reported that in the 1950s, yields approaching 85 tons/hectare were obtained at several locations where sugarcane was farmed intensively, i.e., using fertilizer and irrigation [Arredondo 1969:91]).

Despite these impressive gains, availability of sugarcane is the most significant constraint on sugar production in revolutionary Cuba. An econometric analysis of the performance of the sugarcane agricultural sector over the period 1970–85 concluded that increases in sugarcane output occurred because of increases in land under cultivation rather than improvements in agricultural yields (Ojeda Fagundo and Fiandor Rosario 1988). A Cuban economist has opined that sugarcane agriculture is the Achilles' heel of the Cuban sugar economy (Díaz-Vázquez 1980, 149). The 1986–90 plan calls for agricultural yields of no less than 68.6 tons/hectare by 1990 (Lineamientos económicos 1986, 54), a 15.5 percent increase over the peak yield of 58.0 tons/hectare recorded in 1983. Accomplishment of this goal is likely to be quite a challenge, for agricultural yields actually declined sharply in 1985–86, when they averaged about 51 tons/hectare, and recovered slightly in 1987.

## State Versus Nonstate Sugar Agricultural Yields

An examination of agricultural yields for the state and nonstate sugar sectors (table 3) suggests that there are significant differences in productivity between the two. Between 1962 and 1968 (with the exception of 1966), yields in the state sector exceeded those in the nonstate sector, in some cases by a considerable margin (e.g., by 20 percent in 1968). However, according to one researcher, in 1962 yields in the private sector were higher than in the public sector (i.e., sugarcane cooperatives), despite the superior quality of the cooperatives' lands and the preferential treatment they received in the allocation of machinery and fertilizer (Bianchi 1964, 133).

Beginning in 1969, yields in the nonstate sector are higher than in the state sector in every year, and significantly higher in some years (e.g., about 20 percent in 1976–77). On the basis of an analysis of data for 1971–76, it has been noted that the higher sugarcane yields in the nonstate sector occur despite the more intensive use of agricultural services (e.g., nitrogen fertilizers, irrigation, mechanical harvesting) in the state sector (Forster 1982, 119–20). More recent data on the

# TABLE 3
## Sugarcane Yields, 1952–1987
*(in tons/hectare harvested)*

| Zafra | Total | State | Nonstate |
|---|---|---|---|
| 1952 | 41.3 | | |
| 1953 | 39.9 | | |
| 1954 | 40.5 | | |
| 1955 | 41.2 | | |
| 1956 | 36.7 | | |
| 1957 | 34.9 | | |
| 1958 | 43.3 | | |
| 1959 | 44.4 | | |
| 1960 | 40.6 | | |
| 1961 | 37.2 | | |
| 1962 | 32.2 | 35.8 | 31.5 |
| 1963 | 28.9 | 30.6 | 27.8 |
| 1964 | 35.6 | 36.8 | 33.3 |
| 1965 | 47.8 | 48.2 | 46.8 |
| 1966 | 38.8 | 38.5 | 39.7 |
| 1967 | 46.9 | 47.3 | 45.8 |
| 1968 | 42.0 | 41.2 | 34.2 |
| 1969 | 44.2 | 42.8 | 48.2 |
| 1970 | 55.8 | 54.7 | 59.9 |
| 1971 | 41.7 | 41.1 | 44.1 |
| 1972 | 37.5 | 37.1 | 39.1 |
| 1973 | 45.0 | 44.4 | 47.1 |
| 1974 | 45.6 | 45.0 | 48.7 |
| 1975 | 44.4 | 43.6 | 48.0 |
| 1976 | 44.0 | 42.7 | 50.3 |
| 1977 | 53.1 | 51.1 | 62.8 |
| 1978 | 56.3 | 55.3 | 61.2 |
| 1979 | 58.9 | 57.8 | 64.6 |
| 1980 | 46.0 | 45.2 | 50.5 |
| 1981 | 55.1 | 53.8 | 61.3 |
| 1982 | 55.1 | 53.9 | 61.0 |
| 1983 | 58.0 | 56.7 | 63.6 |
| 1984 | 57.4 | 57.3 | 57.6 |
| 1985 | 50.0 | 49.8 | 50.7 |
| 1986 | 51.6 | 51.3 | 52.7 |
| 1987 | 52.1 | 51.7 | 54.5 |

SOURCES: 1987—AEC 1987, 309; 1985–86—AEC 1986, 305; 1968–84—AEC 1984, 192; 1965–67—AEC 1980, 69; 1962–64—AEC 1978, 68; 1958–61—AAC 1961, 24; 1952–57—AAC 1958, 115.

disparity in yields and on the distribution of agricultural services between the two sectors—continuing to favor the state sector—strengthen the earlier finding (Benjamin et al. 1984, 171).

As Fry has correctly pointed out (1988, 8), sugarcane yield statistics at the national level tend to magnify productivity differences between the state and nonstate sectors; these differences are much less significant when the data are examined at the provincial level. Thus the larger disparities in yield at the national level reflect the concentration of nonstate producers in La Habana, Matanzas, and Villa Clara provinces, where sugarcane yields historically have tended to be higher than elsewhere in the nation. Differences in productivity across regions result from disparities in average rainfall, intensity of application of irrigation and other agricultural services, quality of soil, variety of cane planted, etcetera (Blume 1987, 135).

Table 4 reports sugarcane yields at the provincial level for the 1977 and 1981 *zafras,* the two harvests when the disparity in national yield between state and nonstate producers was largest in the most recent decade (11.7 and 7.5 tons/hectare, respectively), and for 1986, a recent *zafra* for which these data are available. These data support Fry's observations: yield differentials between the two sectors are less significant at the provincial level than at the national level. Moreover, sugarcane yields in La Habana, Matanzas, and Villa Clara provinces tend to be among the highest in the nation, both for state and nonstate producers. Nonstate producers tend to be concentrated in these three provinces: in 1977, 56 percent of the sugarcane land harvested by nonstate producers, and 60 percent of the cane they produced, originated there (AEC 1977, 66); in 1981, the corresponding shares were 49 and 51 percent (AEC 1981, 87), respectively, and in 1986, 46 and 50 percent (AEC 1986, 304), respectively.

## Sugarcane Research

One of the ways in which Cuba has improved its sugarcane yields is through plant genetics. The objective has been to select varieties that are able to thrive in Cuba's natural setting and are resistant to disease.

In prerevolutionary Cuba, government support for research institutions studying sugarcane genetics was very modest; a great deal of the research in this area was conducted by individual sugar mills (CERP 1965b, 356–57; Arredondo 1969, 92). A high-yield variety of

TABLE 4
SUGARCANE YIELDS, STATE AND NONSTATE SECTORS,
BY PROVINCE, 1977–1981, AND 1986
*(in tons/hectare harvested)*

|  | 1977 State | 1977 Nonstate | 1981 State | 1981 Nonstate | 1986 State | 1986 Nonstate |
|---|---|---|---|---|---|---|
| Pinar del Río | 60.9 | 69.5 | 61.6 | 74.4 | 55.8 | 54.8 |
| La Habana | 75.8 | 73.9 | 68.1 | 69.4 | 71.4 | 62.3 |
| Matanzas | 61.4 | 68.6 | 60.0 | 63.4 | 58.1 | 55.1 |
| Villa Clara | 56.4 | 58.5 | 53.9 | 55.8 | 54.2 | 48.4 |
| Cienfuegos | 50.2 | 47.4 | 49.9 | 54.3 | 50.4 | 48.8 |
| Sancti Spíritus | 45.4 | 92.8 | 43.6 | 50.2 | 42.7 | 46.1 |
| Ciego de Avila | 51.9 | 53.6 | 52.4 | 67.9 | 48.5 | 56.3 |
| Camagüey | 53.0 | 60.5 | 49.1 | 55.7 | 45.5 | 46.6 |
| Las Tunas | 47.0 | 49.9 | 50.0 | 56.6 | 47.2 | 45.3 |
| Holguín | 36.0 | 40.2 | 52.7 | 68.1 | 52.5 | 47.3 |
| Granma | 54.8 | 82.9 | 49.6 | 65.0 | 50.0 | 56.0 |
| Santiago de Cuba | 40.3 | 45.3 | 56.4 | 59.1 | 61.9 | 59.8 |
| Guantánamo | 46.7 | 47.5 | 49.1 | 45.7 | 45.8 | 36.1 |
| National average | 51.1 | 62.8 | 52.9 | 60.4 | 51.3 | 52.7 |

SOURCES: 1986—AEC 1986, 304; 1981—AEC 1981, 87; 1977—AEC 1977, 66.

cane developed in Java (POJ-2878) was introduced in 1924 when a mosaic outbreak threatened the sugar industry. This disease-resistant variety spread rapidly, so that by 1940 and 1950 it represented over 45 and 60 percent of plantings, respectively (World Bank 1951, 197; CERP 1965b, 356; Evenson 1976, 212–13). Nevertheless, foreign observers judged that prerevolutionary Cuba's sugarcane agriculture was technologically stagnant, with the state-supported sugarcane Experimental Station (Estación Experimental de la Caña de Azúcar) at Jovellanos poorly funded (despite a levy on sugar production earmarked for research) and largely unable to carry out its work (World Bank 1951, 121, 197–98).

In 1963 the Cuban Academy of Sciences (Academia de Ciencias) established the Institute for Sugarcane Research (Instituto de Investigaciones de la Caña de Azúcar), with technical assistance from the Fiji Sugar Corporation (Madhava 1987, 5). Later, two other institutions were also created, the National Institute for Sugarcane Research (Instituto Nacional de Investigaciones de la Caña de Azúcar

[INICA]), charged with coordinating research on cane cultivation, including genetics (Vázquez 1979b, 34–35; Salomón Llanes 1984, 28), and the Cuban Institute for Research on Sugarcane Derivatives (Instituto Cubano de Investigaciones de los Derivados de la Caña [ICIDCA]), with responsibility for research on sugarcane by-products. In 1981, the Center for the Integrated Development of Sugarcane (Centro para el Desarrollo Integral de la Caña de Azúcar) was created at the Pablo Noriega sugar mill in La Habana province (Sánchez and Scobie 1986, 66).

Precise statistics are not available, but fragmented information suggests that research on sugarcane cultivation and the production of by-products has become increasingly important in Cuba (Miller 1986a; 1986b). Thus, from 1977 to 1987, the only period for which such data are publicly available, the share of the national scientific research budget allocated to MINAZ increased from about 3 to nearly 14 percent. Similarly, MINAZ's share of the national pool of scientists rose over the same period from around 4 to about 9 percent. A great deal of experimentation has taken place to select optimal varieties of sugarcane suited to mechanized harvesting and climatic and drainage conditions in different parts of the island (Gispert 1980; 1981).

In 1979 and 1980 sugarcane production was severely affected by an epidemic of *roya* (rust), a fungal disease that tends to dry up sugarcane stalks and reduce juice content. The disease was first observed in Cuba in late 1978 in plantings of B-4362, one of the more popular varieties cultivated in Cuba, which had been developed in Barbados in 1943 and introduced into Cuba in the 1960s (Chinea and Rodríguez 1982, 11–2). B-4362 was reportedly one of the preferred varieties because of early maturation and high sugar content (Llovio-Menéndez 1988, 311). Interestingly, an encyclopedic work on sugarcane agriculture in Cuba first published in 1982 (Martín Oria et al. 1987) contains detailed information on each of the varieties grown there, including maturation cycle and optimal harvesting time, but does not include such information on B-4362.

The high susceptibility of B-4362 to *roya* had been recorded in the technical literature. Prior to being observed in Cuba in 1978, outbreaks of the disease had affected sugarcane plantings in the Cameroons in 1969 and in Madagascar, the Dominican Republic, and Jamaica (Alfonso and González 1981, 3). According to a former MINAZ official, in 1972 a Cuban technician conducted a study of B-4362 and concluded that it was highly susceptible to *roya;* he recommended that it be planted in small areas, far apart from one another, so that a possible *roya* outbreak could be controlled (Llovio-Menéndez 1988, 311). This warning was ignored by Cuban officials; during 1974–76, for example, 42 percent of total sugarcane plantings consisted of B-4362 (AEC 1977, 67).

*Roya* spread throughout the nation, affecting primarily B-4362 plantings in the Western and central regions, but other varieties (such as My-6426, My-54129, and My-5514) and other regions as well. Agricultural losses from B-4362 plantings affected by *roya* ranged from 10 to 80 percent, depending on the location, and averaged 30 percent nationwide (Chinea and Rodríguez 1982, 12).

According to Castro, *roya* affected one-third of Cuba's sugarcane lands and caused a significant reduction of output in 1980 (F. Castro 1980b, 36). Considering that international sugar prices were high at the time the epidemic hit, Cuban officials have estimated that the *roya* outbreak translated into a loss of $400–$600 million in convertible currency in potential sugar exports (Comparecencia 1981, 3). Although these estimates of revenue loss probably overstate the impact of the *roya* epidemic, as the high world sugar prices were in part the market's reaction to expected lower production levels in Cuba, it is clear that it had significant economic costs: it required massive destruction of infected fields and replanting with fungus-resistant varieties. The share of sugarcane land planted with B-4362, which had averaged about 40 percent in the mid 1970s, had fallen virtually to zero by 1982 (AEC 1977, 67; 1984, 193).

## Sugarcane within Agriculture

During 1953–57 sugarcane production accounted for about one-half of the income generated by the agricultural sector; over this period, sugarcane's share of agricultural income fell from 55.4 percent in 1953 to 48.3 percent in 1957 (CERP 1965a, 84; Arredondo 1969, 77).

Similar estimates of the share of agricultural income generated by sugarcane during the revolutionary period cannot be made because of the lack of data for some years and, more importantly, because of changes in the methodology used by Cuban statisticians to compute national income and product (Mesa-Lago and Pérez-López 1985a, 3–18). However, if gross value of output (GVO) is used as a measure of activity, it can be seen from table 5 that over the period 1967–87,

## TABLE 5
### Gross Value of Output of Agriculture and of Sugarcane Production, 1962–1987
*(in millions of pesos)*

|  | At Current Prices ||| At Constant Prices[a] |||
|---|---|---|---|---|---|---|
|  | Agriculture | Sugarcane | Sugarcane/Agriculture (%) | Agriculture | Sugarcane | Sugarcane/Agriculture (%) |
| 1962 |  |  |  | 940.6 | 283.8 | 30.2 |
| 1963 |  |  |  | 904.2 | 235.1 | 26.0 |
| 1964 |  |  |  | 958.5 | 265.5 | 27.7 |
| 1965 |  |  |  | 1,074.0 | 367.1 | 34.2 |
| 1966 |  |  |  | 1,041.9 | 268.6 | 25.8 |
| 1967 | 1,111.9 | 352.9 | 31.7 |  |  |  |
| 1968 | 1,352.4 | 394.2 | 29.1 | 1,206.4 | 474.0 | 39.3 |
| 1969 | 1,289.2 | 406.3 | 31.5 |  |  |  |
| 1970 | 1,182.4 | 559.2 | 45.5 |  |  |  |
| 1971 | 1,091.6 | 471.0 | 43.1 |  |  |  |
| 1972 | 1,151.5 | 457.5 | 39.7 |  |  |  |
| 1973 | 1,206.6 | 482.1 | 40.0 |  |  |  |
| 1974 | 1,258.4 | 480.2 | 38.1 |  |  |  |
| 1975 | 1,537.7 | 553.6 | 36.0 | 1,399.6 | 513.4 | 36.7 |
| 1971–75 | 1,249.2 | 488.9 | 39.1 | 1,269.4 | 480.9 | 37.9 |
| 1976 | 1,673.9 | 596.3 | 35.6 | 1,448.6 | 511.7 | 35.7 |
| 1977 | 1,747.9 | 684.2 | 39.1 | 1,502.3 | 583.6 | 38.8 |
| 1978 | 1,849.5 | 745.0 | 40.3 | 1,591.3 | 654.3 | 41.1 |
| 1979 | 1,962.2 | 744.2 | 37.9 | 1,611.9 | 634.4 | 39.4 |
| 1980 | 2,168.6 | 758.6 | 35.0 | 1,587.6 | 610.6 | 38.5 |
| 1981 | 3,498.9 | 1,144.3 | 32.7 | 1,791.8 | 701.3 | 39.1 |
| 1982 | 3,393.3 | 1,056.1 | 31.1 | 1,692.6 | 654.5 | 38.7 |
| 1983 | 3,361.0 | 970.3 | 28.9 | 1,675.1 | 633.1 | 37.8 |
| 1984 | 3,566.1 | 1,003.3 | 28.1 | 1,750.6 | 643.7 | 36.8 |
| 1985 | 3,686.4 | 1,009.6 | 27.4 | 1,726.4 | 607.1 | 35.2 |
| 1986 | 3,884.3 | 1,051.4 | 27.3 |  |  |  |
| 1987 | 3,947.1 | 1,065.3 | 27.0 |  |  |  |

SOURCES: 1987—AEC 1987, 115; 1986—AEC 1986, 114; 1978–85—AEC 1985, 112, 279; 1975–77, 1971–75 constant-price average—AEC 1978, 50, 64; 1968–74—AEC 1974, 35; 1968 (constant price)—AEC 1977, 62; 1967—AEC 1972, 30, 62; 1962–66—BEC 1970, 30, 32.

a. At constant prices of 1965.

sugarcane's share of agricultural GVO ranged from nearly 46 percent in 1970 to around 27–29 percent in 1983–87. These figures suggest that, over the twenty-year period, sugarcane cultivation declined sharply in significance within the agricultural sector.

In contrast, other data also presented in table 5, which refer to GVO of the agricultural sector and of sugarcane cultivation at constant prices of 1965, suggest a slower rate of decline and, in fact, a gain in the importance of sugarcane within agriculture in the 1970s and 1980s compared to the early 1960s. Unfortunately, neither set of data is available for the entire period 1962–87, and therefore comparisons over the longer period cannot be made. Moreover, the most recent issues of the Cuban statistical yearbook (AEC 1986 and 1987), omit GVO at constant prices of 1965 for agriculture, signaling that it will not be possible to make these comparisons in the future.

During the 1970s and 1980s, the periods for which both current- and constant-price GVO data are available, the constant-price data in table 5 suggest that there was no significant change in sugarcane's share of agricultural output—this share remained remarkably stable at around 37 percent for the fifteen-year period 1971–85. Meanwhile, the current-price data show a marked decline (32 percent) in sugarcane's importance within the agricultural sector, from a peak share of 40.3 percent in 1978 to 27.0 percent in 1987.

# CHAPTER 3

•

## Industry

As SUGARCANE CULTIVATION was dominant in prerevolutionary Cuba's agricultural sector, so was sugar production in the industrial sector. In the 1950s the sugar industry controlled around one-third of capital stock in industry in the form of 161 sugar mills, 21 sugar refineries, and numerous other related plants. Production capacity of sugar mills was essentially stagnant from 1927 through the early years of the revolution, when a few mills were shut down. More recently, Cuba has carried out an ambitious investment program in the sugar industry whereby most of the mills have been modernized and several new ones built. The objective of the plan is to obtain a substantial increase in sugar output through the year 2000.

### THE SUGAR MILL COMPLEX

In 1959 the Cuban sugar industry was composed of 161 mills and 21 refineries. Most of the mills were located in the sugarcane-producing eastern half of the island: 50 in Las Villas province, 40 in Oriente, and 24 in Camagüey. The sugar mill complex dated from the expansionary stage of the industry, which lasted through the first quarter of the twentieth century. Thus the most recently built mills in operation in 1959 were completed in 1927; in all, 11 were built during 1921–27, 73 during 1902–20, and the rest (77) before 1900 (CERP 1965a, 126; 1965b, 237; Ferrán 1972, 115).

Some analysts have equated the age of the sugar mill complex with its level of technology. They implicitly assume that the mills in operation in the 1950s uniformly embodied machinery and equipment representing technology 30 or more years old. Thus Brundenius writes (1987, 87):

> The obsolescence of the Cuban sugar industry was disastrous: the most "modern" plant dated from 1927, and 40 percent of the *centrales*

(sugar mills) had been built during the 19th century. This obsolescence meant that much of the machinery, equipment and spare parts for this industry were no longer produced on the world market and therefore had to be produced nationally in order to guarantee continuing supplies.

Not only is this judgment contradicted by statements by Cuban officials indicating that the 1960 ban on imports from the United States adversely affected the sugar industry (see below), but it is also at odds with Fidel Castro's assessment of the efficiency of "old" sugar mills.

In a major speech in May 1970, in which he announced that the country would fail to reach the goal of 10 million tons of sugar in the 1970 *zafra,* Fidel Castro commented on the factors that influence sugar mill efficiency, as measured by industrial yield. He pointed out that during the 1970 campaign, two "old" mills—México (formerly Alava) and Caracas (formerly Caracasa)—not modernized since they were taken over by the state, consistently exceeded the performance of renovated mills, even when grinding low-quality sugarcane. Castro stated (1970, 9):

> Three factors have had an influence in the low yields [recorded by renovated mills]: number one, the new equipment; number two, maintenance, which was not up to par in many mills; and number three—and to tell the truth, it's an open question whether this is really factor number three or the principal factor—inefficient management of the mills.
>
> Naturally, our sugar mills are now 18 years older than they were in 1952 [when the largest level of sugar production before 1970 was recorded]. They are carrying the weight of an additional 18 years. But we are of the opinion that age is not the fundamental factor, since all of these mills, such as the Caracas, are of the same age and have a much higher sugar yield than they had in capitalist times.
>
> In other words, even an old mill that has good maintenance and good management, with a good variety of cane, will reach whatever sugar yield is desired. Now, then, a good number of mills that were grinding the same cane, even without new machinery, were getting a yield of 14; others got 12 and others 11. [The national yield in the 1970 *zafra* was 10.71 (AEC 1973, 124).] . . . Nevertheless, a number of the mills prove that mills that are managed well and given adequate maintenance can get a yield as high as 13.5 and 14 grinding the new varieties of cane during February, March, April and even May.

Thus, the most significant conclusion to be drawn from the fact that no sugar mills had been built in Cuba since 1927 was that production capacity of the industry was stagnant because of the lack of demand for sugar. Mills underwent annual maintenance during the off-season (*tiempo muerto*), however, and were periodically overhauled, with modern equipment installed in an on-going basis.

Nearly 40 percent (61 mills) of sugar mills active in 1959 had grinding capacity in the 2,000–3,000 tons/day range; altogether, close to 75 percent of the mills (116 units) had grinding capacity in the 1,000–4,000 tons/day range, suggesting that this might have been the optimal mill size given the land tenure system and other conditions. At either extreme were a few small units with grinding capacity of around 900 tons/day and very large mills with grinding capacity of over 9,000 tons/day.

On the basis of data from the *Anuario Azucarero de Cuba*, grinding capacity in 1958 can be estimated at 561,000 tons/day (AAC 1958, 91–93). A somewhat higher estimate of grinding capacity in 1959 of 569,752 tons/day has also been put forth (Gatria 1959, 107), as has a considerably lower one of 525,971 tons/day in 1962 based on 160 mills (Menéndez Cruz 1962a, 1). Using prerevolutionary Cuba's industrial yield of about 12.8 percent and the 561,000 ton/day estimate of grinding capacity, it can be estimated that the Cuban sugar mill complex in 1958 could produce just under 72,000 tons of raw sugar per day. An estimate of 67,000 tons/day raw sugar production capacity in 1962, based on grinding capacity of 525,971 tons/day, has been given in the literature (ibid. 1).

The value of the sugar mill complex in 1952 (including sugar refineries, alcohol distilleries, and other plants producing sugar derivatives, but excluding the value of land) has been estimated at 1,159 million pesos, over one-third of the total capital stock of the manufacturing sector estimated at 3,269 million pesos (CERP 1965c, 67–83). Another source (El desarrollo industrial 1966b, 113) reported the value of capital stock in the sugar industry under the control of the state around 1963 as 551.8 million pesos at acquisition prices (i.e., undepreciated value)—roughly one-half of the earlier estimate—or 43.8 percent of total capital stock in the state manufacturing sector. This source reports the capital stock of the sugar industry as being distributed as follows:

| | |
|---|---|
| transportation equipment | 22.0 percent |
| buildings and structures | 17.5 percent |
| equipment | 56.5 percent |
| other | 4.5 percent |

Since by 1963 the entire sugar mill complex was under state control and it was largely unchanged from 1952, no explanation is readily available for the wide disparity between the 1952 and 1963 capital stock estimates.

Using the historical high sugar production in each of the mills, one can estimate the annual raw sugar production capability of the industry. In most mills, 1952 was the most productive year. Thus the peak production figures are predicated on a *zafra* of 120 days, the length of the 1952 campaign, or less than four months of operation. Annual production capability of the Cuban sugar industry in 1958, in a less than four-month *zafra,* can be estimated at about 7.5 million tons of raw sugar.

## Changes since 1959

State control over sugar mills began formally in February 1960, when 14 mills were taken over by the Ministry for the Recovery of Misappropriated Assets (Ministerio de Recuperación de Bienes Malversados) (Charadán López 1982, 120). By the end of that year, the entire sugar industry had been nationalized. Management of the sugar mill complex was entrusted to the Sugar Consolidated Enterprise (Empresa Consolidada del Azúcar), created in 1961, reporting to the Ministry of Industries (Ministerio de Industrias). In 1964, when the Ministry of Industries was broken up, jurisdiction over the industrial side of sugar production was transferred to the newly established MINAZ (ibid. 125; A. Rodríguez 1979, 18).

In 1960 and 1961, nine relatively small sugar mills, with combined nominal daily grinding capacity of about 15,000 tons (or about 2.7 percent of national grinding capacity), were shut down and dismantled (CERP 1965a, 90). The closures were justified on the basis of industry rationalization. Reportedly, the equipment in those mills was technologically obsolete and, moreover, difficulties had arisen in supplying the mills with sugarcane and manpower (AAC 1961, 7–8; CERP 1965a, 90). Several of these mills also operated refineries. After 1962, 152 mills and 16 sugar refineries were in operation (Manual Azucarero 1971).

In 1963 MINAZ developed a multiyear plan for the sugar sector spanning the period 1965–70. The so-called Prospective Sugar Industry Plan was to culminate in the production of 10 million tons of sugar in

1970 and comparable levels in subsequent years. To be able to reach that annual level, the plan foresaw the need to make significant investments in sugarcane agriculture, sugar industrial plant and equipment, transportation facilities, and shipping terminals (F. Castro 1986, 17–18). Overall, investments on the order of 1 billion pesos over the period 1965–69 were anticipated, with approximately 465 million devoted to agriculture, 320 million to industry, and 235 million to transportation and shipping (table 6). About 60 percent of investments (630 million pesos) would correspond to imported machinery, equipment, and services, and 40 percent to local supplies. Socialist countries were expected to provide about 75 percent of imported investment goods and services, and capitalist countries the rest.

Specifically, the 1965–70 sugar plan called for a 22 percent increase in grinding capacity of mills, from an estimated 550,000 tons/day in 1960 to 670,000 tons/day in 1970 (T. Martínez 1967, 4); over 100 mills were slated to undergo modernization and expansion, and 2 or 3 new ones were to be built. According to a Cuban economist, investments in the sugar industry represented 70 percent of national investment programmed for the period 1966–70 (Borrego Díaz 1965, 22; 1966, 165). The modernization and expansion of sugar mills was to be partially financed by the Soviet Union through an agreement concluded in September 1965 (Díaz-Vázquez 1980, 152; del Monte 1983, 20).

TABLE 6
SUGAR SECTOR INVESTMENT PLAN, 1965–1969
*(in millions of pesos)*

|  | Total | Domestic | Imported from Socialist Countries | Imported from Capitalist Countries |
|---|---|---|---|---|
| Agriculture | 465 | 205 | 253 | 7 |
| Industry | 170 | 80 | 65 | 25 |
| New capacity[a] | 150 | 30 | 45 | 75 |
| Transportation | 190 | 50 | 100 | 40 |
| Shipping terminals | 45 | 25 | 18 | 2 |
| Total | 1,020 | 390 | 481 | 149 |

SOURCE: Gutelman 1970, 213–9.
 a. Based on construction of three new sugar mills.

The concentration of investment resources during 1966–70 in the expansion of sugar capacity meant that maintenance expenditures were given a lower priority (Charadán López 1982, 134–41). In addition, many of the modernization and expansion projects ran into difficulties and were not completed in a timely fashion. The plan to build two (or three?) new mills was set aside, and instead construction of a large mill (in the Cauto Valley) was proposed; immediate construction of this new mill was later discarded (Mesa-Lago 1971, 306–07).

During 1971–75 substantial efforts were made to complete outstanding sugar industry investments and to continue the modernization of plant and equipment (Charadán López 1982, 169–91). In the mid 1970s, the Cuban sugar mill complex consisted of 148 mills, with combined daily sugarcane grinding capacity of about 538,000 tons/day (appendix 2). Four small mills, with combined grinding capacity of 4,275 tons/day, were shut down between 1967 and 1976.

The process of modernization of the sugar industry was again a high priority during 1976–80, when investments in it reached 970 million pesos and more than 40 mills were overhauled (Vázquez 1981, 38); the Soviet Union assisted in the overhaul of 21 mills (Lazo 1975, 39). In 1974, Cuba and the Soviet Union formed the Permanent Group for the Development of the Cuban Sugar Industry, with responsibility for coordinating Soviet assistance for industry modernization (del Monte 1983, 21).

The five-year plan 1981–85 once again called for heavy investments in the sugar industry, including modernization of 18 mills, expansion of 23 others, and start-up of construction of 7 new ones. It was anticipated that by 1985 potential grinding capacity of the industry would be on the order of 690,000 tons/day (Lineamientos económicos 1981, 80). Sugar production was projected to increase by 20–25 percent with respect to the period 1976–80, or to about 9.5–10.0 million tons by 1985 (ibid., 79–80; Mesa-Lago 1982, 118). In reality, according to Fidel Castro (1986, 51–52), by the end of 1985, 38 mills had been expanded and modernized and 4 new ones had been completed; potential grinding capacity had increased by about 57,000 tons/day compared to 1980. In 1985, potential grinding capacity was around 624,000 tons/day, 9.6 percent short of the 690,000 tons/day anticipated in the plan.

During the period 1986–90, Cuba planned to continue to modernize and expand existing sugar mills and build three new ones; potential grinding capacity was planned to increase by nearly 65,000 tons/day. Sugar production was anticipated to increase by 15 percent compared to the previous five-year period, presumably to about 11 million tons per annum; grinding capacity utilization was projected at 85 percent (roughly the same rate reached during 1980–85) for a *zafra* of 150 effective grinding days. The long-term plan for the sugar industry foresees production of over 11 million tons of sugar in 1990 and annual production of 13–14 million tons by the year 2000 (Comparecencia 1981, 2).

Cuba began to publish systematic statistics on investment by industry in the 1980s, and retrospective data for as early as 1975 have been released. Examination of these data suggests, as expected, that the sugar industry has been the target of a very large share of investment resources allocated to the industrial sector. Table 7 presents the distribution of investment by branches of the industrial sector for selected years in the 1970s and 1980s. It is clear that over the entire period covered by the table, the sugar industry was the heaviest recipient of investment resources within the industrial sector, receiving over 20 percent of total investment in three of the years.

## New Sugar Mills

In May 1980 the Batalla de las Guásimas sugar mill, in Vertientes, Camagüey, was completed, the first green field sugar manufacturing capacity built in Cuba in over five decades (since 1927). Three other sugar mills were under construction at that time: 30 de Noviembre in San Cristóbal, Pinar del Río province; 5 de Septiembre in Cartagena, Cienfuegos province; and Grito de Yara in Cauto, Granma province (Vázquez 1978b, 6–7; 1981, 38–41; Ramos 1982, 2; AEC 1986, 226). All four of these started operation in the early 1980s. Three additional mills—Jesús Suárez Gayol in Camagüey province, Batalla de Santa Clara in Villa Clara province, and Majibacoa in Las Tunas province—were completed during 1985–86 (Morales 1985; Varela Pérez 1986a). Overall, the current expansion plan for the industry foresees construction of fifteen new mills by the end of the century (Vázquez 1981, 41).

The new mills were designed by Cuban technicians. Each of the mills has nominal daily sugarcane grinding capacity of 7,000 tons and can produce 100,000 tons of sugar per annum with a *zafra* of 150 days (Vázquez 1978b, 5; 1979b, 35; and 1981, 41). Grinding capacity of

TABLE 7
DISTRIBUTION OF INVESTMENT BY BRANCHES OF THE INDUSTRIAL SECTOR, 1975–1987
*(in percentages)*

|  | 1975 | 1980 | 1981 | 1984 | 1985 | 1986 | 1987 |
|---|---|---|---|---|---|---|---|
| INDUSTRY |  |  |  |  |  |  |  |
| Electricity | 8.3 | 12.3 | 9.9 | 19.0 | 15.7 | 22.5 | 23.8 |
| Fuels | 1.3 | 3.5 | 5.2 | 6.7 | 5.9 | 5.7 | 7.1 |
| Ferrous mining & metallurgy | 4.3 | 1.5 | 0.9 | 3.0 | 4.3 | 4.4 | 5.1 |
| Nonferrous mining & metallurgy | 1.4 | 16.6 | 14.7 | 12.4 | 13.3 | 16.0 | 14.6 |
| Nonelectrical machinery | 8.1 | 11.4 | 9.6 | 7.3 | 6.6 | 5.7 | 6.6 |
| Electronics | 0.6 | 2.1 | 1.7 | 0.9 | 0.9 | 1.2 | 2.1 |
| Metal products | 1.3 | 0.8 | 0.8 | 1.3 | 1.9 | 2.0 | 1.4 |
| Chemicals | 8.5 | 2.6 | 2.5 | 2.6 | 4.1 | 3.5 | 3.5 |
| Paper and cellulose | 0.5 | 5.6 | 10.4 | 2.0 | 1.4 | 1.6 | 1.9 |
| Printing | 0.5 | 0.4 | 0.2 | 0.1 | 0.1 | 0.1 | 0.1 |
| Wood products | 5.3 | 0.5 | 0.3 | 0.5 | 0.2 | 0.3 | 0.6 |
| Construction materials | 8.2 | 8.0 | 5.3 | 7.3 | 5.9 | 5.7 | 4.6 |
| Glass & ceramics | 0.1 | 1.2 | 1.1 | 0.6 | 0.8 | 1.0 | 1.0 |
| Textiles | 0.4 | 10.6 | 7.1 | 2.9 | 2.3 | 1.2 | 1.1 |
| Apparel | 0.4 | 0.2 | 0.3 | 0.2 | 0.4 | 0.5 | 0.2 |
| Leather | 0.1 | 0.2 | 0.2 | 0.6 | 0.4 | 0.4 | 0.3 |
| Sugar | 20.6 | 13.7 | 17.8 | 20.1 | 23.8 | 15.6 | 15.5 |
| Food | 5.3 | 5.9 | 5.0 | 4.7 | 3.5 | 4.4 | 4.3 |
| Fishing | 22.8 | 1.7 | 1.6 | 1.9 | 2.3 | 2.6 | 3.2 |
| Beverages & tobacco | 1.2 | 0.8 | 1.0 | 3.0 | 3.1 | 2.5 | 1.3 |
| Others | 0.8 | 0.4 | 4.4 | 2.9 | 3.0 | 3.4 | 1.6 |

SOURCE: 1987—AEC 1987, 216; 1986—AEC 1986, 215; 1984–85—AEC 1985, 206; 1975, 1981—AEC 1984, 122; 1980—AEC 1982, 136.

the new mills has also been reported as 6,800 tons/day (BNC 1985; AEC 1986, 226). When fully operational, each will employ 500–600 workers, compared to the more than 700 who would be required in a mill of similar capacity but older technology (Vázquez 1981, 41–42; Otra batalla 1979, 20; Alvarez Rosell and Cruz Lemus 1981).

The mills are quite large by Cuban standards. Though not in the same class as the Cuban industrial giants—such as Brasil (about 13,600 tons/day grinding capacity), Ciro Redondo (11,340 tons/day), Antonio Guiteras (10,150 tons/day), and Panamá (10,090 tons/day)—the new mills are nevertheless more than twice as large as the mode sugar mill size (2,000–3,000 tons/day). Moreover, out of the 148 mills active in the mid-1970s, only 14 had nominal grinding capacity exceeding 7,000 tons/day (see appendix 2).

According to Cuban sources (Danilo Rodríguez 1982, 19), the size of the new mills was carefully chosen to minimize unit costs of sugar production within a relatively simple design. This is consistent with empirical findings by a Cuban researcher (R. Hernández 1974, 98) that, assuming no bottlenecks in cane supplies and a satisfactory industrial yield, giant mills of 13,600 tons/day grinding capacity would result in lowest sugar unit costs, with those of about 7,900 tons/day a close second.

However, a study of the performance of sugar mills during the 1984 *zafra* by Radell (1987, 145–47) showed that relatively large mills (i.e., those with grinding capacity exceeding 6,000 tons/day) tended to perform less satisfactorily with respect to capacity utilization and technical efficiency (measured by the recovery rate, or the percentage of potential sugar actually extracted from sugarcane). He attributed the relatively poorer performance of the larger mills to a higher susceptibility to breakdowns and hastily scheduled downtime (ibid. 151–52). Not only do breakdowns and downtime directly affect output—by taking units out of operation—but they also affect yields, since cane already cut, or scheduled to be cut, has to be diverted to another mill. Particularly when large mills suffer interruptions, it is burdensome to divert large amounts of sugarcane to alternative mills.

Investment in each of the mills is probably in the range of 50–70 million pesos. For example, plant and equipment for the 5 de Septiembre mill reportedly cost 51 million pesos (Ramos 1982, 2). This figure probably does not include infrastructure construction, transportation equipment, etcetera, which would result in markedly higher costs. In some cases, for example the Batalla de las Guásimas mill, a new town has also been built to accommodate workers (Vázquez 1981, 42). Total investment in the four new mills that began operation during 1981–86 (5 de Septiembre, Grito de Yara, Jesús Suárez Guayol, and Batalla de Santa Clara) ranged from 60.9 to 66.6 million pesos (AEC 1986, 226).

For the mills built during 1981–85, investment costs were distributed as follows (Vázquez 1978b, 7):

| | |
|---|---|
| machinery and equipment | 54 percent |
| construction and setup | 37 percent |
| other | 9 percent |

By country of origin, total investment in the new mills has been broken down thus (ibid.):

|  |  |
|---|---|
| Cuba | 67.4 percent |
| socialist countries | 19.5 percent |
| capitalist countries | 13.1 percent |

Finally, 42 percent of the value of machinery and equipment used in the new mills reportedly was produced domestically, 36 percent imported from socialist countries, and 22 percent from capitalist countries (ibid.).

For some of the new mills, the following shares of domestically produced machinery and equipment have been reported:

- 60 percent for the 5 de Septiembre mill, with all other machinery and equipment imports originating from socialist countries (Ramos 1982, 2). This same 60 percent share of domestically produced machinery and equipment appears elsewhere in the literature (Vázquez 1981, 38), but there is no confirmation that the mills were constructed without any inputs from capitalist countries.
- 42 percent for the Batalla de las Guásimas mill, with the remaining 58 percent imported; about two-thirds of imported machinery and equipment originated from socialist countries (primarily the Soviet Union) and one-third from Japan, Sweden, Great Britain, West Germany, and Spain (A. Rodríguez 1980a, 17); and
- 77 percent for the Batalla de Santa Clara mill, with 23 percent imported; out of the imported components, only one-eighth originated from capitalist countries (P. Morales 1985, 21).

## Production of Machinery and Equipment

Repair facilities are critical to an industry such as sugar production that uses heavy equipment and machinery. In prerevolutionary Cuba, many sugar mills met these needs through their own foundries and repair shops, while others relied on outside facilities. Some of the foundries and machine shops also built machinery and equipment for sugar mills: they cast mill rolls and other large pieces and fabricated boilers, evaporators, vacuum pans, and tanks. The largest independent foundries were located in the heartland of the sugar industry: Sagua la Grande (Las Villas province), Unión de Reyes (Matanzas province) and Manzanillo (Oriente province). In addition to the foundries that cast iron and steel forms, several smaller ones worked bronze, copper, and aluminum (World Bank 1951, 973–74; U.S. Department of Commerce 1956, 100; Figueras 1985a, 120–22).

According to estimates, 80–90 percent of prerevolutionary Cuba's stock of capital goods (industrial machinery and transportation equipment) originated from the United States (Figueras 1985a, 126). The U.S. embargo on trade with Cuba, which became effective in October 1960, had an immediate effect on the ability of the Cuban industrial sector—including the sugar industry—to purchase machinery, equipment, and spare parts in the United States. Discussing the problems faced by the sugar industry, in June 1961, Minister of Industries Guevara stated that "our principal obstacle has been the impossibility of obtaining repair parts for the U.S. machinery installed in our plants" (CERP 1965a, 132). The Cuban government reacted to this shortage with a three-pronged approach (Figueras 1985a, 126–27):

- seek substitutes in the socialist countries, or contract with producers in the socialist countries to produce the required goods;
- seek substitutes in capitalist countries, to the extent that producers in third countries were willing to supply goods to Cuba in the face of the U.S. embargo and the availability of hard currency; and
- undertake a national program to stimulate domestic production of spare parts, including turning existing machine shops into producers of spare parts and building new capacity to produce machinery and spare parts.

Among the largest industrial investments made by the revolutionary government in the 1960s was the installation of a turnkey metalworking plant from the Soviet Union in Santa Clara. Formally opened in 1964, the so-called Planta Mecánica was capable of producing 4,000 tons per annum of metal products, including spare parts for sugar mills (Planta mecánica 1963). Subsequently the plant was expanded to include foundry facilities and numerically controlled machine tools imported from Western Europe and merged with an adjoining steel mill to form the Fabric Aguilar Noriega Steelworking Complex (Martí 1974; Palezuelos 1979b). In the 1980s annual production capacity of the complex doubled, and additional facilities were built to manufacture "tandems" (roll mills); the first domestically produced roll mill was completed in 1982 (Grant 1982).

Between 1976 and 1978, Cuban specialists, with assistance from the Soviet Union, developed designs for a high-efficiency steam boiler for the sugar industry. Prototypes were built in the Soviet Union and installed in three Cuban mills in the early 1980s. In 1981 a plant capable of producing up to thirty boilers per annum was completed in Sagua la Grande (J. Oramas 1981; Fonseca 1982).

In 1970 all facilities producing machinery and spare parts for the sugar industry were brought together under the Mechanical Production Enterprise (Empresa de Producción Mecánica), which was attached to the Vice-Ministry for Maintenance and Production of MINAZ, and which later, in 1982, was combined with the network of machine shops at each of the was sugar mills to form the Union of Metalworking Enterprises (Unión de Empresas de Producción Mecánica). Around 1982, 11 enterprises, producing a wide range of machinery and spare parts for the sugar industry, were part of the union (Villa Montes 1983, 22). As was noted above, up to 70 percent of the machinery and equipment used in the sugar mills built in Cuba in the 1980s was produced domestically.

In the late 1960s the Fabric Aguilar Noriega complex built domestically designed machinery to harvest sugarcane: in 1968, 25 self-propelled Libertadora combines, and in 1969–70, 140 tractor-mounted Henderson combines (Lazo 1985c, 28). Since 1977, Cuba has mass-produced the KTP family harvesters in the 60 Aniversario de la Revolución de Octubre plant in Holguín (see chapter 4).

Sugar industry technology and equipment have emerged as potentially important sources of export revenues for Cuba (Otra batalla 1979, 21). As is discussed in chapter 11, Cuba designed and built a sugar mill (Victoria de Julio) in Nicaragua that was completed in January 1985, supplying the design, supervisory personnel for construction, and a large share of the machinery and equipment (Varela Pérez 1985b). Cuba had plans to export sugar industry machinery to East Germany valued at 20 million rubles (about $12.7 million converted at the official 1987 exchange rate of 1 ruble = $1.58) during the five-year period 1986–90 (Salomón Llanes 1986c, 32). Directories of Cuban goods available for export list sugar industry machinery and equipment available through the enterprise Cubaindustria (Cámara de Comercio 1982, 59; 1984, 21–22).

## Production and Yields

Table 8 presents key indicators of performance of the Cuban sugar industry over the last three decades: total sugar production, sugarcane ground per day, effective grinding days, and industrial yield.

After declining significantly in the first half of the 1960s, sugar production has shown an upward trend in the 1970s and 1980s,

TABLE 8
Sugar Industry Performance, 1951–1987
*(in thousands of tons)*

| Zafra | Cane Ground per Day | Effective Zafra Days | Industrial yield (%)[a] | Production |
|---|---|---|---|---|
| 1951 | 468.3 | 96 | 12.95 | 5,821.3 |
| 1952 | 495.9 | 120 | 12.56 | 7,298.0 |
| 1953 | 489.0 | 84 | 12.80 | 5,223.9 |
| 1954 | 494.9 | 79 | 12.62 | 4,959.1 |
| 1955 | 504.7 | 69 | 13.20 | 4,597.7 |
| 1956 | 512.5 | 72 | 12.98 | 4,807.3 |
| 1957 | 514.8 | 87 | 12.84 | 5,741.5 |
| 1958 | 545.0 | 84 | 12.82 | 5,862.6 |
| 1959 | 541.5 | 89 | 12.57 | 6,038.6 |
| 1960 | 542.3 | 88 | 12.51 | 5,942.9 |
| 1961 | 522.2 | 104 | 12.66 | 6,875.5 |
| 1962 | 483.4 | 76 | 13.31 | 4,882.1 |
| 1963 | 461.0 | 68 | 12.36 | 3,882.5 |
| 1964 | 454.1 | 82 | 12.03 | 4,474.5 |
| 1965 | 482.0 | 105 | 12.15 | 6,156.2 |
| 1966 | 481.8 | 76 | 12.32 | 4,537.4 |
| 1967 | 502.1 | 101 | 12.26 | 6,236.1 |
| 1968 | 486.5 | 87 | 12.19 | 5,164.5 |
| 1969 | 471.0 | 86 | 11.02 | 4,459.4 |
| 1970 | 557.8 | 143 | 10.71 | 8,537.6 |
| 1971 | 510.0 | 101 | 11.49 | 5,924.8 |
| 1972 | 476.6 | 91 | 9.93 | 4,324.8 |
| 1973 | 514.8 | 92 | 11.07 | 5,252.7 |
| 1974 | 519.8 | 95 | 11.95 | 5,924.9 |
| 1975 | 513.5 | 99 | 12.44 | 6,314.3 |
| 1976 | 526.9 | 99 | 11.84 | 6,155.9 |
| 1977 | 542.5 | 104 | 11.55 | 6,485.0 |
| 1978 | 563.2 | 119 | 10.96 | 7,350.5 |
| 1979 | 571.4 | 128 | 10.94 | 7,991.8 |
| 1980 | 565.8 | 109 | 10.82 | 6,665.2 |
| 1981 | 580.3 | 114 | 11.08 | 7,358.9 |
| 1982 | 594.1 | 124 | 11.17 | 8,210.1 |
| 1983 | 608.9 | 113 | 10.35 | 7,108.6 |
| 1984 | 620.2 | 126 | 10.47 | 8,206.6 |
| 1985 | 646.5 | 103 | 11.99 | 8,003.9 |
| 1986 | 656.6 | 104 | 10.62 | 7,254.6 |
| 1987 | 673.9 | 99 | 10.64 | 7,116.8 |

SOURCES: 1987—AEC 1987, 243; 1985–86—AEC 1986, 242; 1978–84—AEC 1984, 141; 1975–77—AEC 1977, 86; 1951–74—AEC 1973, 124–5

a. Industrial yield was calculated on the basis of production standardized to 96 degrees polarization.

although there have been significant year-to-year fluctuations, which are smoothed out when five-year averages are used:

| | |
|---|---|
| 1956–60 | 5.528 million tons |
| 1961–65 | 4.514 million tons |
| 1966–70 | 5.787 million tons |
| 1971–75 | 5.548 million tons |
| 1976–80 | 6.930 million tons |
| 1981–85 | 7.778 million tons |

Sugar output in 1986 and 1987 was 7.255 and 7.117 million tons, respectively.

Sugarcane ground per day is an indicator of effective grinding capacity of the industry. How much sugar is produced in a given *zafra* is directly related to the utilization of capacity (i.e., the number of days the mill is in operation) and the efficiency of the industrial process (including the quality of the raw material), as reflected in the industrial yield.

As already explained, in prerevolutionary Cuba the length of the *zafra* was largely determined by the external demand for sugar. There was also an incentive on the part of employers to shorten the length of the *zafras* in order to reduce costs, a contentious issue with workers (Chantez Oliva and Fernández Llorens 1985). In most years, production quotas were allocated to mills to limit their output. Thus the 1953–58 *zafras* averaged 78.5 effective grinding days (i.e., actual days mills were in operation, net of stoppages resulting from equipment breakdowns, bad weather conditions, etc.). The average duration of the 1952–58 *zafras*—including the 1952 *zafra*, a campaign in which no production controls were in effect and which lasted 120 effective days—was 84 days, or less than three months. That is, the industry that controlled the largest share of Cuba's capital stock typically used its productive capacity for 2.5–3.0 months per year. In the 1952 *zafra*, when the prerevolutionary sugar production record was set, sugar mills operated for just under four months. Officials of the Cuban revolutionary government saw the policy of restricting sugar output as one of the key problems affecting the national economy. As Minister of Industries Guevara (1964, 617) put it, "The [U.S. import] quota system resulted in the stagnation of sugar production. In the last few years, the full productive capacity of the Cuban sugar industry has only been used in rare occasions."

With the lifting of restrictions on sugar production beginning in 1961, the length of the *zafra* has increased steadily. Cuba's longest, the 1970 campaign, lasted 143 effective days; other lengthy *zafras* were those for 1978 and 1979 (119 and 128 effective days, respectively) and 1982 (124 effective days). The average length of *zafras* for selected periods (in effective days) is:

| | |
|---|---|
| 1961–65 | 86.0 days |
| 1966–70 | 98.6 days |
| 1971–75 | 95.6 days |
| 1976–80 | 111.8 days |
| 1981–85 | 116.0 days |

The 1985–87 *zafras* were quite short by recent standards, averaging 102 effective production days.

The increase of the length of the *zafra* has been partly responsible for the decline in sugar industrial yield in revolutionary Cuba relative to the 1950s. The lower yields work to offset part of the gains derived from the longer *zafras*. From 1952 to 1958, for example, industrial yield averaged 12.8 percent; it remained at about 12.0 percent through 1968 and fell thereafter, bottoming out at 9.9 percent in 1972. More recently, it has varied significantly from year to year, with performance during 1983 and 1984 falling markedly below levels reached during 1978–82. The 1985 *zafra* resulted in the highest industrial yield in a decade (11.99 percent), but yield fell sharply during the 1986 and 1987 campaigns (to 10.62 and 10.64 percent, respectively).

Using data from the 1950s through 1980, Cuban economists have estimated the following inverse relationship between the length of a *zafra* and industrial yield:

$$y = 14.50 - 0.021\,x$$

where $x$ is the duration of a *zafra* campaign in calendar days (not effective days) and $y$ is the industrial yield, standardized to 96 degrees polarization (Morales Rodríguez and Rodríguez Corominas 1986, 98). This means that, on average, each *zafra* day reduces industrial yield by 0.021, or by about 0.15 percent.

The authors have further disaggregated the data and reestimated the above relationship for *zafras* of three different duration: (1) up to 120 days; (2) 21 to 150 days; and (3) 151 days and longer. They conclude that for those lasting beyond 120 calendar days, the reduction in industrial yield incurred for each additional grinding day is 11 times higher than for *zafras* of shorter duration, which points up the inefficiency of those lasting more than four months.

## Organizational Changes

In the 1970s failure to maintain a steady supply of sugarcane far outpaced climatic conditions as the single most important cause of downtime of mills. In the 1972 *zafra,* for example, shortages of cane were responsible for nearly 35 percent of the downtime; in the 1979 and 1980 *zafras,* they accounted for 23 and 28 percent, respectively, of interruptions in sugar mill activities (AEC 1980, 94).

Problems such as interruptions in sugarcane flows and low quality of sugarcane deliveries to mills were attributed to the organizational structure of sugar production, whereby agricultural and industrial activities were not under the same management and often were not well coordinated. A Cuban economist has described the organizational problems of sugar production in the 1960s and 1970s as follows (del Monte 1981, 78–79):

> The current organizational structure consisting of separate management for the two branches of production—sugarcane agriculture and the sugar industry—has made difficult, and in some cases has prevented, the synchronization of tasks and operational measures to achieve the desired goal [i.e., maximize sugar output]. In all cases, it has demanded extraordinary coordination efforts, which would have been unnecessary had there existed joint management of the two phases of production. . . . It is obvious that as long as this organizational structure remains, full congruence between the objectives and interests of sugarcane agriculture and the sugar industry will not be reached at each mill. The harmonization of the two interests, and the full unleashing of their potential, will be reached only under a single strategy and daily joint activities, guided by the principles of socialist economic development.

In early 1980 control over sugarcane agricultural activities—whether carried out by state farms, CPAs, or private farmers—was shifted from the Ministry of Agriculture (Ministerio de Agricultura) to MINAZ (La comercialización 1984, 45; Rizo Alvarez 1981, 41). The rationale for the change was that it was necessary to coordinate agricultural plans more closely with industrial sugar production (H. Pérez 1982, 13).

Gradually, sugar mills have been converted into agro-industrial complexes, patterned after the Bulgarian and Soviet vertical integration model (Allen 1977, 676–82; Tijonov 1981; Yañez González 1981;

Ivanovich Zerashim and Díaz Romero 1985; Bronshtein 1986; Rodríguez Cordova 1986), as agricultural and industrial operations have been brought together under the same management. Reportedly, this organizational change in Cuba was required by the Economic Management and Planning System (SPDE) so that standards of accountability could be established for mills (del Monte Navarro 1981, 76–78; Rizo Alvarez 1981, 39). It was also hoped that the greater coordination between the agricultural and industrial spheres would give the mills greater authority to insist on punctual deliveries of sugarcane, cleaner cane, and higher quality in general (Ghai et al. 1988, 34).

During the 1981 *zafra* four sugar mills operated as agro-industrial complexes, reportedly with a great deal of autonomy from MINAZ and from local authorities (Rizo Alvarez 1981, 41). In 1982, 13 additional mills and sugarcane areas were converted into agro-industrial complexes, and 76 more in 1983. By 1986 all sugar mills and associated agricultural lands had been converted (García Marrero and Morales Pita 1987, 72).

Since the establishment of agro-industrial sugar complexes is a fairly recent development, there is insufficient information at this time to evaluate their performance. In the 1980s the share of downtime of mills that was attributable to lack of cane supplies fell markedly, averaging around 14 percent, and reaching 8 percent in 1983; however, in the 1986 *zafra* lack of sugarcane accounted for 22 percent of downtime (AEC 1986, 245). Fragmentary data suggest that the change in organizational structure has not always turned around laggard performers. For instance, although it became an agro-industrial complex in 1983, the Julio Antonio Mella complex showed steady deterioration in agricultural and industrial performance in 1984 and 1985, suggesting that other factors affected its operation (Estevez Martir and González del Foyo 1987, 47).

## Sugar within Industry

In 1954 sugar production and refining accounted for about 34 percent of income and 37 percent of domestic value added generated by the manufacturing sector (CERP 1965c, 84–86). The sugar industry dominated the industrial sector of the economy of prerevolutionary

TABLE 9
DISTRIBUTION OF GROSS INDUSTRIAL OUTPUT BY BRANCHES
OF THE INDUSTRIAL SECTOR, 1975–1987
*(in percentages)*

|  | 1975 | 1980 | 1981 | 1984 | 1985 | 1986 | 1987 |
|---|---|---|---|---|---|---|---|
| INDUSTRY |  |  |  |  |  |  |  |
| Electricity | 2.1 | 3.4 | 4.8 | 4.6 | 4.3 | 4.6 | 5.5 |
| Fuels | 6.3 | 5.2 | 5.4 | 4.6 | 4.5 | 4.4 | 4.6 |
| Ferrous mining & metallurgy | 0.9 | 0.9 | 1.1 | 1.1 | 1.2 | 1.6 | 1.6 |
| Nonferrous mining & metallurgy | 0.9 | 1.1 | 1.4 | 1.2 | 1.2 | 1.3 | 1.5 |
| Nonelectrical machinery | 4.6 | 6.5 | 5.8 | 7.5 | 7.8 | 7.1 | 6.4 |
| Electronics | 2.3 | 1.7 | 1.1 | 1.2 | 1.2 | 1.4 | 1.2 |
| Metal products | 1.6 | 1.7 | 1.5 | 1.7 | 1.6 | 1.7 | 1.6 |
| Chemicals | 9.7 | 8.0 | 6.6 | 5.8 | 6.2 | 6.2 | 6.0 |
| Paper and cellulose | 1.2 | 1.2 | 1.4 | 1.5 | 1.6 | 1.3 | 1.6 |
| Printing | 1.3 | 1.4 | 0.9 | 0.9 | 0.9 | 1.0 | 0.8 |
| Wood products | 2.0 | 1.9 | 1.4 | 1.4 | 1.3 | 1.2 | 1.2 |
| Construction materials | 4.1 | 4.0 | 3.9 | 3.3 | 3.3 | 3.4 | 3.4 |
| Glass & ceramics | 0.5 | 0.5 | 0.3 | 0.4 | 0.4 | 0.5 | 0.4 |
| Textiles | 2.1 | 1.7 | 1.7 | 1.6 | 1.8 | 2.0 | 2.8 |
| Apparel | 4.3 | 4.9 | 2.1 | 1.9 | 2.0 | 2.1 | 1.9 |
| Leather | 2.7 | 2.1 | 1.6 | 1.4 | 1.4 | 1.3 | 1.3 |
| Sugar | 9.3 | 9.3 | 15.0 | 14.7 | 13.8 | 13.1 | 12.9 |
| Food | 19.2 | 19.5 | 19.6 | 19.3 | 18.7 | 19.0 | 19.1 |
| Fishing | 1.3 | 1.6 | 2.2 | 2.6 | 2.6 | 2.7 | 2.7 |
| Beverages & tobacco | 20.2 | 19.7 | 18.0 | 19.3 | 19.8 | 19.5 | 19.0 |
| Others | 3.3 | 3.7 | 4.3 | 4.4 | 4.4 | 4.6 | 4.3 |

SOURCES: 1987—AEC 1987, 113–14; 1984–86—AEC 1986, 112–3; 1975, 1981—AEC 1984, 90; 1980—AEC 1982, 97.
*Note:* Output is given in producer prices.

Cuba, although nonsugar industrial activities recorded impressive gains after World War II (Pérez-López 1977).

Data limitations do not permit a precise comparison of the relative importance of the sugar industry of prerevolutionary and revolutionary Cuba within the industrial sector, or in the economy at large. However, available data suggest that it continues to be one of the key components of the industrial sector and a mainstay of the economy.

For example, table 9 shows the distribution of GVO generated by various components of the industrial sector for 1975 and selected years in the 1980s, at producer prices. According to these data, sugar production and refining trailed only the food industry and the tobacco and beverage industries in terms of contribution to GVO. Moreover, the contribution of the sugar industry to GVO of the industrial sector, which was under 10 percent in 1975 and 1980, ranged from nearly 13 to 15 percent in the 1980s.

# CHAPTER 4

•

## Labor and Agricultural Mechanization

THE SUGAR INDUSTRY (agricultural and industrial operations combined) is by far Cuba's largest employer. According to the 1970 population census, 183,510 persons were employed in sugarcane agriculture and 97,000 in sugar industrial activities, for total industry employment of over 280,000 workers (Junta Central 1975, 511). In the 1981 census the corresponding numbers of workers were 271,108 in agriculture and 107,347 in industry, for total sugar industry employment of nearly 380,000 workers (Comité Estatal 1984, 263).

Presumably referring to 1982, Sugar Industry Minister Torralbas has stated that his ministry employed close to 450,000 workers, including technicians, engineers, skilled workers, and laborers (Torralbas González 1983, 95). This compares with total civilian employment in 1982 of about 2.8 million (AEC 1986, 192). An analyst has provided yet another way to gauge the importance of the sugar industry; he estimates that in the early 1980s it employed 400,000 workers, who, together with their families, made up perhaps one-sixth of the population (Feuer 1987, 67).

Generally speaking, sugar production from sugarcane is not a labor-intensive process. Sugarcane is a perennial grass, which can be harvested in Cuba for several years without sacrificing yields. Yields improve if fields are weeded and fertilized regularly, but there is considerable slack here. Sugarcane cultivation lends itself to large-scale farming and does not require the intense care and human attention that must be devoted to other crops, such as tobacco or garden vegetables.

At harvesting time, however, cane requires large amounts of labor to cut, load, and transport the bulky crop to mills in a timely fashion. Revolutionary Cuba has made remarkable progress in mechanizing sugarcane harvesting. This has required substantial investments in harvesting machinery, training of workers, and the preparation of fields for mechanical harvesting. Extracting juice from sugarcane and transforming it into sugar in mills is essentially a capital- and energy-intensive process, requiring relatively small inputs of labor.

## Agricultural Labor

Prior to the revolution virtually all sugarcane harvesting in the nation relied on manual labor. Although a patent for a cane cutting machine was filed in Cuba in 1857 (Edquist 1983, 42; 1985, 32; Ruiz Portal 1980, 19), and some experimentation with cutting equipment took place as early as the 1920s (CERP 1965a, 112–13; Edquist 1985, 33), sugarcane mechanization did not catch on. To some extent this may have been related to the structure of sugarcane production (dominated by small *colonos,* who were not large enough to afford expensive cane-cutting machinery) and opposition from workers, who feared that their jobs would disappear as a result of the new technology (Edquist 1983, 42; 1985, 33).

Cuban workers' opposition to mechanization ran deep. In 1925, tobacco workers went on strike to block the introduction of cigar-making machinery (CERP 1965b, 265). Trade unions fought—and essentially blocked—the introduction of cane harvesting and loading machinery (CERP 1965a, 113) and export of sugar in bulk form (i.e., not bagged).

Harvesting of the sugar crop without mechanized means required large quantities of labor. Although no systematic data on the number of sugarcane field workers are available, estimates (CERP 1965b, 352) suggest that during the 1928–40 *zafras* it ranged from 250,000 to 360,000, depending on the size of the harvest; 85 percent of these field workers were *macheteros* (cane cutters). There are no reliable estimates of field work employment during subsequent *zafras*. It has been estimated by Cuban officials that there were 370,000 "professional" cane cutters in 1958 (Roca 1976, 19), but it is not clear that this estimate is comparable to those for 1928–40, which referred to workers actually employed, whereas those for the later period refer to workers "available" to perform cane-cutting tasks.

Compensation of agricultural workers for cutting and loading cane—traditionally paid on a piece rate basis—and other agricultural wages were established by law, using a formula that took into account the export price of sugar. Labor law also regulated the frequency (every two weeks) and form (cash) of payment for agricultural and industrial workers, obligated sugar mills and *colonos* to set aside land for the establishment of workers' consumer cooperatives, and provided for mills and *colonos* to devote a portion of their lands to workers during the off-season (*tiempo muerto*) for production of crops for their own consumption (CERP 1965b, 345–47).

Though cutting and loading of sugarcane were done almost exclusively by manual labor in prerevolutionary Cuba, there is evidence that mechanization had spread in clearing and preparing the soil for planting. In addition, 80 percent of the cane cut in the late 1950s was reportedly transported to railroads or directly to sugar mills on trucks or tractors with trailers. Cuba's stock of agricultural tractors grew quickly after World War II: in 1945 the national stock numbered 1,888, whereas 14,471 were imported from the United States during 1947–58 (CERP 1965b, 524).

One of the chronic problems of the economy of prerevolutionary Cuba was the strong seasonal nature of employment. During the *zafra* period (approximately four months, from January to April), harvesting and processing of the sugarcane crop demanded large quantities of labor. Significant numbers of these agricultural workers tended to be underemployed or unemployed during the rest of the year. Data for 1943–47 indicate that only 52 percent of agricultural workers were employed for four months or more (CERP 1965c, 126). Thus, depending on the time of year when it was measured, unemployment could vary substantially; for example, it was estimated at 20.7 percent in the midst of the off-season in 1956–57 and 9 percent during the *zafra* (Mesa-Lago 1981, 121).

The problem of the seasonality of employment was most acute in the three eastern provinces (Las Villas, Camagüey, and Oriente), where the sugar industry was concentrated. According to surveys conducted by the National Economic Council (Consejo Nacional de Economía) during 1956–58, unemployment in these provinces peaked during *tiempo muerto* and declined to less than one-half during the *zafra* in Oriente, to less than one-third in Las Villas, and to one-seventh in Camagüey; in fact, during the *zafra* period, Camagüey province drew large numbers of workers from other areas of the nation (Mesa-Lago 1972, 25).

Early policies of the revolutionary government resulted in a reduction in seasonal unemployment, as the number of agricultural (largely sugarcane) workers was slashed by large rural-to-urban migration, recruitment into the armed forces, availability of educational opportunities, and year-round work on state farms (Mesa-Lago 1981, 125). The result was a significant shortage of agricultural workers to harvest sugarcane, which developed as early as the 1961 *zafra* (Menéndez Cruz 1961, 44–45), while there was a surplus of workers in the tertiary (services) sector. The National Sugar Commission (Comisión Nacional Azucarera) estimated that for the 1963 *zafra*, 352,000 experienced cane cutters were needed to maintain a normal flow of sugarcane to mills, compared to the 260,000 who were available (Menéndez Cruz 1963, 12).

To address the labor shortage in sugarcane harvesting, the government turned to "voluntary" labor. These "volunteers" included employed workers performing cane harvesting tasks in addition to their regular duties, unemployed women, students, prisoners, and military recruits (Mesa-Lago 1969c, 340–41; Domínguez 1968, 357–60; Menéndez Cruz 1961, 44–45; 1962a, 3–4). The government also began an aggressive program to mechanize harvesting.

There are no systematic data on employment in sugarcane agriculture in revolutionary Cuba. Regularly published employment statistics are available only at the level of sectors of the economy (e.g., agriculture, industry), but not for branches within those sectors, and they refer only to employment in state enterprises. Working from fragmentary data, one researcher (Roca 1976, 19) has assembled the following series—with some gaps—on the number of professional cane cutters for 1958–71:

| | |
|---|---|
| 1958 | 370,000 |
| 1963 | 210,000 |
| 1964 | 160,000 |
| 1967 | 143,368 |
| 1968 | 105,598 |
| 1969 | 88,300 |
| 1970 | 79,752 |
| 1971 | 72,986 |

Thus the number of professional cane cutters declined by over 40 percent from 1958 to 1963; the number in 1971 (72,986) was roughly one-third of the number active in 1971 (210,000) (see also Pollitt 1973, 260–61). Presumably, the number continued to decline in the 1970s and 1980s.

It is clear, however, that in addition to the professional cane cutters, many other workers (some of them permanently assigned to sugarcane agricultural tasks) have also been drawn into harvesting

TABLE 10
CANE CUTTERS DEPLOYED IN
SELECTED *ZAFRAS*, 1963–1985

| Zafra | No. of Cane Cutters |
|---|---|
| 1963 | 260,000 |
| 1967 | 243,000 |
| 1970 | 350,000 |
| 1971 | 274,000 |
| 1972 | 210,500 |
| 1973 | 229,000 |
| 1974 | 200,300 |
| 1975 | 175,600 |
| 1976 | 153,300 |
| 1977 | 139,100 |
| 1978 | 153,900 |
| 1979 | 126,400 |
| 1980 | 128,000 |
| 1981 | 119,000 |
| 1982 | 110,000 |
| 1985 | 70,000 |

SOURCES: 1985—F. Castro 1986, 52; 1980–82—Varela Pérez 1983, 3; 1970–79—Pollitt 1982, 17; 1963, 1967—Clemens and de Groot 1988, 26.

activities. Table 10 presents estimates of the number of cane cutters in selected *zafras* from 1963 to 1985. The 1963 *zafra* employed about 260,000 cane cutters, of which 210,000 were so-called professionals; the additional 50,000 workers most likely were unpaid "volunteers." In the 1967 campaign, 160,000 professionals were supplemented by 100,000 volunteers.

During the giant 1970 *zafra*, 350,000 cane cutters were deployed; the number declined quite steadily through the 1980s, so that by 1985 harvesting was accomplished by only 70,000 cane cutters. President Castro has stated that cutting, loading, and transporting sugarcane to the sugar mills during the 1954–58 *zafras* required 387,000 workers, whereas these functions were carried out during the 1976–80 *zafras* by 190,000 workers (F. Castro 1980a, 12). Sugar Minister Herrera has stated that about 8,000 cane cutters participated in the 1987 campaign (Lazo 1987, 49).

The sugarcane agricultural sector draws cane cutters from several sources, principally the following:

- workers who are temporarily assigned to sugarcane harvesting activities by their workplaces. These workers fall into two categories: "habitual" cane cutters, who have cut cane in previous campaigns, and "volunteer" cane cutters, who most likely have not engaged in the task previously;
- members of the Youth Labor Army (Ejército Juvenil del Trabajo), a paramilitary organization established in 1973 that consists of military draftees; members typically have no previous experience in cane cutting; and
- workers of state-owned sugarcane farms; since 1985 these workers have been organized in so-called permanent production brigades (brigadas permanentes de producción). In the sugar agricultural sector the brigades specialize in a variety of tasks in addition to manual cane cutting: sugarcane cultivation, weeding, machine repair, or mechanized harvesting (González Fontes and Ramírez Reyes 1984). In 1985 there were 104 brigades in the sugar agricultural sector (L. Domínguez 1986, 58) consisting of 20,800 workers (Ghai et al. 1988, 59).

In the 1985 *zafra* mobilized workers represented 32 percent of cane cutters, workers of state sugar farms 29 percent, and Youth Labor Army members 22 percent.

For the period 1980–87 only, official statistics are available on employment, average salary, and worker productivity in sugar agriculture in the state sector (table 11). State sugarcane agriculture employed 260,000 workers in 1980, compared to about 225,000 in 1987. Over this period around 40 percent of all state agricultural workers were engaged in sugarcane cultivation. Apparently these figures refer to field workers and do not include labor engaged in related activities, for example, transporting cane from fields to mills. In 1985 the MINAZ vice minister in charge of transportation reported that about 30,700 workers were engaged in sugarcane transportation; these represented roughly 10 percent of total employment in sugarcane agriculture, which suggests that overall employment in sugarcane agriculture in 1985 was around 300,000 (Salomón Llanes 1985b).

The average salary of sugarcane workers rose from 130 pesos/month in 1980 to 205 pesos/month in 1986, nearly a 60 percent increase, the bulk of the increase coming in 1981 as part of a general wage reform. As a result of that reform, wages of the lowest-paid workers in agriculture rose by 30 percent (Ghai et al. 1988, 38); salaries of sugar agricultural workers increased in 1981 by 35 percent (table

## TABLE 11
### Selected Labor Indicators for Sugarcane Agriculture 1980–1987

|      | Employment (thousands) | Average Monthly Salary (pesos) | Productivity per Worker (pesos) |
|------|------------------------|--------------------------------|---------------------------------|
| 1980 | 260.6                  | 130                            | 2,533                           |
| 1981 | 258.4                  | 176                            | 3,840                           |
| 1982 | 258.5                  | 185                            | 3,532                           |
| 1983 | 240.4                  | 181                            | 3,371                           |
| 1984 | 211.1                  | 192                            | 4,061                           |
| 1985 | 202.4                  | 200                            | 4,301                           |
| 1986 | 218.0                  | 205                            | 4,160                           |
| 1987 | 224.9                  | 203                            | 4,068                           |

SOURCE: 1987—AEC 1987, 306; 1980–86—AEC 1986, 301.

11). In 1987, the average salary of sugarcane workers declined to 203 pesos/month.

Interestingly, the salary premium of sugarcane workers over other agricultural workers, which was 2.8 percent in 1980 (130 vs. 128 pesos/month), grew to 8–10 percent after the 1981 wage reform; in 1986 the premium was about 13 percent (205 vs. 182 pesos/month) (AEC 1986, 301) and 14 percent in 1987 (203 vs. 178 pesos/month) (AEC 1987, 306). These differentials are probably attributable to wage premium funds for enterprises exceeding productivity targets that were established in state sugarcane enterprises beginning in 1981. By 1982, 41 out of 138 sugarcane enterprises had created such funds (Rizo Alvarez 1981, 39–40).

Worker productivity (average annual value of output per worker) in sugarcane agriculture grew 52 percent in 1981, probably as a result of the wholesale price reform implemented that year. Worker productivity declined in 1982 and 1983 but rose strongly in 1984 and 1985; in 1986, it dropped by 3.3 percent and in 1987 by an additional 2.2 percent.

## Agricultural Mechanization

In the short run, Cuba addressed its severe labor shortage in sugarcane harvesting by relying on voluntary workers. As a long-term strategy, however, it embraced an ambitious plan to mechanize sugarcane agriculture, in particular cutting and loading (Pollitt 1982b, 19). This endeavor required substantial investments in equipment and field preparation and basic changes in the way sugarcane was cultivated and harvested. Mechanization has contributed to overall low industrial yields, a problem that has not been resolved to date.

SUGARCANE HARVESTING MACHINERY

As shortages of cane cutters began to develop in the 1961 *zafra,* the Ministry of Industries, at the time headed by Ernesto Che Guevara, set up a group of technicians to tackle large-scale mechanization of the sugarcane harvest. An experimental machine (the MC-1), which cut the cane at ground level, took the tops off the plants, and deposited the stalks in the furrow, was tested in the 1962 *zafra* and produced massively for the 1963 campaign (Edquist 1985, 34–35). As many as 867 of these mechanical cutters were produced. Apparently the MC-1 worked quite well in cutting cane; however, since it could neither load the cut cane stalks nor clean them (i.e., separate leaves, weeds, and other trash from the stalks), it still required that workers separate the stalks from the trash and load them onto carts (Menéndez Cruz 1963, 17–18).

Cuban-Soviet cooperation in the design and construction of sugarcane harvesting equipment began in 1962 (Pino-Santos and Martínez 1979, 74). In 1963 a Soviet-designed loader, the PG 0.5-CT, was introduced. In that year, Cuba and the Soviet Union entered into an agreement concerning mechanization of sugarcane harvesting: henceforth, Cuba imported large numbers of loaders from the Soviet Union (del Monte 1983, 18), and domestic design and production of harvesting machinery was discontinued, a decision that "had important consequences for Cuba's future technical skills and capabilities" (Edquist 1983, 46), presumably of a negative nature.

The first two combine harvesters to emerge from Cuban-Soviet collaboration, the KCT-1, called the Druzhba (Friendship), towed by a tractor, and the KT-1, a self-propelled machine, were tested in 1964; both cut stalks at ground level, topped them, eliminated leaves, cut the stalks into pieces, and loaded them on a cart. Cuba imported over 450 of these machines, mostly KCT-1s, for the 1965 *zafra;* by the end of the *zafra,* only 10 percent were in operation (Betancourt 1970, 8). The KCT-1 required flat land, had difficulty in cutting cane that was not straight, and was so heavy that it did damage to the roots of the plants, thereby affecting future production from the same fields. It has been reported that Castro said of the Soviet-made KCT-1, "It is a great destroyer; where it has been, nothing will grow for a long time to come" (Karol 1970, 412). In the context of describing the problems that had plagued the 1970 *zafra,* Labor Minister Risquet admitted that, up to that time, efforts to mechanize sugarcane harvesting had been unsuccessful (Roca 1976, 56).

A prototype harvester designed by Cuban technicians and improved upon by their Soviet counterparts evolved into the KTP (Kombain Trasnikouroshniy Priamatoshniy, or single row, continuous-flow cane harvester) line of combine harvesters. Two Cuban engineers, together with a number of Soviet engineers, were awarded the Soviet Union's Lenin Prize for Science and Technology in 1982 for their contributions to the design and development of the KTP harvesters (Despegue 1983, 15; La revolución 1987, 217).

The KTP-1 was first built in the Soviet Union at the Ujtomski plant for export to Cuba (Vladimirov 1974, 26–27) and eventually produced in Cuba (Edquist 1983, 55–56; Mesa-Lago 1978, 51–52; Pino-Santos and Martínez 1979, 75). A self-propelled machine, the KTP-1 was theoretically capable of harvesting both burnt and "green" (i.e., unburnt) cane. The KTP-1 was extensively tested in Cuba in the 1972 *zafra*. It has been reported in Cuban sources that each KTP-1 harvester could perform the work of either 40 (Barreda Sánchez 1982, 44) or 50 (Ruiz Portal 1980, 20) cane cutters.

In July 1977 production of KTP-1s began at the 60 Aniversario de la Revolución de Octubre plant in Holguín. The turnkey plant, purchased from the Soviet Union, represented an original investment of 46 million pesos; it was projected to produce 600 harvesters and 1,000 tons of spare parts per annum (Paneque Brizuelas 1976; Vázquez 1977b; Díaz-Vázquez 1980, 149). In 1977, 60 KTP-1 harvesters were turned out (Bianchi Ross 1985, 40); a total of 545 were built during 1977–79, with a production target of 350 units set for 1980 (Palezuelos 1979a, 20). Another source has reported that 3,500 combines were produced during 1977–84 (Díaz-Vázquez 1985, 48), a figure that would suggest production levels in 1981–84 that would consistently exceed the rated capacity of the plant (600 units per annum). The Holguín plant reportedly fulfilled its production plan of 3,000 KTP-1 harvesters over the period from 1981 to 1985 (Rojas Aguilera 1985). The Soviet Union stopped producing the KTP-1 for export to Cuba in 1979 or 1980 because Cuba gained the ability to produce it domestically (Edquist 1983, 56).

Since 1979 an improved and more efficient version of the KTP-1, the KTP-2, has also been produced at the Holguín plant (Vázquez 1979a). The KTP-2 was specifically designed to harvest green cane (Palezuelos 1979a, 17). Apparently, problems arose in the production of KTP-2s, and in 1984, Cuba again imported combine harvesters from Australia (Clemens and de Groot 1988, 24). In December 1986 production of the KTP-1 was discontinued and the Holguín plant retooled to produce exclusively the KTP-2. In 1987, the first year of full production of the KTP-2, the plan called for the assembly of 620 units (Assembly Line, 1987). Meanwhile, technicians at the Center for the Development of Agricultural Machinery (Centro de Desarrollo de la Maquinaria Agrícola) are reportedly well on their way to designing a new generation of harvesters, the KTP-3, expected to take over around 1990 (Bianchi Ross 1985, 40; Ochocientas 1987). A prototype KTP-3 was tested in the 1987–88 *zafra* with promising results (Rojas Aguilera 1988).

In addition to designing the basic model that became the KTP, in the late 1960s Cuban engineers designed another self-propelled harvester called the Libertadora. This model, which was specifically designed to harvest green cane and could operate effectively both in high-yield fields and in those with lodged or tangled cane—two conditions frequently found in Cuban cane fields—consistently outperformed the KTPs and imported Australian Massey-Ferguson harvesters in cutting green cane. And yet, in its mechanization drive, Cuba did not adopt this particular machine, choosing instead the Soviet-redesigned KTPs.

That the Libertadora was a good product has been proven in the marketplace. Since the early 1970s, it has been produced in West Germany by Claas Maschinefabrik, a world-class producer of grain harvesters. During 1977–82 about 700–800 Claas Libertadoras (or Claas CC 1400) harvesters were produced and exported to more than 44 countries, including Cuba (169 units) and the United States (99 units) (Edquist 1985, 128–30).

Arguably, the decision made in the 1960s by the Cuban leadership to rely on the Soviet Union to resolve technical problems associated with large-scale mechanization of the sugarcane harvest resulted in substantial opportunity costs for Cuba and probably slowed down mechanization. As has been noted by one analyst (Edquist 1985, 125–

27), very little sugarcane is grown in the Soviet Union, and in the 1960s it had no experience in the design and production of a sugarcane harvester. Soviet-designed sugar harvesting machinery introduced in Cuba in the 1960s performed poorly and was one of the factors adversely affecting sugar production.

By hitching its horse to the Soviet Union, Cuba missed out on technological developments in sugarcane harvesting machinery that were occurring elsewhere, particulary in Australia. In the 1960s, while Soviet-designed machinery failed miserably in Cuba, Massey-Ferguson, an Australian company, had already produced a chopper harvester, towed by a standard tractor, that performed very well in Queensland, an area very similar to Cuba with respect to sugarcane characteristics, soil conditions, and topography. A strong case can be made that cooperation with an experienced producer of harvesters would have permitted Cuba to mechanize sooner and with better results. Edquist has judged that reliance on technology transfers from the Soviet Union implied large opportunity costs for Cuba by delaying the breakthrough of cutting mechanization by five to eight years (Edquist 1985, 127).

AGRICULTURAL CHANGES

The Cuban experience has demonstrated that mechanization of sugarcane harvesting goes beyond developing (or importing, as the case may be) machinery to cut, load, and transport the cane. It also entails laying out, preparing, and planting fields with varieties that enhance the operation of the equipment.

Because sugarcane was grown by small operators (*colonos*) in prerevolutionary Cuba, fields were not suitable for large-scale harvesting. Over time, fields have been put together that are of sufficient size and are planted in such a way as to permit more efficient utilization of harvesting equipment. This has required, in many instances, eliminating trees, roads, ditches, and other obstacles that might impede the continuous operation of machinery, and the clearing of stones to reduce the incidence of equipment breakdowns and the picking up of extraneous matter (El desarrollo de la mecanización 1976, 6–7, 15; A. Rodríguez 1973). In addition, varieties of sugarcane that tend to have straighter stalks, and therefore are more suitable for mechanical harvesting (such as C-8751, B-4362 and J-60-5), have been planted (Vázquez 1974, 46; Escobar Casas 1978, 69).

To try to cut back on extraneous matter picked up by harvesting equipment, Cuba developed in the mid-1960s a system of dry-cleaning stations, the *centros de acopio,* where sugarcane loaded mechanically at the fields was sorted out and extraneous matter removed. Toward the end of the 1970s, nearly 500 of these stations were in operation (Alonso 1977, 17; Edquist 1983:50–51). By the early 1980s, 607 cane cleaning stations were in operation (David Posada 1983, 103).

Evidently, the establishment of the *centros de acopio* was not sufficient to bring the problem of extraneous matter under control. In the 1970s, Cuba began experimenting with the Australian system of burning sugarcane fields prior to cutting. The rationale behind this method is that the tops and leaves of the cane, as well as weeds, are burned off, and therefore the amount of extraneous matter is reduced. However, the system has drawbacks (Centro de Investigaciones 1972; 1973; Departamento de Investigaciones 1972; Pozo 1970; A. Rodríguez 1976b; Hernández et al. 1985; Tan 1986, 19):

- tops and leaves that could be used for other purposes (e.g., cattle feed) are lost;
- trash generated by green cane harvesting, which provides ground cover and helps preserve moisture in nonirrigated areas, is also lost;
- the amount of bagasse is reduced substantially;
- burnt sugarcane is more time-sensitive to processing after cutting than green cane;
- green cane yields 7 percent more sugar per ton of cane milled than burnt cane; and
- burnt fields have to be replanted more frequently.

Reportedly, 70 percent of the sugarcane fields harvested in the 1972 *zafra* were burnt beforehand as a way to reduce extraneous matter and more efficiently use manual labor and the stock of harvesters, particularly the Australian-made Massey-Ferguson 201s. In the 1987 *zafra* only 20 percent of sugarcane harvested mechanically was burnt beforehand (Salomón Llanes 1986d, 9).

MECHANIZATION AND YIELDS

According to official sources, virtually all of the loading and 66 percent of the cutting of sugarcane harvested in 1986 was done mechanically (table 12). Mechanical loading began in 1963 and in-

TABLE 12
SUGARCANE MECHANIZATION AND YIELDS, 1962–1988
*(in percentages)*

|      | Loading | Cutting | Industrial Yield[a] |
|------|---------|---------|---------------------|
| 1962 | 0       | 0       | 13.31               |
| 1963 | 1       | 0       | 12.36               |
| 1964 | 20      | 0       | 12.03               |
| 1965 | 26–32   | 1–2     | 12.15               |
| 1966 | 45–46   | 2–3     | 12.32               |
| 1967 | 53–57   | 2–3     | 12.26               |
| 1968 | 61–68   | 3       | 12.19               |
| 1969 | 65–74   | 2       | 11.02               |
| 1970 | 82–85   | 1–2     | 10.71               |
| 1971 | 87      | 2       | 11.49               |
| 1972 | 89–96   | 7       | 9.93                |
| 1973 | 93–94   | 11      | 11.07               |
| 1974 | 96      | 18      | 11.95               |
| 1975 | 96      | 25      | 12.44               |
| 1976 | 97      | 32      | 11.84               |
| 1977 | 97      | 36      | 11.55               |
| 1978 | 98      | 39      | 10.96               |
| 1979 | 98      | 42      | 10.94               |
| 1980 | 98      | 50      | 10.82               |
| 1981 | 98      | 50      | 11.08               |
| 1982 | 98[b]   | 50      | 11.17               |
| 1983 | 98[b]   |         | 10.35               |
| 1984 | 98[b]   | 64      | 10.47               |
| 1985 | 98[b]   | 62      | 11.96               |
| 1986 | 98[b]   | 66      | 10.62               |
| 1988 | 98[b]   | 67      |                     |

SOURCES: Loading—1982–88, estimated as the same rate as during 1978–81; 1963–81, Edquist 1982, 47. Cutting—1988, Varela Pérez 1988; 1986, Varela Pérez 1985e, 1; 1985, F. Castro 1986, 52; 1984, Salomón Llanes 1985, 31; 1971–82, García Giraldino 1983, 11; 1963–70, Edquist 1982, 47. Industrial yield—1985–86, AEC 1986, 242; 1980–84, AEC 1984, 141; 1973–79, AEC 1980, 90; 1962–72, AEC 1973, 122.

a. On the basis of production standardized to 96 degrees polarization.
b. Estimated.

creased rapidly thereafter. Since the mid 1970s, nearly all of the cane harvested has been loaded mechanically.

Machine cutting of sugarcane began in 1965; during 1966–71, the percentage cut mechanically hovered around 2–3 percent. Since 1972 the participation of machines in cutting increased steadily, with the share of cane cut mechanically reaching one-half in 1980 and about two-thirds by 1986. In the mid 1980s the pace of mechanization slowed down, suggesting that areas where mechanized harvesting was easily introduced have already been converted and that additional gains in mechanization may require substantial investments to prepare fields.

Table 13 presents estimates, based on the average productivity of manual workers in cutting and loading, of labor savings associated with mechanization of the sugarcane harvest. It is clear from the estimates that, though mechanical loaders contributed substantial labor savings (ranging from 50,000 to 100,000 man-seasons, excluding 1963), the bulk of the labor savings is attributed to combines capable of performing both cutting and loading functions. In 1985 labor savings associated with mechanical harvesting were of the order of 300,000 man-seasons, of which 20 percent was attributable to loaders and 80 percent to combines. In 1985 nearly all (98 percent) of loading and about 60 percent of cutting were mechanized.

Although Cuba plans in the longer term to continue to increase the share of sugarcane harvested mechanically, it is not likely that mechanization will do away with the *macheteros*. Harvesters cannot operate effectively in hilly areas; in some cases, operation of harvesters is not cost-effective because preparation of certain fields may be prohibitively costly (e.g., rocky fields), or fields may be too small or too far apart to justify the use of machinery (P. Morales 1985, 44). Moreover, efficiency of the KTP harvesters drops off in high-yield fields, e.g., those yielding more than 90,000 *arrobas* (1 *arroba* = 25 pounds or 11.5 kilograms) of sugarcane per *caballería* (de Armas et al. 1983). In the immediate future, Cuba is most likely to rely on mechanical harvesting in some areas and hand cutting and mechanical loading and transport in others, a combination that has been found to be best in terms of cost and quality in other settings (Brown 1987, 42).

Thus far an intractable problem associated with sugarcane mechanization has been an increase in extraneous matter (e.g., dirt, rocks, sugarcane tops, dried leaves) delivered to mills together with cane

TABLE 13
LABOR SAVINGS ASSOCIATED WITH SUGARCANE
HARVEST MECHANIZATION, 1958–1985
*(in worker-seasons)*

|  | Number of Cane Cutters[a] | Labor Saved by Machines |  |  |
|---|---|---|---|---|
|  |  | Loaders[b] | Combines[c] | Total |
| 1958 | 370,000 |  |  |  |
| 1963 | 260,000 | 1,000 |  | 1,000 |
| 1967 | 243,000 | 64,000 | 6,000 | 70,000 |
| 1970 | 350,000 | 96,000 | 3,000 | 99,000 |
| 1973 | 229,000 | 92,000 | 31,000 | 123,000 |
| 1976 | 153,300 | 82,000 | 102,000 | 184,000 |
| 1979 | 126,400 | 71,000 | 134,000 | 205,000 |
| 1982 | 105,000 | 71,000 | 200,000 | 271,000 |
| 1985 | 70,000 | 57,000 | 243,000 | 300,000 |

SOURCE: Clemens and de Groot 1988, 26.
  a. Includes professional cane cutters plus unpaid labor.
  b. Estimated on the basis of productivity of 3.15 tons/day, excluding loading by combines.
  c. Estimated on the basis of 1.26 tons/day of cutting and loading.

stalks. In the first instance, extraneous matter can cause harm to mill machinery; more generally, it slows down mill operations or lowers efficiency or the quality of the outputs (González Eguiluz 1977, 11; García López et al. 1977; Santos and Castro 1970, 83). The increase in extraneous matter was not a serious problem in the 1960s because the share of the harvest subject to mechanization was small; however, as mechanization became more generalized, the poor quality of cane delivered to mills, and ways to improve it, became a priority (Pollitt 1982a, 14–15).

Concerns about the high proportion of extraneous matter in mechanically loaded cane were expressed in 1963, the first year mechanical loaders were used. Thus the experience of the "manual cutting and mechanical loading brigades" showed that mechanically loaded cane tended to contain considerably higher percentages of soil, leaves, and tops than manually loaded cane (Risquet Valdés 1964, 69–70). A Cuban official estimated that while manually cut and loaded sugarcane might contain 2–4 percent extraneous matter, the corresponding percentage for mechanically harvested cane was 5–10 percent (David Posada 1976, 22–23). MINAZ officials have estimated the proportion of extraneous matter in deliveries to mills according to harvesting method to be (Martín Oria et al. 1987, 555):

| | |
|---|---|
| Manual cutting and loading for direct processing | 0–2 percent |
| Manual cutting and loading to be cleaned in the *centros de acopio* | 4–10 percent |
| Mechanical cutting and loading using combines | 10–20 percent |

An analysis of the quality of sugarcane harvested mechanically during 1966–68 yielded the following percentages of extraneous matter (Betancourt 1970, 9):

| | |
|---|---|
| 1965 | 11.17 percent |
| 1966 | 13.74 percent |
| 1967 | 12.93 percent |
| 1968 | 13.08 percent |

Though cleaning in the *centros de acopio* apparently was able to reduce some kinds of extraneous matter (e.g., rocks, soil), it did not resolve the problem of low quality; sugarcane processed in the centers during 1965–68 still averaged about 9.5 percent extraneous matter when delivered to mills (Betancourt 1970, 21). In the 1979–80 *zafra* mechanically harvested cane contained 12.74 percent extraneous matter (González Carrillo 1982, 15).

Partially as a result of the high incidence of extraneous matter, the industrial yield (the ratio of sugar produced to sugar cane milled) in revolutionary Cuba has tended to be low, reaching disturbingly low levels in some years. Cuban agronomists estimate the relationship between extraneous matter and yield as −0.20, that is to say, each 1 percentage point increase in extraneous matter decreases the industrial yield rate by 0.2 percentage points (Peralta et al. 1979, 46; Martín Oria et al. 1987, 555); a factor of −0.25 has also been cited in the literature (Lodos 1977, 16).

During the periods 1951–55 and 1956–60, the average sugar industrial yield (based on production standardized to 96 degrees polarization) was 12.83 and 12.74 percent, respectively (table 12). In 1962, a year during which the Cuban sugar crop was still being harvested manually, it rose to 13.31 percent. However, it declined sharply in 1963 (to 12.36 percent) and more gradually thereafter—as mechanization increased—to 10.71 in 1970 and, following improvement in 1971, to 9.93 in 1972. During the 1978–80 *zafras* yield fell below 11 percent, rose to slightly over 11 percent in 1981–82, and dipped to about 10.4–10.5 percent in 1983 and 1984. In the 1985 and 1986 *zafras,* industrial yield showed a great deal of variability, from 11.96 in 1985—the highest in a decade—down to a mediocre 10.62 percent in 1986.

Another problem associated with mechanization is excessive amounts of cut cane left in the fields. Whereas a loss of up to 5 percent is within tolerance limits for mechanized harvesting—compared to 2 percent for manual harvesting—in the ten *zafras* from about 1975 to 1985, the share of cane left behind in mechanically cut fields was 6.94 percent (Lazo 1985a, 44). In certain agro-industrial complexes the percentage was substantially higher, for example, 9.80 percent in Sandino and 8.78 percent in Venezuela in the 1985 *zafra* (Lazo 1985b, 57). MINAZ has estimated that sugarcane losses from cane left in fields that have been mechanically harvested could have supported production of an additional 750,000 tons of sugar (over 10 percent of output) in 1986 (Varela Pérez, 1986b).

To address this problem, agro-industrial complexes have organized platoons of eight workers each to trail harvesters to collect cane left behind by the machines. For example, the Diez de Octubre complex, which recorded cane losses of 12–20 percent after mechanical cutting, saw such losses fall to about 3 percent after each of its 16 harvesters was assigned an eight-worker platoon (Varela Pérez 1985d, 3). In the 1986 *zafra* the use of manual cane collectors was extended to most agro-industrial complexes (Varela Pérez, 1986c).

Productivity of sugarcane harvesters used prior to 1970 was relatively low, averaging less than 34.5 tons/day (i.e., for an eight-hour shift); in 1972 it was 69 tons/day, with improvements recorded annually thereafter (Alonso 1977, 18). Over the 1975–79 *zafras* productivity of KTP-1 harvesters was reported to have been (Díaz Hernández and Alvarez Portal 1981, 57):

|      |              |
|------|--------------|
| 1975 | 120.6 tons/day |
| 1976 | 144.0 tons/day |
| 1977 | 143.3 tons/day |
| 1978 | 130.3 tons/day |
| 1979 | 132.2 tons/day |

Presumably these figures refer to work performed on burnt cane. Rated productivity of KTP-1s working on burnt cane has been given as 113.4–136.1 tons/day (Vázquez 1979a, 9).

For more recent periods the following figures on productivity of harvesters in operation (primarily KTP-1s) have been given (Varela Pérez 1985e,1; 1988):

| | |
|---|---|
| 1981 | 89.6 tons/day |
| 1982 | 86.2 tons/day |
| 1983 | 74.8 tons/day |
| 1984 | 83.9 tons/day |
| 1985 | 83.9 tons/day |
| 1987 | 80.3 tons/day |

These results are considerably lower than those reported above for the late 1970s. The principal reason for the disparity appears to be that the more recent data refer to productivity harvesting green cane, and therefore the two sets of data are not comparable. For the 1984–86 *zafras* the goal was for machines to harvest the following volumes of cane (Varela Pérez 1984c; 1984d; 1985e):

| | |
|---|---|
| 1984 | 103.2 or 108.8 tons/day |
| 1985 | 100.9 tons/day |
| 1986 | 100.8 tons/day |

Actual productivity in 1984 fell below the goal by 19.5 or 22.9 percent, depending on which of the two goals is used as the base; for 1985 the shortfall was 16.8 percent.

In the 1988 *zafra* productivity of sugarcane combines through March has been reported at 95.9 tons/day (Varela Pérez, 1988). The significant improvement in productivity over 1987 and earlier periods reflects, in part, the addition to the stock of harvesters of more efficient KTP-2 machines, whose productivity in green cane has been reported as being comparable to that of the KTP-1 in burnt cane, that is, 113.4–136.1 tons/day (Vázquez 1979a, 9). Another source has given the rated productivity of the KTP-2 in green cane as 141.75 tons/day (Ochocientas 1987).

Undoubtedly, Cuba's experience with mechanization, purely in terms of the volume of sugarcane subject to mechanical harvesting and the swiftness with which the shift from manual to mechanical harvesting took place, has been a success. Assessing whether the same is true from an economic cost-benefit standpoint is more difficult. As Hagelberg has pointed out, the conditions under which Cuba started sugarcane mechanization were far from auspicious and should be considered as parameters within which Cuba could operate (Hagelberg 1979, 34):

> [The revolutionary policy makers] could and did nationalize foreign properties and transfer the entire sugar complex, with the exception of small cane growers, to the public sector. They could and did alter

the supply of the factors of production, which among other things unexpectedly provoked an acute shortage of labor during harvests and hastened the need for machines to cut and load cane, in the midst of an economic blockade and at a time when there was yet little international experience in sugar cane mechanization.

But the revolution provided exceptional opportunities as well: Cuba could tackle large-scale mechanization because the revolution both destroyed fears of workers that mechanization would eliminate their jobs and provided a longer planning horizon for capital investment than private enterprise could (Turits 1987, 168).

Edquist points out that, in his extensive research on the topic, he has not found any evidence that the Cuban government carried out a cost-benefit analysis of sugarcane mechanization prior to embarking on it. In his view, Cuban decision makers seem to have had an overly optimistic view of the benefits of mechanization and of the time needed to achieve it, while greatly underestimating its costs. Although he was unable to estimate the costs and benefits of mechanization in Cuba because of the lack of information on prices and production costs of machinery, he suggests that the costs during the 1960s exceeded the benefits and that in more recent periods the balance of costs and benefits has been closer. He is uncertain, however, whether cumulative costs and benefits had balanced by 1980 or 1985 (Edquist 1985, 140–44).

## Industrial Labor

Cuba's 161 sugar mills and 22 sugar refineries active during the 1950s employed substantial numbers of workers in industrial operations and transportation activities. Employment tended to be subject to severe seasonal fluctuations, although some year-round employment existed in maintenance and administrative areas.

In the 1970 population census (Junta Central 1975, 511) over 97,000 workers indicated they were associated with sugar industrial activities. Most likely, this figure refers strictly to employment in sugar mills (and refineries), for another source has reported industry employment (including transportation, port operations, maintenance activities, research, etc.) during the period 1972–75 at about 106,000

TABLE 14
EMPLOYMENT IN SUGAR INDUSTRIAL OPERATIONS,
1975–1987
*(in thousands)*

|      | Sugar Industrial | Total Industrial | Sugar Industrial/ Total Industrial (%) |
|------|------|------|------|
| 1975 | 95.7  | 527.9 | 18.1 |
| 1978 | 91.6  | 552.9 | 16.6 |
| 1979 | 92.2  | 553.7 | 16.7 |
| 1980 | 91.9  | 546.1 | 16.8 |
| 1981 | 94.5  | 576.4 | 16.4 |
| 1982 | 100.5 | 599.9 | 16.8 |
| 1983 | 110.6 | 630.5 | 17.5 |
| 1984 | 133.1 | 683.5 | 19.5 |
| 1985 | 138.0 | 709.3 | 19.5 |
| 1986 | 135.8 | 725.9 | 18.7 |
| 1987 | 138.7 | 726.9 | 19.1 |

SOURCES: 1987—AEC 1987, 239; 1986—AEC 1986, 238; 1982–85—AEC 1985, 225; 1981—AEC 1983, 141; 1980—AEC 1985, 225; 1979—AEC 1983, 141; 1978—AEC 1982, 151; 1975—AEC 1986, 238.

workers (Charadán López 1982, 228). In the 1981 census 107,347 workers identified themselves as associated with sugar industrial activities (Comité Estatal 1984, 263).

Cuba began to publish statistics on employment in sugar industrial activities in the early 1980s. Table 14 presents all available data on such employment for 1975 and 1978–87. Employment rose from about 96,000 in 1975 to 138,700 in 1987, or by 44 percent. Employment gains were particularly significant in the 1980s as a fourth shift was introduced in sugar mills in order to permit workers to have time off (Comparecencia 1981, 2; F. Castro 1986, 52) and as new sugar mills became operational. Sugar industrial salaries averaged 166 pesos/month in 1980 and 212 pesos/month in 1981, both higher than the average salary of industrial workers (Comparecencia 1981, 2).

Sugar industrial workers represented 18.1 percent of workers employed in the state industrial sector in 1975 (table 14). Their relative importance in relation to total industrial workers fell to below 17 percent during 1978–82 but recovered during 1983–87. In 1984–87 sugar workers accounted for nearly one-fifth (19.2 percent) of total employment in the industrial sector.

Cuba's sugar mills are the largest industrial employers in the nation. In 1987, 94 percent (140 out of 148) of the mills in operation employed more than 1,000 workers, compared to 40 percent of plants in the industrial sector at large (AEC 1987, 240). Most sugar mills (112, or 76 percent) employed between 1,000 and 3,000 workers, compared to about one-third for all industrial plants. Of the largest industrial employers in the country, that is, those employing over 4,000 workers in one location, 20 out of 29 were sugar mills (ibid).

A factor that has affected the industrial side of sugar production is the tightness of the labor market for skilled workers, particularly in certain areas of the country perceived as being less desirable to live in. Las Tunas, the province with the fourth largest potential sugarcane grinding capacity in the nation, is a case in point (Luzón 1987, 294–302).

Industrial efficiency of the six mills in Las Tunas province in the 1970s and 1980s (the Majibacoa mill, the seventh mill in the province, is not included since it became operational in 1986) was consistently below the national average in terms of industrial yield. The situation prevailed despite heavy investments to modernize the physical plant. In some *zafras,* such as that of 1981, the disparity was very significant: industrial yield of 10.12 for Las Tunas compared to a national average of 11.08 percent (AEC 1986, 248).

In the 1970s the population of Las Tunas underwent both net outmigration (to other provinces) and migration from rural to urban areas within the province (Luzón 1987, 295). These migratory trends contributed to a high turnover in the labor force of sugar mills, a shortage of qualified workers, and low efficiency in sugar production. A Cuban journalist reported the situation in the mills of Las Tunas in 1981 (A. Rodríguez 1980b, 20):

> While modern centrifuges, large boilers and powerful electrical grinding machinery were being installed, the labor force of those mills gradually declined as a result of retirements, transfers, resignations. Between 1970 and 1979, . . . 1,450 workers quit the sugar enterprise Amancio Rodríguez, of which 535 were skilled workers; out of these [skilled workers], 428 were between 18 and 27 years of age. Over the same period, only 101 workers were added. In five years,

1975 to 1979, the sugar enterprise Jesús Menéndez lost, for different reasons, 227 skilled workers, while it added 82 workers over the same period.

Undoubtedly, the new Majibacoa sugar mill must have brought additional pressure to an already tight labor market for skilled sugar workers in Las Tunas.

# CHAPTER 5

•

## Energy and Transportation

SUGAR PRODUCTION is an energy-intensive process, particularly those steps that involve condensing cane juice by heating. Raw sugar is produced in Cuba from sugarcane through an industrial process whereby: (1) crushing machines burst sugar cane stalks to extract cane juice; (2) the cane juice is heated and filtered; (3) the clear juice is run through evaporators and vacuum pans to remove excess water until a thick syrup is formed; and (4) sugar crystals are separated from the syrup by centrifuging. Harvesting and transporting sugarcane to mills also use a great deal of oil products, as does transporting sugar to export terminals.

## ENERGY

The sugar industry is Cuba's largest energy producer and probably its largest consumer. Bagasse, the moist mass of stalks and leaves left behind when cane is ground to extract its juice, is the leading domestic energy source. Because its bulkiness and low caloric value make it uneconomical to transport, bagasse is used as a fuel exclusively in sugar mills. In addition to consuming virtually all of the bagasse produced, the sugar industry also uses fuelwood and oil products.

### BAGASSE PRODUCTION

Although there are no official statistics on bagasse production, estimates of the amount produced in each *zafra* can be made from data on the volume of sugarcane ground and the historical average relationship between that and bagasse output. Moreover, estimates of the oil-equivalent value of bagasse production can be made using standard conversion factors based on caloric content.

Table 15 presents estimates of the oil-equivalent value of bagasse production over the period 1959–87. According to these estimates, bagasse contributed the equivalent of 1.4–to 3.6 million tons of oil annually to Cuban energy supplies during the period. On average, bagasse represented about three-quarters of domestically produced energy supplies, although its relative importance dropped to below 70 percent in 1985–87 as domestic oil production shot up. To put these figures in context, Cuba's historical high oil production was 770,400 tons in 1984, 847,600 tons in 1985, 938,000 in 1986, and 895,000 in 1987 (AEC 1987, 251); imports of oil and oil products during 1959–87 ranged from 3 to over 13 million tons per annum.

It should be stressed that the estimates in table 15 are based on a number of assumptions: that the bagasse-to-milled-cane ratio is .250; that all bagasse is used as fuel in sugar mills; that bagasse has a moisture content of 50 percent; and that one ton of medium-gravity oil is equivalent, in terms of caloric value, to 5.6 tons of bagasse with 50 percent moisture. The rationale for these assumptions is as follows:

1. The average bagasse-to-milled-cane ratio of .250 used in the calculations is in line with a study of sugar mills in prerevolutionary Cuba that found ratios in the range of .244 to .324 (Ruiz 1952, 52); a study of the 1959 crop that yielded a ratio of .254 (Junta Nacional 1960); and a reported national average for 1968 of .279 (Quesada González 1969, 6). It is the same ratio used in several technical studies conducted by Cuban sugar technicians (e.g., García López and Clark 1969, 29; López Guzmán and de Armas Casanova 1979, 21). Production of bagasse may be overstated since no adjustment has been made to account for potentially lower bagasse-to-milled-cane ratios of cane fields burnt prior to harvesting.

2. It has been assumed in the calculations that all of the bagasse produced is used for fuel in sugar mills. This simplifying assumption is necessary because there are no systematic data on the volume of bagasse used outside mills. Cuban statistical yearbooks do contain statistics on bagasse deliveries for industrial, nonfuel uses, but such data are available only beginning with 1972 and are not available for some years (e.g., 1982–83). As can be seen from table 16, when compared to estimates of total bagasse production, the share of bagasse used in industrial activities outside the sugar mills ranged from 2.0 to 2.6 percent in the 1970s and early 1980s. For the more recent years 1984–87, 4.6 percent of estimated bagasse production was used for nonfuel industrial purposes.

3. The moisture content of bagasse has been assumed to be 50 percent. To be sure, if bagasse were dried prior to burning, its caloric

## TABLE 15
### Bagasse in Domestic Energy Supply, 1959–1987
*(in thousands of tons of oil equivalent)*

|      | Bagasse | Domestic Energy Supply[a] | Bagasse/Supply (%) |
|------|---------|--------------------------|---------------------|
| 1959 | 2,000   | 2,177                    | 91.9                |
| 1960 | 2,124   | 2,453                    | 86.6                |
| 1961 | 2,428   | 2,877                    | 84.4                |
| 1962 | 1,642   | 2,041                    | 80.5                |
| 1963 | 1,410   | 1,775                    | 79.4                |
| 1964 | 1,660   | 2,103                    | 78.9                |
| 1965 | 2,267   | 2,682                    | 84.5                |
| 1966 | 1,642   | 2,106                    | 78.0                |
| 1967 | 2,267   | 2,764                    | 82.0                |
| 1968 | 1,892   | 2,508                    | 75.4                |
| 1969 | 1,821   | 2,472                    | 73.7                |
| 1970 | 3,570   | 4,067                    | 87.8                |
| 1971 | 2,303   | 2,797                    | 82.3                |
| 1972 | 1,946   | 2,441                    | 79.7                |
| 1973 | 2,124   | 2,659                    | 79.9                |
| 1974 | 2,213   | 2,789                    | 79.3                |
| 1975 | 2,250   | 2,862                    | 78.6                |
| 1976 | 2,321   | 2,980                    | 77.9                |
| 1977 | 2,500   | 3,237                    | 77.2                |
| 1978 | 3,000   | 3,767                    | 79.6                |
| 1979 | 3,260   | 4,078                    | 79.9                |
| 1980 | 2,750   | 3,542                    | 77.6                |
| 1981 | 2,960   | 3,697                    | 80.1                |
| 1982 | 3,280   | 4,299                    | 76.3                |
| 1983 | 3,067   | 4,286                    | 71.6                |
| 1984 | 3,498   | 4,754                    | 73.6                |
| 1985 | 2,980   | 4,313                    | 69.1                |
| 1986 | 3,046   | 4,458                    | 68.3                |
| 1987 | 2,987   | 4,347                    | 68.7                |

SOURCES: 1979–87—Updated with data from AEC 1987 and earlier issues, and methodology in Pérez-López 1981; 1959–78—Pérez-López, 1981, 117.

a. Includes oil, natural gas, hydroelectricity, bagasse, ethanol, fuelwood and charcoal.

## TABLE 16
### Sugarcane Milled, Estimated Bagasse Production, and Bagasse for Industrial Use, 1972–1987
*(in thousands of tons)*

|      | Sugarcane Milled | Bagasse Produced | Bagasse for Industrial Use | Bagasse for Industrial Use/Bagasse Produced (%) |
|------|---------|---------|-------|-----|
| 1972 | 43,500  | 10,875  | 217   | 2.0 |
| 1973 | 47,500  | 11,875  | 281   | 2.4 |
| 1974 | 49,600  | 12,400  | 322   | 2.6 |
| 1975 | 50,600  | 12,650  | 328   | 2.6 |
| 1976 | 52,000  | 13,000  | 294   | 2.3 |
| 1977 | 56,200  | 14,050  | 331   | 2.4 |
| 1978 | 67,000  | 16,750  | 363   | 2.2 |
| 1979 | 73,000  | 18,250  | 359   | 2.0 |
| 1980 | 61,600  | 15,400  | 311   | 2.0 |
| 1981 | 66,400  | 16,600  | 376   | 2.3 |
| 1982 | 73,500  | 18,375  |       |     |
| 1983 | 68,700  | 17,175  |       |     |
| 1984 | 78,400  | 19,600  | 1,049 | 5.4 |
| 1985 | 66,800  | 16,700  | 982   | 5.9 |
| 1986 | 68,300  | 17,075  | 547   | 3.2 |
| 1987 | 66,900  | 16,725  | 648   | 3.9 |

SOURCES: Cane milled—AEC 1987, 243 and earlier issues. Figures have been rounded to closest 100,000 tons. Bagasse produced—estimated on the basis of a .250 bagasse-to-milled-cane ratio. Bagasse for industrial use—1982–87, AEC 1987, 255; 1978–81, AEC 1984, 153; 1976–77, AEC 1982, 167; 1974–75, AEC 1980, 97; 1972–73—AEC 1977, 153.

value would be higher (Arrascaeta Recano et al. 1982; F. Castro 1984, 56; Friedman and Arrascaeta 1984). In Cuban sugar mills, however, bagasse is generally burned directly; additional handling for sun or steam drying is avoided, but higher moisture levels result. The 50 percent moisture content is in line with reported moisture content in the 1951 *zafra* ranging from 44.10 to 50.79 percent (Ruiz 1952, 35); for 1968 of 49.36 percent (Quesada González 1969, 6); and for 1974 and 1975 of 47.76 percent and 49.67 percent, respectively (Rodríguez and Gutiérrez 1978, 22). The estimate of 50 percent moisture content has also been used by Cuban sugar industry experts in technical studies (e.g., de Armas Casanova and López Guzmán 1978, 45).

4. The conversion factor of 5.6 tons of bagasse to 1 ton of oil of medium gravity was obtained from a Cuban technical study dealing with the caloric value of bagasse (Quesada González 1969, 3). This conversion factor is in line with one of 6 tons of moist bagasse equivalent to 1 ton of oil given elsewhere in the Cuban literature (Noa Silverio 1978, 25) and reportedly used by the Economic Commission for Latin America (ECLA) and the Food and Agriculture Organization (Papel 1955, 506), and with a conversion factor of 3 tons of dried bagasse (30 percent moisture) equivalent to 1 ton of oil used in the United States (U.S. Federal Energy Administration 1977, 16–7; Danilo Rodríguez 1977, 3).

It is inconsistent, however, with a conversion factor of 4 tons of bagasse equivalent to 1 ton of fuel oil used by Fidel Castro (1984, 52) and with his implied conversion factor of 4.4 tons of bagasse equivalent to 1 ton of oil: "we are currently using about 20 million tons of bagasse, equivalent to about 4.5 million tons of oil" (ibid. 56). This same 4.4:1 ratio also is given elsewhere in the Cuban literature (Pernas 1965, 68).

Apparently on the basis of the 4:1 conversion factor, Fidel Castro (1984, 57) has announced that for *zafras* producing about 9 million tons of sugar, Cuba intends to "save" the equivalent of 2.5 million tons of oil per annum through more efficient use of bagasse in sugar mills. This level of savings appears inordinately ambitious, for it would probably imply slashing bagasse consumption in sugar mills by at least 50 percent. That is, for a *zafra* of 9 million tons of sugar with an industrial yield of 11 percent, approximately 82 million tons of sugarcane would be milled, producing about 20.5 million tons of bagasse. If one uses the 4:1 ratio, 20.5 million tons of bagasse would be equivalent to 5.1 million tons of oil and bagasse use would have to be reduced by 50 percent to meet the announced savings. If one uses the 5.6:1 ratio, the reduction in bagasse use by sugar mills needed to free up the equivalent of 2.5 million tons of oil would have to be even more drastic, by about two-thirds.

ENERGY CONSUMPTION

The sugar industry is probably Cuba's largest energy consumer, utilizing virtually all of the bagasse it produces and significant volumes of fuelwood and oil products as well. Gasoline, fuel oil, and diesel fuel are used in the agricultural, transportation, and industrial aspects of sugar production. In the late 1960s the sugar industry was second only to the public service electricity industry in consumption of oil products, a position it probably maintained in the 1970s (Pérez-López 1981, 131–32). A more precise assessment of the position of the sugar industry relative to others in terms of energy consumption is not possible since Cuba does not publish statistics on energy consumption by industry.

The sugar industry is a large consumer and producer of electricity. Sugar mills generally are equipped with their own electricity generation plant, supplemented with power from the national electrical grid. Statistics on electricity generation by the sugar industry are available only for 1970–87. In the giant 1970 *zafra* the sugar industry generated—and consumed—880,500 gigawatt-hours of electricity, or about 18 percent of the electricity produced nationwide. In the 1970s electricity generation by the sugar industry fell below the 1970 level, and the share of total electricity produced declined to 10–12 percent.

Since 1978 the sugar industry has regularly surpassed the level of electricity produced in the 1970 *zafra;* for the first time, in 1982 it produced over 1 million gigawatt-hours of electricity. However, its share of total electricity produced has continued to decline, as generation by other producers (public service plants, other industries) has grown at a faster pace. In the mid 1980s the sugar industry accounted for about 9 percent of total electricity generated in the nation.

Prerevolutionary Cuba's sugar industry generated sufficient volumes of bagasse to achieve energy self-sufficiency. Sugar mill boilers were designed to be fueled by bagasse or by fuelwood, the latter being used at the start-up of the *zafra,* before bagasse had been produced. Because there was an overabundance of bagasse, there was little incentive to install efficient boilers. In fact, mills were designed to ensure that all the bagasse produced during a *zafra* was burned, in order to avoid having to dispose of any excess (David Posada 1979, 12). Economic incentives to burn bagasse more efficiently were introduced in the 1950s with the coming on line of plants to produce paper and paperboard using bagasse as raw material (chapter 6). However, because the volumes of bagasse involved were small—in 1959 reportedly 226,000 tons or 1.7 percent of bagasse production (Junta Nacional 1960, 17)—there was a lack of economic incentive for more efficient use.

In the 1960s a bagasse shortage—or perhaps more accurately, a bagasse imbalance—developed, and many sugar mills turned to fuel oil and fuelwood to supplement bagasse in operating their boilers. Thus, during the 1965–67 *zafras,* 0.5–0.7 gallons of fuel oil were used per ton of sugarcane milled (Medidas 1970, 5; Vázquez 1968, 3), for an average consumption of 70,000–100,000 tons per annum (table 17). In 1968, at a time when the Soviet Union slowed down oil shipments and Cuba instituted oil rationing, an energy conservation program was put into place. Curbing the use of fuel oil in sugar mills was assigned a very high priority. This aspect of the program was not successful, however, for fuel oil consumption rose to almost 3 gallons/ton of sugarcane milled during 1969–73 and became a serious drain on imported oil resources (Varela Pérez 1978, 3).

The jump in fuel oil consumption during the 1960s and 1970s has been attributed primarily to problems in the agricultural sector, namely to the inability of maintaining steady sugarcane flows to mills because of bottlenecks in harvesting and transportation. A secondary concern was the condition of boilers—because adequate maintenance had not been performed, the boilers were operating at very low levels of efficiency (Vázquez 1968, 3).

In the 1968 *zafra* sugar mills met their energy needs from these sources:

|  |  |
| --- | --- |
| bagasse | 97.00 percent |
| oil products | 2.16 percent |
| fuelwood | 0.84 percent |

However, very large mills (i.e, those with grinding capacity exceeding 10,000 tons/day) relied on fuel oil for 3.8 percent of their needs, compared to 1.4 percent for smaller mills (under 2,000 tons/day grinding capacity) (Quesada González 1969, 5). To compound the problem, as was noted earlier, boilers in Cuban sugar mills were designed to use bagasse or fuelwood, not fuel oil. Thus, although hydrocarbons such as fuel oil are substantially more efficient than biomass in operating boilers, they were used with remarkably low efficiency in the mills (ibid. 6).

After peaking in 1972 at 2.94 gallons/ton, or over 400,000 tons of fuel oil, consumption of fuel oil in sugar mills began to decline in the next three *zafras,* falling to about 270,000 tons in 1975. When fuelwood is also taken into account, total consumption of nonbagasse fuels by sugar mills during 1971–75 has been estimated by MINAZ

TABLE 17
FUEL OIL CONSUMPTION IN SUGAR MILLS, 1965–1984

|         | Fuel Oil Consumption (gallons/ton) | Sugarcane Milled (millions of tons) | Total Fuel Oil Consumption (thous. of tons) |
|---------|---|---|---|
| 1965–67 | 0.5–0.7 | 46.1 | 73.1–102.4 |
| 1971    | 2.09  | 52.6 | 342.4 |
| 1972    | 2.94  | 43.5 | 406.0 |
| 1973    | 2.07  | 47.5 | 312.1 |
| 1974    | 1.88  | 49.6 | 296.0 |
| 1975    | 1.67  | 50.6 | 268.3 |
| 1976    | 2.04  | 52.0 | 336.7 |
| 1977    | 2.05  | 56.1 | 365.1 |
| 1978    | 2.08  | 67.0 | 442.4 |
| 1979    | 1.62[a] | 73.1 | 375.0[a] |
| 1980    | 0.97[a] | 61.6 | 189.6[a] |
| 1981    | 0.70[a] | 66.4 | 147.1 |
| 1982    | 0.28[a] | 73.5 | 66.2 |
| 1983    | 0.09[a] | 68.7 | 19.9 |
| 1984    | 0.02[a] | 78.4 | 4.8 |

SOURCES: Fuel oil consumption/ton of sugarcane milled—1979–84, estimated on the basis of total fuel oil consumption (see below); 1971–78, Varela Pérez 1978; 1965–67—Vázquez 1968, 3. Sugarcane milled—AEC 1984 and earlier issues. Total fuel oil consumption—1981–84, Varela Pérez 1985a; 1980, Sugar Industry, 1981, 39; 1979, estimated on the basis of Castro's statement that 1,709,000 tons of fuel oil were used by sugar mills during 1976–80, Castro 1986, 51; 1965–78, calculated as the product of columns 1 and 2, converted to metric tons on the basis of 42 gallons to a barrel and 7.5 barrels of fuel oil to a ton.

a. Estimated.

(in oil equivalents) at 370,300 tons in 1971; 462,300 tons in 1972; 335,400 tons in 1973; 335,900 tons in 1974; and 315,220 tons in 1975 (Charadán López 1982, 155). During 1976–78, fuel oil consumption climbed to about 2 gallons/ton, with total consumption ranging from 340,000 to 440,000 tons per annum.

In the 1980s, Cuba effected a remarkable reduction in consumption of fuel oil in sugar mills. Fuel oil consumption has been reported at 0.70 gallons/ton in 1981 and 0.26 gallons/ton in 1982 (Rodríguez Pérez 1982, 55). Thus, less than 200,000 tons of fuel oil were used in the 1980 *zafra;* about 5,000 tons in 1984; and only 3,000 tons in 1985, with the bulk of the fuel oil consumed in 1985 associated with the start-up of new mills (Varela Pérez 1985a).

Among the economic accomplishments of the period 1981–85 cited by Fidel Castro (1986, 51) in his central report to the Third Congress of the Cuban Communist party was that Cuba had totally eliminated the use of fuel oil in the production of raw sugar, a move that "saved" 1.7 million tons of oil products. Presumably that figure represents the volume of fuel oil that was consumed in these activities during 1976–80, a figure in line with estimates of consumption for 1976–78 and 1980 in table 17.

To be sure, for all practical purposes, Cuba did eliminate the use of fuel oil in sugar mills in 1985—when only about 3,000 tons were reportedly consumed—but consumption *was not* eliminated during the entire five-year interval. Thus about 320,000 tons of fuel oil were probably used by sugar mills during the 1981–85 *zafras,* for a "savings" of about 1.4 million tons of oil products compared to 1976–80 consumption, rather than the 1.7 million tons reported by Castro.

While energy conservation measures have been quite successful in curbing consumption of oil products in raw sugar production, they have been less so in sugarcane agriculture and in the production of refined sugar. In the mid 1980s consumption of oil products in sugarcane harvesting continued to be quite high (J. Oramas 1984; Varela Pérez 1984a). Lack of adequate training and controls were given as some of the reasons for excessive use of fuel and lubricants by KTP operators (Varela Pérez, 1985f). Just prior to the start of the 1987 *zafra,* a sugar industry official noted that energy consumption in cane cultivation had grown "extraordinarily" in recent years, with energy consumption per ton of sugarcane produced in the first half of 1986 higher by 30 percent than the corresponding rate for a like period in 1980 (Varela Pérez 1986e).

In the 1985 *zafra* consumption of oil products in sugar refining averaged 59.6 gallons/ton, compared to planned consumption of 42.3 gallons/ton and a consumption level of 50.4 gallons/ton in 1984; in two of the refineries consumption exceeded 100 gallons/ton (Varela Pérez 1985a). Since in 1984 and 1985 Cuba produced 845,500 and 910,300 tons of refined sugar, respectively (AEC 1986, 253), it can be estimated that refineries consumed approximately 135,000 tons of oil products in 1984 and 172,000 tons in 1985.

Sugar refineries are heavy users of oil products because they tend to operate beyond the duration of the *zafra,* when sugar mills are active and bagasse is available (chapter 6). To conserve oil products, the Camilo Cienfuegos refinery, the largest in the nation (see appendix 3), has been retrofitted to use natural gas from local fields (González Jordán 1986, 137).

## Transportation

The bulkiness of inputs and outputs and the necessity to move the lion's share of output to ports for export give transportation a strategic role in Cuban sugar production and marketing. The railroad traditionally has been the industry's preferred mode of transportation, although road transportation has gained in importance in recent years.

### RAILROAD TRANSPORTATION

So close has been the association between the sugar industry and the railroads that the impetus behind the construction of a railroad in Cuba (the first in Latin America), a 27.2 kilometer line from Bejucal to Havana completed in 1837, was to be able to ship sugar from the booming area of Güines to Havana for export (Marrero 1984, 11:158). Reportedly, railroad transportation reduced the cost of transporting sugar to Havana by 70 percent (Moreno Fraginals 1978, 1:151). According to a Cuban historian, it was the railroad—rather than the steam boiler—that transformed Cuban sugar production and ushered in the industrial revolution in the island (ibid. 1:151). By 1860, Cuba had over 1,200 kilometers of railroads, linking sugar-producing areas in the central and eastern parts of the nation with ports (Marrero 1984 11, 198–210). To complement the public railroads, sugar companies built an extensive system of private railroads to move sugarcane from fields to mills and to link mills with the public railroads.

In 1957, Cuba had 15,300 kilometers of railroads, of which 6,000 kilometers (39 percent) were public and 9,300 kilometers (61 percent) were privately owned, primarily by sugar mills (Lechuga 1972, 14). During the 1955–57 *zafras,* around 90 percent (by weight) of the load carried by public railroads was associated with the sugar industry;

TABLE 18
ROLLING STOCK OF THE RAILROAD SYSTEM, 1987

|  | Public Use | Sugar Industry Use |
|---|---|---|
| LOCOMOTIVES | 398 | 1,036 |
| Diesel | 386 | 562 |
| Steam | — | 474 |
| Electric | 12 | — |
| FREIGHT CARS | 9,748 | 35,186 |
| Box cars | 2,668 | — |
| Sugar cars[a] | — | 28,996 |
| Flatcars | 1,844 | 1,145 |
| Tank cars | 1,599 | 1,241 |
| Gondola cars | 1,592 | 2,164[b] |
| Other | 2,045 | 1,640 |
| PASSENGER AND OTHER CARS | 697 | — |

SOURCE: AEC 1987, 372.
a. Generally referred to as *carros jaula*.
b. *Tolvas,* modified gondola cars used to transport sugar in bulk from mills to shipping terminals.

sugar-related cargoes accounted for about two-thirds of the revenue of the public railroads during this period (AAC 1958, 160–61).

In the early 1980s, Cuba's sugarcane transportation system controlled 9,000 kilometers of railroads (David Posada, 1983:105), compared to about 13,200 for the nation as a whole (AEC 1986, 351). Around that time, the rolling stock of the sugar industry consisted of 450 steam locomotives, 350 diesel locomotives, 20,000 railroad cars of 30-ton capacity, and 8,000 cars of 10-ton capacity (David Posada 1983, 105). It is clear from data for 1987 (table 18) that the sugarcane transportation system dwarfs the public service railroad system: 1,036 locomotives for sugar transportation compared to 398 for public use, and 35,186 freight cars compared to 9,748.

ROAD TRANSPORTATION

In the 1950s trucks began to be important in sugar transportation, particularly in moving cut cane from fields to mills. To some extent, the shift from railroad to truck transportation was related to costs: maintenance and operation of private railroads were a heavy burden on sugar mills. It has been estimated that in 1958 no fewer than 64 sugar mills, controlling 1,309 kilometers of railroad, faced considerable financial difficulties maintaining the infrastructure required and were considering shifting to trucks (Arredondo 1969, 116; CERP 1965a, 124.) According to data from around 1963, 22.5 percent of the capital stock of the Cuban sugar industry was in transportation infrastructure and equipment, primarily railroads (El desarrollo industrial 1966b, 113).

The use of trucks for sugarcane transportation has grown in revolutionary Cuba. The following reasons have been given for the change (Cordovés Herrera 1979, 10):

- the very high initial investments associated with railroad transportation make it difficult to justify them in economic terms, particularly if they are used only for sugarcane transportation;
- railroads are not flexible in terms of being able to handle loads that originate from areas other than the ones the railroad has been built to serve; and
- the time lag between cutting and grinding sugarcane is longer when it is transported by railroad than when it is transported by truck.

Notwithstanding the gradual shift to truck transportation, railroads continue to be the main mode of transportation associated with the sugar industry. In the early 1970s, 70–75 percent of cane harvested was transported by railroads (Charadán López 1982, 191; Lechuga 1972, 14); in 1981 over 60 percent was transported by railroad (Varela Pérez 1981b, 3).

Among the factors that contributed to the failure to reach a production level of 10 million tons of sugar in the 1970 *zafra* were bottlenecks in transportation (Roca 1976, 22). An analysis by Cuban transportation officials identified substantial problems in the operation of the railroads, maintenance and repair of equipment, and condition of railroad beds. It has been estimated that transportation bottlenecks were responsible for over 1 percentage point of the downtime of sugar mills in the 1970 sugar campaign.

A broad effort to improve railroad transportation of cane began in 1971, and significant investments were made in the improvement of road beds, imports of railroad stock, and construction of maintenance and repair facilities. Downtime of sugar mills attributable to railroad bottlenecks reportedly declined from 1.78 percentage points in 1972 to 0.26 percentage points in 1974 as the fulfillment of the railroad transportation improvement plan rose from 56 percent in 1971–72 to 80 percent in 1974–75 (Charadán López 1982, 191–205).

However, railroad transportation problems have not been eliminated, and, at times, their contribution to downtime has again risen, for example to 0.42 percentage points in 1978 and 0.40 percentage points in 1984 (AEC 1984, 144). In 1981–85 investments amounting to over 60 million pesos to improve railroad transportation of sugarcane were projected, including the importation of 190 large Soviet locomotives, manufacture of 2,500 railroad cars, and construction of several repair facilities (Varela Pérez 1981b, 3).

BULK SHIPPING FACILITIES

Prerevolutionary Cuba's ability to rely on bulk shipping of sugar was severely restricted by worker opposition to bulk handling (World Bank 1951, 394). As early as the 1920s, Cuba shipped some sugar in bulk (i.e., not in bags), but it had to be bagged at the mills and transported to ports in that form, then the bags had to be opened at shipside and the sugar dumped in the holds; presumably the bags were reused. Despite the heavy costs associated with bags, bagging, handling of bagged sugar, opening of the bags, and so on, bulk shipping gradually increased in importance as customers demanded that the product be shipped in this form. In 1958, 25 percent of sugar exports were shipped in bulk (Salomón Llanes 1978, 14).

In 1962 the revolutionary government began to ship sugar in bulk from mills to domestic refineries and export terminals. Around 1964 several mills began to ship sugar for export in bulk. Raw sugar was loaded directly onto special railroad wagons called *tolvas,* carrying about 30 tons each, and transported to warehouses located at export terminals. The share of sugar exports shipped in bulk rose from an insignificant 1.2 percent in 1962 to 66 percent in 1970. During 1971–75, the share of bulk exports rose to 69 percent (Salomón Llanes 1978, 15), and in 1984 it reportedly reached 80 percent (La comercialización 1984, 45). In 1987, 136 sugar mills were exclusively shipping raw sugar in bulk form (Varela Pérez 1987).

In addition to two bulk sugar shipping terminals each capable of shipping 1.2 million tons per annum—at Guayabal and Matanzas—whose construction began before 1959, in the 1960s Cuba built a giant terminal in Cienfuegos capable of handling 2.3 million tons of sugar per annum. The Cienfuegos terminal was completed in 1967 (Molina 1977, 5); at the time it was built, it was the largest in the world and represented an investment of nearly 11 million pesos (R. Morales 1967, 60). In 1984, Cuba had a total of seven bulk shipping terminals for sugar (La comercialización 1984, 45; Blanco Díaz 1986, 54). Besides the three mentioned above, similar installations have been built at Boquerón, Ceiba Hueca, Mariel, and Carúpano (Varela Pérez 1986d).

# CHAPTER 6

•

## Refined Sugar and Sugarcane Derivatives

IN ADDITION to producing very large quantities of raw sugar, the Cuban sugar industry also produces significant volumes of refined sugar. Because refined sugar is a higher value-added product than raw sugar, its production and export are more beneficial to the domestic economy. Over the years, Cuba has had difficulty in becoming an important producer of refined sugar primarily because of the lack of international demand for that product. Significant sugar importing countries typically demand raw sugar to be refined domestically.

At the time the government established the Cuban Institute for Research on Sugarcane Derivatives (Instituto Cubano de Investigaciones de los Derivados de la Caña de Azúcar [ICIDCA]) in 1963, then Minister of Industries Guevara said (Cuba Económica 1971, 176; Pereira 1975, 33):

> The experiences of our scientists have already demonstrated that sugarcane derivatives may have a significant economic impact on the country. It may be that over time and as new technologies are developed, sugar is turned into a by-product, a marginal product, and chemical products derived from sugarcane—and industrial products made from them—will have the greater weight in terms of our overall production.

Twenty-five years later, Guevara's vision is far from having been realized, and raw sugar continues to be dominant in the Cuban economy and among sugarcane derivatives. Nevertheless, significant progress has been made in the development and commercialization of other derivatives.

### REFINED SUGAR

In 1958, Cuba had 21 sugar refineries capable of producing nearly 7,000 tons/day of refined sugar (AAC 1958, 194). With two exceptions, the refineries were integrated with mills. Sugar refining capacity had been virtually unchanged since the early 1930s, when a period of fast expansion of refining capacity—to take advantage of the favorable tariff treatment of refined sugar in the U.S. market—came to a close (CERP 1965b, 352–53). After 1937, when U.S. sugar legislation introduced quantitative limits on imports of refined Cuban sugar, the Cuban refining industry operated at very low levels of capacity. In 1958 about 17 percent of refined sugar produced was consumed domestically, and the rest was exported (AAC 1958, 144).

In the 1950s, Cuba was able to increase exports of refined sugar to developing nations. However, opportunities for substantial expansion of refined sugar exports continued to be limited because of the preference on the part of major sugar purchasers—in addition to the United States, Japan, Canada, the Netherlands, France, West Germany, and the United Kingdom—for importing raw sugar to be refined domestically (CERP 1965b, 513–14). The Soviet Union, Cuba's current primary market for sugar and a significant purchaser in the 1950s, also prefers to purchase raw sugar, thus restricting Cuba's ability to move more intensively into this higher value-added product. Eastern European nations, also important markets for Cuban sugar exports, have insisted on maintaining domestic sugar refining capacity and import raw sugar almost exclusively (Luzón 1987, 137).

## CAPACITY AND PRODUCTION TRENDS

Sugar refining capacity declined by about 1,200 tons/day or 17 percent in the early 1960s as rationalization of the sugar industry led to the shutdown of several mills that incorporated refineries. In 1960–61, 17 refineries were in operation, and 16 beginning in 1963 (Manual Azucarero 1971, 1170). There are no readily available statistics on refining capacity in the 1960s and early 1970s. However, on the basis of refining capacity in 1958, it can be estimated that the 16 refineries in operation after 1962 were capable of producing about 5,700 tons of refined sugar per day (see appendix 3).

Table 19 presents available data on production of refined sugar in revolutionary Cuba. To highlight that country's degree of specialization in raw sugar production, table 19 also compares output of refined and raw sugar on an annual basis. Between 1960 and 1987, annual output of refined sugar fluctuated severely, from 616,000 tons in 1960 to over 1.1 million tons in 1967. When five-year averages are used to smooth these annual fluctuations, the results are:

| | |
|---|---|
| 1961–65 | 849,600 tons |
| 1966–70 | 954,300 tons |
| 1971–75 | 743,600 tons |
| 1976–80 | 814,700 tons |
| 1981–85 | 922,300 tons |

Thus refined sugar production reached its highest levels in the second half of the 1960s and declined markedly (by 22 percent) in the early 1970s. In subsequent five-year periods it recovered, average production levels during 1981–85 approaching those reached during the second half of the 1960s. In 1986–87, refined sugar output did not continue the rising trend that had begun in the late 1970s.

An examination of the ratio of refined to raw sugar output suggests that the production of refined sugar has not kept pace with that of raw sugar and therefore revolutionary Cuba's specialization as a raw sugar producer has deepened over time. Thus the refined-to-raw sugar output ratio in the 1960s ranged from 10 to 22 percent, in the 1970s from 11 to 16 percent, and in the 1980s from 9 to 14 percent.

Beginning with 1978, Cuba has released some information on the capacity and performance of the sugar refining industry (table 20). Daily refining capacity remained basically unchanged at about 5,800–5,900 tons/day during 1978–83 but declined in subsequent years, so that by 1986 it stood at 5,300 tons/day, probably the lowest capability since the 1930s. Daily effective refining capacity—which takes into account downtime for maintenance, breakdowns, and so on—was reported as 4,700 tons/day in 1986. In 1987 refining capacity was reported at 6,000 tons/day, and effective refining capacity at 4,900 tons/day.

In 1978–84 sugar refineries operated, on average, about 230 days per year. This compares with an average of 159 calendar days (AEC 1984, 144; 1986, 245) and 119 effective days (table 8) for raw sugar mills over the same period. Thus sugar refineries operated concurrently with sugar mills—that is, over the *zafra* period—with additional time at either end. From an energy use standpoint (chapter 5), this is not efficient, as refineries operating outside the *zafra* period cannot draw on the electric power generated by the mills—from burning bagasse—and must rely on oil-fueled equipment to produce electricity. In 1985–87, refineries were in operation for a much shorter

TABLE 19
Production of Refined Sugar, 1960–1987
*(in thousands of metric tons)*

|      | Refined | Raw | Refined/Raw (%) |
|------|---------|---------|------|
| 1960 | 616.3   | 5,942.9 | 10.4 |
| 1961 | 694.4   | 6,875.5 | 10.1 |
| 1962 | 741.0   | 4,882.1 | 15.2 |
| 1963 | 842.8   | 3,882.5 | 21.7 |
| 1964 | 947.7   | 4,474.5 | 21.2 |
| 1965 | 1,022.1 | 6,156.2 | 16.6 |
| 1966 | 735.9   | 4,537.4 | 16.2 |
| 1967 | 1,128.0 | 6,236.1 | 18.1 |
| 1968 | 1,012.2 | 5,164.5 | 19.6 |
| 1969 | 892.9   | 4,459.4 | 20.0 |
| 1970 | 1,002.7 | 8,537.6 | 11.7 |
| 1971 | 910.7   | 5,924.8 | 15.4 |
| 1972 | 671.3   | 4,324.8 | 15.5 |
| 1973 | 712.0   | 5,252.7 | 13.6 |
| 1974 | 746.2   | 5,924.9 | 12.6 |
| 1975 | 677.9   | 6,314.3 | 10.7 |
| 1976 | 700.1   | 6,155.9 | 11.4 |
| 1977 | 742.5   | 6,485.0 | 11.4 |
| 1978 | 860.6   | 7,350.5 | 11.7 |
| 1979 | 898.7   | 7,991.8 | 11.2 |
| 1980 | 871.6   | 6,665.2 | 13.1 |
| 1981 | 944.5   | 7,358.9 | 12.8 |
| 1982 | 945.0   | 8,210.1 | 11.5 |
| 1983 | 966.7   | 7,108.6 | 13.6 |
| 1984 | 845.5   | 8,206.6 | 10.3 |
| 1985 | 910.3   | 8,003.9 | 11.3 |
| 1986 | 820.2   | 7,254.6 | 11.3 |
| 1987 | 661.1   | 7,116.8 | 9.3  |

SOURCES: Refined sugar—1987, AEC 1987, 249; 1985–86, AEC 1986, 253; 1978–84, AEC 1984, 147; 1971–77, AEC, 1977, 88; 1966–70, AEC 1974, 126; 1964–65, BEC 1966, 87; 1960–63, *Manual Azucarero* 1971, 1170. Raw sugar—table 8.

period (178, 175, and 173 days, respectively); production of refined sugar in 1985 was quite high (910,000 tons) despite the shorter time of operation, but it dropped off substantially in 1986 (820,000 tons) and 1987 (661,000 tons).

The ratio of raw-to-refined sugar produced is a key efficiency

## TABLE 20
### Selected Indicators of the Sugar Refining Industry, 1978–1987

|      | Refining Capacity (000 tons/day) | Effective Refining Capacity (000 tons/day) | Days in Operation | Raw Input/ Refined Output |
|------|------|------|------|------|
| 1978 | 5.8 | 5.0 | 203 | 1.10 |
| 1979 | 5.9 | 5.1 | 238 | 1.14 |
| 1980 | 5.8 | 5.1 | 230 | 1.12 |
| 1981 | 5.8 | 5.1 | 231 | 1.11 |
| 1982 | 5.8 | 5.1 | 237 | 1.14 |
| 1983 | 5.8 | 5.1 | 227 | 1.11 |
| 1984 | 5.6 | 5.0 | 240 | 1.11 |
| 1985 | 5.7 | 5.1 | 178 | 1.12 |
| 1986 | 5.3 | 4.7 | 175 | 1.12 |
| 1987 | 6.0 | 4.9 | 173 | 1.12 |

SOURCES: 1987—AEC 1987, 250; 1980–86—AEC 1986, 249; 1978–79—AEC 1984, 148.

indicator of sugar refining. In 1978 this ratio was 1.10, meaning that 1.10 tons of raw sugar input into the refinery process yielded 1 ton of refined sugar. In 1978–87 the raw-to-refined ratio ranged from 1.10 to 1.14, a variation of about 3.6 percent. In 1983 and 1984, the ratio was 1.11, but it rose slightly to 1.12 in 1985–87.

### REFINED SUGAR IN THE 1980S

Generally speaking, Cuban sugar policies during the 1960s and 1970s emphasized increasing raw sugar production and neglected the refined sugar sector. This seems to have changed in the 1980s, when refining was identified as a potential source of increased export revenue and given a higher priority. Cuba appears to be trying to avoid the repetition of situations such as one that developed in 1981, when lack of refining capacity forced it to send over 75,000 tons of raw sugar to Canada for refining and eventual delivery to Mexico (UNCTAD 1982, 37).

During 1981–85 it was planned to overhaul the sixteen existing refineries, expand the capacity of two (España Republicana and Ecuador) by 200 tons/day each, and build two new ones, expected to become operational in 1985, in Cienfuegos and Santiago de Cuba; the new plants, located in port cities, would have refining capacity of 560 tons/day each and would produce for export (Varela Pérez 1981a). The objective was for Cuba to be able to export over 1 million tons per annum of refined sugar by 1984 (UNCTAD 1982, 37); according to data in table 19, total *production* of refined sugar in 1984 was 845,500 tons.

The 1986–90 plan called for refined sugar output to rise by 25 percent over 1981–85 (Lineamientos 1986, 55); this would mean a projected average annual production level during 1986–90 of about 1.15 million tons, compared to the 922,000 tons per annum produced during 1981–85. Production in 1986, the first year of the new plan period, was 820,200 tons, nearly 29 percent below the projected level, and 661,100 tons in 1987, 43 percent below the projected level.

The Cuban press reported the completion in late 1985 of a new refinery (Julio Antonio Mella) in Santiago de Cuba capable of producing 700 tons/day of refined sugar; total investment in the plant, which incorporates French technology, was roughly 30 million pesos (Sánchez del Toro 1985). Alternatively, the Santiago de Cuba refinery has been reported as representing an investment of 22 million pesos and producing 90,000 tons of refined sugar per annum (BNC 1985, 66). Although the new plant was officially pronounced operational in November 1985, in time for the 1986 *zafra*, it clearly was not: in the 1986 campaign, the Julio Antonio Mella plant produced 3,195 tons of refined sugar, by far the lowest level of output of any of the refineries, and a minuscule proportion (0.4 percent) of the 820,200 tons produced nationwide (AEC 1986, 248). The second new refinery, slated to be built in Cienfuegos, was not completed within the time originally specified; an article on the sugar refining industry published in November 1985 is totally silent on the projected Cienfuegos refinery (Sánchez del Toro 1985).

As data in table 21 indicate, domestic consumption of refined sugar increased steadily in the 1970s and 1980s despite limits on retail sales imposed by the rationing system in place since March 1962. (The monthly ration of refined sugar for adults in the 1980s was 4 pounds; in the central provinces, where fewer processed foods are available, an additional pound of sugar per month was distributed [Benjamin et al. 1984, 36; Ghai et al. 1988, 49].) Domestic consumption accounted for about 20 percent of output in 1965–69, about 22 percent in the 1970s, and nearly 27 percent in the 1980s.

To augment the availability of refined sugar for export, high

TABLE 21
DOMESTIC CONSUMPTION OF REFINED SUGAR, 1965–1987
*(in thousands of tons)*

|      | Consumption | Production | Consumption/ Production (%) |
| --- | --- | --- | --- |
| 1965 | 160.3 | 1,022.1 | 15.7 |
| 1966 | 191.0 | 735.9   | 26.0 |
| 1967 | 210.1 | 1,128.0 | 18.6 |
| 1968 | 214.9 | 1,012.2 | 21.2 |
| 1969 | 168.1 | 892.9   | 18.8 |
| 1970 | 176.5 | 1,002.7 | 17.6 |
| 1971 | 171.9 | 910.7   | 18.9 |
| 1972 | 136.2 | 671.3   | 20.3 |
| 1973 | 149.1 | 712.0   | 20.9 |
| 1974 | 166.2 | 746.2   | 22.3 |
| 1975 | 145.0 | 677.9   | 21.4 |
| 1976 | 179.9 | 700.1   | 25.7 |
| 1977 | 183.7 | 742.5   | 24.7 |
| 1978 | 203.0 | 860.6   | 23.6 |
| 1979 | 220.4 | 898.7   | 24.5 |
| 1980 | 215.3 | 871.6   | 24.7 |
| 1981 | 219.9 | 944.5   | 23.3 |
| 1982 | 225.8 | 945.0   | 23.9 |
| 1983 | 233.7 | 966.7   | 24.2 |
| 1984 | 236.9 | 845.5   | 28.0 |
| 1985 | 232.5 | 910.3   | 25.5 |
| 1986 | 241.9 | 820.2   | 29.5 |
| 1987 | 232.5 | 661.1   | 35.2 |

SOURCES: Consumption—1987—AEC 1987, 387; 1980–86, AEC, 1986, 379; 1978–79, AEC 1984, 264; 1975–77, AEC 1981, 162; 1971–74, AEC 1977, 132; 1966–70, AEC 1974, 177; 1965, AEC 1972, 185. Production—table 19.

*Note:* Consumption is defined as the volume of refined sugar entering the domestic wholesale distribution system.

priority has been given during 1986–90 to increase and improve the quality of *blanco directo* (direct whites, mill whites, or plantation whites), an intermediate product between raw and refined sugar sold domestically as a substitute for the latter (Lineamientos 1986, 54–55; F. Castro 1986, 62). Direct whites offer significant cost savings compared to conventionally refined sugar (Fry 1985, 3–4; Pickett and Robson 1986, 120–27; Greater Availability 1981, 11). Cuban sources estimate that *blanco directo* results in oil savings of $30–40 per ton compared to refined sugar (Norniella 1985).

Production of *blanco directo* apparently began in Cuba around 1980–81 (Varela Pérez 1981a). At first, mills had difficulty in adapting to the production of *blanco directo*; for example, in 1984 the Orlando Nodarse mill met only 13 percent of the output target for that product (Norniella 1985). Around 1985 approximately 150,000 tons of *blanco directo* were being produced annually in six mills; in 1986 the Argelia Libre mill was scheduled to begin production of 85,000 tons per annum (Fernández Font 1986, 205).

## Sugarcane Derivatives

Over the last twenty-five years, ICIDCA has been responsible for the bulk of research and development on sugarcane derivatives in Cuba. ICIDCA, which reported to the vice minister for development of MINAZ, in 1982 had a staff of 700, including 120 university graduates and 210 technicians, working in 30 laboratories, 5 pilot plants and 2 semicommercial plants (Noa Silverio 1983, 130). ICIDCA also maintains a clearinghouse for technical information on sugarcane derivatives and publishes a technical journal, *Sobre los Derivados de la Caña de Azúcar*. Reportedly, ICIDCA is unique, the only institution of its kind in the world where all aspects of the production of sugarcane derivatives are being studied (Miller 1986a, 73).

Cuba's economic development plan for 1986–90 highlights the development and commercialization of sugarcane derivatives other than raw sugar. The plan states (Lineamientos 1986, 55):

> Give priority attention to the fulfillment of the sugarcane derivatives program, in particular with regard to higher value-added products and those with strong links to other sectors of the economy, with the objective of increasing the weight of these products within the national economy and especially within the export sector. To this effect, take special note of production of furfural, lysine, alcohols, *miel protéica* [a type of animal feed], dextran, artificial wood panels, paper, paper pulp, torula yeast, oils, wax, hormones, etcetera.

The economic rationale for assigning a high priority to research, development, and commercialization of sugarcane derivatives other than sugar is twofold: (1) world market prices for sugar in the 1980s have been low and may continue to be so in the future if Cuba and other producers are successful in increasing production through the year 2000; and (2) sugar production generates huge volumes of by-products that heretofore have not been utilized in the most economically efficient fashion.

A rough notion of the volume of by-products generated in the process of sugar production can be obtained from estimates published in Cuban sources. On average, 100 tons of green sugarcane harvested yield the following volumes of products (Noa Silverio 1983, 127):

| raw sugar | 12.5 tons |
| cane tops | 18.4 tons |
| leaves and straw | 42.9 tons |
| final molasses | 3.6 tons |
| filter mud | 3.4 tons |
| bagasse (50% moisture) | 27.5 tons |

Although these data seem to be in error—the products, including sugar, add up to 108.5 tons, higher than the 100-ton sugarcane input—they nevertheless highlight the relatively small amount of sugar, or conversely the very large amounts of by-products, obtained from sugarcane in the sugar manufacturing process. Over one-half of cane harvested (by weight) is composed of cane tops, leaves, and straw that do not—or should not, if the cane is properly cleaned—enter the industrial process.

Another way to look at the relative importance of sugar in relation to by-products is to examine the volume of each that is generated in conjunction with sugar production. According to Cuban sources (Almazán del Olmo 1988, 53), the following volumes of by-products are associated with production of 100 tons of raw sugar:

| bagasse (50% moisture) | 216.6 tons |
| final molasses | 28.3 tons |
| filter mud | 27.5 tons |
| green leaves | 85.0 tons |
| dry leaves | 74.1 tons |
| cane tops | 74.1 tons |

That is, for each 100 tons of raw sugar produced, 505.6 tons of potentially usable by-products are also generated.

In the discussion that follows a distinction is made between sugar by-products and sugarcane derivatives. By-products are those products that are obtained directly from the harvesting or industrial processes associated with sugar production and are the raw materials for the production of derivatives. Examples of by-products are cane tops, straw, bagasse, molasses, filter mud (*cachaza*), and raw sugar. Sugarcane derivatives are obtained from by-products. Table 22 provides an illustrative list of the sugarcane derivatives that are produced, or could be produced, in Cuba from by-products generated in the sugar manufacturing process.

AGRICULTURAL DERIVATIVES

Sugar cane tops, leaves, and trash (straw) are used primarily as livestock feed. In 1987 tops and leaves gathered at the *centros de acopio* were used to feed 939,000 head of cattle; in that year, Cuba had 9 plants that produced cattle feed from sugarcane straw mixed with molasses and urea (Almazán del Olmo 1988, 71). ICINAZ technicians have developed a plan to export dried sugarcane leaves and tops, packed in bales, to earn hard currency (Santana Palenzuela and Cordovés Herrera 1988). Cuba has experimented with the extraction of protein (for animal feed) from sugarcane tops and leaves (Romero Revuelta 1985) and is also considering using sugarcane straw as a substitute for bagasse in sugar mills, a move that would free up additional quantities of bagasse to be used for industrial purposes; according to Cuban estimates, 1.4 tons of sugarcane straw have the equivalent caloric value of 1 ton of bagasse (Gálvez Taupier and Noa Silverio 1985, 126).

Thus far, Cuba has not produced ethanol directly from sugarcane juice (*guarapo*) through fermentation—as is done extensively in Brazil—in commercial quantities (David Posada 1981). Ethanol plants using this technology wash and crush sugarcane; separate bagasse (to be used as fuel) from cane juice; concentrate, sterilize, and ferment the juice with yeast; and filter and distill the fermented mash to obtain 94 percent ethanol (World Bank 1980, 22–23). As opposed to production of ethanol from molasses, as is customary in Cuba, production from cane juice has a more positive energy balance (estimated at 3–8 times as much energy generated, in terms of caloric value, as is consumed) since the sugar production process that yields molasses as a by-product is quite energy intensive.

In the wake of the formal reestablishment of diplomatic relations between Cuba and Brazil in June 1986, prospects have improved for

TABLE 22
Sugarcane Derivatives

|  | Derivative |
|---|---|
| *Raw sugar* | Refined sugar |
|  | Dextran |
|  | Sorbitol |
| *By-product* |  |
| Tops, leaves, straw | Animal feed |
|  | Fuel |
| Cane juice (*guarapo*) | Alcohol (for beverages) |
|  | Alcohol (for synthetic rubber) |
|  | Ethanol |
|  | Sugar fodder |
|  | Lactates |
|  | Dextran |
|  | Other fermentation products |
| Bagasse (*bagazo*) | Newsprint |
|  | Paper pulp |
|  | Particleboard & fiberboard |
|  | Molded products |
|  | Textile fiber and yarn |
|  | Activated carbon |
|  | Carboxymethylcellulose |
|  | Cellophane |
|  | Furfural |
|  | Animal feed (*bagacillo*) |
| Molasses | Alcohol (for beverages) |
|  | Ethanol |
|  | Torula yeast |
|  | Citric acid |
|  | Lysine |
|  | Monosodium glutamate |
| Filter mud (*cachaza*) | Fertilizers |
|  | Wax |
|  | Animal feed (*gicabú*) |

SOURCES: AAC 1958, 193; Fox 1986, 39; Almazán del Olmo 1988.

possible Cuban adoption of Brazilian ethanol production technology. In mid 1985, before diplomatic relations were reestablished, the Cuban international news service reported that Brazil was promoting exports of ethanol distilleries to Cuba and Australia (Cuba-Brasil 1985, 21). Around this time, a Brazilian company announced that it was negotiating with Cuba over the sale of an ethanol distillery (Nazario 1986, 79), and the Cuban international news service later confirmed that a deal involving an experimental distillery had been consummated (Brasilia 1985, 8).

BAGASSE DERIVATIVES

Currently the most economically significant sugarcane derivatives produced in Cuba are those obtained from bagasse. As was discussed earlier (chapter 5), bagasse has traditionally been the principal energy source of sugar mills. In recent years significant amounts of it have been used as raw material in the industrial sector (table 16). Clearly, diverting bagasse from sugar mills and into the industrial sector can affect the mills' demand for alternative energy sources, most likely oil products.

Experimentation and small-scale production in Cuba of paper and particleboard from bagasse goes back to 1915, when kraft paper was produced at a plant attached to the Preston (currently Guatemala) sugar mill in Holguín; particleboard was first produced in Cuba in 1928 (Olema 1980, 40). In 1959, Cuba was already producing a broad range of bagasse-derived products: newsprint, particleboard, acoustical tiles, bagasse-pulp fine papers, and office furniture, with a bagasse paperboard plant scheduled to start production in mid 1959 (Papel 1955, 505–06; Arellano 1959; Harbron 1959, 38; Ruiz 1959).

In 1966 there were three bagasse pulp and paper plants in operation, with annual production capacity of 53,500 tons of paper and paperboard; all three plants were built before 1959 (Pernas 1965, 68) and relied on a combination of bagasse pulp and imported wood pulp. A large plant capable of producing 60,000 tons of bagasse pulp per annum and several qualities of writing and printing paper was constructed adjacent to the Uruguay sugar mill, in Sancti Spíritus province, which generally produced bagasse in excess of its needs for fuel purposes; the plant, named Panchito Gómez Toro, represented an investment of 136 million (Vázquez 1980, 13) or 188 million pesos (A. Rodríguez 1983, 7). Reportedly it began operations in 1986 (Almazán del Olmo, 1988:55).

Bagasse pulp and paper production capacity of the three plants in operation in 1982 can be estimated at 43,200 tons/year of pulp, 51,000 tons/year of paper, and 21,000 tons/year of cardboard (see appendix 4). Official Cuban data on production of bagasse pulp, paper, and

TABLE 23
PRODUCTION OF SELECTED SUGARCANE DERIVATIVES, 1970–1987
*(in thousands of tons)*

|  | 1970 | 1975 | 1980 | 1981 | 1982 | 1983 | 1984 | 1985 | 1986 | 1987 |
|---|---|---|---|---|---|---|---|---|---|---|
| Paper pulp | 33.7 | 36.3 | 29.9 | 31.6 | 33.4 | 34.1 | 38.5 | 49.1 | 58.8 | 51.5 |
| Writing paper | 18.9 | 32.0 | 36.7 | 40.4 | 36.5 | 33.8 | 43.6 | 58.9 | 66.4 | 57.3 |
| Gray cardboard | 11.7 | 15.9 | 13.8 | 14.7 | 14.0 | 12.6 | 10.7 | 11.4 | 10.6 | 12.1 |
| Cardboard for corrugated boxes | 8.5 | 11.8 | 8.0 | 10.5 | 12.3 | 8.7 | 8.1 | 4.9 | 10.8 | 7.2 |
| Ethanol[a] | 910.1 | 670.5 | 841.2 | 781.2 | 867.2 | 866.2 | 887.7 | 936.9 | 969.5 | 1,005.5 |
| Rum[a] | 137.9 | 181.7 | 283.6 | 275.2 | 427.7 | 430.7 | 489.7 | 465.0 | 408.4 | 456.9 |
| Torula yeast | — | 8.0 | 40.9 | 35.6 | 40.2 | 62.2 | 68.4 | 58.4 | 62.3 | 52.9 |

SOURCE: 1986–87—AEC 1987, 252–55; 1970–85—AEC 1986, 252–54.
a. Thousand hectoliters.

cardboard in 1970–87 (table 23) indicate that pulp production was stagnant through 1983, at about 30,000–35,000 tons/year, but increased significantly in 1984–87; meanwhile, cardboard production (gray cardboard plus cardboard for corrugated boxes) peaked in 1981–82 at about 26,000 tons and declined in 1983–87.

Production of paper averaged over 38,000 tons in 1980–81 and dropped in the next two years to an average of 35,000 tons. Beginning in 1984, production increased significantly, with output reaching over 66,000 tons in 1986 and declining to 57,000 tons in 1987. The operating rate of paper-making machinery was 76 percent in 1980 (AEC 1982, 174), over 84 percent in 1981–83 (AEC 1983, 165; 1984, 161), and it fell to under 74 percent in 1984–85 (AEC 1986, 249), suggesting that production capacity increased sharply in those two years. The very high paper production level in 1986 may reflect, in part, the coming on line of the Panchito Gómez Toro plant, which increased national bagasse pulp production capacity to about 100,000 tons/year and paper production capacity to about 110,000 tons/year.

Exports of bagasse paper products were supposed to begin in 1981, when sales contracts were signed with Mexico and Austria; these contracts were not fulfilled by Cuba, however. Cuba did export 300 tons of bond and semibond paper (0.8 percent of output) in 1982, 495 tons (1.5 percent) in 1983, and 1,895 tons (4.3 percent) in 1984 to Nicaragua and the Netherlands. The export plan for 1985 was 17,000 tons of bond, semibond, and offset paper, which would have represented nearly 29 percent of total output (Vidal Valdés 1985, 142–43).

In the 1970s, Cuba tackled—apparently with considerable success—the technical problems of producing bagasse newsprint. Although the first plant in the world to produce 100 percent bagasse newsprint was built in Cuba and started operation in 1958, the output was reportedly too costly, and for this reason the revolutionary government discontinued production in 1960 (Gutiérrez et al. 1976, 25–26; López Guzmán 1982, 18; Navarrete 1980, 2).

In 1974, with financial and technical assistance from the United Nations Development Program (UNDP) and the United Nations Industrial Development Organization, Cuba began research on the feasibility of producing pulp and newsprint from bagasse. It has been reported that the research has resulted in a method to obtain high-quality pulp from bagasse, which yields output with qualities very similar to those of wood pulp (López Guzmán 1983, 44).

As part of the project, a pilot plant (called Cuba-9), was attached to the Pablo Noriega sugar mill in Quivicán, La Habana province (Hernández Serrano 1979). Investment costs have been estimated at $25 million, financed jointly by Cuba ($14.8 million), UNDP ($5.7 million), and Canada and Finland ($4.5 million) (García and Pérez 1988, 21; Pérez-Alcina 1988, 21). Originally scheduled to be completed by the first half of 1978 and to produce 30 tons of newsprint per day (Caballero Almeida 1978, 22; A. Rodríguez 1976; Vázquez 1977a, 6), the plant was not completed until mid 1981 (Montero 1981; A. Rodríguez 1982a, 29). Semicommercial production at the Cuba-9 plant started in 1983 (Gálvez Taupier 1987, 15).

Cuba has expanded the production capacity of three of the four particleboard and fiberboard plants that existed in 1959 and built three others relying on technology and equipment imported from West Germany (La Serna and Carvajal 1983, 22; Varela Rojas 1984, 32–33) (see appendix 4). For example, the Camilo Cienfuegos plant, completed in 1978, was built by the West German firm Bison Werke. It can produce particleboard with plastic or wood veneer finish, suitable for furniture manufacturing; 50 percent of the output of the plant (it has annual capacity of 36,000 tons of product) was earmarked for export (Pérez Alcina 1987, 46–47). In 1987 national production capacity of particle- and fiberboard was estimated at 235,000 (Almazán del Olmo 1988, 67) or 240,000 cubic meters per annum (Gálvez

Taupier 1987, 15). Production of molded bagasse products—a plug for bobbins used to roll paper being produced at the Panchito Gómez Toro mill—began in 1986 at one of the particleboard plants (Salomón Llanes 1986a, 78).

Cuba does not publish statistics on output of particleboard and fiberboard. However, the 1986 statistical yearbook for the first time published data on "production for export" of a number of industrial products, including bagasse particleboard. According to these data, Cuba produced over 5,200 cubic meters of particleboard for export in 1985, 12,500 cubic meters in 1986, and nearly 20,000 cubic meters in 1987 (AEC 1987, 268). These export volumes represented 2.2, 5.4, and 8.5 percent, respectively, of annual production capacity. In 1986 the six particle- and fiberboard plants were exceeding their output plans and yet were operating at 40 percent of capacity (Varela Pérez 1986f, 1).

Another sugarcane derivative from bagasse produced in Cuba is furfural, a compound used to produce furfuryl alcohol and a host of other chemical products. Furfural is used as a solvent in the production of lubricating oils, plastics, anticorrosive materials, herbicides, insecticides, pharmaceutical products, and nylon, among others. An experimental plant to produce furfural, reportedly designed by Cuban specialists and using primarily domestically produced equipment, began operations in 1988 in the sugar mill Amancio Rodríguez, in Las Tunas province; the plant's capacity is 1,000 tons of furfural per annum (Pérez Viera and Castellanos 1988). A second plant, to be built in Camagüey province at a cost of 25 million pesos, is scheduled to be completed before 1990 (Salomón Llanes 1986b, 56).

Finally, bagasse is also being used in Cuba to produce predigested pith (*bagacillo*) for cattle feed. *Bagacillo,* a mixture of sugarcane pith, sodium hydroxide, and molasses, is particularly well suited as feed for dairy cattle (Pagés 1986). In 1982 there were 18 plants producing *bagacillo,* with combined annual production capacity of 80,000 tons (appendix 4); by 1987, 57 *bagacillo* plants were reportedly in operation nationwide.

MOLASSES DERIVATIVES

The most developed sugarcane derivative produced in prerevolutionary Cuba was alcohol (fuel alcohol, or ethanol, and alcohol for beverages) distilled from molasses. Production of alcohol from molasses began in Cuba as early as the middle of the nineteenth century, and distilleries were typically built adjacent to sugar mills. During World War II shortages of imported oil led to the production of gasohol (an ethanol–gasoline–lubricating oil mixture called *carburante nacional*) as an alternative to gasoline. The production of gasohol used significant volumes of domestically produced ethanol (the original mixture called for 70 percent ethanol, 25 percent gasoline, and 5 percent lubricating oil; the proportions were later changed, ethanol's share falling significantly).

Spurred by the demand created by the production of *carburante nacional*, ethanol production capacity and output rose rapidly; during 1943–45, 50 new distilleries were built and capacity trebled. Many of these distilleries were later dismantled when oil supplies again were plentiful and production of *carburante nacional* was discontinued. In 1958, Cuba had 48 alcohol distilleries, with production capacity of nearly 5.2 million hectoliters of alcohol per annum, although almost half were not running because it was not economically feasible to operate them given prices of molasses and of alcohol (CERP 1965b, 514–17). In 1967 only 18 distilleries were in operation, compared to 19 a year earlier (Manual Azucarero 1971, 1202).

It has been reported that in 1987, Cuba had 17 distilleries capable of producing 2.5 million hectoliters per annum of ethanol and alcohol for beverages and pharmaceutical uses (Almazán del Olmo 1988, 56). Another source has given industry capacity in the same year as 1.5 million hectoliters in 16 plants (Gálvez Taupier 1987, 14). Yet a third source indicates that in 1982 there were 15 distilleries in operation, with annual production capacity of 1.4 million hectoliters of ethanol and 330,000 hectoliters of rum (appendix 4). Ethanol production in 1981–85 averaged about 870,000 hectoliters per annum and reached 970,000 hectoliters in 1986 and over 1 million hectoliters in 1987; rum production averaged nearly 420,000 hectoliters per annum in 1981–85, fell to 408,000 hectoliters in 1986 and recovered to 457,000 hectoliters in 1987 (table 23). In 1985–87 production of ethanol for export was 113,000, 269,000 and 250,000 hectoliters respectively, roughly 12–27 percent of output; production of alcoholic beverages for export was 14,200 hectoliters in 1986 (3.5 percent of rum production) and 17,700 hectoliters in 1987 (3.9 percent) (table 23 and AEC 1987, 268).

Utilization of alcohol-producing capacity has been officially reported as 73.7 percent in 1982, 79.1 percent in 1983, and 81.3 percent in 1984 (AEC 1984, 162); it was 75 percent in 1986 (Varela Pérez

1986f). Consumption of molasses in the production of alcohol was 434 kilograms of molasses per hectoliter of alcohol in 1982, 446 kilograms in 1983 and 434 kilograms in 1984 (AEC 1984, 162); in 1986 it was 423, compared to the norm of 408 (Varela Pérez 1986f).

Another important use for molasses in Cuba that competes with the alcohol distilleries for raw material is animal feed production. In the 1950s the relative prices of molasses and alcohol were such that molasses sold for cattle feed brought a higher return than that sold to make alcohol. As a result, the bulk of the available molasses was devoted to animal feed production, and that industry expanded at the expense of the alcohol production industry (CERP 1965b, 515).

The emphasis placed by the revolutionary government on the expansion of the cattle industry further eroded the alcohol industry, as molasses was increasingly diverted from alcohol to cattle feed production. In 1969, for instance, Cuba undertook a program to convert from domestically produced ethanol to imported kerosene as a home cooking fuel. The rationale for the switch was that it was more profitable to devote molasses to cattle feed than to alcohol production. This conversion was essentially completed by the time of the 1973 oil embargo and the ensuing quadrupling of world market prices for oil and oil products (Pérez-López 1981, 127).

In 1965 a pilot plant was built to manufacture torula yeast, a form of animal feed (for cattle, poultry, and pigs), from molasses. On the basis of the positive results obtained, Cuba undertook a program to build ten additional plants at a cost of 100 million pesos; presumably, a significant part of the investment was in convertible currency, as six of the plants were to be imported from France and four from Austria (Díaz Sosa 1981, 30; Marsán 1977, 17–19).

By 1980 there were nine torula yeast plants in operation (H. Pérez 1982, 12); in 1982 there were ten, with combined production capacity of 120,000 tons per annum (appendix 4). Torula yeast production rose from 8,000 tons in 1975 to 68,400 tons in 1984, with production declining to 58,400 tons in 1985, rising to 62,300 in 1986, and again declining to 52,900 in 1987 (table 23). Cuba produced 22,870 tons of torula yeast for export (39 percent of output) in 1985, 22,300 tons (36 percent of output) in 1986 and 24,000 tons (45 percent of output) in 1987 (table 23 and AEC 1987, 268).

Two Cuban sugar mills have facilities to produce about 5,600 tons of baker's yeast per annum, while five alcohol distilleries can recover up to 7,200 tons of saccharomyces yeast annually (appendix

4). Sacchoramyces yeast, a product with high protein value, is used as animal feed.

Also with financial and technical assistance from the UNDP, Cuba has built a pilot plant to study the use of fermented molasses for animal feed. The first stage of the project (called Cuba-10), an industrial fermentation plant, went into operation in 1983; other installations to produce aminoacids for cattle feed were to be completed at a later date (Savall 1984; Vázquez 1977a, 6–7). Cuba is also producing a mixture of molasses and torula yeast called *miel protéica* used as pig feed; in 1987 there were eight plants capable of producing this (Almazán del Olmo 1988, 58)

FILTER MUD DERIVATIVES

Cuba has also produced derivatives from *cachaza,* the filter mud produced in the clarification or purification of cane juice. Three plants to produce wax from *cachaza* were established in the 1950s adjacent to the Jaronú (currently Brasil), Delicias (Antonio Guiteras) and Chaparra (Jesús Menéndez) sugar mills. All three plants sent the wax to the United States for refining. In 1978, two of the plants were shut down (A. Rodríguez 1982b, 12) and only the Jesús Menéndez plant, by now capable of producing refined wax, remained in operation. In 1982 production capacity of the Jesús Menéndez plant was given as 115 tons of refined wax per annum (appendix 4). More recently, it has been reported that the capacity of the Jesús Menéndez plant was 120 tons of crude wax and 30 tons of refined wax per annum and that a new plant, capable of producing 500 tons of refined wax per annum, would be installed by 1990 at the Antonio Guiteras sugar mill (Aumentará 1986).

In 1983 experimental production of a cattle feed product derived from *cachaza* invented by a Cuban chemist was started. The product, *gicabú,* is obtained by exposing filter mud to the sun to evaporate excess moisture (Pagés 1984). Based on the favorable results obtained in tests, construction of 170 evaporation areas, capable of processing all the *cachaza* produced in the country, was planned (Pagés 1985).

RAW SUGAR DERIVATIVES

Commercial production in Cuba of derivatives from raw sugar is limited to refined sugar and dextran. Commercial production of dextran began in 1963 at a plant adjacent to the España Republicana mill, with production capacity of 450 tons per annum (see appendix 4). Dextran is used domestically in the preparation of muds for oil drilling and in the food and cosmetics industries (Almazán del Olmo 1988, 69). In 1986 and 1987, Cuba exported 200.8 tons and 95.8 tons, respectively, of dextran (AEC 1987, 268).

# CHAPTER 7

•

## Production Costs

THE LITERATURE on costs of producing sugar in Cuba is so thin as to be almost nonexistent. It appears that no industrywide information on production costs was collected in prerevolutionary Cuba, and no systematic data or analyses of production costs are available for that period. There are estimates of production costs for two years, 1939 and 1949, obtained from a survey of three prototype sugar mills, but no information is available on costs in the 1950s. This lack may be partially attributable to the structure of the industry: privately owned and fragmented.

Although the structure of the industry changed radically after 1960, when it was nationalized by the revolutionary government, there has been no change with regard to the publication of production cost statistics. The literature suggests, however, that an accounting system is in place within MINAZ that produces cost statistics for internal use. An international consulting company, Landell Mills Commodities Studies, has produced estimates of sugar production costs in different countries, including Cuba.

### COSTS IN PREREVOLUTIONARY CUBA

To my knowledge, the only estimates of sugar production costs in prerevolutionary Cuba in the public domain are those that were produced by a mission (the Truslow Mission) from the International Bank for Reconstruction and Development—the official name of the World Bank—that visited Cuba in 1950. According to information developed by the mission, average production costs of sugar (including transportation to a port for export) in Cuba in three sugar mills in 1949 ranged from $11.93 to $15.43 per 325-pound bag (see table 24), or 3.67–4.75 cents/pound; in 1939 the comparable figures ranged from $4.54 to $6.92 per 325-pound bag, or 1.40–2.13 cents/pound. For the two dozen American-owned mills, the reported average cost

## TABLE 24
### Sugar Production Costs, 1939 and 1949
*(in pesos/325-pound bag)*

|  | Mill A 1939 | Mill A 1949 | Mill B 1939 | Mill B 1949 | Mill C 1939 | Mill C 1949 |
| --- | --- | --- | --- | --- | --- | --- |
| Cost of cane at sugar mill | 2.28 | 7.40 | 2.81 | 8.43 | 2.84 | 9.35 |
| Direct manufacturing cost | 0.14 | 0.39 | 0.48 | 0.71 | 0.26 | 0.86 |
| Bags and bagging | 0.17 | 0.60 | 0.18 | 0.59 | 0.33 | 0.57 |
| Direct taxes | 0.35 | 0.61 | 0.28 | 0.28 | 0.28 | 0.34 |
| Indirect costs | 0.77 | 1.44 | 0.60 | 2.45 | 2.39 | 3.59 |
| Depreciation | 0.99 | 0.47 | 0.01 | 0.15 | 0.60 | 0.43 |
| Transportation to seaboard | 0.65 | 1.02 | 0.18 | 0.85 | 0.22 | 0.29 |
| Total | 5.35 | 11.93 | 4.54 | 13.46 | 6.92 | 15.43 |

SOURCE: World Bank 1951, 808.

of production in 1949 was 4.20 cents/pound (World Bank 1951, 807–08). It should be noted that over this period, the Cuban peso was exchanged at par with the U.S. dollar.

The data in table 24 reveal that sugar production costs in Cuba more than doubled between 1939 and 1949; for Mill B, they almost trebled (increase of 196 percent). Costs tended to rise across all items in table 24, but the most significant increases were in the cost of raw material—sugarcane—already the most important single cost factor in sugar production. Thus the cost of cane delivered to mills rose threefold between 1939 and 1949. The structure of costs in 1949 (as a percentage of total cost) for three sugar mills was as follows (World Bank 1951, 808):

|  | Mill A | Mill B | Mill C |
| --- | --- | --- | --- |
| Cost of cane at mill | 62.0 | 62.6 | 60.6 |
| Direct manufacturing cost | 3.3 | 5.3 | 5.6 |
| Bags and bagging | 5.0 | 4.4 | 3.7 |
| Direct taxes | 5.1 | 2.1 | 2.2 |
| Indirect costs | 12.1 | 18.2 | 23.3 |
| Depreciation | 3.9 | 1.1 | 2.8 |
| Transportation to seaboard | 8.6 | 6.3 | 1.9 |

It should be noted that these figures refer to average total costs and therefore include a return to fixed assets (capital).

By far the most significant operating cost (60–62 percent of total) incurred by sugar mills in 1949 was the purchase of sugarcane. Thus the efficiency of the sugarcane agricultural sector was important in overall sugar production costs. Medium-sized cane farms, that is, those producing between 2,250 and 4,500 tons per annum, were reportedly optimal in prerevolutionary Cuba from a cost standpoint—they were able to prosper when international sugar prices were high and to withstand periods of low prices better than the very large or very small farms (CERP 1965c, 137).

A comparison of sugar production costs in Louisiana and Cuba, presumably for around 1940, showed costs of 4.08 cents/pound in Louisiana, 77 percent higher than the 2.31 cents/pound estimated for Cuba. The bulk of the difference resulted from much higher sugarcane costs in Louisiana (122 percent higher), whereas manufacturing costs were not dramatically different (21 percent higher in Louisiana). Cuba's cost advantage was attributed to the fact that sugarcane there could be harvested for several years (reportedly up to seven) without replanting, whereas in Louisiana annual replanting was necessary (Alienes Urosa 1950; CERP 1965c, 138; Acosta 1972, 79).

A significant factor in sugar production costs identified by the Truslow Mission that, in its view, could be substantially reduced or eliminated altogether was that of bags and bagging. As noted above, bags and bagging represented 3.7–5.0 percent of total sugar production costs in 1949. For raw sugar being transported to domestic refineries or for export, this cost could have been eliminated by relying on bulk shipping, a method that would probably also have reduced overall transportation costs. As was discussed earlier, bulk shipping was not politically feasible in prerevolutionary Cuba because of opposition from organized labor.

## Costs in Revolutionary Cuba

A reading of the literature (e.g., Albuerne 1974; Fernández Martín et al. 1984; Suárez Guerra 1983) suggests that Cuba has in place, and has had in place since the mid 1970s, a sophisticated system of economic data collection and control for the sugar industry that is probably capable of yielding reliable production cost estimates. However, to my knowledge, Cuba has not published official statistics on sugar production costs.

Information on the costs incurred by a given industry can generally be obtained from input-output matrices, which contain data for each industry on the value of its purchases from and sales to all other industries. Cuban statisticians have produced at least three input-output tables: for the first half of 1963, for 1965, and for 1981. Only the 45 × 45 table for 1963 has been published, however (González Maicas 1964), and unfortunately, it did not treat the sugar industry as a separate entity. Moreover, since the table dealt only with enterprises under the jurisdiction of the Ministry of Industries, agricultural (including sugarcane agricultural) operations were not included.

Some insights into the structure of sugar production costs in revolutionary Cuba may be gleaned from articles in the Cuban literature dealing with accounting systems and methods of estimating sugar production costs. According to the then director of the Consolidated Sugar Industry Enterprise of the Ministry of Industries, a uniform accounting system for all sugar mills was put in place on 1 July 1961 (all mills were under state control by that date). For 1962 the structure of costs of producing raw sugar (in percentages) was (Menéndez Cruz 1964, 6):

| | |
|---|---|
| raw materials and direct inputs | 60.04 |
| indirect inputs | 3.16 |
| energy | 1.68 |
| labor | 24.82 |
| social security | 3.05 |
| debt service and depreciation | 5.99 |
| other production costs | 1.26 |

Interestingly, for the 1962 *zafra*, Menéndez Cruz (1964, 7) presents data on production costs by size (i.e., grinding capacity per day) of sugar mills. These data, in index number form, with production costs of mills capable of grinding between 2,836 and 4,535 tons of cane per day as 100, are as follows:

| | |
|---|---|
| less than 1,700 tons per day | 105.45 |
| 1,701–2,835 tons per day | 100.21 |
| 2,836–4,535 tons per day | 100.00 |
| 4,536–6,800 tons per day | 102.57 |
| More than 6,800 tons per day | 104.60 |

These figures for 1962 point out quite clearly that medium-sized sugar mills were the most cost-efficient units, as the smallest mills did not benefit from economies of scale and the largest were adversely affected by sugarcane supply problems.

Beginning around 1966, Cuba eliminated financial transactions among state-owned enterprises and replaced the existing accounting systems with a loose system of statistical reporting. The central plan ceased to have a directive nature, and annual national budgets, as well as the entire Ministry of Finance, were abolished (Mesa-Lago 1981, 23–24). In the sugar industry, this translated into a lack of attention to costs and inadequate financial information. In the 1970s these policies were reversed, with the implementation beginning in 1975 of the Economic Management and Planning System (Sistema de Dirección y Planificación de la Economía) which emphasized physical planning and financial controls (Suárez Guerra 1984, 219–22).

As might be expected, there is no information on sugar production costs in Cuba over the late 1960s and early 1970s. For 1984 several Cuban researchers (Fernández Martín et al. 1984, 29) have developed the following structure of costs for an integrated sugar mill complex producing raw sugar, molasses, and bagasse for industrial use:

|  | % of Cost |
|---|---|
| sugarcane | 66.58 |
| transportation and *acopio* of sugarcane | 5.18 |
| raw materials | 0.47 |
| energy | 18.29 |
| direct labor | 5.06 |
| maintenance (incl. depreciation) | 18.42 |
| administration | 6.26 |
| Total | 118.27 |
| less sales of by-products (bagasse, molasses) | 18.27 |
| Total | 100.00 |

This structure of costs is as it appears in the Cuban source, although there appears to be an error in the figures; the sum of the costs associated with sugar production yields 120.26 percent, rather than 118.27 percent.

The cost data for 1962 and 1984 are structured sufficiently differently from the estimates for prerevolutionary Cuba discussed earlier not to permit extensive comparisons. While the cost data developed by the Truslow Mission for 1939 and 1949 related to payments for tasks performed, the more recent data are loosely based on payments to each of the factors of production. The one category that appears roughly equivalent in both sets of data is sugarcane input cost. The more recent data suggest that the cost of sugarcane continues to be the most important single factor affecting overall sugar production costs, representing over 60 percent of total costs.

One area in which revolutionary Cuba appears to have made progress in reducing costs is transportation: movement of sugar from mills to refineries or to export ports and loading onto ships for export. As was noted in chapter 5, in prerevolutionary Cuba sugar had to be bagged at sugar mills and transported in this form. The cost of bags and bagging was not insignificant: 3.5 to over 5.0 percent of total production costs in 1949, according to estimates. Virtually all of the bags were imported, manufactured in the United States from Indian jute (World Bank 1951, 394). The Truslow Mission reported that in 1950, imported sugar bags cost 59 cents each. In fact, recognizing that Cuban labor's opposition to bulk shipping was not likely to be reversed, the mission recommended the establishment of a bag mill in Cuba using at first imported jute and eventually domestically produced kenaf. This move would aid the trade balance, create a market for a domestic fiber, and generate employment (ibid. 1031–36).

In revolutionary Cuba sugar is transported from mills to refineries or to export terminals predominantly in bulk, eliminating costs associated with bags and bagging. In the mid 1960s it was estimated that the cost of shipping, transporting, and warehousing one ton of bulk sugar was 2.34 pesos, compared to 7.03 pesos for the same volume bagged, for a cost saving of 4.69 pesos per ton. For export shipments of 5.3 million tons, by relying on bulk shipping Cuba could reduce costs by approximately 21 million pesos, including over 16 million pesos in hard currency for bags, which cost 38 cents each (R. Morales 1967, 62). The Cienfuegos shipping terminal, built at a cost of 14 million pesos, reportedly saved 37 million pesos in imported bags alone in its first ten years of operation (Molina 1977, 5). Bulk transportation also reduces costs associated with loading sugar onto ships.

Some fragmentary information on absolute production costs in revolutionary Cuba has appeared in the literature:

1. The cost of production at a sugar mill in Camagüey province around 1963 was reported to be 4.37 centavos/pound, a figure that presumably excluded depreciation, maintenance, and overhead costs and did not take into account actual labor costs because of voluntary labor; if wage rates prevailing in 1958 had been paid, cost of production would have exceeded 5 centavos/pound (CERP 1965a, 133).

2. In August 1977 a Cuban official stated publicly that world market prices for sugar had fallen so low that they barely covered Cuban production costs (Milián, 1977, 2). Since the world market price in mid 1977 was about 8 U.S. cents/pound (it averaged 8.80

U.S. cents/pound in the second quarter of 1977 and 7.48 U.S. cents/pound in the third), it can be inferred that Cuban production costs in mid 1977 were in the range of 7–8 U.S. cents/pound.

3. In April and May 1977, Marcelo Fernández Font, the Cuban foreign trade minister, proposed that a new International Sugar Agreement (ISA) being negotiated in Geneva establish a price range of 15–25 U.S. cents/pound; the lower price, he stated, "logically should cover production costs and provide a reasonable profit margin" (Convenio Azucarero 1977, 12; Alvarez Quiñones 1977, 2; Fernández Colino 1977a). It can be inferred from Fernández Font's statements that Cuban sugar production costs in early 1977 were not anywhere near 15 U.S. cents/pound since he noted that the price range was negotiable and that his concern about accepting a lower price range (such as the 10–20 U.S. cents/pound proposed by importing countries or 11–21 U.S. cents/pound developed by the president of the conference as a compromise position—which ultimately prevailed) was that inflation would soon bring the real price down to the 8–9 U.S. cents/pound range.

4. From an article by a Cuban technician dealing with the optimal length of the *zafra,* it may be inferred that sugar production costs in Cuba in the late 1970s, in an efficient mill, were slightly over 9 centavos/pound (Morales Pita 1983, 11).

5. Adjusting the estimate in (4) to account for lower overall efficiency of sugar mills, two Cuban authors have estimated average sugar production costs in 1984 at 10.4 centavos/pound. These costs were distributed evenly between inputs produced domestically and imported inputs; hard currency imports accounted for 60 percent of imported inputs, with soft currency inputs accounting for the other 40 percent (Miranda Torres and Rodríguez Valdés 1984, 123–24).

## Other Cost Estimates

At least two estimates of production costs in Cuba made by outside sources have appeared in the Cuban literature without comment: an estimate of 12 U.S. cents/pound in 1979 attributed to the Latin American and Caribbean Sugar Exporters Group (Rodríguez Corominas and Likichev 1984, 229), and a range of 12–17 U.S. cents/pound in 1982 attributed to the British consulting firm Landell Mills Commodities Studies (Castell 1985, 18). However, also relying on data developed by Landell Mills, a U.S. source has estimated that in 1982 sugar production costs of the principal cane-based sugar exporting countries (Cuba, Brazil, Australia, the Dominican Republic, India, the Philippines, Thailand, South Africa, and Fiji) ranged from 10.73 to 15.32 U.S. cents/pound (Hoff and Lawrence 1985, 15).

Using an engineering cost methodology, Landell Mills has estimated sugar production costs for a range of countries and regions, including countries producing sugar from both cane and beets. The estimates are for crop years 1979/80–1982/83; a four-year average has been chosen to obtain an estimate akin to a normal, or long-term, cost of production and to discount exchange rate fluctuations. Table 25 presents the estimates, in index number form, with world average production cost during the 1979/80–1982/83 harvests equal to 100.

Data in table 25 suggest that Cuba was among the low-cost sugar producers, with costs about 30 percent below the world average. However, production costs (also from sugarcane) were lower in South Africa, Brazil (Central/South region), Fiji, Australia, St. Kitts, and the Dominican Republic than in Cuba.

According to the Landell Mills estimates, about 55 percent of the costs of sugar production in Cuba were attributable to field costs, 28 percent to factory costs, and 17 percent to administrative costs. Fixed costs accounted for about 70 percent of total costs, and variable costs for the remaining 30 percent (Landell Mills 1985, 67).

The Landell Mills study also compares production costs of the principal sugar exporters: Brazil, Cuba, the Dominican Republic, Thailand, the Philippines, Australia, South Africa, and France. With the exception of France, the major exporters all produce sugar from sugarcane. While all eight have production costs below the world average, there are marked differences across countries:

- Brazil (Central/South region) and South Africa have the lowest production costs (index value of 57), followed by Australia (62) and the Dominican Republic (69).
- Cuba's production costs (71) were slightly lower than those of France (73), the Philippines (75) and Brazil (North/Northeast region) (79).
- Thailand's production costs (90) were highest among the major exporters, but still 10 percent below the world average.

Landell Mills further estimates that all the major sugar exporters except Australia and France have variable costs that are below 20 percent of the world average cost, primarily because wages—a major

TABLE 25
WORLD SUGAR PRODUCTION COSTS,
1979/80 TO 1982/83
*(weighted world average cost=100)*

| Country/Region | Input | Index Value |
| --- | --- | --- |
| Japan | Cane | 229 |
| Puerto Rico | Cane | 183 |
| Japan | Beet | 170 |
| Trinidad | Cane | 158 |
| Italy | Beet | 155 |
| Poland | Beet | 141 |
| Guyana | Cane | 118 |
| Panama | Cane | 117 |
| Barbados | Cane | 113 |
| United States (mainland) | Beet | 111 |
| Costa Rica | Cane | 109 |
| United States (mainland) | Cane | 107 |
| Hawaii | Cane | 103 |
| United Kingdom | Beet | 102 |
| Jamaica | Cane | 97 |
| West Germany | Beet | 92 |
| Nicaragua | Cane | 92 |
| Belize | Cane | 91 |
| Mexico | Cane | 90 |
| India | Cane | 90 |
| Thailand | Cane | 90 |
| Guatemala | Cane | 86 |
| El Salvador | Cane | 81 |
| Honduras | Cane | 79 |
| Argentina | Cane | 79 |
| Brazil[a] | Cane | 79 |
| Colombia | Cane | 76 |
| Philippines | Cane | 75 |
| Mauritius | Cane | 75 |
| France | Beet | 73 |
| Cuba | Cane | 71 |
| Dominican Republic | Cane | 69 |
| Saint Kitts | Cane | 66 |
| Australia | Cane | 62 |
| Fiji | Cane | 60 |
| Brazil[b] | Cane | 57 |
| South Africa | Cane | 57 |

SOURCE: Landell Mills 1985, 53–75.
  a. North-Northeast region.
  b. Central-South region.

component of variable costs—tend to be low in these countries. The study concludes (Landell Mills 1985, 76):

> The very low level of variable costs, equivalent to 3 to 4 c/lb [U.S. cents/pound], raw value, for most of these countries, helps to provide an answer to one of the great paradoxes of the recent behavior of the sugar market. This is the willingness of producers to continue to grow beet or sugar to supply sugar to the free market, even when prices have fallen to the 3 c/lb [U.S. cents/pound] range.

# CHAPTER 8

•

## Foreign Trade

Throughout the twentieth century the Cuban sugar industry has been, and remains, export-oriented: the vast majority of production is earmarked for export, and sugar is the premier export commodity and generator of foreign exchange. The external orientation of the industry has made Cuban governments sensitive to the ill effects of swings in international sugar prices. As a result, Cuba has played a leading role in international price stabilization agreements.

To avoid the uncertainties of the market, Cuba has continuously sought favorable terms for its sugar exports. This has resulted in special trading relationships with major sugar purchasers—before 1960 with the United States, and since then with the Soviet Union and other socialist countries. Despite these special arrangements, the world market continues to affect the terms at which Cuba can sell its sugar exports.

This chapter reviews a number of issues related to the Cuban sugar trade: the structure of the international sugar market and the volatility of prices in that market, patterns of Cuban sugar trade, including preferential trade relationships, and the importance of the sugar trade to the economy. The next three chapters deal with other aspects of Cuba's sugar trade and foreign aid: chapter 9 discusses specifically the complex issue of subsidies in Cuban-Soviet sugar trade; chapter 10 analyzes multilateral cooperation related to the stabilization of sugar trade; and chapter 11 discusses Cuba's sugar diplomacy in the Third World.

## THE STRUCTURE OF THE INTERNATIONAL SUGAR MARKET

Because sugar-producing crops can be grown in both tropical (sugarcane) and temperate (sugar beet) climates, sugar is produced in a large number of countries. According to data developed by the United Nations Statistical Office, 111 countries produced significant volumes of sugar in 1983–84, making it one of the most geographically dispersed commodities. Interestingly, in the 1970s and 1980s, Cuba was active in assisting African and Latin American countries in increasing sugar production, a policy that most likely affects sugar trade flows. This aspect of revolutionary Cuba's foreign policy is discussed in chapter 11.

Closely related to the diffuse nature of sugar production is the tendency toward self-sufficiency. As data in table 26 indicate, over the period 1954–87 only about one-third of world sugar production entered world trade, two-thirds being consumed in the countries where it was produced. In the mid 1970s the share of world sugar production that entered world trade fell to about one-fourth; in the most recent six-year period (1982–87), under 30 percent of world sugar output was traded internationally.

A longstanding practice in international sugar trading has been the negotiation of long-term bilateral arrangements between importers and exporters about quantities and/or prices. These arrangements benefit importers by assuring access to supplies; exporters benefit from revenue stabilization. Long-term bilateral arrangements are typically of a preferential nature, conferring to specific exporting countries more favorable terms (e.g., access to a protected market, higher price) than those that prevail in the open market. Examples of preferential arrangements in sugar trading are the United States Sugar Program, the Commonwealth Sugar Agreement (succeeded by the Lomé Agreement between the European Economic Community (EEC) and the African, Caribbean, and Pacific nations), and Cuban sales to the Soviet Union and other socialist nations. In the parlance of the international sugar trade, the "world" or "free" market refers to transactions outside these long-term preferential arrangements.

One of the effects of the segmentation of world sugar trade into preferential and nonpreferential (world) markets is the compression of the latter. In the 1970s and 1980s only 13–21 million tons were marketed annually through the world market, approximately 65–76 percent of total sugar exports (table 27) or no more than 16–23 percent of world output.

The tendency toward domestic consumption (which results in relatively small percentages of sugar being traded compared to production), coupled with the strong preference on the part of exporters to sell their output through long-term arrangements, shape the world or free sugar market into a residual market. A substantial portion of

## TABLE 26
### WORLD SUGAR PRODUCTION AND TRADE, 1954–1987
*(in thousands of tons)*

|      | Production | Exports | Exports/Production (%) |
|------|-----------:|--------:|----:|
| 1954 | 37,372  | 15,357 | 41.1 |
| 1955 | 38,925  | 14,496 | 37.2 |
| 1956 | 40,217  | 14,127 | 35.1 |
| 1957 | 43,992  | 15,383 | 35.0 |
| 1958 | 47,210  | 15,715 | 33.3 |
| 1959 | 49,791  | 16,678 | 33.5 |
| 1960 | 52,302  | 19,282 | 36.2 |
| 1961 | 54,710  | 22,328 | 40.8 |
| 1962 | 51,478  | 20,940 | 40.7 |
| 1963 | 52,015  | 19,382 | 37.3 |
| 1964 | 59,213  | 18,844 | 31.8 |
| 1965 | 64,863  | 20,509 | 31.6 |
| 1966 | 64,044  | 20,326 | 31.7 |
| 1967 | 66,380  | 21,930 | 33.0 |
| 1968 | 66,794  | 22,227 | 33.3 |
| 1969 | 69,544  | 19,906 | 28.6 |
| 1970 | 72,951  | 23,020 | 31.6 |
| 1971 | 73,957  | 20,956 | 28.3 |
| 1972 | 75,731  | 21,786 | 28.8 |
| 1973 | 77,900  | 22,420 | 28.8 |
| 1974 | 78,918  | 21,934 | 27.8 |
| 1975 | 81,545  | 20,478 | 25.1 |
| 1976 | 86,573  | 22,534 | 26.0 |
| 1977 | 91,286  | 28,216 | 30.9 |
| 1978 | 90,832  | 25,072 | 27.6 |
| 1979 | 89,327  | 25,985 | 29.1 |
| 1980 | 84,489  | 28,832 | 34.1 |
| 1981 | 92,764  | 29,142 | 31.4 |
| 1982 | 101,810 | 30,427 | 29.9 |
| 1983 | 96,901  | 28,981 | 29.9 |
| 1984 | 99,411  | 28,497 | 28.7 |
| 1985 | 98,371  | 27,750 | 28.2 |
| 1986 | 100,488 | 27,165 | 27.0 |
| 1987 | 104,010 | 28,243 | 27.2 |

SOURCE: ISO 1988 and earlier issues.

TABLE 27
SIZE OF THE WORLD SUGAR MARKET
*(in thousands of tons and percentages)*

|      | World Market[a] | World Market as a % of World Exports | World Market as a % of World Output |
|------|---------|---------|---------|
| 1971 | 14,455 | 69.0 | 19.6 |
| 1972 | 16,567 | 76.0 | 21.9 |
| 1973 | 16,482 | 73.5 | 21.2 |
| 1974 | 16,074 | 73.3 | 20.4 |
| 1975 | 13,211 | 64.5 | 16.2 |
| 1976 | 15,481 | 68.7 | 17.9 |
| 1977 | 20,760 | 73.6 | 22.7 |
| 1978 | 17,491 | 69.8 | 19.3 |
| 1979 | 18,271 | 70.3 | 20.5 |
| 1980 | 19,418 | 67.3 | 23.0 |
| 1981 | 20,627 | 70.8 | 22.2 |
| 1982 | 21,652 | 71.2 | 21.3 |
| 1983 | 20,555 | 70.9 | 21.2 |
| 1984 | 19,197 | 67.4 | 19.3 |
| 1985 | 18,984 | 68.4 | 19.3 |
| 1986 | 18,185 | 66.9 | 18.1 |
| 1987 | 18,509 | 65.5 | 17.8 |

SOURCES: World market—ISO 1988 and earlier issues. World market as a percentage of world exports or world production—calculated from column 1 and data in table 26.

a. World market means the total arrived at by adding together each country's net exports after deducting net exports under special arrangements.

the sugar exported to the world market is of cane origin, which has a low elasticity of production adjustment. Because it takes 12–24 months for newly planted cane to reach maturity, by the time production adjusts to high prices market conditions might have changed (Tsadik 1982, 139). As a result, the sugar world market is very volatile, subject to wild price swings.

Over the period 1950–86, world sugar prices fluctuated severely, annual average prices reaching as low as 1.86 cents/pound in 1966 and as high as 29.96 cents/pound in 1974 (table 28 and figure 1). Prices nearly tripled in 1963, 1974, and 1980 and fell by more than 50 percent in 1965 and 1982 relative to a year earlier. The average year-to-year percentage deviation (based on absolute values) was nearly 39 percent. Three- and five-year moving averages smooth out some of the year-to-year price fluctuations, but deviations from the trend are still quite significant: an average of 24 percent per annum for the three-year moving average and 16 percent for the five-year moving average (computed from the absolute value of percentage changes).

As Fry (1985, 9–10) has pointed out, sugar exporters are caught in a dilemma. To the extent that they are successful in insulating themselves from world market price fluctuations by increasing sales through long-term arrangements, they reduce the size of the world market and thus contribute to its instability. For example, with a residual free market of the order of 20 percent of total world output (well within the range that obtained in the 1970s and 1980s), the coincidence in a given year of a 5 percent upward deviation in world production from long-term trend and a 5 percent downward deviation in world consumption increases the volume of sugar entering the world market by 50 percent; according to this scenario, world prices most likely would tumble. Alternative scenarios that could lead to tightness in the world market, and rising prices, can also be constructed.

## Markets for Cuban Sugar

Like most major sugar producers and exporters, Cuba has traditionally marketed its output both through long-term preferential relationships and through the world market. Preferential markets have been the more significant to Cuba in both quantitative and qualitative terms; nevertheless, the world market has also been of strategic significance, particularly as an important source of hard currency during the revolutionary period.

During 1954–59, Cuba disposed of about 55 percent of its sugar exports in preferential markets (United States) and 45 percent in the world market (table 29 and figure 2). As will be discussed below, it made some sugar sales to the Soviet Union and other socialist countries over this period, but these were conducted at world market prices and were considered to be world market sales.

In 1960 the Soviet Union and the socialist countries became major purchasers of Cuban sugar, and the United States' share of Cuban sugar exports fell to 35 percent. By 1961, the United States was no longer a purchaser, and the Soviet Union and the socialist countries had become the predominant buyers, taking as much as three-fourths

TABLE 28
PRICES IN THE WORLD SUGAR MARKET, 1950–1988
*(in U.S. cents/pound)*

|      | Market Price | % Change | 3-Year Average | % Change[a] | 5-Year Average | % Change[a] |
|------|------|-------|-------|-------|-------|-------|
| 1950 | 4.98 |       |       |       |       |       |
| 1951 | 5.67 | 13.9  | 4.94  |       |       |       |
| 1952 | 4.17 | −26.5 | 4.42  | −10.6 | 4.30  |       |
| 1953 | 3.41 | −18.2 | 3.61  | −18.2 | 3.95  | −8.1  |
| 1954 | 3.26 | −4.4  | 3.30  | −8.6  | 3.51  | −11.1 |
| 1955 | 3.24 | −0.6  | 3.32  | 0.6   | 3.71  | 5.6   |
| 1956 | 3.47 | 7.1   | 3.96  | 19.1  | 3.73  | 0.5   |
| 1957 | 5.16 | 48.7  | 4.04  | 2.2   | 3.67  | −1.5  |
| 1958 | 3.50 | −32.2 | 3.88  | −4.0  | 3.65  | −0.5  |
| 1959 | 2.98 | −14.9 | 3.21  | −17.4 | 3.54  | −3.1  |
| 1960 | 3.14 | 5.4   | 3.01  | −6.1  | 3.10  | −12.3 |
| 1961 | 2.91 | −7.3  | 3.01  | 0     | 4.10  | 32.2  |
| 1962 | 2.98 | 2.4   | 4.80  | 59.4  | 4.68  | 14.1  |
| 1963 | 8.50 | 185.2 | 5.78  | 20.6  | 4.48  | −4.4  |
| 1964 | 5.87 | −30.9 | 5.50  | −5.0  | 4.27  | −4.7  |
| 1965 | 2.12 | −63.9 | 3.28  | −40.3 | 4.08  | −4.5  |
| 1966 | 1.86 | −12.3 | 2.00  | −39.0 | 2.77  | −32.0 |
| 1967 | 2.03 | 9.1   | 1.96  | −2.3  | 2.27  | −18.0 |
| 1968 | 1.98 | −2.5  | 2.46  | 25.7  | 2.60  | 14.4  |
| 1969 | 3.37 | 70.2  | 3.03  | 23.3  | 3.13  | 20.6  |
| 1970 | 3.75 | 11.3  | 3.88  | 28.0  | 4.21  | 34.5  |
| 1971 | 4.53 | 20.8  | 5.24  | 34.8  | 5.74  | 36.3  |
| 1972 | 7.43 | 64.0  | 7.20  | 37.4  | 11.06 | 92.6  |
| 1973 | 9.63 | 29.6  | 15.67 | 117.8 | 14.41 | 30.3  |
| 1974 | 29.96 | 211.1 | 20.03 | 27.8 | 15.82 | 9.8   |
| 1975 | 20.50 | −31.6 | 20.68 | 3.2  | 15.95 | 0.8   |
| 1976 | 11.57 | −43.6 | 13.39 | −35.3 | 15.59 | −2.2 |
| 1977 | 8.09 | −30.1 | 9.17  | −31.5 | 11.53 | −26.0 |
| 1978 | 7.84 | −3.1  | 8.53  | −6.9  | 13.17 | 14.2  |
| 1979 | 9.66 | 23.2  | 15.39 | 80.4  | 14.23 | 8.1   |
| 1980 | 28.67 | 196.8 | 18.41 | 19.6 | 14.29 | 0.5   |
| 1981 | 16.89 | −41.1 | 17.99 | −2.3 | 14.42 | 0.9   |
| 1982 | 8.41 | −50.2 | 11.26 | −37.4 | 13.53 | −6.2 |
| 1983 | 8.47 | 0.7   | 7.36  | −34.6 | 8.60  | −36.4 |
| 1984 | 5.20 | −38.6 | 5.91  | −19.7 | 6.44  | −25.2 |
| 1985 | 4.05 | −22.1 | 5.10  | −13.7 | 6.10  | −5.1  |
| 1986 | 6.05 | 49.4  | 5.62  | 10.2  | 6.45  | 5.6   |
| 1987 | 6.75 | 11.6  | 7.67  | 36.4  |       |       |
| 1988 | 10.19 | 50.7 |       |       |       |       |

SOURCE: World market price data from IFS, various issues.
   a. Calculated from unrounded figures.

FIGURE 1
WORLD SUGAR MARKET PRICES
U.S. CENTS PER POUND

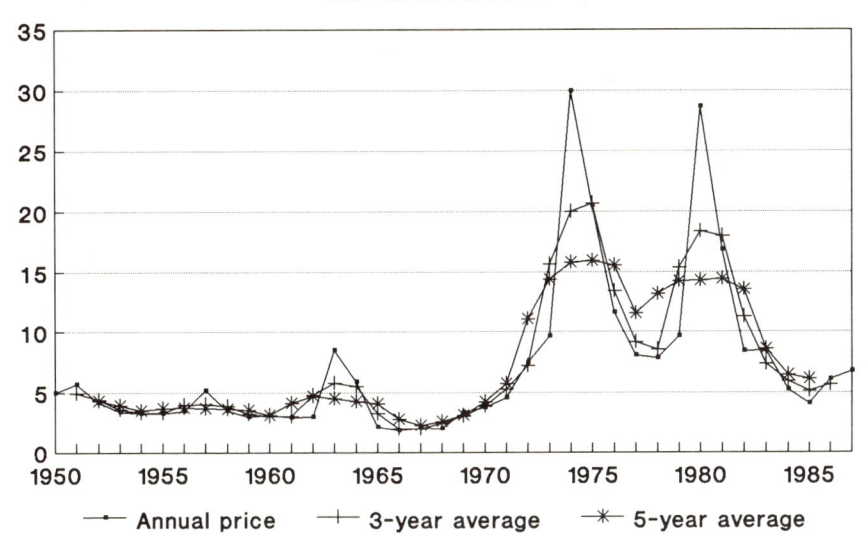

SOURCE: Table 28.

of total exports in 1961–62 and becoming a preferential market for Cuban sugar exports. The share of Cuba's sugar exports to the socialist countries (including the Soviet Union) subsequently fell to about two-thirds but has risen in recent years. During 1982–86, over three-fourths of Cuban sugar exports went to socialist countries—the Soviet Union alone accounting for over one-half of the total—and the remaining one-fourth to the world market. In 1987, 85 percent of Cuban sugar exports were destined for the socialist countries—60 percent to the Soviet Union alone—and 15 percent to the rest of the world.

Cuba's preferential sugar trade relationship with the United States and the socialist countries and participation in the world sugar market are described briefly below. Appendix 5 contains detailed statistics on the volume of exports by partner country for the period 1954–87 that are culled from information provided by Cuba to the International Sugar Organization (ISO); a summary of these data, grouping Cuban exports by major partner country or area, is given in table 29.

UNITED STATES

Preferential treatment of Cuban sugar by the United States began shortly after the establishment of the Cuban Republic on 20 May

TABLE 29
Cuban Sugar Exports by Destination, 1954–1987
*(in thousands of tons)*

|  | Total Exports | United States | % | Socialist Countries[a] All | % | USSR | % | Other | % |
|---|---|---|---|---|---|---|---|---|---|
| 1954 | 4,236 | 2,410 | 57 | 10 | 0 | 10 | 0 | 1,817 | 43 |
| 1955 | 4,644 | 2,574 | 55 | 485 | 10 | 456 | 10 | 1,585 | 34 |
| 1956 | 5,393 | 2,813 | 52 | 269 | 5 | 213 | 4 | 2,311 | 43 |
| 1957 | 5,275 | 2,753 | 52 | 387 | 7 | 358 | 7 | 2,135 | 40 |
| 1958 | 5,632 | 3,241 | 58 | 251 | 4 | 188 | 3 | 2,139 | 38 |
| 1959 | 4,953 | 2,937 | 59 | 274 | 6 | 274 | 6 | 1,742 | 35 |
| 1960 | 5,635 | 1,949 | 35 | 2,281 | 40 | 1,578 | 28 | 1,406 | 25 |
| 1961 | 6,414 | 0 | 0 | 4,825 | 75 | 3,303 | 51 | 1,588 | 25 |
| 1962 | 5,131 | 0 | 0 | 3,733 | 73 | 2,112 | 41 | 1,398 | 27 |
| 1963 | 3,521 | 0 | 0 | 2,066 | 59 | 973 | 28 | 1,454 | 41 |
| 1964 | 4,176 | 0 | 0 | 2,650 | 63 | 1,937 | 46 | 1,526 | 37 |
| 1965 | 5,316 | 0 | 0 | 3,544 | 67 | 2,456 | 46 | 1,771 | 32 |
| 1966 | 4,435 | 0 | 0 | 3,245 | 73 | 1,815 | 41 | 1,190 | 27 |
| 1967 | 5,683 | 0 | 0 | 3,885 | 68 | 2,473 | 44 | 1,798 | 32 |
| 1968 | 4,613 | 0 | 0 | 3,150 | 68 | 1,832 | 40 | 1,463 | 32 |
| 1969 | 4,799 | 0 | 0 | 2,815 | 59 | 1,352 | 28 | 1,983 | 41 |
| 1970 | 6,906 | 0 | 0 | 4,746 | 69 | 3,105 | 45 | 2,161 | 31 |
| 1971 | 5,511 | 0 | 0 | 3,275 | 59 | 1,581 | 29 | 2,236 | 41 |
| 1972 | 4,140 | 0 | 0 | 2,263 | 55 | 1,097 | 27 | 1,877 | 45 |
| 1973 | 4,797 | 0 | 0 | 2,947 | 61 | 1,661 | 35 | 1,850 | 39 |
| 1974 | 5,491 | 0 | 0 | 3,239 | 59 | 1,975 | 36 | 2,252 | 41 |
| 1975 | 5,744 | 0 | 0 | 4,004 | 70 | 3,187 | 55 | 1,739 | 30 |
| 1976 | 5,764 | 0 | 0 | 4,256 | 74 | 3,036 | 53 | 1,508 | 26 |
| 1977 | 6,239 | 0 | 0 | 4,684 | 75 | 3,790 | 61 | 1,555 | 25 |
| 1978 | 7,231 | 0 | 0 | 5,101 | 71 | 3,936 | 54 | 2,130 | 29 |
| 1979 | 7,269 | 0 | 0 | 5,094 | 70 | 3,842 | 53 | 2,175 | 30 |
| 1980 | 6,191 | 0 | 0 | 3,958 | 64 | 2,726 | 44 | 2,233 | 36 |
| 1981 | 7,072 | 0 | 0 | 4,722 | 67 | 3,204 | 45 | 2,350 | 33 |
| 1982 | 7,743 | 0 | 0 | 6,167 | 80 | 4,426 | 57 | 1,576 | 20 |
| 1983 | 6,792 | 0 | 0 | 5,118 | 75 | 3,315 | 49 | 1,675 | 25 |
| 1984 | 7,017 | 0 | 0 | 5,549 | 79 | 3,650 | 52 | 1,467 | 21 |
| 1985 | 7,182 | 0 | 0 | 5,447 | 76 | 3,709 | 52 | 1,735 | 24 |
| 1986 | 6,703 | 0 | 0 | 5,214 | 78 | 4,020 | 60 | 1,488 | 22 |
| 1987 | 6,482 | 0 | 0 | 5,534 | 85 | 3,863 | 60 | 948 | 15 |

source: Calculated from ISO data in appendix 5.
a. Albania, Bulgaria, PRC, Czechoslovakia, German Democratic Republic, Hungary, Mongolia, North Korea, Poland, Romania, Soviet Union, Vietnam, and Yugoslavia.

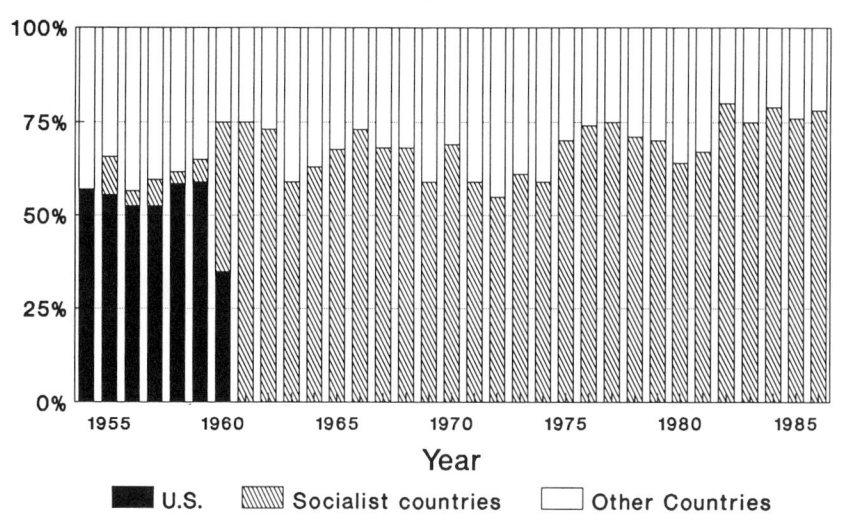

FIGURE 2
CUBAN SUGAR EXPORTS BY DESTINATION
PERCENT OF EXPORTS

SOURCE: Table 29.

1902. In 1894 the United States discontinued a system of bounties (payments) to domestic sugar producers aimed at protecting them from lower-cost foreign producers and introduced a tariff on sugar imports instead. The general, or most-favored-nation (MFN), tariff rate was set at 1.685 cents/pound (U.S. Congress 1962, 19).

The reciprocity treaty of 1902, which became effective in December 1903, reduced the tariff faced by Cuban sugar in the U.S. market by 20 percent relative to the MFN tariff. The lower tariff (1.348 cents/pound for Cuban sugar vis-à-vis the MFN tariff of 1.685 cents/pound—table 30) permitted Cuban producers to realize a higher price for their product in the U.S. market. Thus the price of Cuban raw sugar in New York, duty excluded, was generally the same as the world price in New York plus approximately the 20 percent tariff preferential received by Cuba in the U.S. market (United States Cuban Sugar Council 1948, 67)

Over the next decade, Cuba established itself as the dominant foreign sugar supplier to the United States. U.S. sugar imports from Cuba surpassed 1 million tons in 1903, when Cuban sugar took 38 percent of the U.S. market; with the exception of 1905, annual U.S. sugar imports from Cuba remained above the 1 million ton mark,

# TABLE 30
## Tariff Treatment of Cuban Sugar in the U.S. Market
*(in cents/pound and thousand metric tons)*

|  | U.S. Sugar Tariff General | U.S. Sugar Tariff Cuba | U.S. Imports from Cuba | Cuba as a % of U.S. Market |
|---|---|---|---|---|
| 1900 | 1.685 | 1.685 | 320 | 14.6 |
| 1901 | 1.685 | 1.685 | 499 | 18.6 |
| 1902 | 1.685 | 1.685 | 446 | 19.1 |
| 1903 | 1.685 | 1.348[a] | 1,087 | 38.1 |
| 1904 | 1.685 | 1.348 | 1,279 | 46.6 |
| 1905 | 1.685 | 1.348 | 934 | 33.0 |
| 1906 | 1.685 | 1.348 | 1,262 | 40.7 |
| 1907 | 1.685 | 1.348 | 1,468 | 44.8 |
| 1908 | 1.685 | 1.348 | 1,048 | 28.8 |
| 1909 | 1.685 | 1.348 | 1,298 | 43.8 |
| 1910 | 1.685 | 1.348 | 1,592 | 49.0 |
| 1911 | 1.685 | 1.348 | 1,519 | 42.1 |
| 1912 | 1.685 | 1.348 | 1,445 | 47.5 |
| 1913 | 1.685 | 1.348 | 1,956 | 53.2 |
| 1914 | 1.256[b] | 1.0048[b] | 2,234 | 53.7 |
| 1915 | 1.256 | 1.0048 | 2,170 | 48.5 |
| 1916 | 1.256 | 1.0048 | 2,336 | 45.6 |
| 1917 | 1.256 | 1.0048 | 2,118 | 40.9 |
| 1918 | 1.256 | 1.0048 | 2,068 | 53.8 |
| 1919 | 1.256 | 1.0048 | 3,033 | 50.8 |
| 1920 | 1.256 | 1.0048 | 2,614 | 52.1 |
| 1921 | 2.000[c] | 1.60[c] | 2,350 | 45.4 |
| 1922 | 2.206[d] | 1.7648[d] | 4,107 | 56.7 |
| 1923 | 2.206 | 1.7648 | 3,108 | 55.4 |
| 1924 | 2.206 | 1.7648 | 3,349 | 58.2 |
| 1925 | 2.206 | 1.7648 | 3,559 | 52.8 |
| 1926 | 2.206 | 1.7648 | 3,883 | 58.0 |
| 1927 | 2.206 | 1.7648 | 3,311 | 55.0 |
| 1928 | 2.206 | 1.7648 | 2,948 | 47.0 |
| 1929 | 2.206 | 1.7648 | 3,764 | 51.9 |
| 1930 | 2.50[e] | 2.00[e] | 2,400 | 43.9 |
| 1931 | 2.50 | 2.00 | 2,252 | 37.2 |
| 1932 | 2.50 | 2.00 | 1,625 | 28.2 |
| 1933 | 2.50 | 2.00 | 1,427 | 25.4 |
| 1934 | 1.875[f] | 0.90[f] | 1,693 | 24.6 |
| 1935 | 1.875 | 0.90 | 1,660 | 30.7 |
| 1936 | 1.875 | 0.90 | 1,907 | 29.8 |
| 1937 | 1.875 | 0.90 | 1,955 | 31.4 |
| 1938 | 1.875 | 0.90 | 1,761 | 29.3 |

TABLE 30 *(continued)*

|  | U.S. Sugar Tariff | | U.S. Imports from Cuba | Cuba as a % of U.S. Market |
|---|---|---|---|---|
|  | General | Cuba | | |
| 1939 | 1.875 | 0.90[g] | 1,751 | 25.9 |
| 1940 | 1.875 | 0.90 | 1,588 | 27.1 |
| 1941 | 1.875 | 0.90 | 2,449 | 33.7 |
| 1942 | 1.875 | 0.75[h] | 1,629 | 32.3 |
| 1943 | 1.875 | 0.75 | 2,592 | 44.2 |
| 1944 | 1.875 | 0.75 | 3,282 | 52.1 |
| 1945 | 1.875 | 0.75 | 2,543 | 46.7 |
| 1946 | 1.875 | 0.75 | 2,070 | 40.3 |
| 1947 | 0.9375 | 0.75 | 3,577 | 50.8 |
| 1948 | 0.6875[i] | 0.50[i] | 2,655 | 41.3 |
| 1949 | 0.6875 | 0.50 | 2,815 | 41.0 |
| 1950 | 0.6875 | 0.50 | 2,961 | 39.6 |
| 1951 | 0.625[j] | 0.50 | 2,673 | 38.0 |
| 1952 | 0.625 | 0.50 | 2,703 | 37.4 |
| 1953 | 0.625 | 0.50 | 2,504 | 33.4 |
| 1954 | 0.625 | 0.50 | 2,410 | 33.1 |
| 1955 | 0.625 | 0.50 | 2,754 | 34.0 |
| 1956 | 0.625 | 0.50 | 2,813 | 34.4 |
| 1957 | 0.625 | 0.50 | 2,754 | 35.1 |
| 1958 | 0.625 | 0.50 | 3,241 | 37.9 |
| 1959 | 0.625 | 0.50 | 2,937 | 34.8 |
| 1960 | 0.625 | 0.50 | 1,949 | 25.1 |
| 1961 | 0.625 | 0.50 | 0 | 0.0 |

SOURCES: Tariffs—1900–58, AAC 1958, 226–27; 1959–61, U.S. Congress, 1962, 37–38. U.S. imports from Cuba—1900–53, U.S. Congress, 1962, 3; 1954–61, ISO data from appendix 5. Cuban market share—1900–05, U.S. Congress, 1962, 3, 37–38; 1906–58, AAC, 1958, 225–27; 1959–61, U.S. Congress, 1962, 3, 37–38.

a. Preferential tariff rate effective 13 December 1903. Prior to that date, tariff was 1.685 cents/pound.
  b. Effective 1 March 1914.
  c. Effective 28 May 1921.
  d. Effective 30 September 1922.
  e. Effective 18 June 1930.
  f. Effective 8 June 1934. The proclaimed rate for Cuban sugar was 1.50 cents/pound; it was reduced to 0.90 cents/pound effective 4 September 1934.
  g. During the period 12 September to 26 December, duty reverted to 1.5 cents/pound.
  h. Effective 20 January 1942.
  i. Effective 1 January 1948.
  j. Effective 6 June 1951.

with Cuba's share of the U.S. market rising to over 40 percent in some years. During World War I, Cuban sugar made larger inroads in the U.S. market: exports rose above 2 million tons/year. Cuba entered into an agreement with the International Sugar Committee, a group created by the Allies to manage the purchase and distribution of sugar, to sell the entire crops of 1918 and 1919 at a fixed price (Grupo Cubano 1963, 463). In 1919, U.S. imports of Cuban sugar exceeded 3 million tons. Over the war years (1914–19), Cuba had supplied nearly 50 percent of the imported sugar needs of the United States (table 30).

In 1921 and again in 1922, the United States increased the tariff on sugar imports to protect domestic beet sugar producers. Cuban sugar continued to dominate the U.S. import market during the 1920s, its share climbing to nearly 60 percent in 1924 and 1926, when it shipped 3.3 and 3.8 million tons, respectively.

However, world market prices for sugar weakened considerably in the 1920s as world production outstripped demand. As the premier world exporter, Cuba assumed a leadership position in attempting to return prices to higher levels, including taking unilateral steps (beginning in 1926) to cut back on domestic production to prop up world prices (see chapter 10).

The Smoot-Hawley Tariff Act of 1930 again raised U.S. sugar tariffs. Upon its enactment, the U.S. MFN duty for raw sugar rose to 2.5 cents/pound, while the rate applicable to Cuba (by virtue of the 20 percent tariff preference) went to 2.00 cents/pound. The result of these tariff increases—which virtually doubled the duty rate on imported sugar—coupled with the Great Depression in the United States, was a severe reduction in overall U.S. sugar imports, including imports from Cuba. In response to record low sugar prices—averaging well under 2 cents/pound during 1929–35 and falling below 1 cent/pound in 1932—Cuba slashed sugar production and exports. U.S. sugar imports from Cuba fell below 2 million tons per year beginning in 1932, with Cuba's share of the U.S. sugar market tumbling to about 25 percent in 1933–34.

The Sugar Act of 1934, also known as the Jones-Costigan Act, profoundly changed the mechanism for limiting sugar imports into the U.S. market, setting aside the system of tariffs in place since 1894. The act required the secretary of agriculture to determine annually the sugar consumption requirements of the United States, and each producing area—domestic and foreign—was permitted to fill a designated percentage of this requirement based on its participation in the U.S. market during the three-year period 1931–33. The act also authorized the imposition of a consumption tax on sugar, the proceeds to be used to support domestic sugar beet producers.

With the adoption of a quota system as the device to provide protection to the domestic U.S. industry, Cuba could not take full advantage of the tariff preference its sugar exports held in the U.S. market (made even more signifcant by tariff reductions for Cuban sugar granted by the Reciprocal Trade Agreement of 1934, to 0.90 cents/pound, compared to the then general tariff of 1.875 cents/pound) to increase its export volume. However, as quota holders, Cuban producers often, although not always, benefited from the generally higher price that U.S. purchasers paid for imported sugar in the face of an overall supply restriction.

The Sugar Act of 1934 allocated to Cuba 28.6 percent of the U.S. market, a substantially lower share than in recent history, with the exception of 1932–34. As was noted above, this particular allocation came about because the U.S. legislation chose the period 1931–33 as the base to set the quotas. Cuba's allocation of 28.6 percent of the U.S. market was continued by the Sugar Act of 1937 and remained in place until 1948, subject to significant annual adjustments (e.g., between April 1942 and December 1947, when quotas were suspended because of war conditions and Cuba sold the totality of its sugar exports to the United States). During 1943–47, U.S. sugar imports from Cuba again exceeded 2 million tons per year, and Cuba supplied over 45 percent of U.S. demand.

The Sugar Act of 1934 also provided that no more than 22 percent of Cuban sugar shipments to the United States under the quota could consist of refined sugar. This resulted in substantial cutbacks, from a high of 504,000 short tons (1 short ton = 2000 pounds) in 1932 to 423,000 short tons in 1934 and 387,000 short tons in 1935. The Sugar Act of 1937 imposed an absolute quota (375,000 short tons per annum) on Cuban refined sugar exports to the United States, a move that stunted the island's sugar refining industry.

The Sugar Act of 1948 maintained the system of quantitative restrictions first introduced in the Sugar Act of 1934 but changed the method of establishing quotas to Cuba's benefit. Rather than establishing fixed quotas based on a percentage of consumption for each producing area, the 1948 act assigned fixed quantities to domestic areas and the Philippines and variable quotas to Cuba and other foreign suppliers. The allocation to domestic areas (including Hawaii, Puerto Rico, and the Virgin Islands) was 4,268,000 short tons, and to the Philippines 952,000 short tons, for a total of 5,250,000 short tons. The difference between that amount and overall sugar consumption in any given year—a variable amount, depending on demand—was to be covered by imports from Cuba and other foreign suppliers, with Cuba allotted 98.64 percent of these imports. Moreover, Cuba would be allocated a proportional share of any shortfall in U.S. domestic production and 95 percent of any shortfall in exports from the Philippines.

Amendments to the Sugar Act in 1951 and 1956, the latter extending the legislation through 31 December 1960, made some adjustments to the quota system that had an adverse effect on the participation of Cuban sugar in the U.S. market. Nevertheless, under the variable quota system established by the Sugar Act of 1948, in 1948–52, Cuba supplied about four-tenths and in 1953–59 about one-third of the United States' growing sugar market. Cuba's sugar exports to the United States during 1955–59 averaged nearly 2.9 million tons per annum.

In July 1960 the Sugar Act was extended by an amendment that would permit the U.S. president to cut any foreign quota if such action was in the national economic interest. Shortly after the legislation was enacted, President Eisenhower used this new authority to reduce purchases of Cuban sugar during the second half of 1960 to just under 40,000 tons—a reduction of some 700,000 tons from anticipated import levels—on the grounds that Cuba's sugar sales to the Soviet Union and other socialist countries (see below) put into question Cuba's ability to continue to be a reliable sugar supplier to the U.S. market. After Cuba retaliated by nationalizing U.S.-owned investments in Cuba, President Eisenhower set Cuba's quota for 1961 at zero (Heston 1987, 418–23).

As was noted above, the restrictions on sugar supply imposed by the Sugar Act of 1934 and subsequent U.S. legislation tended to make the price of raw sugar in the United States higher than it would have been otherwise. In such situations, quota holders (i.e., the parties entitled to sell sugar in the protected U.S. market, including domestic producers and Cuban exporters) are able to appropriate the difference between the price in the restricted market and that in a free market. This difference is referred to by economists as the quota rent; others refer to it as the quota premium or the subsidy in the U.S. sugar program (U.S. Congress 1962, 14).

The impact of participation in the U.S. quota program on the price of Cuban sugar sales to the United States may be estimated by comparing the average price Cuba received from sales to the United States and the world market price. This price difference, taken over the volume of U.S. imports of Cuban sugar, provides an estimate of the impact of quota participation on Cuban foreign exchange earnings.

As data in table 31 indicate, the price Cuban sugar commanded in the U.S. market over the period 1934–60 was generally higher (20 out of 27 years) than the world market price; the exceptions were the World War II and immediate postwar years (1942–47), when the United States purchased the entire Cuban export crop at fixed prices, and a fifteen-month period in 1950–51 when world market prices shot up because of the Korean War and the Suez incident (U.S. Congress 1962, 14). In some cases, the price differential in favor of Cuba was quite significant: for example, 1953 and 1959–60, when there was a premium for Cuban sugar of over 2 cents/pound.

Over the entire time span when Cuban sugar exports were subject to the U.S. sugar quota regime (1934–60), participation in the system resulted in a cumulative subsidy by U.S. sugar consumers to Cuban exporters of over $1.1 billion. For example, during 1953–56, the preferential price Cuban sugar received in the U.S. market translated into additional Cuban export revenue of about $100 million per annum; in 1958 and 1959, the gain in export revenues was nearly $137 and $154 million, respectively. The gains were partially offset by subsidies from Cuban producers to U.S. consumers in 1941–47 and 1951, when the price Cuban sugar received in the U.S. market was lower than the world market price.

SOCIALIST COUNTRIES

Through the first three quarters of 1959, the only official contacts between the Soviet Union and the Cuban revolutionary government—in power since 1 January of that year—appear to have been related to sugar sales, reportedly two sales amounting to 500,000 tons (Torres Ramírez 1971, 15). In themselves, these commercial contacts were not extraordinary, for the Soviet Union and other socialist

## TABLE 31
### Cuba-U.S. Sugar Trade, 1934–1960

|  | U.S. Price Paid for Cuban Sugar (cents/pound) | World Price of Sugar (cents/pound) | U.S. Price Premium (cents/pound) | U.S. Imports (000 tons) | Subsidy ($ million) |
|---|---|---|---|---|---|
| 1934 | 1.37 | 0.91 | 0.46 | 1,693 | 17.2 |
| 1935 | 2.21 | 0.88 | 1.33 | 1,660 | 48.7 |
| 1936 | 2.56 | 0.88 | 1.68 | 1,907 | 70.6 |
| 1937 | 2.35 | 1.13 | 1.22 | 1,955 | 52.6 |
| 1938 | 1.90 | 1.00 | 0.90 | 1,761 | 34.9 |
| 1939 | 1.74 | 1.43 | 0.31 | 1,751 | 12.0 |
| 1940 | 1.67 | 1.11 | 0.56 | 1,588 | 19.6 |
| 1941 | 2.09 | 1.46 | 0.63 | 2,449 | 34.0 |
| 1942 | 2.48 | 2.69 | −0.21 | 1,629 | −7.5 |
| 1943 | 2.46 | 2.69 | −0.23 | 2,592 | −13.1 |
| 1944 | 2.59 | 2.69 | −0.10 | 3,282 | −7.2 |
| 1945 | 2.65 | 3.14 | −0.49 | 2,543 | −27.5 |
| 1946 | 3.42 | 4.24 | −0.82 | 2,070 | −37.4 |
| 1947 | 4.97 | 5.03 | −0.06 | 3,577 | −4.7 |
| 1948 | 4.64 | 4.23 | 0.41 | 2,655 | 24.0 |
| 1949 | 4.94 | 4.16 | 0.78 | 2,815 | 48.4 |
| 1950 | 5.09 | 4.98 | 0.11 | 2,961 | 7.2 |
| 1951 | 5.07 | 5.67 | −0.60 | 2,673 | −35.4 |
| 1952 | 5.35 | 4.17 | 1.18 | 2,703 | 70.3 |
| 1953 | 5.43 | 3.41 | 2.02 | 2,504 | 111.5 |
| 1954 | 5.21 | 3.26 | 1.95 | 2,410 | 103.6 |
| 1955 | 5.00 | 3.24 | 1.76 | 2,754 | 106.9 |
| 1956 | 5.10 | 3.48 | 1.62 | 2,813 | 100.5 |
| 1957 | 5.30 | 5.16 | 0.14 | 2,754 | 8.5 |
| 1958 | 5.41 | 3.50 | 1.91 | 3,241 | 136.5 |
| 1959 | 5.35 | 2.97 | 2.38 | 2,937 | 154.1 |
| 1960 | 5.35 | 3.14 | 2.21 | 1,949 | 95.0 |
| Cumulative Subsidy 1934–60 |  |  |  |  | 1,123.0 |

SOURCES: U.S. price paid for Cuban sugar and world market price of sugar—U.S. Congress 1962, 14–15; U.S. imports—table 30.

countries had frequently purchased sugar from prerevolutionary Cuba.

According to official trade statistics, during 1949–58, Cuba exported sugar to the Soviet Union, Albania, Bulgaria, Czechoslovakia, Hungary, Poland, Romania, Yugoslavia, and the PRC. Cuba sold sugar to the Soviet Union in every year during 1953–58 (Comercio Exterior 1953–54, 501; 1955–56, 558; 1957–58, 604), including substantial volumes in 1955 (456,000 tons or about 10 percent of total exports in that year) and 1957 (358,000 tons or 7 percent of total exports) (table 29).

By the time the first trade and payments agreement between revolutionary Cuba and the Soviet Union was signed on 13 February 1960, the Soviet Union had already contracted to buy 575,000 tons of Cuban sugar for delivery in 1960. The February agreement obligated the Soviet Union to purchase an additional 425,000 tons for delivery in 1960 (to make up 1 million tons) and 1 million tons during each of the years 1961–64; the Soviet Union also agreed not to reexport such sugar to Cuba's traditional markets. As Cuban sugar exports during 1954–59 had averaged about 5 million tons per annum, the 1 million tons per annum contracted for by the Soviet Union were significant for Cuba.

The 1960 Cuban-Soviet trade agreement called for payment for the additional 425,000 tons to be purchased in 1960 to be made totally in the form of Soviet goods; in subsequent years, 20 percent of the price would be payable in convertible currency and 80 percent in Soviet goods (Convenio de intercambio 1960, 5737). Critics of the agreement noted that the payment provisions represented a significant departure, for Cuban-Soviet commercial relations prior to 1960 had been one-sided, with Cuba running a very large trade surplus; in fact, Cuban trade statistics do not record any imports from the Soviet Union during 1953–58 (CERP 1965, 701).

Although the 1960 agreement is silent on this point, it is reasonable to assume that Cuban sugar sales to the Soviet Union were to be made at, or near, prevailing world market prices. Since in 1960 the world market price was around 3 cents/pound, this meant that sales to the Soviet Union would be effected at prices significantly below the preferential price paid by the United States in that year—5.35 cents/pound (table 31). Cuban sugar sales to the Soviet Union in the mid 1950s had also been made at prices below the preferential U.S. price (presumably, the sales were made at the world market price), a move that had angered some U.S. legislators who perceived such transactions as awarding "special privileges to an enemy country" (Heston 1987, 410).

In fact, the evidence strongly suggests that sugar sales to the Soviet Union in 1960 were made at prices *below* the world market price. For example, a sale of 345,000 tons announced in February 1960 was made at 2.78 cents/pound, compared to a world market price at the time of 2.90 cents/pound (Cepero Bonilla 1960, 43, 39). Sales to the Soviet Union during 1959 had also been made at below-market prices, presumably at a discount of 15 points (i.e., 15 one-hundredths of a cent) from the prevailing market price (ibid. 37-38).

That price discounting on sugar sales to the Soviet Union went on in 1959 is confirmed by official Cuban trade statistics, which report that the unit value of sugar exports to the Soviet Union in 1959 was 2.65 cents/pound (Comercio Exterior 1959, 174), compared to an average world market price of 2.97 cents/pound and an export unit value to the United States of 5.11 cents/pound. The foreign trade minister, and sugar expert, Raúl Cepero Bonilla (1960, 9) defended the decision to sell sugar to the Soviet Union at below-market prices:

> Cuba does not wish high prices [in sales to the Soviet Union] because they encourage sugar production in other areas, and, believes that price policies play a secondary role in plans to expand sugar exports. International economic policies [i.e., an international sugar agreement], rather than price policies of the Cuban government, will determine whether Cuba will be able to increase its sugar exports.

When the United States cut back Cuba's 1960 quota by 700,000 tons in July 1960, the Soviet Union and other socialist countries moved in swiftly to purchase the stranded sugar. The PRC agreed in July to buy 2.5 million tons over a five-year period; agreements negotiated in 1960 with Poland, East Germany, Bulgaria, Hungary, Czechoslovakia, and Romania also contained commitments to purchase Cuban sugar (Grupo Cubano 1963, 1499–1501). Subsequently these agreements were modified and the quantities increased.

From 1960 forward, then, the Soviet Union and the socialist nations became Cuba's primary sugar purchasers, a radical shift in export patterns played out over a very brief period of time. In 1960 the Soviet Union and the socialist countries took 2.9 million tons of Cuban sugar (40 percent of total exports in that year) and in 1961 about 4.8 million tons (75 percent of exports), compared to the average 280,000 tons per annum (5.5 percent of exports) they took in 1954–59.

Detailed Cuban import statistics for 1960 and 1961 are not available. Unit value of Cuban sugar exports to the Soviet Union for 1962 and of Soviet imports of Cuban sugar for 1960–62 (table 32) suggest that the Soviet Union paid a price of about 3 cents/pound in 1960 and about 4 cents/pound in 1961–62, compared to world market prices of around 3 cents/pound. The figure of 4 cents/pound in 1961–62 is also confirmed by other sources (e.g., Arredondo 1969, 140; Boorstein 1969, 198, 202). Cuban authors assert that the Soviet contract price for 1961–62 was 4.09 cents/pound (Pino-Santos and Martínez 1979, 57; M. T. Valdés 1984, 136). The PRC, Cuba's second most important sugar customer among the socialist countries, paid the same price as the Soviet Union in 1962 (Comercio Exterior 1962, 5).

As is discussed in more detail in chapter 10, since the 1930s, sugar-producing and consuming nations have concluded multilateral pacts to attempt to regulate the world market for sugar and stabilize world market prices. The system of quotas to allocate world market sales in the several international sugar agreements (ISAs) negotiated between 1931 and 1958 excluded Cuban sugar sales to the United States from the definition of the world market because of their preferential nature. However, Cuban sales to the Soviet Union and socialist countries in the 1950s had been made at, or near, world market terms and fitted within Cuba's permissible level of world market sales established by the international agreements in force.

Cuba argued that its sales to the Soviet Union in 1960 were not typical world market sales (i.e., were of a long-term nature and payable mostly with Soviet merchandise) and therefore should not be counted against its world market allocation of about 2.4 million tons. An international conference held in Geneva in 1961 to allocate world market shares for 1962 and 1963—under the 1958 ISA—broke down because of Cuba's insistence that it be awarded a sufficiently large world market allocation to accommodate its customary level of sales to the United States in addition to growing sales to the Soviet Union and the socialist countries. A new ISA negotiated in 1968 recognized Cuban sugar sales to the Soviet Union and socialist countries as preferential and therefore exempted them from its control. Such sales have been treated as preferential in subsequent international sugar pacts.

With world market prices for sugar soaring in 1963—as high as 10.36 cents/pound in December, averaging 8.50 cents/pound for the entire year—the 4 cents/pound price contracted by the Soviet Union was out of line with market conditions. As early as May 1963, the Soviet Union agreed to increase the sugar purchase price to 6 (Torres

## TABLE 32
### PRICES IN CUBAN-SOVIET SUGAR TRADE AND IN OTHER MARKETS
*(In U.S. cents/pound)*

|  | Cuban-Soviet Trade ||||| Prices in Other Markets |||||
|---|---|---|---|---|---|---|---|---|---|---|
|  | Contract Price ||| Cuban Export Unit Value | Soviet Import Unit Value | World Market Price | U.S. Import Unit Value | Preferential Prices || Cuban Exports to Market Economies[a] ||
|  | A | B | C |  |  |  |  | U.S. | EEC | Unit Value | Constructed Price |
| 1960 | 4.09 |  |  | 3.10[a] | 3.20 | 3.14 | 5.4 | 6.30 | 5.62 |  |  |
| 1961 | 4.09 |  |  | 3.97[a] | 4.07 | 2.91 | 5.4 | 6.45 | 5.62 |  |  |
| 1962 | 6.11 |  |  | 4.15 | 4.14 | 2.98 | 5.6 | 8.18 | 5.75 |  |  |
| 1963 | 6.11 |  |  | 6.21 | 6.23 | 8.50 | 6.8 | 6.90 | 5.75 |  |  |
| 1964 | 6.11 |  |  | 6.22 | 6.04 | 5.87 | 6.4 | 6.75 | 5.82 |  |  |
| 1965 | 6.11 |  |  | 6.09 | 5.90 | 2.12 | 5.7 | 6.99 | 5.94 |  |  |
| 1966 | 6.11 |  |  | 6.07[a] | 6.17 | 1.86 | 5.9 | 7.28 | 5.86 |  |  |
| 1967 | 6.11 |  |  | 6.03 | 6.14 | 2.03 | 6.3 | 7.52 | 5.09 |  |  |
| 1968 | 6.11 |  |  | 6.03 | 6.12 | 1.98 | 6.5 | 7.75 | 5.09 |  |  |
| 1969 | 6.11 |  |  | 5.94 | 6.12 | 3.37 | 6.7 | 8.07 | 5.09 |  |  |
| 1970 | 6.11 | 5.94 |  | 5.94 | 6.11 | 3.75 | 7.0 | 8.52 | 5.16 |  |  |
| 1971 | 6.11 | 6.41 | 6.11 | 5.90 | 6.23 | 4.53 | 7.2 | 9.09 | 6.79 | 4.66[a] | 4.68[c] |
| 1972 | 6.11 | 6.45 | 6.66 | 6.46 | 6.09 | 7.43 | 7.9 | 10.29 | 6.66 | 6.88 | 7.24[d] |
| 1973 | 12.02 | 11.82 | 11.83 | 11.71 | 12.34 | 9.63 | 8.8 | 29.50 | 10.66 | 8.51 | 8.54[d] |
| 1974 | 19.64 | 19.30 | 19.70 | 19.33 | 19.69 | 29.96 | 19.5 | 22.47 | 25.79 | 18.99 | 19.02 |
| 1975 | 30.40 | 26.36 | 30.38 | 26.48 | 28.69 | 20.50 | 24.5 | 13.31 | 14.82 | 29.74 | 26.64 |
| 1976 | 30.95 | 27.43 | 28.18 | 27.64 | 27.90 | 11.57 | 12.6 | 11.00 | 12.46 | 17.28 | 14.71 |
| 1977 | 35.73 | 26.94 | 28.43 | 27.99 | 28.30 | 8.09 | 9.2 | 13.93 | 15.11 | 11.76 | 11.51 |
| 1978 | 40.78 | 36.71 | 36.69 | 36.15 | 36.92 | 7.84 | 8.6 | 15.56 | 19.29 | 7.61 | 8.15[b] |
| 1979 | 44.00 | 37.17 | 37.74 | 36.87 | 38.16 | 9.66 | 10.1 |  |  | 8.79 | 10.32 |

| | | | | | | | | |
|---|---|---|---|---|---|---|---|---|
| 1980 | 47.45 | 47.39 | 48.56 | 47.53 | 49.03 | 28.67 | 22.3 | 30.11 | 22.09 | 24.06[b] | 28.47[b] |
| 1981 | 33.73 | 35.10 | 35.19 | 35.13 | 37.20 | 16.89 | 21.2 | 19.73 | 18.93 | 16.13 | 13.82 |
| 1982 | 33.73 | 39.00 | 35.82 | 34.04 | 36.70 | 8.41 | 15.3 | 19.92 | 18.12 | 8.59 | 8.23 |
| 1983 | | 46.00 | | 45.95 | 49.72 | 8.47 | 17.6 | 22.04 | 17.57 | 7.17[b] | |
| 1984 | | 44.00 | | 44.50 | 51.04 | 5.20 | 18.8 | 21.74 | 16.04 | 5.09[b] | |
| 1985 | | 45.00 | | 48.79 | 48.93 | 4.05 | 13.0 | 20.34 | 16.12 | 3.64[b] | |
| 1986 | | 50.60 | | 47.56 | 51.57 | 6.05 | 16.2 | 20.96 | 18.61 | 6.77[d] | |
| 1987 | | 41.90 | | 38.67 | 56.13 | 6.76 | 15.0 | 21.83 | 21.44 | 5.40[d] | |

SOURCES:
Contract price:
A: 1973–82—M. T. Valdés 1984, 136. 1961–72—Pino-Santos and Martínez 1979, 57.
B: ECLAC 1988, 18.
C: 1978–82—AEC 1985, 470; 1974–77—AEC 1980, 206. 1972–73—AEC 1977, 200. 1971—AEC 1976, 186. Contract price C converted to U.S. dollars at the following official exchange rates (in U.S. dollars per peso): 1960–71, $1.00; 1972, $1.09; 1973, $1.19; 1974, $1.21; 1975, $1.21; 1976, $1.22; 1977, $1.26; 1978, $1.33; 1979, $1.38; 1980, $1.41; 1981, $1.28; and 1982, $1.20.

Cuban export unit value: 1986–87—AEC 1987, 471; 1985—AEC 1985, 433; 1981–84—AEC 1984, 336–7; 1975–80—AEC 1980, 184–5; 1971–74—AEC 1977, 179; 1967–70—AEC 1971, 240–1; 1965—AEC 1985, 430; 1964—Comercio Exterior 1964, 4; 1963—Comercio Exterior 1963, 4; 1962—Comercio Exterior 1962, 5; Converted to U.S. dollars at official exchange rates. The exchange rates (in U.S. dollars per peso) are 1983, $1.16; 1984, $1.13; 1985, $1.09; 1986, $1.21; and 1987, $1.00.

Soviet import unit value: Vneshniaia Torgovlia, various issues. Converted to at the following exchange rates (in U.S. dollars per ruble): 1960–71, $1.11; 1972, $1.21; 1973, $1.35; 1974, $1.32; 1975, $1.39; 1976, $1.35; 1977, $1.36; 1978, $1.46; 1979, $1.53; 1980, $1.54; 1981, $1.39; 1982, $1.38; 1983, $1.35; 1984, $1.23; 1985, $1.20; 1986, $1.42; and 1987, $1.58.

World Market Price: IFS, various issues.
U.S. import unit value: U.S. Bureau of the Census, various issues.
Preferential prices: U.S.–Contract No. 12, c.i.f. duty paid, New York. From IFS, various issues. EEC—Negotiated export price from African, Caribbean and Pacific countries under the Sugar Protocol, Lomé Convention, from IFS, various issues.
Cuban exports to market economies: Cuban export unit value to market economies—calculated from AEC 1987 and earlier issues. Constructed price of exports to market economies pursuant to contracts—calculated from data in AEC 1982 and earlier issues, weighted by corresponding volume of exports from the same sources.

a. Estimated.
b. Japan, Canada, and Spain, unless otherwise noted.
c. Japan only.
d. Japan and Canada only.

Ramírez 1971, 59) or 6.11 cents/pound (Pino-Santos and Martínez 1979, 57). This reported change tends to be confirmed by both Soviet and Cuban official trade statistics, as the unit value of Soviet sugar imports from Cuba was 6.23 cents/pound and the unit value of Cuban exports to the Soviet Union 6.21 cents/pound in 1963 (table 32). Cuba has given the following version of how the change in price came about (En el décimo 1963, 8):

> As comrade Fidel explained upon his return from the Soviet Union [in mid 1963], as a result of the spontaneous initiative of the Soviet government, particularly of Cuba's great friend Nikita Khrushchev, the Soviet Union decided to raise the price of the sugar purchased from Cuba to 6 cents/pound, taking into account the rise in world sugar prices and in order to benefit our economy.

Cuba's 1963 sugar crop (production of 3.9 million tons—table 8) was the poorest on record since 1945 (AAC 1958, 96). Exports in that year were only 3.5 million tons, compared with 5.1 million tons in 1962 and 6.4 million tons in 1961. Exports to socialist countries in 1963 amounted to under 2.1 million tons, compared to 3.7 and 4.8 million tons in 1962 and 1961, respectively. Exports to the Soviet Union in 1963 were below 1 million tons (973,000 tons), less than one-half of the previous year's deliveries and one-third of the level of deliveries in 1961.

In January 1964, Cuba and the Soviet Union entered into a new long-term sugar supply agreement, which called for Soviet purchases of 24.1 million tons during 1965–70: 2.1 million tons in 1965, 3.0 in 1966, 4.0 in 1967, and 5.0 in each of the years 1968–70 (Texto del convenio 1964, 166). Cuba's performance under the pact was dismal. As data in table 33 substantiate, it shipped a total of 13.1 million tons to the Soviet Union in 1965–70, about 54 percent of the agreed levels; in 1968 and 1969, Cuba fulfilled only 35 and 28 percent, respectively, of sugar supply commitments to the Soviet Union.

The 1964 Cuban-Soviet agreement also fixed sugar prices at 6 cents/pound for the entire period 1964–70 (Texto del convenio 1964, 166). According to other sources (Pino-Santos and Martínez 1979, 57; M. T. Valdés 1984, 136–38), however, the contracted price for 1964–72 was 6.11 cents/pound. Yet a third contract price for 1970— 5.94 cents/pound—also has been given in the literature (ECLAC 1986, 18).

Available evidence suggests that over this period, prices of Cuban

TABLE 33
Cuban-Soviet Sugar Trade, 1965–70
*(in millions of tons)*

|      | Planned | Actual | Actual/Planned (Plan=100) |
|------|---------|--------|---------------------------|
| 1965 | 2.1 | 2.5 | 119 |
| 1966 | 3.0 | 1.8 | 60 |
| 1967 | 4.0 | 2.5 | 63 |
| 1968 | 5.0 | 1.8 | 35 |
| 1969 | 5.0 | 1.4 | 28 |
| 1970 | 5.0 | 3.1 | 62 |
| Cumulative total | 24.1 | 13.1 | 54 |

SOURCES: Planned—Texto del convenio 1964; actual—table 29.

sugar sales to the PRC and several Eastern European socialist nations followed those in Cuban-Soviet trade very closely. For example, in 1965 the average price (export unit value, in centavos per pound) of Cuban sugar exports was 6.09 to the Soviet Union, 6.17 to East Germany, 6.10 to Czechoslovakia, and 6.06 to the PRC; similarly, in 1970 the average price received by Cuba in sugar sales to the Soviet Union (in centavos/pound) was 5.94, while it was 5.62 to East Germany, 6.00 to Czechoslovakia, and 6.06 to the PRC. Prices in sugar sales to Bulgaria, Hungary, and Romania diverged from the others, however. Moreover, prices close to world market prices obtained in sales to less developed socialist countries, that is, North Korea and Vietnam (AEC 1985, 430). Meanwhile, world market prices for sugar remained relatively high in 1964—averaging 5.87 cents/pound—but again tumbled during 1965–70, averaging around 2 cents/pound in 1965–68, and rising to an average of about 3.5 cents/pound in 1969–70.

The contract price of Cuban sugar exports to the Soviet Union remained at 6.11 centavos/pound during 1971 and 1972; this is confirmed by data in official Cuban statistical yearbooks (AEC 1977, 200; 1976, 186); with the devaluation of the U.S. dollar in 1972 (by about 10 percent), the contract price of Cuban sugar sales to the Soviet Union in that year was closer to 6.7 cents/pound. By the end of 1972, the world market price had again gone well above the contracted price.

A new Cuban-Soviet agreement, concluded in December 1972,

set the sugar export price for 1973–80 at 200 rubles/ton, or about 11 cents/pound (F. Castro 1973, 2; Pino-Santos and Martínez 1979, 70). (There is some confusion in the literature regarding the contract price for 1972. Whereas Castro and others [e.g., Gouré and Rothenberg 1975, 51] have reported it as 11 cents/pound, an official Cuban source has given it as 12.02 cents/pound [BNC 1975, 32]. Both figures seem to have a basis: though, at the time the agreement was signed, the price in terms of U.S. dollars was indeed 11 cents/pound, the devaluation of the dollar in 1973 meant that the dollar price in that year was 12.02 cents/pound. Other sources [table 32] have given the 1973 contract price as 11.82 or 11.83 cents/pound.)

World market prices for sugar continued to rise through 1973, so that by December of that year they had once again risen above the price contracted with the Soviet Union. The climb continued through 1974, peaking at about 65 cents/pound in November 1974. The agreed delivery price to the Soviet Union for 1974 was adjusted upward to 325 rubles/ton, or 19.64 cents/pound (BNC 1975, 31–32; Pino-Santos and Martínez 1979, 70), compared to an average world market price of 29.96 cents/pound in that year.

In late January 1975 the CMEA executive committee met in Moscow to review issues related to trade and cooperation among members. The communiqué of the session (Adopta el Comité 1975, 8) stated that "measures to stabilize prices in commercial contracts among members for the five-year period 1976–80 [were adopted] . . . to create favorable conditions for the development of trade." The thrust of the new measures was the establishment of a policy whereby prices in intra-CMEA trade would be adjusted annually, rather than only during the first year of each five-year period, as had been customary since the adoption of the so-called Bucharest formula in 1958 (Marer 1972, 6–7). This modification in pricing policy was reportedly forced on other CMEA members by the Soviet Union in an effort to reduce opportunity costs incurred in exporting raw materials (especially oil) at fixed prices (Kohn and Lang 1977, 139–43; Pérez-López 1979, 286).

Consistent with the move toward more flexible pricing, in 1975 the Soviet Union guaranteed Cuba a "minimum" price for sugar of 500 rubles per ton (about 30.40 cents/pound), the price to be adjusted *upward* in step with changes in the prices of Cuban imports from the Soviet Union (F. Castro 1979, 4; Pino-Santos and Martínez 1979, 70);

by comparison, the average world market price for sugar in 1975 was about 20.5 cents/pound.

The Cuban-Soviet long-term commercial agreement for 1976–80, signed in February 1976, extended the use of the minimum price indexation formula through 1980. For this five-year period, the minimum price of Soviet sugar imports from Cuba was to be maintained at 500 rubles/ton (30.40 cents/pound), and the price in each subsequent year was to be increased proportionally to increases in the prices of Soviet exports to Cuba relative to the prices these products commanded in 1975 (F. Castro 1976, 3; 1979, 4; 1981, 3; ECLA 1980, 194; S. Pérez 1984, 118; J. L. Rodríguez 1982, 121; 1984a, 234; 1984b, 126; Sánchez García-Calzadilla 1982, 80).

Reportedly, the price of a "basket" of imports from the Soviet Union consisting of over 100 products is used to calculate the annual "upward" adjustment (Pino-Santos and Martínez 1979, 71). Although the components of the basket, their base-period price levels, and their weights have not been made public, it has been reported that oil plays a prominent role. Thus, in explaining the adjustment mechanism of the sugar price in April 1976, Vice President Carlos Rafael Rodríguez suggested that it merely related sugar export prices to prices of oil imports from the Soviet Union (M. Rivero 1976, 8). At variance with this, on the basis of discussions with Cuban officials, one researcher (Domínguez 1989, 85) has reported that the price adjustment mechanism was related "in part to the average price of Cuban exports (basically sugar, nickel, and citrus fruits) in the world market over the past five years, and in part to the five-year average of selected Cuban imports from the USSR (especially petroleum)."

A Soviet source has reported that during 1981–85, the preferential price arrangement for Cuban sugar remained unchanged from that in effect during 1976–80 (Burmistrov 1982, 11). However, in its *Economic Survey of Latin America 1980* ECLA noted that, presumably beginning in 1979, the indexation formula for the sugar price underwent significant modification, with the price the Soviet Union pays for Cuban sugar "de-linked" from prices of Soviet exports to Cuba (ECLA 1980, 194; Zimbalist 1982, 141). Not only has this assertion not been corroborated by any other analyst or by ECLA in subsequent issues of the *Survey,* but in a more recent publication in this series (for 1983), ECLA (1983, 21) notes that, for 1981–85, Cuban sugar exports to the Soviet Union were to be made at a minimum price of

35.4 cents/pound (effective in 1980), the price to be adjusted annually from that base "through an indexation mechanism whereby *increases* [emphasis added] in the prices of manufactured goods and other goods imported [from the Soviet Union] are applied to the price of Cuban sugar so that bilateral trade relations remain stable." This recent statement, added to the lack of corroboration in the literature, puts into question the earlier ECLA claim that the price indexation mechanism applicable to sugar exports to the Soviet Union was abandoned in 1979.

The effect of the minimum price indexation provision in place since 1975 has been to sever the link between the price in Cuba's bilateral sugar sales to the Soviet Union and the world market price. Thus, over the period 1975–86, contract prices nearly doubled, from 26 to 51 cents/pound, while world market prices fell from about 20 to 6 cents/pound. In 1987 the price in sugar contract sales to the Soviet Union was nearly 42 cents/pound, over six times the world market price of about 7 cents/pound (table 32).

As was noted earlier, available evidence suggests that during the 1960s, sugar export prices that Cuba negotiated with the Soviet Union were also applicable to sales to its major purchasers in Eastern Europe and to the PRC. However, in the 1970s this system broke down, and the price paid by the Soviet Union far exceeded that paid by Eastern Europe and the PRC.

For the period 1971–82, Cuba has published information on the price at which Cuban sugar was sold pursuant to contracts to selected socialist and capitalist nations. Table 34 presents such data for sales to the Soviet Union and main markets among the socialist countries: East Germany, Bulgaria, Czechoslovakia, and the PRC. The data in table 34 are given in terms of centavos/pound, to avoid the influence on the data of changes in the U.S. dollar-peso exchange rate.

For 1971 and 1972 the contract price of Cuban sugar sales to the Soviet Union was 6.11 centavos/pound; sales to East Germany, Bulgaria, Czechoslovakia, and the PRC were made at the identical price. In 1973 the contract price with the Soviet Union, Bulgaria, and the PRC jumped to 9–10 centavos/pound, while it remained unchanged with East Germany and Czechoslovakia. In 1974 prices rose across the board to a level of about 16.4 centavos/pound. Starting in 1975—when the Soviet Union began to guarantee a minimum price for Cuban sugar and introduced a price indexation mechanism—the uniformity in pricing across socialist countries ceased to exist.

TABLE 34
CONTRACT PRICE OF CUBAN SUGAR EXPORTS, 1971–1982
(*in centavos/pound*)

|  | Soviet Union | East Germany | Bulgaria | Czechoslovakia | PRC |
|---|---|---|---|---|---|
| 1971 | 6.11 | 6.11 | 6.11 | 6.11 |  |
| 1972 | 6.11 | 6.11 | 6.11 | 6.11 | 6.11 |
| 1973 | 9.94 | 6.11 | 10.08 | 6.11 | 9.42 |
| 1974 | 16.28 | 16.38 | 16.38 | 16.38 | 16.45 |
| 1975 | 25.11 | 16.34 | 16.34 | 16.34 | 22.77 |
| 1976 | 23.10 | 16.34 | 16.34 | 16.34 | 15.85 |
| 1977 | 22.56 | 16.34 | 17.32 | 16.34 | 12.86 |
| 1978 | 27.57 | 16.34 | 18.26 | 16.34 | 10.24 |
| 1979 | 27.33 | 16.34 | 19.21 | 16.34 | 9.63 |
| 1980 | 34.42 | 19.86 | 20.15 | 19.86 | 16.37 |
| 1981 | 27.48 | 22.96 | 22.44 | 16.64 | 19.27 |
| 1982 | 29.84 | 22.96 | 23.37 | 20.86 | 16.49 |

SOURCES: 1978–82—AEC 1985, 470; 1974–77—AEC 1980, 206; 1972–73—AEC 1977, 200; 1971—AEC 1976, 186.

Contract prices for Cuban sugar sales to the Soviet Union rose in 1975 to over 25 centavos/pound, dropped to about 23 centavos/pound in 1976–77, climbed to over 34 centavos/pound in 1980, and fell to about 28–30 centavos/pound in 1981–82. In contrast, contract prices remained fixed at about 16.4 centavos/pound with Bulgaria during 1974–76 and East Germany and Czechoslovakia during 1974–79. Annual adjustments in contract prices with Bulgaria began in 1977 and with East Germany and Czechoslovakia in 1980. Apparently beginning around 1975–76, the PRC shifted to a policy of buying Cuban sugar at the prevailing world market price of the previous year (Fernández Font 1986, 198).

An examination of official Soviet and Cuban official sugar trade statistics for 1971–87 raises some interesting issues:

1. According to the literature, since 1975 the Soviet Union has paid a minimum price for Cuban sugar of 500 rubles/ton. And yet, according to the data on import unit values in table 35, the average "price" the Soviet Union paid for Cuban sugar in 1975, 1976, and 1977 was well below that level, averaging about 455 rubles/ton.

2. The possibility that the above difference might be attributable to freight costs, that is, that the contract price might refer to landed

TABLE 35
UNIT VALUES OF SOVIET SUGAR IMPORTS FROM CUBA AND OF CUBAN
CRUDE OIL IMPORTS FROM THE SOVIET UNION, 1971–1987

|  | Sugar | | Oil | |
| --- | --- | --- | --- | --- |
|  | Rubles/MT[a] | % Change | Pesos/MT[a] | % Change |
| 1971 | 120.9 | — | 16.37 | — |
| 1972 | 119.9 | −0.8 | 18.28 | 11.7 |
| 1973 | 201.5 | 68.1 | 21.55 | 17.9 |
| 1974 | 329.2 | 63.4 | 22.81 | 5.8 |
| 1975 | 453.4 | 37.7 | 38.53 | 68.9 |
| 1976 | 455.7 | 0.6 | 40.16 | 4.2 |
| 1977 | 458.7 | 0.7 | 50.51 | 25.8 |
| 1978 | 557.5 | 21.5 | 62.90 | 24.5 |
| 1979 | 549.8 | −1.4 | 74.04 | 17.7 |
| 1980 | 701.9 | 27.7 | 81.56 | 10.2 |
| 1981 | 590.1 | −15.9 | 104.00 | 27.5 |
| 1982 | 586.2 | −0.7 | 129.05 | 24.1 |
| 1983 | 811.9 | 38.5 | 153.17 | 18.7 |
| 1984 | 914.8 | 12.7 | 178.54 | 16.6 |
| 1985 | 898.8 | −1.7 | 196.46 | 10.0 |
| 1986 | 800.6 | −10.9 | 197.89 | 0.7 |
| 1987 | 783.2 | −2.2 |  |  |

SOURCES: Soviet sugar import unit values—calculated from *Vneshniaia Torgovlia* 1987 and earlier issues; Cuban crude oil import unit value—calculated from AEC 1987 and earlier issues.
a. Metric ton.

cost in the Soviet Union, including freight, and the unit values to the value at Cuban ports, has been explored. Though no definitive answer can be given, the evidence seems to support the view that the 500 rubles/ton minimum price referred to a price at Cuban ports: (i) in previous agreements, the price that has been publicly reported was the one at Cuban ports. For example, the 1964 agreement, which covered the period 1965–70, expressly states that the sugar contract price is "6 cents of U.S. dollar per British pound FAS [free alongside ship] Cuban ports" (Texto del convenio 1964, 166). Similarly, Cuban economists have noted that the sugar contract price agreed to in 1972 (for the period 1973–80) was "200 rubles per metric ton stowed at Cuban ports" (Pino Santos and Martínez 1979, 68); and (ii) Soviet import statistics refer to the value of imports at foreign ports, that is, they exclude freight costs. In earlier years, the "price" derived from Soviet import data (e.g., 201.5 rubles/ton in 1973) in table 35 corresponded very closely with the reported contract price (200 rubles/ton), corroborating that the contract price was a Cuban port price. In conclusion, on the strength of the current literature, there is no basis for arguing that the differences between contract price and Soviet import unit values for 1975, 1976, and 1977 noted above result from the way in which freight costs are treated.

3. Another possible explanation, and a more likely one, is that differences between contract prices and realized prices (i.e., unit values) may be attributable to sales outside the agreements. Facing shortages of convertible currency, at times Cuba has reportedly sold sugar to the Soviet Union outside the terms of their sugar agreement—at market prices and in convertible currency (ECLAC 1985:18). Since unit values reflect total trade, including sales at market prices, they tend to be lower than contract prices in a period when the contract price exceeds the world market price, as was the case in 1975–77 and in every year since then. There is no systematic information on the volume of Cuban sugar exports to the Soviet Union transacted inside and outside the sugar agreements. According to one source (Radell 1983, 370), Cuba sold 1.7 million tons of sugar to the Soviet Union at less than contract prices during 1975–76; this would correspond to about 27 percent of total sales to the Soviet Union of 6.2 million tons in those two years (see table 29).

4. A close reading of the Cuban literature suggests that the indexation mechanism was supposed to work always to Cuba's benefit, that is, it would operate only when the price of Cuban imports from the Soviet Union rose, so as to maintain constant the terms of trade between the price of sugar and that of a basket of commodities. Again, the unit value data in tables 32 and 35 contradict that assumption. In several of the years (e.g., 1979, 1981, 1982, 1985, and 1986), the average price paid for Cuban sugar was lower than a year earlier, suggesting that the price adjustment mechanism was used also to lower the price. The contract price data (in centavos/pound) in table 34 also show this to be the case.

5. The behavior of the unit values of the Soviet imports puts into question the Cuban contention that the agreements with the Soviet Union have stabilized sugar prices. It is clear from table 35 that substantial fluctuations in the "price" paid occurred, including an

increase of nearly 28 percent in 1981, a decline of 16 percent in 1982, increases of nearly 39 percent in 1983 and 13 percent in 1984, and three straight years of declines in 1985–87.

6. There seems to be little relation between the movement of Soviet oil export prices to Cuba, as measured by the Cuban import unit values given in table 35 (Soviet export unit values cannot be computed since the Soviet Union has not published data on the quantity of oil exports for the relevant period) and changes in unit values of Soviet sugar imports from Cuba, putting into question the statement that oil plays an important role in the price indexing scheme. Essentially the same lack of relationship is evident when changes in the unit value of Cuban sugar exports to the Soviet Union (table 32) are compared with corresponding changes in unit values of oil imports.

The pattern of movement in unit values of Cuban sugar exports to the Soviet Union and of Soviet imports of Cuban sugar described above challenge official Cuban explanations of how the sugar price indexation mechanism operates. Movements over time in Soviet contract prices (tables 32 and 34) also tend to buttress this skepticism. Cuban statistical yearbooks for 1983–87 did not update the data on contract prices, so that the most recent such data available are for 1982. As is clear from figure 3, the contract price and unit value series of sugar sales to the Soviet Union are very highly correlated: they both show substantial year-to-year fluctuations and suggest that the price indexation mechanism also worked to reduce sugar prices from one year to the next.

Press reports circulating in 1986 suggested that the Soviet Union cut the price of sugar imports from Cuba for that year and also for 1986–90 (Minrex 1986, 2). The reduction in sugar prices was reportedly associated with efforts by Soviet leader Gorbachev to tighten trade relations with CMEA nations. According to one report, Cuba had requested that the minimum price of sugar exports for 1986 be set at a higher level than the contract price for 1985 (reported as 915 rubles/per ton, or about 50 cents/pound), and that prices for subsequent years during the five-year period 1986–90 be subject to annual upward adjustment; instead, the Soviet Union agreed to a price of 850 rubles per ton for 1986, 7 percent lower than the ruble price in 1985, and fixed this price for the entire period 1986–90 (Castro the "Non-Smoker" 1986, 42).

Official Soviet trade statistics indicate that the unit value of Soviet

FIGURE 3
PRICES IN CUBAN-SOVIET SUGAR TRADE
U.S. CENTS PER POUND

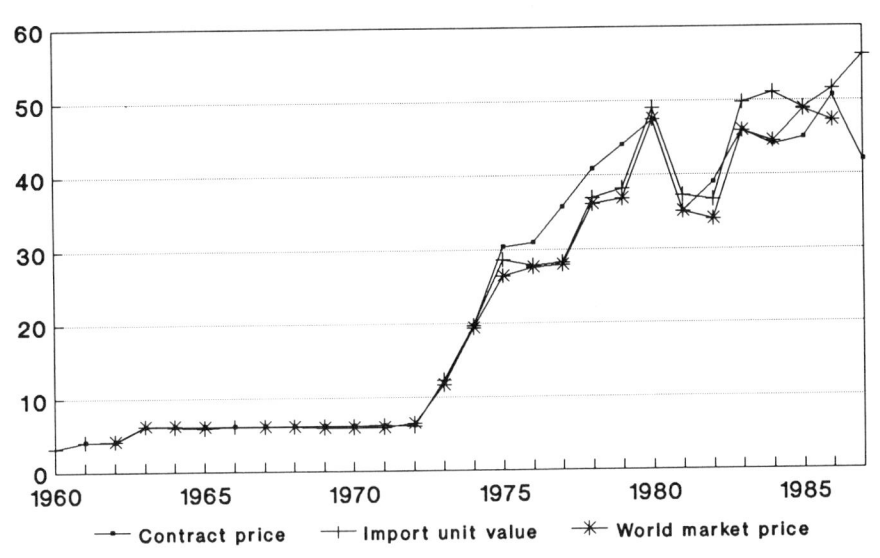

─●─ Contract price   ─+─ Import unit value   ─✶─ World market price

SOURCE: Table 32.

imports of Cuban sugar in 1986 was 800.6 rubles/ton, about 11 percent lower than the corresponding value in 1985, and in 1987 it was 783.2 rubles/ton, a further reduction of 2.2 percent (table 35).

WORLD MARKET

One of revolutionary Cuba's pressing economic problems was how to dispose of the sugar it produced. As is discussed in chapter 10, in the 1920s Cuba instituted a policy of restricting sugar output in an attempt to improve the price at which it could sell it abroad. Despite the self-imposed restrictions, prerevolutionary Cuba regularly produced more than could be consumed domestically or sold to the United States under favorable terms. The outlet that was available for this sugar—40–50 percent of total exports in the 1950s—was the world market. Hence the importance Cuba attached to stabilization of the world sugar market through international agreements and allocation of a sizable share of that market.

In the 1950s, Cuba followed an aggressive policy of expansion of markets for its sugar exports. Efforts were made to increase sales to traditional markets in Western Europe and the Americas while developing new outlets in Eastern Europe and Asia. In 1951, Cuba entered into multiyear agreements with the United Kingdom, West Germany, and Canada to sell substantial quantities of sugar as a quid pro quo for certain tariff concessions (Grupo Cubano 1963, 954–55). A year later an agreement was negotiated with the government of France—acting on behalf of French sugar traders—that gave Cuba access to the Moroccan market and increased sales opportunities in Japan (ibid. 960). As was noted earlier, in the 1950s, Cuba also sold sugar to the Soviet Union, the PRC, and Eastern European nations. All of these sales—whether in the form of long-term arrangements with Western European nations or spot sales to the Soviet Union and the socialist nations—were world market sales and were made at, or near, the world price.

Since 1960, Cuban sugar sales to the Soviet Union and the socialist nations have been deemed to be under special arrangements and therefore have not been considered as being part of the world market. Thus sugar exports to "other countries" in table 29 are a good approximation for Cuban sales to the world market. If one uses Cuban sales to nonsocialist nations as a proxy for world market sales, it is clear that Cuba's participation in the world sugar market has dropped significantly during the revolutionary period.

In the early 1960s, Cuba's sugar exports to the world market accounted for about 25 percent of total exports, a significant drop from the 40–50 percent such sales represented in the 1950s. World market sales accounted for about 33 percent of total Cuban export sales of sugar in the second half of the 1960s, 40 percent in the first half of the 1970s, and about 33 percent again in the second half of the 1970s. During 1981–86, world market sales accounted for just over 20 percent of Cuba's sugar exports, the lowest share since the World War II years, when Cuba sold virtually its entire sugar crops to the United States. In 1987, Cuban sugar exports to the world market fell to a recent historical low of 15 percent.

The significant decline in Cuban participation in the world sugar market is also apparent from data in table 36. In the second half of the 1970s, Cuba supplied 7–12 percent of sugar exports to the world market, compared with 11–15 percent in the first half of the decade. In the most recent five-year period (1982–86), Cuba's share of the

TABLE 36
CUBAN PARTICIPATION IN THE WORLD SUGAR MARKET, 1971–1987
(in thousands of tons)

|      | Total Size of World Market | Cuban Exports to World Market | Cuba/World Market (%) |
|------|---|---|---|
| 1971 | 14,455 | 2,159 | 14.9 |
| 1972 | 16,567 | 1,802 | 10.9 |
| 1973 | 16,482 | 1,774 | 10.8 |
| 1974 | 16,074 | 2,174 | 13.5 |
| 1975 | 13,211 | 1,652 | 12.5 |
| 1976 | 15,481 | 1,383 | 8.9 |
| 1977 | 20,760 | 1,487 | 7.2 |
| 1978 | 17,491 | 2,047 | 11.7 |
| 1979 | 18,271 | 2,057 | 11.3 |
| 1980 | 19,418 | 2,189 | 11.3 |
| 1981 | 20,628 | 2,244 | 10.9 |
| 1982 | 21,652 | 1,697 | 7.8 |
| 1983 | 20,555 | 1,686 | 8.2 |
| 1984 | 19,197 | 1,421 | 7.4 |
| 1985 | 18,984 | 1,756 | 9.2 |
| 1986 | 18,185 | 1,472 | 8.1 |
| 1987 | 18,509 | 918 | 5.0 |

SOURCE: ISO 1988 and earlier issues.
*Note:* World market means the total arrived at by adding together each country's net exports after deducting net exports under special arrangements.

world sugar market was 7–9 percent; in 1987, Cuba's share was 5 percent.

It should be noted that world market exports do not necessarily imply sales at world market prices. Over certain periods, significant volumes of Cuba's world market exports have been made pursuant to long-term contracts at prices higher than those of the world market. For example, during 1964–78, Spain purchased Cuban sugar at prices fixed in advance; in most years, world market prices were lower than the agreed price, and Cuba reaped an additional benefit in the exchange (Recarte 1980, 165–83). Japan also purchased Cuban sugar pursuant to long-term contracts in the 1960s and 1970s; these reportedly expired in 1981, and since then Japan has relied on spot market purchases of Cuban sugar (UNCTAD 1982, 23). According to the Banco Nacional de Cuba, in 1987 Cuba had medium-term sugar sales agreements with Angola, Egypt, Iraq, Libya, and Canada (BNC 1988a, 25).

## Sugar and the Cuban Export Economy

The importance of sugar to twentieth century Cuba's export economy is evident from the ratio of the value of sugar exports to total exports. Sugar sales accounted for the following percentages of Cuba's total exports (decennial averages are used for the sake of brevity) (Mesa-Lago and Pérez-López 1985c, 75):

|         |              |
|---------|--------------|
| 1900–09 | 55.9 percent |
| 1910–19 | 78.6 percent |
| 1920–29 | 85.2 percent |
| 1930–39 | 77.3 percent |
| 1940–49 | 81.4 percent |
| 1950–59 | 81.4 percent |

In revolutionary Cuba sugar has continued to be the backbone of the export economy. For every year during 1958–87, it accounted for over 70 percent of the total value of exports; for certain years, for example 1963–65, 1967, 1974–76, and 1977–79, its share of exports exceeded 85 percent. During the most recent four-year period (1984–87), sugar exports accounted for about 75 percent of the value of Cuban exports, minerals for about 6 percent, tobacco for about 2 percent, and other products (including reexported oil and oil products) for the rest (AEC 1987, 430).

The export orientation of the Cuban sugar industry is also evident from table 37, which presents data on sugar production, consumption, and exports for 1950–87. Over the entire period, Cuba exported on average over 90 percent of the sugar it produced each year. In the 1950s it produced on average about 5.5 million tons of sugar per annum and exported about 5.1 million tons, that is, about 93 percent; annual production in the 1960s averaged 5.4 million tons and exports about 5.0 million tons, or about 92 percent of production. During the 1970s, Cuban sugar production rose to an average of 6.4 million tons per annum and exports to 5.9 million tons, or about 92 percent of production; in 1970, the then record high production year, Cuba exported 6.9 million tons, also a record level; in 1978 and 1979, it exported about 7.2 million tons, the first time that the 7 million ton

## TABLE 37
### Sugar Production, Consumption, and Net Exports, 1950–1987
*(in thousands of tons)*

|      | Production | Consumption | Net Exports | Net Exports/Production (%) |
|------|-----------|-------------|-------------|----------------------------|
| 1950 | 5,558     | 247         | 5,261       | 94.6                       |
| 1951 | 5,759     | 292         | 5,441       | 94.5                       |
| 1952 | 7,225     | 303         | 5,008       | 69.3                       |
| 1953 | 5,159     | 258         | 5,516       | 106.9                      |
| 1954 | 4,890     | 206         | 4,226       | 86.4                       |
| 1955 | 4,528     | 206         | 4,644       | 102.6                      |
| 1956 | 4,740     | 313         | 5,394       | 113.8                      |
| 1957 | 5,672     | 304         | 5,307       | 93.6                       |
| 1958 | 5,784     | 242         | 5,631       | 97.4                       |
| 1959 | 5,964     | 331         | 4,952       | 83.0                       |
| 1960 | 5,862     | 348         | 5,635       | 96.1                       |
| 1961 | 6,767     | 376         | 6,414       | 94.8                       |
| 1962 | 4,815     | 373         | 5,131       | 106.7                      |
| 1963 | 3,821     | 456         | 3,521       | 92.1                       |
| 1964 | 4,590     | 402         | 4,176       | 91.0                       |
| 1965 | 6,082     | 492         | 5,316       | 87.4                       |
| 1966 | 4,867     | 542         | 4,435       | 91.1                       |
| 1967 | 6,236     | 630         | 5,683       | 91.1                       |
| 1968 | 5,315     | 682         | 4,613       | 86.8                       |
| 1969 | 5,534     | 636         | 4,799       | 86.7                       |
| 1970 | 7,559     | 619         | 6,906       | 91.3                       |
| 1971 | 5,950     | 616         | 5,511       | 92.6                       |
| 1972 | 4,688     | 471         | 4,140       | 88.3                       |
| 1973 | 5,383     | 464         | 4,797       | 89.1                       |
| 1974 | 5,926     | 522         | 5,491       | 92.7                       |
| 1975 | 6,427     | 499         | 5,744       | 89.4                       |
| 1976 | 6,151     | 532         | 5,764       | 93.7                       |
| 1977 | 6,953     | 519         | 6,238       | 89.7                       |
| 1978 | 7,662     | 552         | 7,231       | 94.4                       |
| 1979 | 7,800     | 519         | 7,269       | 93.2                       |
| 1980 | 6,805     | 530         | 6,191       | 91.0                       |
| 1981 | 7,926     | 552         | 7,071       | 89.2                       |
| 1982 | 8,040     | 649         | 7,648       | 95.1                       |
| 1983 | 7,460     | 678         | 6,792       | 91.0                       |
| 1984 | 7,783     | 728         | 7,017       | 90.2                       |
| 1985 | 7,889     | 887         | 7,209       | 91.3                       |
| 1986 | 7,467     | 762         | 6,703       | 90.0                       |
| 1987 | 7,231     | 773         | 6,482       | 89.6                       |

SOURCE: ISO 1988 and earlier issues.
*Note:* A net export/production ratio exceeding 100 percent results from the drawing down of existing stocks.

export level was exceeded. Figures available to date for the 1980s show that sugar production has averaged slightly under 7.6 million tons per annum and exports just under 6.9 million tons, or about 91 percent of output.

Finally, sugar exports are crucial as generators of hard currency revenue. In 1981, the first year for which data are available, sugar sales generated $866.3 million, or nearly 62 percent of the nation's hard currency export revenue. Subsequently, sugar's contribution to hard currency earnings dropped significantly—to as low as 14 percent in 1985—as world market prices softened and oil reexports emerged as the main hard currency export earner (BNC 1987, 24). In 1986–87 sugar exports accounted for about 23 percent of hard currency export earnings (BNC 1988b, 17).

# CHAPTER 9

## Subsidies in Cuban-Soviet Sugar Trade

CENTRAL TO THE economic relationship between Cuba and the Soviet Union is sugar trade. Since 1961 the Soviet Union has been Cuba's most important market for sugar exports. In 1987, for example, it took 60 percent of Cuba's physical exports of sugar (table 29), and sugar accounted for 84 percent of the value of total Cuban exports to the Soviet Union (AEC 1987, 423, 471).

As was discussed in chapter 8, in addition to purchasing large quantities of Cuban sugar, beginning in the early 1960s the Soviet Union has paid preferential or concessional prices—that is, above world market prices—for Cuban sugar deliveries. Though preferential prices are common in international sugar trading, the very high margins of preference granted by the Soviet Union to Cuban sugar are unprecedented: for example, the contract price in 1986 was around 51 cents/pound, compared to a world market price of just above 6 cents/pound (table 32).

In the mid 1970s, Cuba and the Soviet Union agreed to a formula for establishing the price of sugar in bilateral trade that essentially severed any relationship between this price and the world market price. A minimum contract price was set at a very high level and automatically adjusted to take into account changes in the prices of a basket of Cuban imports from the Soviet Union. Whereas prices generated by this formula have tended to rise annually, world market prices have been flat or even declined markedly (as in the 1980s). The result has been a skyrocketing in the price premium paid by the Soviet Union and in the magnitude of transfers from the Soviet Union to Cuba in the form of sugar prices.

In view of the very high price that Cuba receives for sugar exports to the Soviet Union, it is relevant to raise two questions. First, does this highly advantageous price represent a subsidy from the Soviet Union to Cuba? And second, how significant are these transfers?

This chapter concentrates on quantitative estimates of the subsidy element in Cuban-Soviet sugar trade. It first examines different views on whether the very high price constitutes a subsidy. Then it critically reviews several sets of estimates of the subsidies that have appeared in the literature. Estimates made by others have been replicated and updated so that they can be compared with each one another and with additional estimates derived here. For the sake of comparability, estimates are in U.S. dollars; conversions from rubles or pesos to U.S. dollars have been made at official exchange rates.

## Soviet Price Subsidies

The Soviet Union provides implicit trade subsidies when it exports commodities (e.g., oil) to CMEA members at prices below world market prices and when it imports commodities (e.g., Cuban sugar, nickel) from CMEA countries at prices above those prevailing in world markets. In recent years an empirically based literature has emerged that attempts to explain—and measure—this phenomenon of implicit subsidies in Soviet trade with its Eastern European allies. To explain why the Soviet Union has engaged in trade at terms that at first glance appear to be unfavorable, Marrese and Vanous (1983a; 1983b) have coined the term *unconventional gains from trade* to refer to military, political, ideological, and economic nonmarket benefits that are secured through preferential trade treatment in bilateral agreements.

Not all analysts of the Cuban economy accept the proposition that the purchase by the Soviet Union of Cuban sugar at above-market prices constitutes a trade subsidy. Cuban economists dismiss the argument, countering that the favorable treatment of developing countries within CMEA is merely evidence of the principles of internationalist socialism and the socialist division of labor at work (Borroto Román and Peñabaz Suárez 1980, 72; Torres Pérez and Carballosa Torres 1985, 209–10). As the former foreign trade minister, Marcelo Fernández Font (1986, 120), puts it:

> With regard to the preferential treatment of Cuban sugar exports to socialist countries, there are—and there could be—no colonialist residues or pretensions of establishing colonial domination. It reflects the application of a principle of internationalist socialism—the equalization of development levels across CMEA member nations—through

which our country receives preferential prices not only for sugar exports, but also for other export products.

Along the same lines, Cuban economists argue that the preferential prices Cuba receives from the Soviet Union are merely a reflection of the type of arrangement—"just" commodity export prices, linked to the price of imported products—developing countries have been demanding as part of the New International Economic Order (NIEO) and the Soviet Union has been willing to grant (J. L. Rodríguez 1985, 91; 1986, 14; Martínez Salsamendi 1984, 142).

Cuban analysts have also minimized the magnitude of the subsidy, arguing that preferential prices paid by the Soviet Union for Cuban sugar are not out of line with internal Soviet prices (Borroto Román and Peñabaz Suárez 1980, 82). They posit that sugar production costs (from sugar beet) in the Soviet Union in 1980 hovered around 30 cents/pound, twice the average cost in developed countries. When compared with the high cost of domestic sugar, the price premium paid by the Soviet Union for Cuban sugar is much less significant. Other Cuban analysts claim that the cost of producing sugar in Eastern Europe and the Soviet Union is four to seven times higher than in Cuba and at times higher than import costs from Cuba (González Maicas and Díaz-Vázquez 1988, 149).

President Castro addressed the issue of preferential pricing by the Soviet Union for Cuban sugar in an interview with a foreign journalist in June 1987. When challenged by the interviewer to explain the importance to the Cuban economy of the reported $1 million-per-day sugar price transfer received from the Soviet Union, Castro responded (Mina 1988, 149):

> Not a million. The United States calculates the difference between the price in the marginal world sugar market—not the price in Europe or the price the United States pays for sugar imports—and the price the Soviet Union and socialist countries pay to us for sugar and call that difference a subsidy. That is, the fact that we have been able to establish the kind of just and fair trading relations that should exist between developing and developed countries, something that we propose for all developing countries in their relations with the developed capitalist world—an objective that is part of the principles of the New International Economic Order that we have achieved with the socialist countries—is used to make erroneous, arbitrary, and manipulated calculations. Sugar is generally sold at prices much higher

TABLE 38
UNIT VALUE OF SOVIET SUGAR IMPORTS FROM ALL SOURCES, 1971–1987
(in rubles/metric ton)

|      | Cuba  | Brazil | Australia | Philippines | Dominican Republic | Nicaragua | Total | Total (excl. Cuba) |
|------|-------|--------|-----------|-------------|--------------------|-----------|-------|--------------------|
| 1971 | 120.9 |        |           |             |                    |           | 120.9 |                    |
| 1972 | 119.9 | 116.6  | 108.3     |             |                    |           | 118.2 | 114.9              |
| 1973 | 201.5 | 162.5  | 144.7     |             | 160.0              |           | 186.1 | 157.9              |
| 1974 | 329.2 |        |           |             |                    |           | 329.2 |                    |
| 1975 | 453.4 | 884.2  | 788.5     |             |                    |           | 485.5 | 834.5              |
| 1976 | 455.7 |        |           | 205.4       |                    |           | 435.5 | 210.9              |
| 1977 | 458.7 |        |           | 127.6       |                    |           | 409.6 | 127.6              |
| 1978 | 557.5 |        |           |             |                    |           | 537.1 | 134.7              |
| 1979 | 549.8 | 208.3  |           |             |                    |           | 544.3 | 203.4              |
| 1980 | 701.9 | 259.7  |           | 231.2       |                    |           | 564.2 | 258.4              |
| 1981 | 590.1 | 451.3  |           | 462.4       |                    |           | 553.3 | 448.2              |
| 1982 | 586.2 | 198.9  | 140.1     | 217.6       |                    |           | 466.8 | 206.5              |
| 1983 | 811.9 | 185.6  | 150.0     | 138.9       |                    |           | 580.6 | 205.9              |
| 1984 | 914.8 | 130.9  | 91.5      | 140.4       |                    |           | 681.8 | 123.7              |
| 1985 | 898.8 | 78.9   |           |             |                    |           | 780.7 | 78.9               |
| 1986 | 800.6 | 126.8  | 107.4     |             |                    | 140.4     | 629.9 | 121.8              |
| 1987 | 783.2 | 92.8   | 93.4      |             |                    | 142.9     | 607.5 | 94.9               |

SOURCE: *Vneshniaia Torgovlia* 1987 and earlier issues.

than the marginal prices of the world market, where prices are depressed because of dumping by the European Community and protectionist measures by the United States. They make this kind of calculation, and then speak about subsidies.

If, in fact, the price the Soviet Union pays for Cuban sugar were a reflection of "just" commodity prices, pursuant to the NIEO, the Soviet Union would be expected to treat other developing countries in the same fashion. As is clear from table 38, this has not been the case through 1987. The very high prices the Soviet Union pays for Cuban sugar has given rise to friction between Cuba and other sugar exporters in the developing world not able to ship their product to the Soviet Union under such advantageous terms (MacDonald and Demetrius 1986, 43).

For instance, according to data in table 38, in 1984, the price (average import unit value, in rubles per metric ton) the Soviet Union paid for Cuban sugar was nearly 7 times that paid to Brazil and 6.5 times that paid to the Philippines, both also developing nations. In

1985 the Soviet Union purchased Cuban sugar at a price 11.4 times as high as that paid to Brazil. In 1986 the average price of Cuban sugar bought by the Soviet Union was 6.3 and 5.7 times the average price paid to Brazil and Nicaragua, respectively; in 1987 the corresponding ratios were 8.4 for Brazil and 5.5 for Nicaragua.

It is no secret that at least since 1984, Cuba has purchased sugar from other sugar-producing nations at depressed world market prices and resold it to the Soviet Union at the preferential price. For example, the BNC (1985, 35) has reported that in 1984–85, Cuba purchased sugar on the world market valued at 201 million pesos; when reexported to the Soviet Union, it generated 1,529 million pesos, for a net gain of 1,328 million pesos or a 661 percent return on investment. In 1986 and 1987, Cuban sugar *imports*—to be reexported—amounted to 89.6 and 189.4 million pesos, respectively (BNC 1988b), roughly 670,000 tons in 1986 and 1.270 million tons in 1987 at the average world market price.

Other authors (Zimbalist 1982, 139–43; 1988, 34–36; Turits 1987, 173–74; Zimbalist and Eckstein 1987, 17) argue that the high prices paid by the Soviet Union for Cuban sugar represent "tied aid," in the form of restricted ruble credits the Soviet Union extends to Cuba automatically to cover bilateral trade imbalances. They reason that Cuba "pays" for the high prices received for its sugar through lack of flexibility in importing, higher than world market prices for goods purchased from the Soviet Union, and other hidden costs.

Among the disadvantages (see Mesa-Lago and Gil 1989, 209–210) for Cuba of its trading relationship with the Soviet Union are:

1. Cuba has very little bargaining power in determining the mix of imported products it receives from the Soviet Union. In 1979, Fidel Castro spoke of the paradox of abundant supplies of Soviet-made television sets for export to Cuba at the same time that there was a shortage of other household items such as bed sheets, towels, and soap. Castro stated (1979, 5):

> Any of you could say: Wouldn't it be better to import more towels and fewer television sets? More bed sheets and fewer television sets? Ah, if only we could! I suspect that we could establish a moratorium on television set imports, or reduce them by half, and instead buy more soap, towels, and bed sheets. But we can't do that, because it is not an option available to us. The friendly countries who supply us with the television sets do not have surplus production of towels, bed sheets, or mattresses for export. On the other hand, they do

have [surpluses of] television sets, and therefore we import television sets. If they have [surplus production of] washers, or refrigerators, or other products, we also import them. Within the kind of trading relationship we have with them, [the socialist] countries export to us those products for which they have surpluses.

2. Cuba may pay higher than world market prices for imports from the Soviet Union. A report attributed to the BNC indicated that, in 1965, prices of Soviet goods imported by Cuba were 50 percent higher than similar products purchased in the international market (Gouré and Weinkle 1972, 75). There is also some evidence (Domínguez 1978, 56–57; Mesa-Lago and Gil 1989, 205–06; Zimbalist 1988, 35–36) that Cuba has paid higher prices in importing certain products (e.g., grains, powdered milk, lumber, tin plate, machinery) from the Soviet Union than it would have paid had it imported them from alternative sources. Since 1986, Cuba has been paying prices higher than those in the world market for imports of Soviet oil (Zimbalist 1988, 35).

3. Soviet goods and services shipped to Cuba are often deficient in quality and not sellable in international markets. Cuba has purchased technologically obsolete products from the Soviet Union, such as the first vintage of mechanical cane harvesters, which worked poorly (Zimbalist 1982, 142). Similarly, quality problems and technological deficiencies have plagued Soviet-designed industrial plants built in Cuba—for example, a textile factory in Santiago de Cuba and two nickel facilities—delaying production and forcing reductions in capacity (Zimbalist 1988, 36–37).

4. Shipments of Soviet goods often fail to meet delivery schedules, thereby disrupting Cuban economic activity. For example, in 1979, Soviet lumber deliveries fell short of agreed levels, adversely affecting the construction industry as well as the production of furniture and packaging materials for perishable products and for exports (F. Castro 1979, 3).

5. Improper loading of ships in the Soviet Union translates into longer unloading time—and higher costs—in Cuban ports (Zimbalist 1982, 142).

Finally, the reliance on the price of sugar as the main mechanism for transferring Soviet aid distorts Cuba's production and investment patterns. Artificially high returns in the sugar industry draw scarce investment resources into sugar production and away from alternative industries; they also tend to perpetuate commodity specialization and prevent economic restructuring away from sugar. Analysts have noted that the very high sugar price paid by the Soviet Union distorts patterns of Cuban agricultural production, encouraging higher sugar output and lower production of other crops than would prevail if Cuban-Soviet sugar trade were conducted at market prices (Eckstein 1981, 188; Sánchez and Scobie 1986, 37). Cuba's growing emphasis on sugar production for export, to the detriment of other agricultural products, is discussed in chapter 12.

On the generosity of nations and the "cost" to Cuba of sugar subsidies, Ernesto Guevara's words in March 1960 regarding the U.S. sugar subsidy are instructive (Guevara 1960, 226):

> With reference to the price of Cuban sugar, we made a statement a few days ago that received the undeserved comment of U.S. spokesman Lincoln Price; they insist that the [subsidy of] 150 million pesos the United States pays for our sugar is a gift to Cuba. That is not so. Cuba has had to sign tariff agreements in return that have forced us to spend $1.15 more or less in the United States for every $1.00 they spend here. This means that in a ten-year period our people have given one billion dollars to the North American monopolies. We don't have to give anyone gifts, but if our money went to the North American people we would be a little more satisfied with the whole arrangement, but our money goes into the vaults of the monopolies. That money serves as an instrument of oppression, used to prevent the enslaved people of the world from initiating their liberation. Cuba has paid 61 cents in interest for every single dollar loaned by the United States and this is only short term—just imagine what it would be over a long term if we had received a loan similar to that of the Soviet Union. That is why we have followed Martí's advice and tried to diversify our foreign trade as much as possible. We do not want to be tied to any one buyer. Our goal is to diversify our foreign trade and internal production in order to get more markets abroad.

## MEASURING THE SUBSIDY

Estimating of the subsidy element in Soviet purchases of Cuban sugar requires establishing the price at which Cuba could have sold its sugar to alternative buyers in the absence of sales to the Soviet Union, that is, the "opportunity price." Most of the disagreement among authors over subsidy estimates for specific years, and over the cumulative size of the subsidy, arise from differences in assumptions about the hypothetical price at which Cuba would have sold its sugar had sales to the Soviet Union not occurred.

A second methodological issue that affects subsidy estimates relates to exchange rates. Methods rely on a comparison between the price the Soviet Union pays for Cuban sugar—or Cuba receives from the Soviet Union—and the price in some alternative market. While the price (import unit value) at which the Soviet Union buys Cuban sugar is denominated in rubles and the price (export unit value) Cuba receives is denominated in pesos, prices in alternative markets are generally denominated in U.S. dollars. The question is, then: What is the appropriate exchange rate to convert either rubles or pesos to dollars (or vice versa) in order to make the required comparisons?

Available estimates of the Soviet sugar subsidy have generally relied on *official* exchange rates. Conventional wisdom has it that these far overstate the value of the ruble or the peso vis-à-vis the dollar or other convertible currencies, but there is no consensus on a more realistic rate. In practical terms, use of official (overvalued) exchange rates to estimate subsidies tends to overstate the price paid by the Soviet Union, or received by Cuba, in bilateral sugar trade, the difference between this price and the price in an alternative market (i.e., the subsidy margin), and the overall estimated magnitude of the subsidy.

### WORLD MARKET PRICE

Estimates of the subsidy payments to Cuba by the Soviet Union related to the purchase of sugar have been made by the U.S. Central Intelligence Agency (CIA) since at least the mid 1970s (USCIA, 1975, 15; 1976, 14; 1981, 39; 1984, 40). Essentially, the CIA calculates the subsidy as the difference between the price at which Cuba sells sugar to the Soviet Union, converted to U.S. dollars at the official exchange rate, and the average world market price for sugar.

This method implicitly assumes that the world market price is the standard against which the opportunity cost incurred by the Soviet Union in purchasing Cuban sugar—rather than sugar available in the world market—is to be measured. Lending credence to this assumption, a well-known sugar expert finds that the world market price "is actively followed and analyzed as the closest equivalent to the opportunity cost of sugar" (Fry 1985, iii). Moreover, much to the dismay of domestic sugar interests in the United States, estimates of the U.S. sugar "quota premium" or subsidy have generally been based on the difference between the U.S. preferential price and the world market price (U.S. Congress 1962, 14).

The CIA has estimated that cumulative Soviet sugar subsidies to Cuba during 1961–83 amounted to nearly $17 billion, or about 50 percent of the estimated total Soviet economic assistance to Cuba over this period (USCIA 1984, 40). The CIA also notes that, unlike other forms of aid (e.g., balance of payments aid, project aid), the sugar subsidies are considered a grant and are not subject to repayment. Relying on the same methodology, Mesa-Lago and Gil (1989, 216) estimated cumulative Soviet sugar subsidies during 1960–84 at $19.5 billion, roughly 70 percent of total Soviet transfers in the form of price subsidies to Cuba during this time.

According to annual estimates made using the CIA methodology—that is, taking the difference between the unit value of Cuban sugar exports to the Soviet Union and the world market price (table 32) times the quantity of sugar sold to the Soviet Union in each year—Soviet sugar subsidies to Cuba during 1960–87 amounted to $29.4 billion; almost 98 percent of the subsidy ($28.7 billion) was bestowed after 1975, when Cuban sugar export prices began to be indexed annually. In 1987, the latest year for which the estimate can be made, the subsidy amounted to $2.7 billion, down from nearly $3.7 billion in 1986. The estimated subsidies for each year are reported in table 39, column 1.

OTHER PREFERENTIAL PRICES

Although the CIA estimates of the sugar subsidy have been widely used, they are not universally accepted. Some analysts have argued that they are flawed and significantly overestimate the magnitude of the Soviet subsidy (e.g., Radell 1983, 366–67; Zimbalist 1982, 141; Turits 1987, 174; Zimbalist and Eckstein 1987, 17).

Radell (1983, 366–67) notes that the world market for sugar is a residual market, used by exporting countries to dispose of material that can not be sold at (higher) preferential prices, and therefore world market prices are not representative of true opportunity costs. A more appropriate standard against which to gauge the opportunity cost of Cuban sugar exports to the Soviet Union, he argues, is another preferential price, for example, the U.S. import price.

Using the U.S. import price for sugar as a reference, Radell finds that Cuba received a "negative" subsidy in sugar sales to the Soviet Union—that is to say, the price at which Cuba sold sugar to the Soviet Union was lower than the one it would have received if the sugar had been sold to the United States at the average U.S. import price—in every year during 1960–63 and 1967–72. However, according to Radell, Soviet sugar subsidies to Cuba in 1975 and 1976 were quite significant, amounting to $288 million and slightly over $1 billion, respectively.

In support of this view, another author has estimated that, had Cuba sold to the United States, at U.S. preferential prices, the volume of sugar sold to the Soviet Union during 1962–72, these exports would have generated about $8.4 billion, compared to the estimated $7.6 billion Cuba actually received from the Soviet Union. Thus Cuban sugar export revenue would have been higher by $800 million had it traded sugar with the United States—at preferential prices—rather than with the Soviet Union (J. Smith 1984, 373–74).

Radell's estimates of Soviet sugar price subsidies to Cuba end with 1976. Estimates updated through 1987 (table 39, column 2) reveal very sizable Soviet sugar subsidies in every year during 1977–87. Over the period from 1960 to 1987, estimates of sugar subsidies to Cuba based on Radell's methodology (i.e., calculated on the basis of differences between the Soviet import unit value for sugar imports from Cuba in U.S. dollars, converted at the official exchange rate, and the average U.S. sugar import price, as given in table 32) amounted to nearly $26.8 billion. Over the period when the sugar price indexation mechanism was in effect (1975–87), the estimated subsidy reached almost $27.1 billion. (This is because under this methodology, the cumulative subsidy through 1974 was negative.)

Both, the Cuban sugar export unit value series to the Soviet Union and average U.S. import price (unit value) series in table 32 are affected by sales at (lower) nonpreferential prices (this occurrence is described in chapter 8). For this reason, alternative subsidy estimates have been made using as the opportunity price two measures purportedly unaffected by the influence of transactions at market prices: the U.S. preferential price and the preferential price at which the EEC purchased sugar from African, Caribbean, and Pacific nations (table 32).

Estimates of Soviet sugar price subsidies to Cuba based on the difference between the Soviet contract price and preferential prices in the United States and the EEC (table 39, columns 3 and 4) during 1961–87 amounted to $21.2 billion when the U.S. preferential price is used as the alternative price, and $24.5 billion when the EEC preferential price is used. For the period over which the price indexation mechanism has been in effect (1975–87), the estimated subsidy amounted to $22.4 billion when gauged against the U.S. preferential price, and $23.8 billion against the EEC preferential price. It should be noted that the preferential price series for the United States in table 32 is based on a landed price in New York, including duty, rather than on a price at the exporter's port. The Soviet contract price, and presumably the EEC preferential price, are the price at the exporter's port, excluding freight and duty. This difference in price basis tends to make each observation of the U.S. preferential price series higher than it would be if it were on an exporter's port basis, narrow the gap between the Soviet contract price and the U.S. preferential price, and understate estimates of Soviet sugar subsidies.

## PRICES PAID BY MARKET ECONOMIES

For similar reasons as Radell, Domínguez (1989, 290) also posits that the CIA methodology tends to overestimate Soviet sugar subsidies. He argues that a more realistic barometer of prices at which Cuba could have disposed of sugar not sold to the Soviet Union would be the price at which it sold to Western nations (Japan, Canada, Spain) under contract and in the spot market. Domínguez relies on Cuban trade statistics and estimates Soviet subsidies in terms of Cuban pesos, thereby avoiding the thorny issue of the appropriate exchange rate to convert to U.S. dollars. In what follows, his subsidy estimates in pesos have been converted to U.S. dollars at the official exchange rate in order to permit comparison with the other estimates.

Using the unit value of Cuban sugar sales to Canada, Spain, Japan, and "other" market economies as a hypothetical opportunity price, Domínguez calculates a "real weighted Soviet subsidy for Cuban sugar" (1989, 86–87). His approach yields dramatically different estimates from those obtained by other methods for certain years, for example, 1975, when the CIA estimates the Soviet subsidy at $577 million, Radell at $288 million, and Domínguez at a negative $316 million. In that year, while the price the Soviet Union paid for Cuban sugar was above the world market price, the U.S. average import price, and the U.S. and EEC preferential prices—a situation that would yield positive subsidies to Cuba under the CIA and Radell methodologies—it was substantially lower than that paid by Japan and Spain, and therefore Cuba incurred an opportunity cost, or a negative subsidy, in selling sugar to the Soviet Union.

Following the approach proposed by Domínguez, unit values of Cuban sugar export sales to the Soviet Union have been compared with two measures of alternative prices in Western markets (i.e., Japan, Canada, and Spain) in table 32: (1) a unit value series derived from official Cuban statistics on sugar sales to the three market economies (these data are not available for years prior to 1971); and (2) a composite price, constructed using official Cuban statistics on contract prices to the three countries, weighted by volume of actual sales (contract prices are available only for 1971–82).

Subsidy estimates developed using either of the two measures of prices in Western markets (table 39, columns 5 and 6) track each other quite closely but are strikingly different in some years from the estimates that use the world market price, the U.S. average import price, or the U.S. or EEC preferential price as the alternative price. In the 1980s these subsidy estimates approximate those obtained from comparing export prices to the Soviet Union with world market prices (table 39, column 1). As was discussed in chapter 8, the tendency for the two sets of estimates to converge arises from the fact that in the 1980s, Spain and Japan no longer purchased Cuban sugar through fixed-price contracts.

Interestingly, in the 1980s subsidy estimates based on export unit values to market economies tend to balloon out—and exceed those made by means of the other approaches—since average export prices to Japan and Canada were lower than alternative prices, including the world market price. (Official Cuban statistics do not record any sugar sales to Spain during 1983–87.)

Using the average unit value of sugar exports to Japan, Canada, and Spain as an alternative to the average price of exports to the Soviet Union, one can estimate the Soviet sugar subsidy to Cuba during 1971–87 at about $28.2 billion. For 1975–87 the estimated subsidy is $28.1 billion.

SOVIET IMPORT PRICE FROM OTHER NATIONS

Yet another way in which the Soviet sugar subsidy may be inferred is by focusing on the opportunity cost the Soviet Union incurs in purchasing sugar from Cuba—at preferential prices—rather than from other producing nations. Table 38 presented the unit values of Soviet sugar purchases from Cuba and from other nations during 1971–87. As is clear from those data, only in one year (1975) during the seventeen-year period did the average price the Soviet Union paid for Cuban sugar fall below that paid to other nations. (Official Soviet trade statistics show the totality of sugar imports originating from Cuba during 1960–71 and 1974, so that this comparison is not applicable.) Converting ruble unit values in table 38 to dollars at the official exchange rate, one can estimate that, by choosing to purchase sugar from Cuba rather than from other producers, the Soviet Union incurred additional costs amounting to nearly $28.4 billion during 1971–87 and $28.3 billion during 1975–87 and transferred these resources to Cuba. These estimates are given in column 7 of table 39.

## Comparing Subsidy Estimates

The empirical evidence is very strong that, at least since 1975, the Soviet Union has subsidized the Cuban economy through very high sugar prices. Disagreements among analysts over whether subsidies were present before 1975, and how large the subsidies have been, arise from different assumptions regarding the hypothetical price at which Cuba would have sold its sugar in the absence of sales to the Soviet Union.

Table 39 summarizes several possible measures, arrived at through different assumptions regarding a hypothetical or alternative price for Cuban sugar, of the magnitude of the subsidies the Soviet Union has bestowed on Cuba by virtue of preferential prices. It should be recalled that subsidy estimates in this table are all given in terms of a common currency, U.S. dollars, and that the conversion from rubles or pesos is made at official exchange rates. To the extent that the official peso/U.S. dollar or ruble/U.S. dollar exchange rate may be overvalued, calculations underlying table 39 may overestimate the magnitude of the subsidies (Turits 1987, 174; Zimbalist and Eckstein 1987, 17; Zimbalist 1988, 33).

At one extreme, one method assumes that, absent sales to the Soviet Union, Cuba would have disposed of that sugar in the world market at prevailing world market prices. Compared to the other methods, this approach yields the largest differences between actual

TABLE 39
ESTIMATES OF SOVIET SUGAR PRICE SUBSIDIES, 1960–1987
(in millions of dollars)

|  | World Market Price | U.S. Import Unit Value | Preferential Prices U.S. | Preferential Prices EEC | Cuban Exports to Market Economies Unit Value | Cuban Exports to Market Economies Constructed Price | Soviet Import Unit Value Differentials |
|---|---|---|---|---|---|---|---|
| 1960 | −1 | −77 | | | | | |
| 1961 | 77 | −97 | −161 | −111 | | | |
| 1962 | 54 | −68 | −110 | −71 | | | |
| 1963 | −49 | −12 | −44 | 8 | | | |
| 1964 | 15 | −15 | −34 | 15 | | | |
| 1965 | 211 | 11 | −35 | 16 | | | |
| 1966 | 169 | 11 | −35 | 7 | | | |
| 1967 | 218 | −9 | −64 | 14 | | | |
| 1968 | 164 | −15 | −57 | 41 | | | |
| 1969 | 77 | −17 | −49 | 30 | | | |
| 1970 | 150 | −61 | −134 | 70 | | | |
| 1971 | 48 | −34 | −84 | 33 | 43 | 43 | |
| 1972 | −23 | −44 | −72 | −16 | −10 | −19 | 7 |
| 1973 | 76 | 130 | 63 | 196 | 117 | 116 | 98 |
| 1974 | −463 | 9 | −429 | 391 | 15 | 14 | 0 |
| 1975 | 420 | 294 | 557 | 324 | −229 | −11 | −1,689 |
| 1976 | 1,076 | 1,024 | 1,181 | 1,080 | 693 | 865 | 1,003 |
| 1977 | 1,662 | 1,596 | 2,066 | 1,944 | 1,356 | 1,377 | 1,707 |
| 1978 | 2,457 | 2,458 | 2,330 | 2,228 | 2,477 | 2,430 | 2,430 |
| 1979 | 2,305 | 2,376 | 2,409 | 2,093 | 2,378 | 2,249 | 2,036 |
| 1980 | 1,133 | 1,606 | 1,042 | 1,524 | 1,411 | 1,146 | 1,862 |
| 1981 | 1,289 | 1,131 | 1,086 | 1,143 | 1,343 | 1,506 | 632 |
| 1982 | 2,501 | 2,088 | 1,862 | 2,037 | 2,483 | 2,518 | 2,319 |
| 1983 | 2,739 | 2,347 | 1,751 | 2,078 | 2,834 | | 2,712 |
| 1984 | 3,162 | 2,594 | 1,791 | 2,250 | 3,171 | | 3,552 |
| 1985 | 3,658 | 2,938 | 2,016 | 2,560 | 3,692 | | 3,649 |
| 1986 | 3,679 | 3,135 | 2,627 | 2,835 | 3,615 | | 3,875 |
| 1987 | 2,718 | 3,503 | 1,709 | 1,742 | 2,833 | | 4,201 |
| 1960–87 | 29,422 | 26,802 | 21,182[a] | 24,461[a] | | | |
| 1975–87 | 28,699 | 27,090 | 22,427 | 23,838 | 28,057 | | 28,289 |

a. 1961–87.

and hypothetical prices and therefore the largest subsidy estimates (table 39, column 1): $29.4 billion for the period 1960–87. The bulk of these subsidies occurred during 1975–87, when the estimated Soviet subsidy reached $28.7 billion. Since Cuban merchandise exports during that time amounted to about $67.8 billion, the estimated subsidy of $28.7 billion corresponded to roughly 42 percent of the total value of Cuban exports.

At the other extreme, several methods assume that the appropriate hypothetical price against which to gauge Soviet preferential prices is another preferential price (for example, the U.S. or EEC preferential price), the average U.S. import price, or the price of Cuban sugar exports to Western markets. These methods yield lower subsidy estimates (table 39, columns 2–6) than those obtained when the world market price is considered as the opportunity price. For 1975–87, estimated subsidies range from $22.4 to $28.1 billion, 33–41 percent of the value of merchandise exports. Estimates based on the difference between the average price the Soviet Union paid for Cuban sugar and for similar imports from other developing countries—$28.3 billion, or 42 percent of total merchandise exports for 1975–87—fall within the range of the other subsidy estimates.

A remarkable finding is how strongly all estimates point to very large transfers from the Soviet Union to Cuba in the form of sugar price subsidies from 1975 to 1987. To be sure, subsidy estimates for specific years, or for brief time spans, vary depending on which estimating method is used, but cumulative estimates are quite consistent, ranging from $23.8 to $28.7 billion over the years 1975–87, a striking result considering the crudeness of the data and methods used.

In light of these above estimates, it is useful to review Fidel Castro's only known reference to the size of the Soviet sugar subsidy cited above: (1) that the Soviet sugar price subsidy to Cuba is less than $1 million per day; and (2) that calculations that yield such subsidy estimates rely on the world market price of sugar as the alternative price, and, if a preferential price in another market were used as the reference price, the estimates would be much lower.

- Estimated subsidy levels in table 39 suggest that since 1976, Soviet sugar subsidy levels have far exceeded the $1 million per day mark. For 1976–80, they ranged from $4.7 to $5.0 million per day, depending on which alternative price is used to make the estimate. For the most recent three-year period (1985–87), subsidy levels ranged from about $6 to $9 million per day.

- Castro is on target when he states that subsidy estimates will vary with the alternative price assumed for Cuban sugar. Indeed, comparing the price paid by the Soviet Union to U.S. and EEC preferential prices does yield the lowest subsidy estimates. However, even when another preferential price is chosen as the alternative price, estimates yield very large subsidy levels, far exceeding the $1 million per day level. Thus in 1987, Soviet sugar subsidy estimates amount to $1.7 billion ($4.7 million per day) when the Soviet purchase price is compared with preferential prices either in the United States or in the EEC.

Finally, how do subsidies in Cuba's preferential sugar trade relationship with the United States compare with those granted by the Soviet Union? Estimates of the subsidy element in Cuban-U.S. sugar trade in table 31 indicate that the cumulative subsidy that accrued to Cuba over the years 1934–60 was $1.1 billion; the subsidy peaked at about $150 million in 1959 and had reached $137 million a year earlier. Regardless of which estimate of Soviet sugar subsidy is used (table 39), it is clear that since 1976 the Soviet subsidy has exceeded the peak U.S. subsidy by a factor of ten. The Soviet sugar subsidy in 1987, the most recent year for which it can be estimated, was 11–27 times the magnitude of the peak U.S. sugar subsidy to prerevolutionary Cuba.

# CHAPTER 10

•

## International Cooperation

Hagelberg has observed (1977, 5) that there is no commodity with a longer history of international agreements aimed at regulating production or prices than sugar. He attributes this dubious accomplishment to the very wide geographic spread of sugar production and the keen interest of governments in sugar production and trade for the purposes of tax collection. With the commercialization of beet sugar at the beginning of the nineteenth century, sugar production was no longer limited to the tropics: potentially every country in the world could have its own sugar industry, and many could go beyond import substitution to become exporters. Because sugar was an important source of revenue, European governments were deeply concerned with changes in the structure of sugar production and trade.

As early as 1864, Belgium, France, the Netherlands, and the United Kingdom negotiated an agreement to phase out subsidies on domestic production and export of sugar. This agreement did not take hold; similar pacts were negotiated in 1875 and 1888 but were not ratified. The Brussels Convention of 1902, signed by ten European countries, committed signatories to eliminate all direct and indirect production and export subsidies on sugar and to impose countervailing duties on imports from countries engaging in subsidization. The convention was extended in 1908 but rendered inoperative by World War I; it was formally annulled in 1920 (Hagelberg 1977, 5).

As a major producer and the premier exporter, Cuba has played a key role in international efforts to stabilize world sugar production and prices in the twentieth century. In 1926 it unilaterally reduced sugar production to try to prop up the world market and the following year convened an international meeting of exporters with the same objective. Cuba was a key participant in the 1929 Brussels Conference, which resulted in a four-year agreement to stabilize prices, as well as in the Chadbourne Agreement of 1931 and the International Sugar Agreements (ISA) of 1937 and 1953 and their extensions. From 1926 to 1958, Cuban sugar production was totally unrestricted in only twelve years, most of them in the periods of World War II and the Korean War.

Revolutionary Cuba has continued to be an important actor in the negotiation of international agreements on sugar price stabilization. It was a moving force behind the International Sugar Conferences held since the 1960s that have culminated in several ISAs. It should be noted, however, that since 1959, Cuba has not imposed restrictions on sugar output aimed at stabilizing world output and prices. Cuba has also been an active participant in the work of a number of international organizations that have attempted to stabilize commodity prices and improve the terms of trade of exporters of raw materials.

## Early Attempts at Price Stabilization

Cuba's sugar industry underwent very rapid expansion in the first quarter of the twentieth century. Production during the 1902–03 *zafra*, the first harvest after the establishment of the Cuban Republic, was roughly 1 million tons; by comparison, the 1924–25 *zafra* resulted in production of over 5.3 million tons. Contributing to the expansion of production capacity and output were free-flowing U.S. investment and increased international demand for Cuban sugar as a result of abnormally low sugar production in war-torn Europe. In 1920 world market prices soared to an annual average of about 12 cents/pound, reaching as high as 22 cents/pound in May 1920 (compared to an annual average of 2–5 cents/pound in 1902–19), and prosperity reigned in Cuba, the so-called *danza de los millones* (Silva León 1975, 19).

It was a short-lived dance, however. By 1925 world sugar stocks had risen to very high levels, Cuban output had increased substantially—as had that of new suppliers (Puerto Rico, Java, the Philippines)—and the European sugar industry had recovered. The result was a market glut and the plummeting of prices.

In 1926, Cuba took the very painful step of unilaterally reducing sugar production (and exports) to try to prop up the world market. The Verdeja Act of May 1926 limited production by each major sugar mill to 90 percent of recent output, granted the government the authority to determine the beginning and ending dates of *zafras,* and empowered the executive to limit output of subsequent *zafras.* As is clear from table 40, the restrictive actions taken in 1926 were only the

TABLE 40
SUGAR PRODUCTION RESTRICTIONS, 1920–1958
(in thousands of metric tons)

| | Zafra Status | Output | % of World Market |
|---|---|---|---|
| 1920–24 | Free | 4,010.6 | 22.3 |
| 1925 | Free | 5,347.1 | 21.4 |
| 1926 | Restricted[a] | 5,082.0 | 20.1 |
| 1927 | Restricted | 4,645.7 | 18.7 |
| 1928 | Restricted | 4,164.7 | 15.4 |
| 1929 | Free | 5,313.0 | 19.8 |
| 1930 | Free/Restricted[b] | 4,813.0 | 16.6 |
| 1931 | Restricted | 3,215.0 | 11.2 |
| 1932 | Restricted | 2,683.5 | 10.2 |
| 1933 | Restricted | 2,003.3 | 8.5 |
| 1934 | Restricted | 2,324.4 | 9.2 |
| 1935 | Restricted | 2,615.1 | 10.1 |
| 1936 | Restricted | 2,634.7 | 9.3 |
| 1937 | Restricted | 3,065.0 | 10.1 |
| 1938 | Restricted[c] | 3,066.4 | 10.1 |
| 1939 | Restricted[d] | 2,806.6 | 9.6 |
| 1940 | Restricted | 2,863.8 | 9.2 |
| 1941 | Restricted | 2,480.1 | 8.0 |
| 1942 | Free | 3,446.7 | 12.1 |
| 1943 | Restricted[e] | 2,929.5 | 10.8 |
| 1944 | Free | 4,370.8 | 15.9 |
| 1945 | Free | 3,610.3 | 15.3 |
| 1946 | Free | 4,117.9 | 18.1 |
| 1947 | Free | 5,932.5 | 21.5 |
| 1948 | Free | 6,141.0 | 21.3 |
| 1949 | Free | 5,302.1 | 16.3 |
| 1950 | Free | 5,636.0 | 17.0 |
| 1951 | Free | 5,840.5 | 15.7 |
| 1952 | Free | 7,326.6 | 18.3 |
| 1953 | Restricted[f] | 5,159.2 | 13.2 |
| 1954 | Restricted[g] | 4,890.4 | 11.9 |
| 1955 | Restricted | 4,527.6 | 11.0 |
| 1956 | Restricted | 4,743.7 | 11.3 |
| 1957 | Free | 5,671.9 | 12.8 |
| 1958 | Restricted | 5,780.6 | 12.3 |

SOURCE: AAC 1958, 109, 96, 219, 223.
   a. Unilateral restrictions pursuant to the Verdeja Act.
   b. Chadbourne Agreement becomes effective.
   c. 1937 ISA becomes effective.
   d. Economic provisions of 1937 ISA are suspended, but Cuban production restrictions remain in place.
   e. Restrictions put in place because of high stocks and scarcity of ships (1943 only).
   f. Unilateral restrictions because of high stocks.
   g. 1953 ISA becomes effective.

beginning of a deliberate policy of production curbs that affected Cuban sugar output—with some exceptions—for the next thirty-three years. In 1927 the so-called Tarafa Act tightened government control over the sugar industry and created a permanent commission to determine annually a level of sugar exports that would not disrupt the international market. The commission was also charged with entering into discussions with other exporters to reach an international arrangement that would stabilize the world sugar market.

In November 1927, Cuba convened a meeting in Paris with representatives of sugar interests from Czechoslovakia, Poland, and Germany, at which the industries of these three nations agreed to reduce their sugar exports provided Cuba continued to exercise self-restraint in production and exports. As nonsignatory countries not bound by the arrangement stepped up their sales, in mid 1928 Cuba announced it would no longer unilaterally restrict production and exports as of 1929 and called for the League of Nations to convene an international conference on the problems of the world sugar industry.

In April 1929 the League of Nations held a conference in Geneva to address sugar production and marketing problems. The conference did not come to an agreement but, on its heels, Cuba and several traditional exporting countries (Germany, Belgium, Poland, and Czechoslovakia) agreed in Brussels in June 1929 to a four-year arrangement aimed at limiting sugar exports and stabilizing world prices. Like its predecessor, this pact was unsuccessful in stabilizing prices because it failed to involve a number of key exporters.

In 1930, Cuba again imposed unilateral restrictions on sugar production and exports (Swerling 1951), using them to encourage international support for a global stabilization plan called the Chadbourne Agreement. In Brussels in 1931 the national sugar industries of Cuba, Czechoslovakia, Poland, Hungary, Belgium, Luxembourg, Germany, Indonesia, and the Netherlands, acting in a quasi-official capacity, signed a five-year stabilization agreement; subsequently Peru and Yugoslavia also became signatories.

The economic provisions of the Chadbourne Agreement (which followed the outlines of the Chadbourne plan) consisted of a system of export quotas to balance world production and consumption and stabilize prices. Cuba was assigned a basic export quota to the free market ranging from 655,000 tons in 1930–31 to 855,000 tons in 1934–35, or about 16 percent of the anticipated free market sales of participants (table 41). Although Cuba's exports to the United States were not considered as part of the free market and therefore were not subject to the quota regime, a precedent followed in subsequent international sugar pacts, implementation of the Chadbourne Agreement meant a reduction of Cuba's sugar production on the order of 25 percent (Pérez-Cisneros 1957, 33). Sugar production in 1931, the first year after curbs were fully in effect, was about 3.2 million tons, compared to 4.8 million tons in 1930; for the 1930s, Cuba's share of world sugar output fell to below 10 percent, compared to about 20 percent in the 1920s.

## International Sugar Agreements

When the Chadbourne Agreement formally expired in September 1936, the situation in the world sugar market was not appreciably different from when the agreement was first concluded. Despite limitations on production and exports by signatories, price stabilization had not been achieved because nonmembers (both exporters and import-substituting countries) had increased their output. Moreover, world sugar consumption over this period had been adversely affected by the world depression.

In 1937 a group of twenty-two countries met in London to consider ways to stabilize the world sugar market. Out of these sessions emerged the first ISA, concluded in May 1937 and effective for five years. Twenty-one countries signed the final protocol: in addition to the ten signatories to the Chadbourne Agreement, South Africa, Australia, Brazil, China, the United States, France, Haiti, India, Portugal, the Dominican Republic, and the Soviet Union also signed the 1937 ISA.

Like the Chadbourne Agreement, the 1937 ISA was based on export quotas: export tonnages were allocated to individual producers annually according to a basic quota adjusted to reflect the expected size of the free market in the following year. Cuba's basic quota was 940,000 tons per annum, or about 26 percent of the anticipated size of the free market for participants in the agreement; in effect, because of annual adjustments, Cuba's quotas were 893,000 tons in 1937–38; 1,018,502 tons in 1938–39; 811,000 tons in 1939–40; and 876,000 in 1940–41.

Unlike its predecessor, however, the 1937 ISA sought to involve sugar consumers—who could also benefit from price stabilization—

TABLE 41
CUBA AND INTERNATIONAL SUGAR AGREEMENTS, 1930–1984
(in metric tons)

|  | Basic Quota | | Free Market Exports | |
|---|---|---|---|---|
|  | Volume | % of Total | Volume | % of Total |
| CHADBOURNE AGREEMENT | | | | |
| 1930–31 | 655,000 | 13.6 | 640,193 | 16.2 |
| 1931–32 | 805,000 | 16.3 | 928,555 | 26.6 |
| 1932–33 | 855,000 | 17.0 | 1,011,499 | 35.1 |
| 1933–34 | 855,000 | 16.6 | 801,296 | 32.8 |
| 1934–35 | 855,000 | 16.3 | 930,982 | 37.3 |
| 1937 ISA | | | | |
| 1937–38 | 940,000 | 25.9 | 897,674 | 29.6 |
| 1938–39 | 940,000 | 25.9 | 1,051,444 | 33.9 |
| 1939–40 | 940,000 | 25.9 | 769,959 | 28.2 |
| 1940–41 | 940,000 | 25.9 | 460,864 | 31.4 |
| 1953 ISA | | | | |
| 1954 | 2,250,000 | 42.3 | 1,871,820 | 50.5 |
| 1955 | 2,250,000 | 42.3 | 2,109,431 | 56.5 |
| 1956 | 2,250,000 | 42.3 | 2,795,398 | 61.1 |
| 1957 | 2,415,000 | 39.1 | 2,532,073 | |
| 1958 | 2,415,000 | 39.1 | 2,433,581 | |
| 1958 ISA | | | | |
| 1959 | 2,415,000 | 39.1 | | |
| 1960 | 2,415,000 | 39.1 | | |
| 1961 | 2,415,000 | 39.1 | | |
| 1962–63 | Suspended | | | |
| 1968 ISA | | | | |
| 1969 | 2,150,000 | 28.0 | 1,923,482 | 25.0 |
| 1970 | 2,150,000 | 28.0 | 2,103,210 | 23.7 |
| 1971 | 2,150,000 | 28.0 | 2,159,040 | 23.2 |
| 1972–73 | Suspended | | | |
| 1977 ISA | | | | |
| 1978 | 2,500,000 | 15.7 | 2,047,429 | 11.7 |
| 1979 | 2,500,000 | 15.7 | 2,159,040 | 11.3 |
| 1980–81 | Suspended | | | |
| 1982 | 2,827,000 | 14.2 | 1,696,852 | 7.8 |
| 1983 | 2,827,000 | 14.2 | 1,685,672 | 8.2 |
| 1984 | 2,827,000 | 14.2 | 1,420,589 | 13.5 |

SOURCES: Chadbourne Agreement—Pérez-Cisneros 1957, 31; 1937 ISA—Pérez-Cisneros 1957, 53; 1953 ISA—Pérez-Cisneros 1957, 104; 1958 ISA—Silva León 1975, 133, 160; 1968 and 1977 ISA—Fernández Font 1986, 173–81; and ISO, various issues.

and to increase the number of participants. The 1937 ISA was successful on both of these counts: its signatories accounted for 85 percent of sugar exports and 88 percent of consumption (Pérez-Cisneros 1957, 54). Like the Chadbourne Agreement, the 1937 ISA made a distinction between the world market and the "free market," the latter being defined as that part of the world market not covered by preferential agreements (such as U.S. imports from Cuba); the economic clauses of the agreement applied only to sugar movements in the free market.

Shortly after the outbreak of World War II, the economic provisions of the ISA were suspended. Cuba sold its entire sugar output from the 1942–47 *zafras* to the United States at fixed prices ranging from 2.65 cents/pound in 1942–44 to 4.96 cents/pound in 1947. After the war, sugar production worldwide recovered, but international sugar prices remained quite firm; prices were boosted temporarily to over 8 cents/pound in the summer of 1951 by the Korean War.

In response to war conditions, in 1942 Cuba suspended curbs on domestic sugar production. Although production curbs were briefly reintroduced in 1943 bcause of the scarcity of ships to transport sugar exports, the next nine years (1944–52) marked the only sustained period of unrestrained production in Cuba since 1925. Output recovered and Cuba's production accounted for about 20 percent of world output in 1946–48. In 1948, Cuba for the first time produced more than 6 million tons of sugar in a single *zafra,* a production level that remained the highest on record until the giant 1952 *zafra* of 7.3 million tons. However, the latter level of output represented only about 18 percent of world output, as sugar production worldwide was increasing rapidly (table 40).

At several international meetings held immediately after the war, Cuba advocated the concept of international agreements to stabilize primary commodity markets, especially the sugar market. Specifically, it proposed the reimposition of the economic provisions (i.e., the export quota system) of the 1937 ISA. However, because market prices were relatively high, other nations showed little interest in entering into restrictive agreements.

The situation changed in 1952 when Cuba, operating without restraints, produced a record high sugar crop of nearly 7.3 million tons. To prevent a market collapse, it set aside 1.75 million tons of sugar produced that year to be supplied to the market over the next five years, and it reintroduced production curbs effective with the 1953 *zafra*.

In June 1953 negotiations on a new ISA began in London. An agreement was concluded in August of that year and became effective 1 January 1954 for five years. The 1953 ISA was also based on export quotas, aimed at stabilizing world market prices within a given price band. Among its economic provisions were (United Nations 1953):

- the objective of the agreement was to stabilize prices in the range of 3.25 to 4.35 cents/pound;
- basic export quotas for each exporting country would be assigned on the basis of an estimate of the size of the free market (5.39 million tons);
- quotas for each country could vary from the basic assigned quota (either higher or lower) depending on whether the price stabilization objective was being met; in any event, quotas could not be set any lower than 80 percent of the basic quota;
- on the basis of a market of 5.39 million tons, Cuba's basic quota was set at 2.25 million tons, with the proviso that Cuba would be assigned the first 50,000 tons of any increase in free market demand; and
- Cuban exports to the United States were excluded from the free market and therefore were not subject to the agreement.

Cuban negotiators, government officials, economic commentators and a range of sugar interests (including the labor union representing sugar workers) hailed the 1953 ISA as being favorable to Cuba, highlighting the benefits to be gained from price stabilization and the very high share of the free market assigned to Cuba via the basic quota (2.25 million tons, or about 42 percent of the anticipated size of the world market—table 41). However, two commentators and sugar experts who were to occupy key economic positions in the revolutionary government—Raúl Cepero Bonilla, revolutionary Cuba's first head of the Ministry of Foreign Trade (Ministerio del Comercio Exterior), and Jacinto Torras, a vice minister in the same ministry—were critical of the pact. Cepero Bonilla argued that, by accepting a basic quota of 2.25 million tons of exports to the free market, Cuba had lost ground, since its free market exports had averaged 2.5 million tons in the previous five-year period (Pérez-Cisneros 1957, 95–96); Torras criticized the agreement the grounds, among others, that its estimate of the size of the free market—and therefore of Cuba's basic quota—was inflated and it lacked control over exports by the British Commonwealth (Torras 1977).

The 1953 ISA was in trouble even before it became effective. In December 1953 basic export quotas for 1954, the first year of operation of the pact, were cut by 15 percent to try to raise prices above the floor; they were again cut by 5 percent in May 1954—and reached the 20 percent reduction limit permitted by the agreement—but prices remained lower than the floor. Prices finally climbed above the floor price in 1955, after allocations for that year were set below anticipated basic levels. In November 1956, during a regularly scheduled review, several modifications were made to the agreement, among them the narrowing of the price band to 3.15–4.00 cents/pound and a readjustment of basic quotas; as a result of the latter, Cuba's basic export quota was increased to 2.415 million tons, or 40.9 percent of the free market estimated at 5.902 million tons. Prices surged in 1957 as a result of the Suez crisis, and the economic provisions of the agreement were suspended for part of that year.

In September–October 1958 a new ISA was negotiated. The 1958 ISA was essentially an extension of the 1953 agreement (as modified in 1956), with some minor changes. The new agreement was to become effective on 1 January 1959 and last for five years; the price band remained at 3.15–4.00 cents/pound; Cuba's basic quota (for the first three years) remained at 2.415 million tons, approximately 39 percent of the anticipated free market; and quotas for the last two years of the agreement were supposed to be established at a review conference to be held in 1961 (Grupo Cubano 1963, 990–92). The Cuban revolutionary government ratified the 1958 ISA in June 1959 (Silva León 1975, 165).

## Revolutionary Cuba and International Sugar Agreements

The shifts in Cuban sugar export patterns away from the United States and toward the Soviet Union, Eastern Europe, and the PRC in 1960–61 essentially brought down the 1958 ISA. In July 1960 the United States set the quota for imports of Cuban sugar at zero for the remainder of 1960 and for subsequent years. Suddenly Cuba lost a preferential market that had traditionally absorbed well over one-half of its sugar exports (53 percent during 1950–58) at higher than market prices. The Soviet Union and other socialist countries reacted by stepping up purchases of Cuban sugar, the Soviet Union committing itself to purchase 1 million tons annually. The United States, in turn, reallocated the quota formerly held by Cuba to over a dozen countries. The net effect of these actions was to shrink substantially the free market governed by the ISA (Mahler 1984, 717).

The conference held in Geneva in 1961 to allocate quotas for 1962 and 1963 under the 1958 ISA provided the first opportunity for revolutionary Cuba to express its views on sugar export policies and on the ISA. Cuba had already had strong differences of opinion with other ISA members regarding the treatment of the 1 million tons of sugar sold to the Soviet Union in 1960. Though most ISA signatories saw these sales as counting toward Cuba's quota for that year, Cuba insisted that they should not, because such sales: (1) were long-term sales; (2) were mostly payable with Soviet merchandise; (3) had not been taken into account when the original quotas had been allocated; and (4) were made to a country that had traditionally been a sugar-importing country and had committed itself not to reexport the sugar, thereby having no effect on the market (Cepero Bonilla 1962, 50). The ISA Council had decided to take up the issue of how to deal with Cuban sales to the Soviet Union in the context of the quota negotiations for 1962 and 1963.

The Cuban delegation, led by the minister of foreign trade, Raúl Cepero Bonilla, demanded an export quota of 6.8 million tons, significantly above the 5.65 million tons initially suggested by the conference (and based on Cuba's basic quota of 2.415 million tons plus an estimated quota to the United States of 3.235 million tons) or the 6.2 million tons offered as a compromise figure by other participants (Cepero Bonilla 1962, 54–56). Cuba reasoned that the lower quota levels would: (1) penalize Cuba for its growing exports to the Soviet Union; (2) reward countries that had benefited from the carving up of the former U.S. quota held by Cuba; and (3) not give Cuban sugar exports sufficient room to grow (Silva León 1975, 164–68). Since the differences between Cuba and other participants could not be bridged, the 1961 Geneva negotiations broke down. Beginning in 1962, the ISA was suspended except for its statistical functions.

To put the Cuban demands in perspective, it should be noted that Cuba's sugar *production* did not reach the *export* quota level it sought in any year during the 1960s—in fact, in 1963 and 1964, production was 3.9 and 4.5 million tons, respectively (table 8). As Hagelberg has pointed out (1979, 35), in the early 1960s, Cuba was able to maintain a reasonable level of exports, in the face of declining production, by disposing of sizable stocks in hand (over 1.2 million tons at the end of 1959, 1.1 million at the end of 1960, and 1.0 million at the end of

1961.) Prior to the late 1970s, Cuba had exceeded annual *production* of 6.8 million tons only twice (1952 and 1970), and, according to statistics of the ISO, it exceeded an annual rate of 6.8 million tons of sugar exports for the first time ever in 1978 (table 37).

World market prices fluctuated severely in the 1960s because the market was wholly unregulated. Prices climbed in 1963 to an average of 8.5 cents/pound in part because of low production in Cuba—production and exports in 1963 were only 3.9 and 3.5 million tons, respectively—but fell precipitously to 2.12 cents/pound in 1965 and remained at very low levels in subsequent years (1.92 cents/pound in 1966, 2.03 in 1967, and 1.98 in 1968).

In view of the increased price instability, a new attempt at an ISA was made in 1968. The resulting agreement, which became effective on 1 January 1969, partly fulfilled Cuba's main objective: it exempted from ISA control Cuban sugar sales to the Soviet Union and other socialist nations (except for sales to certain Eastern European nations beyond some specified levels). The economic provisions of the 1968 ISA included (International Sugar Agreement 1968):

- exemption from the ISA regime of sales made under "special arrangements," including exports under the Commonwealth Sugar Agreement and the Afro-Malagasy Sugar Agreement, exports by Cuba to socialist countries, and exports to the United States;
- a basic export tonnage allocation to Cuba of 2.15 million tons per annum for the first three years of the pact, roughly 28 percent of free market sales estimated at 7.689 million tons;
- a price objective in the range of 3.25–6.50 cents/pound; and
- a commitment on the part of suppliers to sell a certain amount of sugar to member countries at the ceiling price even if world market prices were to exceed that level.

The United States and the EEC chose to remain outside the 1968 ISA, the former because of objections to Cuban participation and the latter because of dissatisfaction with the size of the quota it was allowed under the pact.

A Cuban economist has judged the 1968 ISA negotiations a success since Cuba was able, for the first time, to obtain quota allocations beyond the level of free market sales in the previous five-year period (i.e., a basic quota of 2.15 million tons vs. actual free market exports averaging 1.523 million tons) (Silva León 1975, 172). He neglects to mention, however, that: (1) Cuban exports during 1964–68 were not restricted—since there was no ISA in place—and were held to low levels by Cuba's inability to produce sugar; and (2) the free market quota assigned to Cuba by the 1968 ISA was lower than the one Cuba had rejected during the failed 1962 negotiations (2.415 million tons).

As prices firmed up beginning in 1969 and gradually increased, the 1968 ISA's economic provisions were suspended. In 1973, with market prices in the 9–12 cents/pound range, producers and consumers met again in Geneva to renew the ISA for five years. Cuba proposed an agreement that would:(1) preserve the distinction between preferential and market sales and keep the former out of the control of the ISA; (2) increase Cuba's export quotas; (3) stabilize prices within a 6–9 cents/pound price range; and (4) establish a guaranteed access price of 11 cents/pound contingent on importing countries' acceptance of a minimum purchase price of 5 cents/pound (Silva León 1975, 179–82; Fernández Font 1986, 176–77).

The negotiations broke down, however, for sugar producers were unwilling to agree to a system of quotas in the face of strengthening sugar prices. The Cuban view was that negotiations failed because the industrial countries were unwilling to negotiate on two issues: a realistic price band, in line with production costs, and guaranteed minimum purchase levels to balance the commitment on the part of exporters to a maximum access price (Danilo Rodríguez 1978, 12).

The skyrocketing of world market prices in 1974, and their subsequent sudden drop, brought the parties to the negotiating table once again in 1977. Cuba now sought: (1) a three-year agreement; (2) a price band ranging from 15 to 25 cents/pound; (3) a larger quota for Cuba; and (4) assurances that preferential sales would not fall under the discipline of the ISA (Fernández Colino 1977a, 22–23). The first round of negotiations, held in Geneva in the spring, broke down over differences regarding the price range, the financing (by exporters) of reserve stocks, and the way in which quotas would be implemented (i.e., market share vs. absolute value quotas) (Alvarez Quiñones 1977, 1–3; Fernández Colino 1977b, 17). A second session, held in the fall, resulted in a new ISA.

The 1977 ISA, effective 1 January 1978 for five years, included the following economic provisions (Wasserman 1977; I. Smith 1983, 316–19):

- sales under "special arrangements" remained outside the agreement; all Cuban exports to CMEA members were designated as special arrangements, and sales of up to 650,000 tons to non-CMEA socialist countries (Albania, PRC, North Korea, Vietnam, and Yugoslavia) would

not be charged against Cuba's quota over the first two years of the agreement;
- Cuba was allocated a basic quota of 2.5 million tons, or about 16 percent of a free market estimated at 16 million tons; the basic quota could be reduced by 15–17.5 percent in the event the free market were lower than 16 million tons;
- a price range of 11–21 cents/pound (adjusted later to 12–22 and 13–23 cents/pound) was established; and
- producing countries were required to hold—and finance—stocks equivalent to ten percent of their assigned quotas.

Although the agreement seemed to differ substantially from Cuban objectives, Cuba's negotiator and minister of foreign trade, Marcelo Fernández Font, described the negotiations as a success and the agreement that emerged as "an effective instrument to regulate the market" (Salomón Llanes 1977a, 43).

The EEC again chose to remain outside the 1977 ISA, thereby permitting European producers to continue to rely on export subsidies to dispose of excess amounts of beet sugar in the world market and dooming the 1977 pact. In 1978, Australia and Brazil challenged the EEC's export subsidy regime before the General Agreement on Tariffs and Trade (GATT), arguing that such practices were in violation of Article 16 of GATT that outlaws export subsidies that "seriously prejudice" the interests of contracting parties (I. Smith 1981a). Several other exporters, including Cuba, joined in the GATT proceedings against the EEC (Tabío York 1982, 220–24). Partially in response to a GATT panel decision that found that EEC practices were indeed a source of uncertainty and constituted a threat of serious prejudice to other producers, the EEC modified aspects of its sugar program in 1981 (I. Smith 1981b), although apparently not to the satisfaction of Cuba and other exporting countries (Lazo 1982, 29–30).

In 1982 another round of negotiations on a new ISA began in Geneva, this time with the anticipated participation of the EEC in a final agreement. In order to permit sufficient time for negotiation, participants agreed to a two-year simple extension (i.e., through 31 December 1984) of the 1977 ISA. In May 1983, Cuba proposed a new ISA that would (Cabrizas Ruiz 1984, 90):

- continue to recognize the existence of preferential markets (e.g., Cuban sales to the Soviet Union and Eastern Europe) and exclude sales to them from the ISA;

- establish, and guarantee, minimum export levels;
- provide a mechanism to stabilize the market and world market prices;
- actively involve sugar importers so that they also would have to live by agreed rules; and
- grant special and preferential treatment to developing countries.

As the negotiations unfolded, the most contentious issue was the form that the regulatory mechanism was to take; Australia, Brazil, and Cuba favored a traditional type of ISA, based on export quotas, as opposed to the EEC approach of nationally held but internationally controlled buffer stocks (Navarrete 1983a; 1983b, 7–8; I. Smith 1985, 296). On the issue of preferential market sales, Australia and Cuba differed sharply, Australia arguing that Cuban exports to the Soviet Union and other centrally planned economies were important in determining the size of the world market and should fall under the regulatory mechanism of the ISA (I. Smith 1985, 297).

In an assessment of the negotiations, the Cuban minister of foreign trade, Cabrisas Ruiz, singled out EEC efforts to capture a large share of export quotas (by arguing that actual export performance should be used as the reference to determine allocations, a method that would tend to give the EEC large allocations since exports of its members were not restricted by the 1977 ISA) and Australian insistence that Cuban special arrangements with the Soviet Union be brought under the control of the ISA as the two issues that led to the failure of the negotiations (Lazo 1984, 47–48).

With the expiry of the 1977 ISA on 31 December 1984, the world sugar market once again became unregulated. An administrative arrangement, the 1984 ISA, devoid of economic provisions, was agreed to in order to maintain the operations of the ISO. The 1987 ISA, concluded in September 1987 and effective for three years (with a possible two-year renewal), is similarly an administrative agreement, without any economic clauses (UNCTAD 1987a).

## International Organizations

Revolutionary Cuba has been an active participant in organizations that have promoted reforms in the international economic system benefiting developing countries, among others the improvement of earnings for exports of raw materials through mechanisms such as indexation of commodity prices, and the negotiation of commodity agreements. Three such organizations that are relevant to international trade in sugar are the United Nations Conference on Trade and Development (UNCTAD), the Nonaligned Movement (NAM), and the Latin American and Caribbean Sugar Exporters Group (Grupo de Países Latinoamericanos y del Caribe Exportadores de Azúcar [GEPLACEA]).

UNCTAD

Established in 1964, UNCTAD has been a forum for developing countries to discuss issues related to the link between trade and development policies, particularly for raw material suppliers. The International Sugar Conferences that led to the 1968 ISA and subsequent agreements have been held under the auspices of UNCTAD.

UNCTAD was instrumental in the development of common positions among developing countries that culminated in the adoption by the United Nations General Assembly in 1974 of a set of proposals generally referred to as the New International Economic Order (NIEO). A key element of the NIEO was an Integrated Program for Commodities, aimed at stabilizing commodity prices, financed by a central facility or Common Fund. Cuba played an active role in UNCTAD activities aimed at implementing the NIEO through the North-South dialogue. Cuba has also played an active role in the so-called Group of 77 (or G-77), a coordinating group of developing countries within the United Nations system.

NONALIGNED MOVEMENT

Cuba has participated in the activities of the NAM since that group of countries was established in 1961 (Levi 1979). In the 1970s and 1980s, at a time when Cuba was particularly active in the NAM, the organization heavily promoted economic initiatives put forth by developing countries in the United Nations General Assembly, UNCTAD, and other fora (Cernic 1985, 7–14).

With regard to commodities, for example, the Economic Declaration adopted at the Sixth Summit of the NAM (held in Havana in September 1979) referred to the adverse terms of trade faced by primary commodity exporters and endorsed the Integrated Program for Commodities and the Common Fund (Willetts 1981, 150–54).

Problems faced by developing countries related to depressed international commodity prices were highlighted in Fidel Castro's report to the Seventh Summit Conference of the NAM (1983, 57–63) held in Algiers in 1983.

GEPLACEA

In November 1974, Mexico, Cuba, and eighteen other sugar-producing Latin American and Caribbean countries established GEPLACEA to coordinate policies related to prices and marketing of sugar (Reed 1979, 305–06). The principal objectives of GEPLACEA are (Grupo de Países 1987, 180–81) to:

- provide information and options to member countries that permit the adoption of common positions regarding the sugar industry;
- coordinate policies aimed at obtaining just prices for sugar exports;
- improve cooperation and exchanges of information among foreign trade organizations of member countries; and
- encourage exchanges of technical information regarding sugar agriculture, production of sugarcane by-products, and sugar production.

GEPLACEA has coordinated positions among member countries toward new ISAs beginning with that of 1977.

A founding member, Cuba has played an active role in GEPLACEA activities, hosting the Sixth Plenary Session of GEPLACEA in February 1977, a forum on the status and prospects of the Latin American and Caribbean sugar industries (Nocedo de León 1988, 62) at which members developed a common position for the 1977 ISA negotiations, and the Twenty-Third Plenary Session in October 1987. A Cuban official, Jorge Brioso Domínguez served as executive secretary of the organization from 1975 to 1978 (Vázquez, 1975), and two other Cuban officials served as assistant secretary for marketing and statistics from 1978 to 1981 and from 1981 to 1984.

# CHAPTER 11

## Assistance to Third World Nations

According to statistics of the Food and Agriculture Organization of the United Nations, sugarcane is an important agricultural crop in nearly one hundred developing countries in Africa, Asia, and Latin America. Sugar industries of developing countries vary widely in size and technological sophistication, depending on whether production is for domestic consumption or export, and on the stage of development of the nation.

Generally speaking, efficiency of Third World sugar industries is relatively low, particularly in African nations where independence and other political events resulted in sudden changes in property relations and led to the emigration of foreign technicians. Thus the sugar industries of the Third World are fertile ground for technical assistance in the areas of sugarcane agriculture, sugar production, organization, and human resource development.

A long tradition as a producer and exporter of sugar from sugarcane and a commitment to expand sugar output uniquely qualify Cuba to assist Third World nations in the development of their sugar industries. With an industrial base of over 150 sugar mills, 16 refineries, 7 bulk shipping terminals, and scores of plants producing alcohol, cattle feed, bagasse particleboard, paper, and other sugarcane by-products, Cuba's offers of assistance in sugar-related activities have credibility. Also bolstering its capabilities in this regard is a record of sugar-related research and a large pool of qualified workers ready and willing to undertake foreign assignment.

The impact of Cuban technical assistance on world sugar production and trade is difficult to assess with precision. To be sure, some of the nations whose sugar industries Cuba has assisted represent potential importers of sugar, including Cuban sugar. To the extent that these countries' industries gain in efficiency—and increase output—as a result of the assistance, Cuba may be foreclosing export possibilities. However, in most cases, it appears that Cuban assistance to date has had only marginal impact on production and trade flows.

This could change in the future, however, if Cuba were to become a supplier of turnkey sugar mills.

Cuba's willingness and ability to assist other Third World countries enhance its international stature and serve foreign policy objectives. Cuban technical assistance abroad might also translate into modest commercial benefits in the form of revenues from technical services performed or exports of machinery. On balance, however, Cuban sugar industry assistance to the Third World appears to respond to foreign policy rather than commercial considerations.

## Forms of Cuban Technical Assistance

Cuba's technical assistance abroad is coordinated by the State Committee on Economic Cooperation (Comité Estatal de Colaboración Económica). Established in November 1976, it is responsible for establishing and carrying out economic, scientific, and technical cooperation programs with foreign nations and international organizations. Prior to its establishment, these functions were carried out by the Commission on Economic and Scientific-Technical Cooperation (Comisión de Colaboración Económica y Científico Técnica) and the Ministry of Industrial Development (Ministerio de Desarrollo Industrial) (Gómez 1986b, 2).

Since the mid 1970s, Cuba has been assisting African, Asian, and Latin American countries in the development of their sugar industries. Forms of assistance have included: (1) direct assistance by Cuban personnel, primarily in agricultural and industrial activities (e.g., maintenance and repair of sugar.mill machinery); (2) consulting services related to the construction, repair, or modernization of sugar mills; (3) on-the-job training of host country technicians or skilled workers by visiting Cuban experts; and (4) training in Cuba of foreign sugar technicians and skilled workers. In several instances there is evidence of exports of Cuban-made sugar industry machinery and equipment; this development is to be expected since in designing and maintaining foreign mills, Cuban technicians may have a tendency to specify Cuban-made equipment they are familiar with.

TECNOAZUCAR, the enterprise responsible for providing engineering and technical services to the Cuban sugar industry, provides these services to foreign nations as well (Lazo 1983, 32–33). TECNOAZUCAR is supported by seven specialized enterprises:

- Instituto de Proyectos Azucareros (IPROYAZ)—design, basic engineering, and supervision of construction of industrial facilities.
- Instituto Cubano de Investigaciones Azucareras (ICINAZ)—applied research on sugar technology.
- Instituto Cubano de Investigaciones de los Derivados de la Caña de Azúcar (ICIDCA)—applied research on commercialization of sugarcane by-products.
- Empresa de Automatización Industrial (EDA)—automated management and control systems.
- Union de Empresas de Producción Mecánica (UEMPROMEC)—production of machinery and equipment including agricultural equipment and industrial equipment such as crystallizers, juice heaters, evaporators, pumps, clarifiers, and vacuum pumps.
- Empresa de Construcción y Montaje (ECMI)—construction of sugar mills and bulk shipping terminals.
- Empresa de Procesamiento de Datos de la Industria Azucarera (DATAZUCAR)—support for automated management and control systems for agriculture and industry, including training of personnel.

Whether Cuba receives payment for technical services provided abroad is unclear. According to Cuban sources, through 1977 all civilian assistance to developing countries was free (Felipe 1985, 88). Around 1978, however, Cuba began to offer some for-pay services to countries in a position to pay, for example, oil-exporting countries. Thus it has been reported that since the late 1970s, Cuba has followed a two-tier policy regarding compensation for civilian services performed abroad (Martínez Salsamendi 1984, 144-45):

- Free services: Provided to less developed countries or to those countries that face economic hardship. In general, recipient countries are responsible only for living expenses of Cuban specialists; Cuba pays salaries of workers on foreign assignment in domestic currency (i.e., pesos).
- For-pay services: Provided to countries with the ability to pay. Recipient countries are responsible for all expenses, including salaries, generally payable in convertible currency.

The bulk of Cuba's technical services is reportedly provided free.

## Sugar Industry Assistance

The earliest reference to the sugar industry as an area for Cuban bilateral assistance was in cooperation agreements signed with Somalia and the Congo in 1974. Cuban collaboration with Mexico in sugar-related operations also began in the mid 1970s. Overall, Cuba has lent assistance to the sugar industries of at least fourteen developing countries in Africa (Angola, Benin, Burundi, Congo, Ethiopia, Ghana, Guinea-Bissau, Madagascar, Mauritania, Mozambique, Nigeria, Somalia, Tanzania, and Uganda), six in Latin America (Colombia, Guyana, Jamaica, Mexico, Nicaragua, and Panama), and three in Asia (Laos, Sri Lanka, and Vietnam). In addition, it has been reported that Zaire has discussed with Cuban officials the possibility of assistance in a plan to increase sugar production (Simón 1987).

NICARAGUA

TECNOAZUCAR's most significant activities abroad to date have been in Nicaragua (Abascal López, 1985; Paneque Brizuelas, 1983; Varela Pérez, 1985b; 1985c). In September 1980 the Nicaraguan Ministry of Agricultural Development contracted with TECNOAZUCAR and IPROYAZ to conduct a study to determine the optimal location for a projected agro-industrial sugar complex. Cuban specialists carried out an economic feasibility study and determined that the Tipitapa-Malacatoya region offered the best possibilities. Cuban specialists began preparation of fields for sugarcane cultivation and breaking ground for construction of the Victoria de Julio mill in early 1982.

Cuban technicians were responsible for the design, construction, and start-up of the new mill. In addition to the industrial plant, similar in design to the new mills built in Cuba and capable of grinding 7,000 tons per twenty-four hours, Cuba also assisted in the construction of a dam and irrigation facilities to support sugarcane production. About 400 Cuban workers and technicians worked on the project over a three-year period, and some 700 skilled workers participated during shorter periods. Many of these workers had been involved in the construction of similar sugar mills in Cuba (Muy valiosa 1985). Cuba provided either 60 percent (F. Castro 1985b, 90) or 65 percent (Abascal López 1985, 46) of the mill's equipment.

Cuban assistance to Nicaragua in the design and construction of the Victoria de Julio agro-industrial sugar complex, including equipment and spare parts for the mill, was originally financed through a $50 million intergovernmental loan agreement (Recibe Fidel 1981; Cuba-Nicaragua 1982). At the mill's inauguration ceremony in January 1985, President Fidel Castro (1985b, 90–91) announced Cuba's decision to cancel the loan and donate all the labor, materials, and equipment to Nicaragua. Castro (ibid. 90) estimated the value of goods and services delivered by Cuba for the project at $75 million. The Victoria de Julio mill began operations in April 1985. Cuba reportedly provided operators for sugarcane harvesters for the sugar mill's first *zafra* in 1986 (Serán manejadas 1976).

ANGOLA

In July 1976, MINAZ and the Angola State Secretariat for Industry and Energy signed a direct cooperation agreement establishing the bases for Cuban assistance to Angola in the development of the sugar industry. Cuban technicians were on hand for Angola's 1976–77 harvest, the first after Angola nationalized the sugar industry (F. Castro 1977). Their role was primarily to repair and maintain the four existing sugar mills (López Rivera 1977, 21). Cuban personnel also assisted Angolans in the preparation of fields and in sugarcane cultivation (Avilés 1985, 35).

After disappointing harvests in 1981 and 1982—when sugar output reached only about 30 percent of targets—the Angolan government signed a new agreement with Cuba to increase the level of assistance. Large numbers of Cuban technicians began to arrive in Angola in mid 1983 and were assigned to three of the four existing sugar mills. Under the direction of Cuban specialists, production systems were reorganized, idle equipment repaired, fields prepared for mechanized harvesting, new chemical analysis techniques introduced, and machinery overhauled. Intensive training of Angolan personnel was also instituted (R. Martínez 1983b).

According to a press report, late in 1978 the Angolan government was dissatisfied with Cuban technical assistance in a number of areas of the economy, including the sugar industry, and was seeking aid from Western nations. Of the sugar industry, the report said (Lamb 1978, 7):

> Economists say the Cubans also initially took over the sugar refineries but were unable to run them properly because the equipment the Portuguese left behind was 20 years ahead of what the Cubans were using at home. There, too, [Angolan President Agostinho] Neto is now looking for Western assistance.

MOZAMBIQUE

Cuban assistance to the Mozambican sugar industry began in December 1977 with the arrival of the first group of Cuban technicians, who were initially assigned to direct the operation and maintenance of three sugar mills at that time already under state control. When the Marromeu sugar mill, one of the principal mills, was nationalized, Cuban technicians assumed similar responsibilities there and were instrumental in restarting the mill in 1979.

Cuban technicians have also been involved in organizing and managing sugarcane cultivation and harvesting operations. Cuban-manufactured sugar machinery and equipment have been exported to Mozambique (J. Rodríguez 1983, 42–43). In 1984 the Cuban enterprise IMEXPAL (Empresa Importadora y Exportadora de Plantas Alimentarias) began a series of studies to determine how to optimize sugar production in six Mozambican mills (Experiencia 1984).

ETHIOPIA

Cuban assistance to the Ethiopian sugar industry began in the late 1970s. An agreement concluded in April 1977 provided for training in Cuba of Ethiopian sugar production engineers, chemists, and technicians, and for on-site technical assistance to the Ethiopian Sugar Corporation (ACR 1979–80, B213; Hidalgo 1978, 9). During the academic year 1982–83, Cuba reported that two Ethiopian students graduated from Cuban university-level institutions with degrees in sugar-related disciplines (Lechuga 1982, 38). Several score of Ethiopian sugar technicians have received training in Cuba in management of production processes and in sugar handling (Díaz-Vázquez 1982, 33). Cuban technicians (welders, boilermakers) built three vacuum pans in Ethiopia for the Metahara sugar mill, one of three mills in the country (Carriba 1981).

In 1983 there were twenty-one Cuban engineers and technicians in Ethiopia engaged in sugar industrial and agricultural activities. Cuban technicians were also collaborating with their Ethiopian counterparts in the expansion of the Shoa sugar mill, including the improvement of irrigation systems; it was anticipated that Cuba would supply machinery and equipment for the project (J. Rodríguez 1983, 44).

MEXICO

Cuban-Mexican cooperation in science and technology began in September 1974 with the signature of a government-to-government framework agreement. The Mexican National Science and Technology Council (Consejo Nacional de Ciencia y Técnica) and Cuba's State Committee on Economic Cooperation were designated as the lead agencies in implementing the accord (M. Castro 1984, 22).

In December 1974, Cuba and Mexico entered into an "industrial complementarity" agreement dealing with, among other things, the production of machinery for the sugar industry (Entrevístanse 1974). Subsequently it was announced that Cuban and Mexican technicians would jointly design a sugar mill (Acuerdan 1975) and that Mexico and Cuba would build identical sugar mills relying primarily on each other's technological capabilities and domestically produced equipment (Fernández 1975). Although Cuba has built a number of new sugar mills, it appears that the Mexican twin was not built.

Since 1979 the emphasis of Cuban assistance to Mexico in the sugar sector has been on agriculture, information systems, and technology transfer. Cuban and Mexican scientists have collaborated on research to improve sugarcane varieties. Cuban specialists (from DATAZUCAR) have assisted Mexico in the installation of an automated system for planning and control of the sugar harvest (C. Martínez 1984, 22–23). Cuba has also exported to Mexico sugar harvesting machinery and *acopio* centers. Mexico has aided Cuba in the design of plants to produce the sugar derivative furfural.

In the 1980s, Cuba and Mexico were considering establishing a joint enterprise to produce sugar industry equipment for their respective markets and export to third markets (Díaz-Vázquez 1982, 40). They reportedly entered into a joint venture to sell domestically produced agricultural machinery in third markets (Zimbalist and Eckstein 1987, 17); most likely, among the joint venture's offerings are Cuban-made sugar industry machinery and equipment.

OTHERS

Cuba has also given assistance to the sugar industries of other Third World nations.

*Benin:* Assistance to Benin's sugar industry has been provided in the context of a basic economic and scientific-technical cooperation agreement signed in 1978. Technicians from Benin have pursued sugar-related studies in Cuban institutions (Carriba 1983).

*Burundi:* Cuban assistance to Burundi's sugar industry began in the 1980s as one of the programs supported by an Intergovernmental Economic and Scientific-Technical Cooperation Commission (Cuba-Burundi 1981; ACR 1980–81, B124). As part of the cooperation plan for 1982, Cuba offered training in Cuba for Burundian sugar technicians in sugarcane production (ACR 1984–85, B189). A cooperation protocol signed in October 1983 again identifies the sugar industry as one of the specific areas for Cuban assistance (Cuba-Burundi 1983; ACR 1983–84, B95).

*Congo:* In 1974, Cuba and the Congo entered into a technical, scientific, and cultural cooperation agreement whose objective was to "strengthen bilateral cooperation in the fields of education, health and sugar" (ACR 1974–75, B581). Cuban technicians arrived in the Congo in the mid-1970s to assist in the operation of the agro-industrial sugar complex at Ncayi (R. Martínez 1983a, 11).

*Ghana:* In the early 1980s, Cuba assisted Ghana in the rehabilitation of sugar mills (ACR 1983–84, B437). A protocol signed at the conclusion of the first meeting of the Cuban-Ghanaian Intergovernmental Commission for Economic and Scientific-Technical Cooperation, held in May–June 1983, identified the sugar industry as an area for Cuban assistance (Cuba-Ghana 1983). In mid 1985, the Ghana Sugar Estates Limited signed a contract with Cuban sugar officials regarding the rehabilitation of the Komenda sugar factory. In addition to overhauling the mill, which had been operating at low levels of capacity, Cuban experts were also to assist in the improvement of sugarcane fields (Cuban Sugar Factory 1985).

*Guyana:* Cuban economic assistance to Guyana, including aid related to the sugar industry, began in 1974 (Díaz-Vázquez 1982, 42). In the early 1980s the two countries were negotiating the export of parts and equipment for the Guyanese sugar industry (Colaboración 1983, 13).

*Jamaica:* During the tenure of the Manley government, Cuba gave assistance to the Jamaican sugar industry, primarily in the areas of production of sugarcane derivatives and control of sugarcane diseases (Díaz-Vázquez 1982, 42). Specifically, in the mid 1970s, Cuba provided consulting services on the production of paper from bagasse (Estrecharán 1975).

*Laos:* Cuban assistance to Laos has focused on sugarcane agriculture. Cuban specialists have worked with Laotian counterparts in the identification of cane varieties resistant to drought conditions and to *roya;* the two countries have exchanged high-yield varieties (Gómez 1986a, 29). In 1984 a student from Laos graduated from a Cuban institution of higher learning with a degree in sugar production engineering (Ayuda 1985, 30).

*Madagascar:* The sugar industry has been an important focus of Cuban assistance to Madagascar. Cuban technicians have worked in improving the Sirama mill, the main sugar-producing plant in the northeast region (ACR 1979–80, B257). Cuban personnel have assisted Madagascar in operating mills more efficiently since 1979; sugar technicians from Madagascar have received training in Cuban institutions (J. Rodríguez 1983, 44).

*Panama:* Cuba has assisted Panama in agricultural and industrial aspects of sugar production and has exported sugar industry equipment to that nation (Díaz-Vázquez 1982, 42). In 1975, Cuba donated an *acopio* center to Panama (Felipe 1985, 90). IMEXPAL has also sold spare parts for Panamanian sugar mills (Experiencia 1984, 42). It has also been reported that Cuba and Panama have established a joint sugar refining venture (Zimbalist and Eckstein 1987, 17).

*Somalia:* A scientific-technical cooperation agreement signed in June 1974 provided for the exchange of sugar industry specialists; a subsequent protocol, signed in July 1976, continued such arrangements (Pérez-López and Pérez-López 1980, 57, 78). (Cuban assistance programs in Somalia ended in 1977, when that country broke diplomatic relations with Cuba in response to Cuban military assistance to Ethiopia in the Ogaden War.)

*Sri Lanka:* Cuban specialists carried out a major technical assessment of the sugar industry, including recommendations to make it more efficient (J. Rodríguez 1983, 44).

*Tanzania:* Cuban assistance to the Tanzanian sugar industry, primarily in sugarcane agriculture, apparently began in the late 1970s (M. Rivero 1981, 28; ACR 1977–78, B416).

*Uganda:* In 1979 the Ugandan government reportedly sought Cuban assistance in restoring its crippled sugar industry (ACR 1979–80, B370). In the early 1980s, Cuba sent six technicians to assist in the rehabilitation of the Kinyara sugar works (ACR, 1982–83, B323).

*Vietnam:* Cuba has assisted Vietnam in the areas of sugarcane agriculture and processing. Cuban specialists carried out an economic feasibility study of the Thay-Ming sugar mill (Experiencia 1984, 42).

# CHAPTER 12

•

## Sugar and the Economy

AT THE HEART of the structural problems of the economy of prerevolutionary Cuba were heavy concentration on the production and export of a single commodity—sugar—and the consequent vulnerability to exogenous shocks arising from changes in the world market price for that commodity. Regino Boti, the first head of the Central Planning Board (Junta Central de Planificación) characterized the role of sugar in prerevolutionary Cuba thus (Boti 1961, 24): "The principal factor influencing the growth of the Cuban economy while it was dominated by imperialist monopolies was the volume and price of the sugar crop." Diversification of the agricultural and industrial sectors of the economy away from sugar was high among the economic priorities of the revolutionary government in power since 1959. To what extent have these structural problems been alleviated, or resolved, by economic policies of the revolutionary regime?

Assessing long-term structural changes of the Cuban economy is more difficult than meets the eye. For one thing, the statistical base has significant gaps. Reliable macroeconomic statistics for prerevolutionary Cuba are available only beginning with the late 1940s, when the newly created Banco Nacional de Cuba (BNC) began to publish such statistics; more recently, there is a gap in macroeconomic (and other) statistics for some of the early years of the revolution (e.g., 1960–61). Second, macroeconomic data available for prerevolutionary and revolutionary Cuba are largely not comparable. And third, the extraordinarily high prices the Soviet Union pays for Cuban sugar distort trade statistics, biasing estimates of the importance of sugar exports in relation to total exports.

Mindful of these serious methodological problems, I nevertheless explore in this chapter the question of whether sugar's role in the Cuban economy has changed significantly in the last twenty-five years or so. I do this by examining three aspects of the issue—specialization in production, export concentration, and effect of changes in world market prices of sugar on economic growth. The chapter closes with some tentative conclusions regarding the extent to which the role of sugar in the Cuban economy has changed as a result of policies implemented by the revolutionary government.

## Commodity Specialization

According to official estimates by the BNC, during 1949–58 the sugar sector (agriculture and industry) accounted for 28–29 percent of Cuban GNP (Mesa-Lago 1971, 278; Roca and Hernández 1972, 68). Although there is some evidence that sugar's share of GNP was following a downward trend—for example, it was 25 percent in 1957–58, two years in which sugar output and exports were quite high (table 37)—it is clear that prerevolutionary Cuba's economy was severely skewed toward sugar production and suffered from the economic ills associated with monoculture.

Reviewing the statistical record, Carmelo Mesa-Lago (1986, 301; 1981, 57) concludes that revolutionary Cuba has had little success in reducing the role of sugar in the economy. He points out that sugar's combined industrial/agricultural share of the global social product (GSP) has hovered around one-tenth, with only a slight tendency to decline; sugar's shares of GSP were almost identical in 1962 and 1981, 11.4 percent and 11.5 percent, respectively. (For more recent years, sugar's combined industrial/agricultural shares of GSP are: 1982, 11.0 percent; 1983, 9.9 percent; 1984, 10.3 percent; and 1985–1987, 10.1 percent [AEC 1987, 106, 113–14].) On the basis of these data and others, Mesa-Lago (1981, 64; 1986, 299) concludes that Cuba continues to have a monoculture economy and that sugar monoculture may have been more pronounced in the late 1970s than in prerevolutionary Cuba.

Using the same basic statistical record and his own estimates of Cuban economic performance, Claes Brundenius (1984, 67) draws diametrically opposite conclusions. Although he concedes that changes in the structure of production were modest during the 1960s, he argues that they accelerated during the 1970s. In his view, the relative importance of sugar in the Cuban economy has fallen sharply—according to his estimates, the share of Cuban gross domestic product (GDP) accounted for by sugar (agricultural and industrial operations combined) fell from 14.0 percent in 1970 to 7.9 percent in 1981. How to reconcile these two contradictory views?

MACROECONOMIC STATISTICS

Strictly speaking, it is not possible to trace the changes over time in Cuba's structure of production—and in the relative importance of sugar within the Cuban economy—because the appropriate data are not available (Mesa-Lago and Pérez-López 1985a). Cuban macroeconomic statistics for the prerevolutionary period were based on the System of National Accounts, the accounting system used by Western economies to measure economic activity. In the early 1960s, however, Cuba shifted to another accounting system, the Material Product System, used by centrally planned economies. Through 1959, then, the available measure of overall Cuban economic activity is GNP, whereas after 1962 the available measure is GSP. (Official statistics on macroeconomic activity for 1960 and 1961—under either system—have not been published.) GNP and GSP differ not only with respect to which sectors of the economy are covered (GSP excludes so-called nonproductive service sectors, such as education, housing, etc., which are included in GNP) but also with respect to the very concept of economic activity being measured: GSP includes the value of intermediate outputs, while GNP measures only value added.

In addition to the problem of the absence of a consistent base (i.e., GNP or GSP for both prerevolutionary and revolutionary periods) against which to gauge the development of sectors in the economy, there are other statistical problems that frustrate attempts to determine secular shifts in Cuba's production structure. In fact, a case could be made that the data limitations are so severe that it is not possible to measure with precision changes in the structure of Cuban production even for short time spans *within* the revolutionary period.

First, macroeconomic data for revolutionary Cuba reflect a mixture of sector data at constant and current prices. For some sectors (e.g., agriculture and industry, except for new products), internal prices were fixed in the early 1960s and therefore output of these sectors has been reported primarily at constant prices. For others (e.g., trade, transportation), however, output has been measured at current prices. Thus measures of the composition of output by sector tend to be distorted, with agriculture's and industry's shares probably understating the relative importance of these sectors relative to others.

A second major problem is that, over time, the methodology used by Cuban statisticians to value output has changed, so that consistent time series on the value of output for sectors of the economy, and for the economy at large, are not available. For example, the output valuation method in use during the period 1962–72 was "complete circulation" (*circulación completa*), roughly equivalent to the so-called gross turnover method, which is affected by double counting. Since 1977, the output valuation method in use for most sectors—but not for agriculture, which remains under *circulación completa*—is "enterprise exit" (*a salida de empresa*), equivalent to the so-called enterprise method, which avoids double counting. And third, the price reforms of 1981 (a wholesale price reform in January, followed by a retail price reform in December) introduce further discontinuities in the macroeconomic data; historical series based on the 1981 price structure have not been published.

Notwithstanding the macroeconomic data limitations, Mesa-Lago's contention that sugar continues to be one of the mainstays of the Cuban economy seems to be borne out by the available data. Whether the argument is posed in terms of the contribution of sugar to gross value of output generated by industry or agriculture (which would control for the problem of overvaluation of output of certain sectors, e.g., trade, which report data valued at current prices) or of the contribution of sugar (agriculture and industry) to GSP at current prices, the results are quite similar.

- Sugar's contribution to GVO of the agricultural sector has typically outweighed that of all other nonsugar agricultural activities combined. Data on GVO at current prices (table 5) suggest that sugar's share of agricultural GVO declined sharply after 1967. By 1986, sugar and nonsugar agriculture's shares were virtually identical at about 27 percent.
- However, if the same comparison is made in terms of GVO at constant prices of 1965—available from Cuban official statistics for the agricultural sector, with some gaps—a different picture emerges. The constant price data suggest that sugar gained in importance within agriculture during the 1970s and 1980s, compared to the 1960s. Thus, during 1971–85, sugar's share of agricultural output remained remarkably stable at around 37 percent; its contribution to agricultural output peaked in 1977 at 41.1 percent, and by 1985 it had declined by about 5 percentage points (table 5).
- Within industry, sugar trails only the food and the beverage and tobacco industries in terms of contribution to GVO at producer prices (table 9). No information is available on GVO for the industrial sector at constant prices, however.
- As was noted earlier, in the 1980s sugar industrial and agricultural operations combined accounted for about 10 percent of total GSP (at cur-

rent prices), about the same share they have held during the entire revolutionary period.

Brundenius's contention that the role of sugar in the Cuban economy has fallen precipitously relies on his estimates of the value of output of the sugar sector and of GDP. The methodology he uses appears to introduce a severe downward bias to sugar's share of GDP.

As was discussed above, Cuban official statistics indicate that in 1957–58, sugar accounted for about 25 percent of Cuban GNP. However, on the basis of Brundenius's estimates of the value of production of the sugar sector and of GDP (1984, 39, 174), sugar's share of GDP in 1958 is 12.8 percent, about one-half the share obtained from the official data. Sugar's share of GDP based on his estimates is 12.7 percent for 1959, 12.4 percent for 1960, and 13.7 percent for 1961. At least for these early years, when there is no suggestion that significant structural change had taken place and when sugar production and exports were high—production and exports averaged about 6.2 and 5.7 million tons, respectively (table 37)—Brundenius's estimates of the value of sugar output and of GDP impart a severe downward bias to sugar's share.

It is more difficult to assess whether his estimates for later periods are afflicted by the same biases since there are no comparable official statistics to gauge them against. Brundenius uses three different methodologies for estimating the value of output of the sugar sector and GDP for the periods 1946–61, 1961–68, and 1968–80. Sugar's share of GDP for 1961 based on the estimating methodology he used for 1946–61 is 13.7 percent, but it is 12.6 percent based on the one that he used for 1961–68. It appears, then, that the methodology he used for the more recent periods (1961–68 and 1968–80) also imparts a downward bias to sugar's share of GDP.

RESOURCES DEVOTED TO SUGAR PRODUCTION

Statistics on investment in sugar production (chapter 3) and on area devoted to sugarcane cultivation also support the view that sugar continues to be one of the mainstays of the economy of contemporary Cuba.

A pattern of heavy investment in sugar-related activities—both industrial and agricultural—is apparent. Disaggregated investment data are available only for the years since 1975. During 1975–87 the sugar industrial sector was the largest recipient of investment resources, averaging around 20 percent of total industrial investment (table 7). In 1985 nearly 24 percent of the value of investments in the industrial sector were related to the sugar industry; in 1986 and 1987 sugar's share of industrial investment fell to about 16 percent as investment priorities changed, with projects in electricity generation (including the Juraguá nuclear power plant) and nickel production taking up larger shares of investment resources. Similarly, investments in sugarcane agriculture have been high, taking about one-third of total agricultural investment.

As can be observed from table 42, area under sugarcane cultivation has increased through the 1970s and 1980s. In 1987, 1.778 million hectares of land were devoted to sugarcane cultivation. This is higher than the area devoted to sugarcane cultivation during the prerevolutionary period. The figure for 1987 was nearly 25 percent higher than in the prerevolutionary record-high crop year 1952.

Unfortunately, systematic official statistics are not available on total land under cultivation or on land devoted to other crops, and therefore it is not possible to make comparisons with land devoted to cane cultivation. Selected statistics available from the Food and Agriculture Organization of the United Nations suggest that the growth in area devoted to sugarcane has encroached on area devoted to other crops and intensified dependency on imported food products.

Table 43 presents statistics from the FAO on area under cultivation for three staple agricultural commodities: rice, beans, and corn. For beans and corn, area declined from the early 1960s, so that by 1987 land devoted to corn cultivation had declined by 52 percent relative to 1961 and to beans by about 13 percent relative to 1962. In 1961–62 about 160,000 hectares were devoted to rice production; this area dropped significantly through 1968—as more land was turned over to sugarcane production—and only began to recover in 1969. In the 1970s the area devoted to rice cultivation again matched that of 1961–62 and exceeded it during 1973–77. However, in the 1980s it again fell to levels around those of 1961–62.

FOOD PRODUCTION AND IMPORTS

Partially as a result of the concentration on sugarcane production, Cuban food imports have risen rapidly (table 44). Between 1970 and 1975, food imports (in value terms) more than doubled, from about

TABLE 42
AREA UNDER SUGARCANE CULTIVATION
(*in thousands of hectares*)

|  | *Area under Cultivation* |
|---|---|
| 1952 | 1,425 |
| 1953 | 1,605 |
| 1954 | 1,541 |
| 1955 | 1,444 |
| 1956 | 1,346 |
| 1957 | 1,323 |
| 1958 | 1,583 |
| 1961 | 1,340 |
| 1963 | 1,166 |
| 1968 | 1,417 |
| 1969 | 1,535 |
| 1970 | 1,504 |
| 1971 | 1,436 |
| 1972 | 1,389 |
| 1973 | 1,421 |
| 1974 | 1,450 |
| 1975 | 1,507 |
| 1976 | 1,533 |
| 1977 | 1,630 |
| 1978 | 1,640 |
| 1979 | 1,685 |
| 1980 | 1,659 |
| 1981 | 1,725 |
| 1982 | 1,752 |
| 1983 | 1,743 |
| 1984 | 1,750 |
| 1985 | 1,757 |
| 1986 | 1,763 |
| 1987 | 1,778 |

SOURCE: 1987—AEC 1987, 308; 1978–86—AEC 1986, 284; 1968–77—AEC 1977, 67; 1961, 1963—F. Castro 1976, 17; 1952–58—AAC 1958, 115.

*Notes:* Data for 1952–58 are given in source in *caballerías*; the conversion from *caballerías* to hectares was on the basis of 1 *caballería*= 13.42 hectares. Data for 1952–58 refer to land under sugarcane cultivation and available for each of the *zafras*; for 1968–87 the data refer to sugarcane plantings as of 31 December of the reported year.

TABLE 43
AREA UNDER CULTIVATION
FOR SELECTED CROPS
(*in thousands of hectares*)

|      | Rice | Beans | Corn |
| ---- | ---- | ----- | ---- |
| 1961 | 150  |       | 160  |
| 1962 | 164  | 40    | 153  |
| 1963 | 85   | 40    | 141  |
| 1964 | 71   | 40    | 132  |
| 1965 | 38   | 35    | 120  |
| 1966 | 32   | 35    | 127  |
| 1967 | 44   | 35    | 121  |
| 1968 | 88   | 35    | 120  |
| 1969 | 146  | 35    | 120  |
| 1970 | 128  | 35    | 120  |
| 1971 | 130  | 35    | 120  |
| 1972 | 140  | 35    | 130  |
| 1973 | 190  | 35    | 130  |
| 1974 | 195  | 35    | 130  |
| 1975 | 200  | 35    | 130  |
| 1976 | 205  | 35    | 76   |
| 1977 | 200  | 35    | 76   |
| 1978 | 154  | 35    | 76   |
| 1979 | 142  | 35    | 76   |
| 1980 | 169  | 35    | 77   |
| 1981 | 144  | 35    | 77   |
| 1982 | 143  | 35    | 77   |
| 1983 | 150  | 35    | 77   |
| 1984 | 161  | 35    | 77   |
| 1985 | 159  | 35    | 77   |
| 1986 | 171  | 35    | 77   |
| 1987 | 153  | 35    | 77   |

SOURCE: FAO, *Production Yearbook*, various years.

263 million to 595 million pesos; by 1980 they had reached over 745 million, and they peaked at 890 million in 1985. They fell sharply in 1986 to about 705 million pesos, as overall imports were slashed to try to improve the balance of payments situation, and recovered somewhat in 1987 when they reached 750 million pesos.

Food imports accounted for 15–20 percent of the value of imports during the 1970s, and 9–16 percent in the 1980s. The sharp drop in the 1980s is partially the result of the very high fuel import bill, which

TABLE 44
FOOD IMPORTS, 1970–1987
(in millions of pesos)

|      | Imports |          |        | Food as a % of |          |
|------|---------|----------|--------|----------------|----------|
|      |         |          |        | Total          | Nonfuel  |
|      | Total   | Nonfuel[a] | Food[b] | Imports       | Imports  |
| 1970 | 1,311.0 | 1,195.5  | 262.2  | 20.0           | 21.9     |
| 1975 | 3,113.1 | 2,792.5  | 594.8  | 19.1           | 21.3     |
| 1977 | 3,461.6 | 2,962.2  | 570.4  | 16.5           | 19.3     |
| 1978 | 3,573.8 | 2,917.4  | 596.3  | 16.7           | 20.4     |
| 1979 | 3,687.5 | 2,927.4  | 567.4  | 15.4           | 19.4     |
| 1980 | 4,627.0 | 3,715.5  | 746.1  | 16.1           | 20.1     |
| 1981 | 5,114.0 | 3,947.8  | 766.7  | 15.0           | 19.4     |
| 1982 | 5,530.6 | 4,032.7  | 810.6  | 14.7           | 20.1     |
| 1983 | 6,222.1 | 4,364.6  | 786.7  | 12.6           | 18.0     |
| 1984 | 7,227.5 | 5,008.4  | 822.5  | 11.4           | 16.4     |
| 1985 | 8,035.0 | 5,379.3  | 889.2  | 11.1           | 16.5     |
| 1986 | 7,596.1 | 5,062.6  | 708.9  | 9.3            | 14.0     |
| 1987 | 7,611.5 | 4,973.4  | 749.9  | 9.9            | 15.1     |

SOURCE: AEC 1987, 433 and earlier issues.
Note: Cuban trade statistics distributed by 1-digit SITC Section are available for other years as well. Data for those years are not reported here, however, because a very large percentage of the trade—up to 20 percent in some cases—is unallocated.
  a. Excludes Section 3 of the Standard Industrial Trade Classification (SITC), fuels and lubricants.
  b. SITC 0, food and live animals.

includes substantial volumes of fuel for reexport. Food products' share of nonfuel imports in the 1980s ranged from 14 to 20 percent.

Since 1962, Cuba has maintained a rationing system that limits goods available for purchase by consumers, including a wide range of food products. Partly through the rationing system, a significant change has been effected "in diet away from domestic pulses [beans] and root crops towards imported wheat-based foods such as bread" (Lehmann 1985, 257). Thus there is substantial pent-up consumer demand for food products. Absent the government monopoly over domestic and international commerce, food imports would have been substantially higher than reported in table 44.

Despite favorable agricultural conditions (in terms of climate and soil quality), Cuba ranks near the bottom among CMEA countries in terms of self-sufficiency in food production. A comparative study of CMEA nations published in the leading Cuban economic journal (Jurasek 1987) relied on different methodologies to assess the degree to which member nations produced food to meet the needs of their populations around the end of the 1970s. Regardless of which method was used—calculation of food supplies in terms of caloric content, gross food supplies in value terms, self-sufficiency measured in per capita consumption or in terms of consumption patterns in non-CMEA nations—Cuba ranked behind the Soviet Union, all six European CMEA nations (Bulgaria, Czechoslovakia, East Germany, Hungary, Poland, and Romania), Mongolia, and the CMEA average. Within CMEA, Cuba ranked ahead only of Vietnam in self-sufficiency in food production.

Table 45 presents statistics on domestic production and imports of selected food products: rice, beans, corn, milk, poultry meat, and meat products. Also reported in table 45 is the ratio of imports to apparent consumption (domestic production plus imports), or import penetration ratio, for each of these products.

For beans and corn, the dependence on imports climbed significantly from the 1960s (66 percent for beans in 1962–65 and 48 percent for corn in 1961–65) to the 1980s (over 80 percent for each in 1981–85 and 75–82 percent in 1986–87) as domestic production fell (corn) or stagnated (beans). Rice production increased steadily from the 1960s on, but imports remained quite high. The ratio of rice imports to apparent consumption declined from 50–60 percent in the 1960s to 40 percent in the first half of the 1970s, and to under 30 percent in the second half, where it remained during the 1980s.

With regard to milk and meats, the situation is mixed. Reliance on milk imports (in its powdered, condensed, and evaporated forms) reached over 45 percent of apparent consumption in 1966–75 and fell to about 26–29 percent in 1976–87. These figures understate the significance of imported milk because they do not take into account the milk-equivalent value of imported butter and cheeses and appear not to reflect substantial donations of powdered milk that Cuba has received through the United Nations World Food Program.

Production of poultry nearly tripled between 1974–75 and 1981–87 while imports increased at a slower rate, so that reliance on imports dropped from about 30 to under 20 percent. Domestic output of other meat products (beef, veal, mutton, pork) actually declined in the 1960s and 1970s, with some recovery in the 1980s. The reliance on imports (canned meats) to meet domestic consumption rose from

TABLE 45
PRODUCTION AND IMPORTS OF FOOD PRODUCTS FOR
SELECTED PERIODS, 1961–1987
*(in thousands of tons)*

|  | Domestic Production | Imports | Imports/ Consumption (%) |
|---|---|---|---|
| **RICE** | | | |
| 1961–65 | 152 | 228 | 60 |
| 1966–70 | 164 | 173 | 52 |
| 1971–75 | 374 | 246 | 40 |
| 1976–80 | 425 | 171 | 29 |
| 1981–85 | 516 | 207 | 29 |
| 1986–87 | 521 | 195 | 27 |
| **BEANS** | | | |
| 1962–65 | 29 | 56 | 66 |
| 1966–70 | 22 | 77 | 78 |
| 1971–75 | 24 | 92 | 80 |
| 1976–80 | 25 | 93 | 80 |
| 1981–85 | 27 | 116 | 81 |
| 1986–87 | 28 | 83 | 75 |
| **CORN** | | | |
| 1961–65 | 140 | 128 | 48 |
| 1966–70 | 118 | 158 | 57 |
| 1971–75 | 122 | 252 | 67 |
| 1976–80 | 95 | 397 | 81 |
| 1981–85 | 95 | 425 | 82 |
| 1986–87 | 95 | 440 | 82 |
| **MILK** | | | |
| 1965 | 462 | 285 | 38 |
| 1966–70 | 526 | 386 | 42 |
| 1971–75 | 545 | 492 | 47 |
| 1976–80 | 1128 | 455 | 29 |
| 1981–85 | 1116 | 397 | 26 |
| 1986–87 | 1114 | 414 | 27 |
| **POULTRY MEAT** | | | |
| 1974–75 | 35 | 14 | 29 |
| 1976–80 | 70 | 17 | 20 |
| 1981–85 | 95 | 22 | 19 |
| 1986–87 | 93 | 20 | 18 |
| **MEAT PRODUCTS** | | | |
| 1965 | 245[a] | 6 | 2[a] |
| 1966–70 | 240 | 20 | 8 |
| 1971–75 | 226 | 32 | 12 |
| 1976–80 | 203 | 30 | 13 |
| 1981–85 | 226 | 43 | 16 |
| 1986–87 | 240 | 35 | 13 |

SOURCE: Appendix 6.
a. Estimated.

about 2 percent in 1965 to 16 percent in 1981–85; it declined to about 13 percent in 1986–87. Poultry meat and egg production, and milk and other meat production to a lesser extent, depend on imported feed grains (Sánchez and Scobie 1986, 51).

Two international experts have given this assessment of the Cuban agricultural situation and Cuban dependency on imported products in the 1980s (Sánchez and Scobie 1986, 56–57):

> It is of interest to note that the strongest growth in food consumption has depended on imported foodstuffs. The big increase in livestock products (except beef), higher bean consumption and greatly expanded wheat consumption all depend directly on imports.
>
> The Cuban dependence on imported food has consequences for its non-farm sector. During the years 1979 and 1980 a severe austerity program reduced imports of capital goods and industrial raw materials to save foreign currency for essential food imports. This is a common feature among developing countries dependent on imported goods to sustain a food subsidy scheme. . . .
>
> The distortion in terms of trade [the very high prices paid by the Soviet Union for Cuban sugar] facing Cuban agriculture results in more sugar and less food crops being produced; this results in more imports (especially of rice and beans). At the same time the food rationing system lowers the price of staples and raises the consumption levels, further adding to import requirements. Finally the emphasis on livestock products and wheat consumption greatly increases food imports. . . . Imports of all major food groups are substantial.

## Export Concentration

The export orientation of the Cuban sugar industry has persisted through contemporary times. As has been discussed in chapter 8, over the period 1950–87, Cuba exported on average over 90 percent of its physical output of sugar. In the 1980s about 91 percent of sugar output was exported.

Moreover, the Cuban economy has depended on sugar for the lion's share of its export earnings. For every year from 1958 to 1987, sugar accounted for over 70 percent of the total value of exports, rising to over 85 percent in certain years. During the most recent four-year period (1984–87), it accounted for about 75 percent.

At a gathering of sugar workers in October 1980, President Fidel

Castro (1980a, 3) described the role of the sugar industry in Cuba's external sector:

> The sugar industry is the largest generator of foreign exchange, of soft currency as well as of freely convertible currency. The sugar industry is the great producer of foreign exchange, the producer of the resources the country needs in order to finance operation of the rest of the economy and the services sector. It is true that other sectors of the economy are growing, true that mining, tobacco, and fishing all contribute to the economy, and industry is contributing more, but nothing can be compared with the thousands of million pesos in foreign exchange contributed by the sugar industry.

## SUGAR WITHIN THE EXPORT BASKET

Concentrating on the record through the 1970s, several analysts (e.g., LeoGrande 1979, 8–9; Mesa-Lago 1981, 82–83; 1986, 301; Packenham 1986, 63; Roca 1988, 103) have argued that Cuba's dependency on sugar exports has continued unabated during the revolutionary period. That revolutionary Cuba has enjoyed very modest success in diversifying its export basket is confirmed by statistical measures published by UNCTAD for developed and developing nations.

UNCTAD's indexes of export concentration measure the relative concentration in the export structure of a country; index values range from 0 to 1, the latter indicating maximum concentration. Table 46 reproduces UNCTAD's export concentration indexes for Cuba and other Latin American nations for 1960, 1966, 1970, 1975, and 1983. The countries are listed in order of decreasing value of the concentration index in 1983.

Cuba's export concentration indexes not only tend to be very high in absolute terms (higher than .771 for each of the five years reported in table 46), but also are the highest for Latin America as a whole, with the exception of Suriname and Bolivia in 1960 and Uruguay in 1966. Thus Cuba and oil-exporting Venezuela were the Latin American countries whose export structure was most highly concentrated. At the other extreme, Brazil, Argentina, Peru, and Mexico (before oil exports became significant) tended to have the most diversified export structure in Latin America.

Analysts who have suggested that Cuban sugar export dependency continues to be high have been taken to task by Brundenius (1984, 62–63) for failing to consider that the value of sugar exports is

TABLE 46
EXPORT CONCENTRATION INDEXES

|  | 1960 | 1966 | 1970 | 1975 | 1983 |
|---|---|---|---|---|---|
| Cuba | .766 | .864[a] | .771 | .871 | .733 |
| Venezuela | .725 | .702 | .659 | .688 | .611 |
| Suriname | .821 | .754 | .728 | .491 | .543 |
| Ecuador | .644 | .650[b] | .495 | .564 | .532 |
| Mexico | .272 | .243 | .116 | .174 | .516 |
| Colombia | .743 | .664 | .622 | .530[e] | .488 |
| El Salvador | .712 | .500 | .472 | .448[e] | .488 |
| Bolivia | .795[c] | .738[d] | .542 | .444 | .483 |
| Guyana | .543 | .554 | .582 |  | .472 |
| Jamaica | .560 | .536 | .460 | .509[e] | .462 |
| Belize | .492 | .466 | .524 | .770 | .431 |
| Grenada |  |  | .610 | .565 | .431 |
| Dominican Republic | .541 | .598 | .519 | .563 | .430 |
| Costa Rica | .609 | .462 | .398 | .337[e] | .379 |
| Nicaragua | .460 | .517[a] | .275 | .313[e] | .375 |
| Honduras | .511 | .531 | .431 | .358[e] | .372 |
| Chile | .654[c] | .747[d] | .754 | .547[e] | .350 |
| Paraguay | .318[c] | .345[d] | .231 | .272 | .338 |
| Panama | .561[c] | .592 | .568 | .492 | .316 |
| Guatemala | .694 | .496 | .332 | .306 | .280 |
| Uruguay | .445[c] | .917[d] | .409 | .271[e] | .271 |
| Peru | .293[c] | .832[d] | .350 | .287 | .237 |
| Argentina | .300 | .322 | .222 | .164 | .212 |
| Haiti |  | .406[d] | .386 | .280[e] | .201 |
| Brazil | .580 | .463 | .335 | .237[e] | .133 |

SOURCE: UNCTAD 1985 and earlier issues.
  a. 1965.
  b. 1964.
  c. 1962.
  d. 1968.
  e. 1976.

distorted by fluctuations in the world market price of sugar and, more importantly, by the very high price the Soviet Union pays for Cuban sugar, two factors he claims tend to overstate sugar's contribution to the value of exports. These criticisms are also applicable to the work of economists in Cuba. For example, three recent studies by economists associated with the Cuban government (Díaz-Vázquez 1981, 141–42; Fernández Arner and Plá García 1982, 42; M. T. Valdés 1984, 132)

## Sugar and the Economy

### TABLE 47
### Sugar Export Shares Based on Total Exports and Nonfuel Exports, 1975–1987
*(in millions of pesos and percentages)*

|      | Total Exports | Fuel Exports | Nonfuel Exports | Sugar Exports | Sugar as a % of Total Exports | Sugar as a % of Nonfuel Exports |
|------|---------------|--------------|-----------------|---------------|-------------------------------|---------------------------------|
| 1975 | 2,952.2       | 2.7          | 2,949.5         | 2,655.9       | 90.0                          | 90.1                            |
| 1977 | 2,918.4       | 67.1         | 2,851.3         | 2,438.3       | 83.6                          | 85.5                            |
| 1978 | 3,440.1       | 46.0         | 3,394.1         | 2,981.1       | 86.7                          | 87.8                            |
| 1979 | 3,499.2       | 56.0         | 3,443.2         | 3,011.4       | 86.1                          | 87.5                            |
| 1980 | 3,966.7       | 168.4        | 3,798.3         | 3,327.3       | 83.8                          | 87.6                            |
| 1981 | 4,223.8       | 178.9        | 4,044.9         | 3,346.2       | 79.2                          | 82.7                            |
| 1982 | 4,933.2       | 338.3        | 4,594.9         | 3,813.1       | 77.3                          | 83.0                            |
| 1983 | 5,534.9       | 586.6        | 4,948.3         | 4,102.2       | 74.1                          | 82.9                            |
| 1984 | 5,476.5       | 573.9        | 4,902.6         | 4,130.6       | 75.4                          | 84.3                            |
| 1985 | 5,991.5       | 621.2        | 5,370.3         | 4,471.0       | 74.6                          | 83.3                            |
| 1986 | 5,321.5       | 269.1        | 5,052.4         | 4,105.7       | 77.2                          | 81.3                            |
| 1987 | 5,401.0       | 364.0        | 5,037.0         | 4,019.8       | 74.4                          | 79.8                            |

SOURCE: AEC 1987 and earlier issues.

use data on raw value of exports to make the point that Cuba's export basket consists of a very limited number of products.

Also relying on raw Cuban export statistics, Brundenius and Zimbalist (1985a, 41) have posited that in the 1980s sugar's share of the value of exports dropped significantly—to 79.1 percent in 1981, 77.1 percent in 1982, and 73.8 percent in 1983. More recently, Zimbalist and Eckstein (1987, 16) have made a similar argument, noting that sugar's share of the value of exports fell to 75.7 percent during 1983–84. The declining trend, in these authors' view, is evidence of substantial export diversification during the 1980s.

However, it is not taken into account by these analysts that part of the reduction in sugar's export share results from the anomalous situation whereby Cuban *reexports* of Soviet oil recently became a significant source of export revenue (Pérez-López 1987). If the official export data are adjusted to eliminate oil reexports (table 47), sugar's average export share during 1981–87 rises from 76.1 percent to 82.4 percent.

In a recent work, Zimbalist (1988, 24) accepts that part of the reduction in sugar's share of exports is attributable to oil reexports, but he claims that estimates such as those in table 47 understate the reduction because some of the reexported oil products (e.g., naphtha) are produced in Cuba. This appears to be a meaningless distinction. The overriding consideration is that domestic oil production accounts for a very small percentage of national needs, and the ability to export oil products is directly related to the ability to import oil and oil products from the Soviet Union.

INFLUENCE OF PRICE SUBSIDIES

The very high price the Soviet Union pays for certain Cuban imports, such as sugar and nickel, coupled with Cuba's reexports of Soviet oil, tend to distort official trade statistics and limit their usefulness in exploring secular changes in the composition of the export basket. Conceptually, adjusting the trade data to remove the impact of oil reexports is a straightforward procedure (see table 47). It is much more difficult to adjust the data to factor out the subsidy element from the prices the Soviet Union pays for Cuban imports. To do so requires decomposing the price at which Cuba sells products (sugar, nickel) to the Soviet Union into two components: a "normal" price at which the products are traded; and the subsidy or aid the Soviet Union grants to Cuba via price premiums. (In what follows, nickel sales to the Soviet Union are excluded.)

Chapter 10 discusses in considerable detail the issue of the sugar price subsidy and estimates a range of its possible values using several "opportunity prices": (1) the world market price; (2) the U.S. import price; (3) preferential prices in the United States and the EEC; (4) the price at which Cuba sold sugar to selected market economies (Canada, Japan, Spain) pursuant to contracts; and (5) the price at which the Soviet Union purchased sugar from other countries (e.g., Brazil, the Dominican Republic, the Philippines, Nicaragua.) The subsidy margins—and therefore the level of Soviet subsidization—are largest when the world market price is used as the opportunity price and lowest when preferential prices in either the United States or the EEC are used.

To illustrate the effect of the Soviet sugar price subsidies on the trade statistics, table 48 presents sets of estimates of sugar's share of total Cuban nonfuel exports derived from official trade statistics adjusted to extract the subsidies. These hypothetical estimates are subject to numerous caveats and should be treated merely as illustrative.

## TABLE 48
### Sugar Exports as a Share of Nonfuel Exports, 1962–1987
*(in percentages)*

*Alternative Valuations of Sugar*

|  | Actual | World Price | U.S. Import Unit Value | Preferential Prices U.S. | Preferential Prices EEC | Cuban Export Unit Value[a] | Soviet Import Unit Value |
|---|---|---|---|---|---|---|---|
| 1962 | 82.8 | 80.8 | 84.7 | 85.8 | 84.8 | | |
| 1963 | 86.8 | 87.9 | 87.1 | 87.8 | 86.6 | | |
| 1964 | 85.9 | 85.6 | 86.2 | 86.5 | 85.6 | | |
| 1965 | 85.8 | 79.6 | 85.6 | 86.5 | 85.5 | | |
| 1966 | 84.3 | 78.1 | 84.0 | 85.2 | 84.1 | | |
| 1967 | 71.1 | 60.2 | 71.4 | 73.5 | 70.5 | | |
| 1968 | 76.8 | 69.0 | 77.3 | 78.7 | 75.2 | | |
| 1969 | 75.6 | 72.4 | 76.2 | 77.2 | 74.4 | | |
| 1970 | 76.9 | 73.0 | 78.1 | 79.5 | 75.2 | | |
| 1971 | 76.4 | 75.0 | 77.3 | 78.5 | 75.5 | 75.2 | |
| 1972 | 72.8 | 73.5 | 74.1 | 74.9 | 73.3 | 73.1 | 72.5 |
| 1973 | 75.4 | 73.9 | 72.8 | 74.2 | 71.3 | 73.1 | 73.5 |
| 1974 | 86.5 | 88.5 | 86.5 | 88.4 | 84.2 | 86.4 | 86.5 |
| 1975 | 90.0 | 88.7 | 89.2 | 88.2 | 89.0 | 90.6 | 93.2 |
| 1976 | 88.1 | 82.1 | 82.6 | 81.2 | 82.1 | 84.8 | 82.7 |
| 1977 | 85.5 | 73.0 | 73.9 | 65.9 | 68.4 | 76.7 | 72.4 |
| 1978 | 87.8 | 73.3 | 73.3 | 74.9 | 76.0 | 73.0 | 73.6 |
| 1979 | 87.5 | 75.6 | 74.9 | 74.5 | 77.6 | 74.9 | 78.0 |
| 1980 | 87.6 | 84.3 | 82.3 | 84.6 | 82.7 | 83.2 | 81.0 |
| 1981 | 82.7 | 77.0 | 77.9 | 78.1 | 77.8 | 76.7 | 80.3 |
| 1982 | 83.0 | 68.9 | 72.6 | 74.3 | 73.0 | 69.0 | 70.6 |
| 1983 | 82.9 | 67.3 | 71.1 | 75.4 | 73.2 | 66.2 | 67.6 |
| 1984 | 84.3 | 63.3 | 70.4 | 76.7 | 73.5 | 63.2 | 56.1 |
| 1985 | 83.3 | 55.4 | 66.4 | 74.5 | 70.2 | 54.7 | 55.5 |
| 1986 | 81.3 | 46.7 | 61.5 | 67.1 | 65.1 | 54.2 | 48.9 |
| 1987 | 79.8 | 56.1 | 33.7 | 69.4 | 69.1 | 53.9 | [b] |

SOURCES: Actual—based on official trade data from AEC 1987 and earlier issues adjusted to extract sales of fuel exports (see table 47). Alternative valuations—based on official trade data adjusted to extract Soviet sugar price subsidies calculated from table 39.
a. Exports to Canada, Spain, and Japan.
b. Estimated subsidy for 1987 exceeds value of sugar exports.

Column 1 of Table 48 presents sugar's share of nonfuel exports as computed from the official (i.e., actual) trade data. Columns 2–7 contain estimates of sugar's share based on adjusted trade data, where the adjustment has been to assume that the sugar sold to the Soviet Union in each year was traded at some hypothetical price different from the actual price, that is to say, extract the estimated value of the Soviet sugar subsidy. For example, column 2 presents estimates of sugar's share assuming that Cuban sugar exports to the Soviet Union during each year were made at world market prices, while columns 4 and 5 do the same under the assumption that sales were effected at the prices the United States and the EEC paid to preferred exporters. For the calculations underlying table 48, subsidy estimates in dollars from table 39 were converted to pesos at official exchange rates.

The estimates of sugar's share of nonfuel exports in table 48 are quite close for 1962–75 regardless of which alternative price is used to value sugar exports to the Soviet Union. In fact, for some years (e.g., 1963, 1974), sugar shares derived using the world market price or the U.S. or EEC preferential price are higher than those derived from actual data. This is the case because actual prices in Cuban-Soviet sugar sales in those years were below prices in other markets, that is, Cuba subsidized sugar sales to the Soviet Union. The estimates in table 48 suggest that there was a dip in sugar's export share toward the end of the 1960s, but by the mid 1970s, Cuba's dependence on sugar for the generation of export revenues was probably at its peak.

After 1976, the year when a new pricing mechanism for Cuban sugar sales to the Soviet Union began to operate—a method that set a very high floor price, indexed annually proportionally to increases in the prices of Soviet exports to Cuba relative to the prices they commanded in 1975—and Soviet aid to Cuba via sugar price subsidies began to escalate, estimates of sugar's share of exports differ significantly depending on which hypothetical price is used. These differences are most acute for the 1980s: whereas the official data (i.e., including the subsidies) show sugar's share of exports at above 80 percent for 1981–87 (column 1), this share would have been under 65 percent had Cuba sold its exports to the Soviet Union at prevailing world market prices (column 2). However, if either the U.S. or EEC preferential prices were used as the hypothetical price for exports to the Soviet Union, sugar's share of exports for 1981–87 would have been around 75 percent (columns 4 and 5).

Even if the official trade data are adjusted to extract Soviet sugar price subsidies, the statistical record is quite strong that sugar continues to play a predominant role in the Cuban export basket. If one uses the U.S. preferential price as the hypothetical price at which to value exports to the Soviet Union—there is some logic in using this method since presumably it yields estimates comparable with those for the prerevolutionary period, when Cuba sold the bulk of its sugar exports to the United States at U.S. preferential prices—data in table 48 suggest that sugar's share of the value of exports in revolutionary Cuba has tended to behave cyclically, varying from 67 to 88 percent. Sugar's share of the value of exports was over 80 percent in 1962–66, dipped in 1967–73 to about 75 percent, recovered in 1974–76, and dropped again to the 75 percent range after 1977 (with the exception of 1980, when it climbed to nearly 85 percent and 1986 and 1987 when it fell to 67 and 69 percent, respectively).

Brundenius (1984, 75) and, more recently, Zimbalist (1988, 25–27) have argued that in order to gauge the true extent of production (and presumably of export) diversification that has taken place in revolutionary Cuba, it is necessary to express the value of sugar and other exports in constant prices. Doing so would "adjust for the manifold increase in sugar prices paid by the Soviet Union after the midseventies" (Zimbalist 1988, 25). Both authors have chosen the year 1965 as the base and derive constant price shares for principal export products. According to Zimbalist's calculations (1988, 27), constant price sugar export shares (based on the 1965 distribution of trade) were 84.5 percent in 1965, 86.7 in 1970, 82.2 in 1975, and about 88 percent in 1980; in the 1980s sugar's share declined gradually, reaching about 68–75 percent in 1985.

Trends in constant-price sugar export shares generally coincide with the adjusted sugar export shares derived by subtracting sugar subsidies from trade data (table 48). Conceptually, the constant price approach—which freezes prices of products in the export basket at the levels they commanded in 1965—appears to be more appropriate to address the impact of fluctuations in world market prices on the structure of output and exports than that of the high prices paid by the Soviet Union, as claimed by the proponents of this approach.

## World Prices and Economic Performance

International commodity markets are characterized by price volatility. Swings in world market prices can have a severe impact on export revenues, and on the economic performance, of countries specializing in commodity exports.

As is discussed in chapter 11, Cuba's efforts to stabilize world production and prices of sugar date from the 1920s. In 1926 it unilaterally reduced production to try to prop up world market prices, and the following year it convened the first international meeting of sugar exporters with the same purpose. Cuba was a key participant in the 1929 Brussels Conference, which resulted in a four-year agreement aimed at stabilizing international sugar prices, as well as in each of the ISAs that have been in effect since the early 1930s.

The volatility of international sugar prices has been demonstrated in table 28 by means of percentage changes in the world market price from year to year and from a trend line. Indices of commodity price instability developed by UNCTAD clearly point out that, over the period from 1962 to 1987, sugar showed by far the highest degree of price instability among primary commodities—a variation index of 74.0 percent (based on the percentage deviation from exponential trend levels), compared to 19.3 for all primary commodities, 28.7 for food products, 24.7 for tropical beverages, 17.8 for agricultural raw materials, and 16.3 percent for minerals, ores, and metals (table 49). For shorter periods (1962–80 or 1980–87), variation in sugar market prices also outstrip those of any other primary commodity.

A recent econometric study of Cuban sugar trade (Tan 1986, v–vi) has estimated the long-run elasticity of world sugar price with respect to Cuba's export share to be about –0.7 in the historical period. That is, a 1 percent increase (decrease) in Cuba's share of the world market induced a 0.7 percent decline (increase) in the world sugar price in nominal terms. Should Cuba succeed in its ambitious plans to increase sugar production over the rest of the century, and should demand for sugar from socialist nations fail to keep pace, substantial quantities of Cuban sugar are likely to gravitate toward the world market and put downward pressure on world prices to the detriment of Cuba and all exporting countries relying on the world market. One analyst (Turits 1987, 177) has questioned whether the Soviet Union can absorb increasing quantities of Cuban sugar exports implied by Cuba's ambitious production plans.

REEXPORTS BY SOCIALIST COUNTRIES

It has been suggested in the literature that Cuban trade with the Soviet Union and socialist nations may have added to world sugar

## TABLE 49
### INSTABILITY INDEXES IN MONTHLY MARKET PRICES FOR SELECTED PRIMARY COMMODITIES
*(percentage variation)*

|  | 1962–87 | 1962–80 | 1980–87 |
|---|---|---|---|
| ALL COMMODITIES | 19.3 | 15.2 | 7.0 |
| FOOD | 28.7 | 24.4 | 12.5 |
| Sugar | 74.0 | 67.4 | 36.0 |
| Rice | 30.5 | 23.2 | 11.2 |
| Palm kernels | 30.5 | 23.7 | 32.1 |
| Palm oil | 27.8 | 22.0 | 23.5 |
| Groundnuts | 27.9 | 17.6 | 11.6 |
| Maize | 20.2 | 17.2 | 11.9 |
| Palm kernel oil | 31.9 | 24.3 | 32.4 |
| Sunflower oil | 29.5 | 23.6 | 19.7 |
| Wheat | 23.0 | 21.8 | 5.9 |
| Copra | 31.3 | 25.9 | 32.5 |
| Coconut oil | 29.2 | 22.0 | 35.2 |
| Fishmeal | 26.3 | 22.4 | 12.7 |
| Soybean oil | 27.7 | 22.6 | 21.9 |
| Soybean meal | 21.5 | 17.2 | 10.3 |
| Groundnut oil | 27.2 | 18.9 | 25.9 |
| Soybeans | 21.0 | 16.9 | 9.5 |
| Beef | 14.4 | 11.7 | 5.3 |
| Bananas | 16.3 | 15.7 | 12.7 |
| Pepper | 20.4 | 14.5 | 22.7 |
| TROPICAL BEVERAGES | 24.7 | 25.5 | 12.4 |
| Tea | 21.4 | 20.9 | 19.0 |
| Cocoa | 32.9 | 27.7 | 10.3 |
| Coffee | 26.5 | 28.4 | 13.3 |
| AGRICULTURAL RAW MATERIALS | 17.8 | 16.6 | 8.6 |
| Linseed oil | 34.6 | 33.2 | 15.3 |
| Rubber | 24.7 | 25.9 | 14.7 |
| Cotton | 19.9 | 15.3 | 12.4 |
| Sisal | 36.6 | 41.3 | 4.6 |
| Wool | 24.1 | 26.3 | 9.6 |
| Hides and skins | 26.0 | 25.2 | 12.0 |
| Tropical timber | 16.6 | 16.9 | 8.7 |
| Jute | 16.4 | 10.4 | 30.4 |

TABLE 49
(continued)

|  | 1962–87 | 1962–80 | 1980–87 |
|---|---|---|---|
| MINERALS, ORES AND METALS | 16.3 | 12.3 | 5.9 |
| Tungsten | 48.5 | 30.0 | 9.5 |
| Tin | 26.9 | 21.5 | 14.7 |
| Lead | 31.1 | 20.9 | 19.3 |
| Phosphate rock | 37.3 | 34.4 | 8.4 |
| Copper | 21.5 | 23.1 | 9.1 |
| Manganese ore | 20.7 | 21.1 | 4.7 |
| Iron ore | 12.4 | 11.6 | 3.6 |
| Aluminum | 16.1 | 14.7 | 17.3 |
| Zinc | 26.0 | 26.5 | 9.5 |

SOURCE: UNCTAD 1987, 67.

price volatility because the latter reexported substantial amounts of Cuban sugar to the world market. Radell (1983, 373) has observed that the Soviet Union faces a chronic shortage of convertible currency; at times, it might have found it beneficial to import sugar from Cuba—bartered for Soviet products—to be reexported later to the world market for hard currencies. Moreover, such Soviet sales were often made at distressed prices, thereby depressing world market prices. According to Goldman (1967, 110), the Soviet Union often behaved in this manner in trading relations with developing countries in the 1960s:

> The second criticism of commodity repayment is that the Russians frequently resell the bartered merchandise for hard currency at a reduced price. By doing this the Russians, not the Indians [reference is to cashew nuts and other Indian commodity exports to the Soviet Union], obtain the hard currency, and the Indians face a reduced world price for the commodities that remain. Burma has had similar problems with its rice, as have Egypt with cotton and Cuba with sugar.

The evidence is very strong that, at least through the 1960s, imports of Cuban sugar by the Soviet Union and other socialist countries were not exclusively for internal consumption, and a share of those sugar imports were reexported (Sugar Economy 1974–75). According to one analyst, over 40 percent of the average 3.4 million tons of Cuban sugar exported annually to the socialist countries in 1961–68 were reexported (González Cofiño 1976, 696).

A second analyst states that during 1966–70 socialist countries (CMEA members plus the PRC) reexported to the world market about 52 percent of the sugar they imported from Cuba pursuant to long-term contracts. These resales increased the availability of sugar in the world market, contributed to lower world market prices, and affected Cuba's ability to generate hard currency from world market sales (J. T. Smith 1984, 369). Also referring to the 1966–70 period, a third analyst (Grissa 1976, 31) has written:

> It should be noted that the Comecon [CMEA] countries plus China reexport on the average the greater part of their sugar imports from Cuba. In 1966–70, the quantities reexported by these countries to the free market amounted to an annual average of 1,874 thousand tons of raw sugar. This was 56 percent of their average imports from Cuba.

Moreover, the issue of reexports of Cuban sugar by the Soviet Union and other socialist countries played an important role in the negotiation of the ISA of 1968. One of Cuba's objectives was to have its sales to the Soviet Union and socialist countries considered as taking place under "special arrangements" and thereby excluded from the world market, which would permit Cuba to retain its relatively large allocations to export to other nations (for hard currency). However, other exporters opposed the Cuban proposal, arguing that a substantial portion of Cuban sugar sales to socialist countries found its way into the world market. At the end of the negotiations, a compromise was struck (International Sugar Agreement 1968, 11):

> Under Article 36 [of the 1968 International Sugar Agreement] the exports of Cuba to socialist countries are not to be charged to its quota for the free market except in the particular circumstances discussed below. The U.S.S.R., Cuba's main export market, and a number of other socialist countries which import Cuban sugar, export or reexport large quantities to the free market. In 1966 and 1967, for instance, Cuba exported, on average, 1.54 million metric tons to the free market and 3.52 million tons to socialist countries, including 2.14 million to the U.S.S.R. The U.S.S.R., in turn, exported an average of 1.18 million tons, of which 1.04 million tons were shipped to the free market. Other socialist countries, so far as is known, exported about 1.7 million tons, mainly to the free market. . . .
> 
> Under the provisions of Article 39 [of the 1968 International Sugar

Agreement] the U.S.S.R. is to undertake, on becoming a party to the agreement as an importing member, to limit its total exports to the free market to 1.1 million tons in 1969. Any limitation on its exports to socialist countries is specifically excluded. . . . Article 36 provides that if Cuba's exports to Czechoslovakia, Hungary and Poland exceed 250,000 tons in any quota year, the excess will be charged to the Cuban quota. This should limit the extent to which these three countries could use Cuban sugar to make up shortfalls in their own production for export.

Exports, or reexports, by other socialist countries are not subject to regulation under the agreement, but it provides for an eventual indirect check on reexports to the free market by China (Mainland) and Eastern Germany which have accounted for most, but not all, of the remaining exports by socialist countries. In 1966 and 1967 their exports to the free market appear to have averaged nearly 600,000 tons. Article 36 states that if the exports of China (Mainland) and Eastern Germany to the free market exceed, in any quota year, 300,000 tons, the excess is to be deducted from the Cuban quota in effect for the following year but only if, and to the extent that, Cuba's exports to these countries in the same quota year were more than 910,000 tons. Cuban exports to them have not exceeded this figure since 1962 and in 1966–67 averaged 816,000 tons.

Table 50 presents statistics for 1960–87 on Soviet and PRC sugar exports and on the magnitude of such exports relative to imports from Cuba. Since over this period both the Soviet Union and the PRC were net sugar importers, and important markets for Cuban sugar, their sugar exports represent, to a large extent, reexported Cuban sugar.

Data in table 50 suggest very strongly that in the 1960s and early 1970s, the Soviet Union exported a significant proportion of the sugar it imported from Cuba: as high as 92.3 percent in 1963, 104.2 in 1969 (meaning that Soviet exports exceeded total imports from Cuba), and 91.2 in 1971. Soviet reexports of sugar dropped off drastically after 1971, from 1.4 million tons in 1971 to only 64,000 tons in 1972. There are indications that the Soviets have been active in the world sugar market in more recent periods as well (Fowler 1974, 63–64). Since 1973 Soviet sugar reexports have ranged from 50,000 to 300,000 tons, the equivalent of 2–8 percent of imports from Cuba, the highest level (302,000 tons, or 7.8 percent of imports from Cuba) occurring in 1986.

Data in table 50 also suggest that, particularly in the mid 1960s,

TABLE 50
SOVIET UNION AND PRC SUGAR EXPORTS, 1960–1987
*(in thousands of metric tons and percentages)*

|      | Soviet Union Total | Soviet Union % of Cuban Imports | PRC Total | PRC % of Cuban Imports |
|------|------|-------|-------|-------|
| 1960 | 262   | 17.8  | 12  | 2.6   |
| 1961 | 951   | 28.4  | 104 | 10.1  |
| 1962 | 901   | 40.3  | 282 | 30.1  |
| 1963 | 920   | 92.3  | 214 | 42.6  |
| 1964 | 433   | 25.1  | 524 | 135.6 |
| 1965 | 731   | 32.4  | 427 | 107.1 |
| 1966 | 1,163 | 63.2  | 501 | 80.9  |
| 1967 | 1,201 | 48.4  | 338 | 60.8  |
| 1968 | 1,461 | 83.5  | 265 | 61.5  |
| 1969 | 1,388 | 104.2 | 167 | 37.5  |
| 1970 | 1,518 | 50.5  | 88  | 16.5  |
| 1971 | 1,402 | 91.2  | 117 | 25.2  |
| 1972 | 64    | 5.8   | 156 | 52.8  |
| 1973 | 46    | 2.9   | 155 | 51.3  |
| 1974 | 117   | 6.3   | 153 | 42.7  |
| 1975 | 59    | 2.0   | 199 | 108.8 |
| 1976 | 79    | 2.6   | 153 | 60.2  |
| 1977 | 87    | 2.4   | 173 | 75.9  |
| 1978 | 174   | 4.6   | 120 | 22.5  |
| 1979 | 244   | 6.6   | 115 | 23.6  |
| 1980 | 165   | 6.2   | 235 | 45.9  |
| 1981 | 183   | 5.9   | 145 | 25.3  |
| 1982 | 267   | 6.3   | 150 | 16.4  |
| 1983 | 148   | 4.9   | 130 | 16.9  |
| 1984 | 204   | 5.8   | 130 | 18.4  |
| 1985 | 175   | 4.8   | 250 | 36.8  |
| 1986 | 302   | 7.8   | 290 | 94.5  |
| 1987 | 201   | 5.4   | 490 | 80.1  |

SOURCE: ISO 1988 and earlier issues.

the PRC reexported Cuban sugar; during 1964–66, it reexported essentially all of the sugar it imported from Cuba. In the 1970s and 1980s, it continued to reexport a significant portion, including the equivalent of all of its imports of Cuban sugar in 1975.

The effect on world market prices of reexports of Cuban sugar by the Soviet Union and socialist countries is difficult to assess. To the extent that they added to supplies entering the world market, these reexports tended to depress prices. Indeed, world market prices of sugar were quite low during the 1960s, especially during 1965–67 (world market prices hovered around 2 cents/pound), when Soviet and PRC reexport activity was high, but clearly the low level of market prices during the 1960s cannot be attributed solely, or principally, to reexporting. Interestingly, in 1963, a year when the world market price of sugar rose to 8.5 cents/pound (compared to under 3 cents/pound in 1962), the Soviet Union reexported 920,000 tons of sugar, the equivalent of 92.3 percent of imports from Cuba in that year, which it had purchased at just over 6 cents/pound (table 32).

IMPACT OF WORLD MARKET PRICES

To be sure, Cuba has traditionally sold the bulk of its sugar exports under preferential arrangements—first to the United States, and currently to the Soviet Union and socialist nations—at more stable, and higher, prices than the world market price. Nevertheless, the level of sugar prices in the world market influences Cuban economic performance. This is so because, over certain periods, preferential prices received by Cuba have borne some relationship to world market prices. Moreover, in addition to sales pursuant to preferential arrangements, Cuba has traditionally disposed of substantial quantities of sugar in the world market (Eckstein 1980, 264). In 1981–87, about 23 percent of Cuban sugar exports went to other than socialist countries, presumably at world market prices (table 29). Over this period, Cuba accounted for 8.1 percent of sugar sold through the world market (table 36).

Because of the very limited basket of hard currency exports, Cuba's ability to generate hard currency revenues to operate the segment of the economy that depends on imports from capitalist countries is closely associated with international sugar prices. It has been observed that the makeup of Cuba's import basket is sensitive to prices in the world sugar market; when world market prices are high (as in 1974) and hard currency from sugar sales is available, Cuba tends to increase its share of imports from capitalist countries, and the opposite is the case when world market prices are low (J. T. Smith 1984, 369; Carciofi 1983, 217).

In contemporary Cuba sugar sales to the world market carry strategic significance since they generate convertible currency—

which Cuba cannot typically obtain from its socialist trading partners—necessary to finance the import of goods and services from market economies and service the hard currency debt. The mechanism through which changes in international sugar prices affect Cuban economic performance may be as follows: changes in export prices of sugar affect export revenue, which in turn affects the ability to import necessary intermediate goods (and thus production in the short term) as well as capital goods (and future production); export revenue in excess of import needs finances consumption from abroad in earlier periods (in the form of repayment of export credits) and enhances the ability to finance future consumption from abroad (by improving creditworthiness and the ability to obtain additional export credits) (Mesa-Lago and Pérez-López 1985c, 59; J. L. Rodríguez 1982, 115).

While preferential arrangements have insulated the Cuban economy from the vagaries of the world sugar market, the insulation has not been by any means total. As Vice President Carlos Rafael Rodríguez remarked in 1977 (Collar Fraguela 1977, 31):

> Our preferential agreements with the Soviet Union and other socialist nations that are members of CMEA regarding prices eliminate the unequal exchange relation that affects exporters of raw materials in developing countries and permit us to plan, with certainty, our steady development.
>
> But Cuba cannot escape totally the uncertainties of the capitalist market, still an important destination of our sugar exports and a key source of technology that we can not renounce. As a result, although a fall in [world market] sugar prices cannot ruin us, as it could during the times of foreign domination, negative conditions in the world market, such as we are experiencing now, deeply affect our foreign earnings, over 30 percent of which originate from capitalist markets.

The adverse impact of low sugar prices in the world market on Cuban economic performance and the beneficial impact of high prices have been noted by numerous officials and analysts. Speaking in September 1976—at a time when sugar prices in the world market had softened after reaching record high levels—President Fidel Castro (1976, 2) said:

> It is sad that the time when we are making the greatest efforts to undertake these steps forward in the political, state [organization] and social fields should coincide with an unfavorable economic situation.

... These problems are mainly caused by the fact that there has been an extraordinary drop in the market price of sugar. ... These ... price fluctuations on the world market are really hair-raising. And such things as the price of sugar are truly beyond the control of our revolution.

In a report issued to Western creditors in mid 1982, the BNC (1982, 34) gave the following explanation for the economic problems that had necessitated a request for a renegotiation of the hard currency debt:

The most important factor continues to be the behavior of sugar prices. Its typical cycle—in the absence of an effective international agreement—affects foreign exchange planning and, consequently, that of foreign expenditures. . . . At times price declines at short notice have been so severe that not even conservative estimates of price trends have been able to discount their effects. . . . [A] sudden price drop in the latter months of 1975, just before the plan was implemented, made a quick adjustment necessary, with a four-cent reduction in the planned price. This logically led to a revision of national economic plans. Moreover, the unpredictability of the change had a negative effect on the balance of trade during the initial years of the Plan period.

Referring to the same period, Domínguez (1978, 148) made this assessment:

The extraordinary increase in the world price of sugar [during the first half of the 1970s] became a powerful stimulant to the Cuban economy, dramatically improving terms of trade. . . . Cuba launched the first sustained period of real growth in per capita income in revolutionary history. Capitalist sugar-price inflation at last rescued the Cuban economy in the early 1970s. The decline of the world price of sugar in 1975 ended the bonanza: Cuban annual economic-growth rates for the second half of the decade are expected to slow down by 40 percent, compared to the 1971–75 period, under the 1976–80 five-year plan. But it is plain that the sustained increase of the world price of sugar from 1968 to 1974 had rescued the Cuban economy.

A report on industrialization in Cuba by the United Nations Industrial Development Organization (UNIDO 1986, 3–4) states:

The Cuban economy experienced deceleration when the price of sugar began descent from the $0.65 high of November 1974 and collapsed to about $0.08 a pound in mid-1976. The price of this key component of Cuba's export soared in 1980, but fell by almost 70 percent in the early 1980s. The change in sugar prices largely attests to the change in economic conditions. . . . Despite advances in economic diversification, sugar continues to remain the backbone of the Cuban economy.

A study that attempted to estimate Cuban GDP per capita in dollars using the physical indicators approach (Mesa-Lago and Pérez-López 1985b) concluded that this technique may not be suitable to economies such as Cuba's that depend heavily on a single export commodity subject to highly volatile price behavior. Thus estimates of Cuban GDP per capita in dollars based on the behavior of consumption-oriented, relatively stable, physical indicators failed to reflect the impact on the economy of external shocks, such as a drop in world market prices of sugar that occurred in 1976–78. In support of this view, a simple correlation between the absolute levels of international sugar prices and GSP at current prices (GSP at constant prices was not available) for 1962–81 yielded a coefficient of .68, and with a one-year time lag the coefficient was .76, figures that suggest a significant statistical relationship between world market prices of sugar and GSP (Mesa-Lago and Pérez-López 1985c, 59). Criticisms of this test that argue, for instance, that it is invalid because of a time trend in both variables (Brundenius and Zimbalist 1985b, 129) have been rebutted by demonstrating that the world market price of sugar does not exhibit a clear time trend (Mesa-Lago and Pérez-López 1985d, 79).

In a more recent work, Domínguez (1989, 101–02) observes that for the first time in revolutionary Cuba's history, the economy was able to grow during the first half of the 1980s despite very low prices in the world sugar market. He attributes the change in historical relationship between sugar prices in the world market and domestic economic performance to the generosity of the Soviet Union. Not only did that country transfer massive amounts of resources to Cuba during this period via sugar price subsidies—which assured Cuba's ability to maintain adequate levels of imported goods from the Soviet Union and socialist countries—but it also provided Cuba with an alternative hard currency export commodity (oil), which made up for the hard currency shortfall associated with low prices for sugar in the world market. Indeed, during 1983–85, oil reexports were Cuba's principal hard currency export earner, generating almost twice as much as sugar exports (BNC 1985, 31). In 1986, although the world market price of sugar increased from 4.05 to 6.05 cents per pound, the Cuban economy went into a recession, as the Soviet Union cut the price it paid for Cuban sugar (in pesos) by over 12 percent; in 1987, Cuba actually reported a negative rate of economic growth, as the Soviet Union cut the sugar price by an additional 1.6 percent. Domínguez (1989, 102) describes the current relationship between the international price for sugar and economic growth as follows:

> Thus the "rhythm" of the Cuban economy may still reflect in part the effects of world sugar prices, but now it may also be affected by the "exigencies" of the Soviet economy. At times, as in 1984 and in 1987, this new factor may be more important than the trend in the world price of sugar. If this is the case, the nature but not the fact of Cuba's vulnerability to the international economy has changed.

## Sugar and Structural Change

Management of the Cuban economy by the revolutionary government over the last twenty-five years appears to have had a marginal impact in changing the structure of the economy to reduce the role of the sugar industry. Although precise measurement and comparisons with prerevolutionary Cuba are not feasible for a host of methodological reasons, the record suggests that sugar (industry plus agriculture) has continued to be one of the key sectors of the economy and the backbone of the export economy.

Moreover, Cuba's plans to increase sugar production and exports through the end of the century virtually assure that the industry will continue to play a predominant role in the economy. Unlike other sugar-exporting countries, which have made serious efforts to restructure their economies, Cuba has cast its lot with sugar. Officials speak of the imperative to increase sugar production not only to meet the anticipated needs of socialist countries but also to regain "historical participation levels" in the world market.

It does appear that by virtue of arrangements with the Soviet Union that guarantee very high prices for sugar exports regardless of the behavior of the world market price, Cuba has been able to stabilize sugar export revenue in soft currency and mitigate the severity of economic cycles associated with swings in world market prices of sugar. However, because efforts to diversify the hard currency export basket have not been wholly successful, the economy continues to depend on sugar sales to nonsocialist countries—typically at world market prices or at prices related to them—to generate hard currency and therefore remains somewhat vulnerable to volatile world market prices.

APPENDIXES
REFERENCES
INDEX

# APPENDIX 1

## Cuban Sugar Statistics

THE IMPORTANCE of sugar to the Cuban economy is reflected in the abundance, regularity of publication, and general high quality of sugar statistics. Nonsugar production statistics in prerevolutionary Cuba were relatively scarce and not readily obtainable because of the lack of a regular publication that might have brought together statistics collected by a myriad of government bureaus, departments, ministries, and offices, or by private organizations (Pérez-López 1977, 45). Attempts at publishing a statistical yearbook were made by the General Statistics Directorate (Dirección General de Estadística); however, the *Anuario Estadístico* that resulted was published very irregularly (1914, 1952, 1956, 1957), and therefore its usefulness was severely limited.

### AVAILABILITY OF SUGAR STATISTICS

Since the beginning of the republic, detailed sugar production statistics for each *zafra* were published annually in *Industria Azucarera y sus Derivados* (1903–31); this publication was superseded in 1937 by an annual yearbook published by the private journal *Cuba Económica y Financiera*. The *Anuario Azucarero de Cuba* (AAC 1937–62) was published uninterruptedly from 1937 through at least 1962 in essentially the same format; the issues for 1961 and later years were published by the Ministry of Foreign Trade. There is some question as to when publication of the *Anuario Azucarero* stopped; the latest copy available to researchers in the United States is for 1962, although there are references in the literature to an issue for 1963 in the holdings of Havana's Biblioteca Nacional José Martí (Chilcote 1986, 751) and also to an issue for 1965 (Mesa-Lago 1969a:85).

Issues of the *Anuario Azucarero de Cuba* contain a wealth of statistics on industrial and agricultural aspects of sugar production in Cuba. For industrial activities the statistics were derived from annual censuses of the industry and reported at the level of each individual mill. Thus, for each mill, the following statistics were available: grinding and sugar production capacity; actual cane ground and sugar produced; days in operation during each *zafra*; and industrial yield. For agricultural activities, sugarcane production quotas assigned to each medium and large private producer (*colono*) were also reported. Cuban historical sugar production statistics, obtained from the *Anuario Azucarero* and its predecessors, were included in two major studies of the world sugar market released in the early 1960s by international organizations (FAO 1961; International Sugar Council 1963).

Since the mid 1960s, Cuba has regularly published annual statistical compendia, first the *Boletín Estadístico de Cuba* (BEC 1964–71) and, more recently, the *Anuario Estadístico de Cuba* (AEC 1972–87). While the level of detail is not as fine as in the *Anuario Azucarero* and data on specific production units are not reported, the yearbooks nevertheless contain a great deal of information on agricultural and industrial aspects of sugar production. Overall, Cuba is rated by an authority on international sugar statistics as being among the top dozen countries of the world in terms of the comprehensiveness of sugar industry information it disseminates (Fry 1988, 10).

For example, the most recent issue of the yearbook—*Anuario Estadístico de Cuba 1987*—contains data on area devoted to sugarcane plantings (broken down by state and private sector); plantings by variety of sugarcane; production of sugarcane (also broken down by state and private sector); new plantings; and agricultural services (irrigation, fertilizer application) related to sugarcane agriculture (broken down by state and private sector). Regarding industrial aspects of sugar production, data are provided on volume of sugarcane ground (nationally and by province); cane ground per *zafra* day and per "effective" grinding day (effective grinding time is the difference between *zafra* days and downtime); potential grinding capability of sugar mills; length of the *zafra*, effective grinding days, and downtime of mills according to reason for the interruption; sucrose content of sugarcane; sucrose losses in the industrial process; production of raw sugar (in physical terms and in terms of production standardized to 96 degrees polarization); and production of refined sugar.

Sugar trade statistics tend to be superior, in terms of quality and availability, to other Cuban economic statistics. To a considerable extent, this is so because of the reporting requirements of the ISO, the implementing arm of the international sugar stabilization agreements. As was discussed in chapter 10, Cuba has been a participant in each of the ISAs that have been negotiated since the 1930s.

The *Anuario Azucarero* also contained summary statistics on sugar exports, including statistics by port of export and country of destination. More detailed export statistics on the basis of the export nomenclature were available in the annual foreign trade statistical volumes, *Comercio Exterior* (1902–64). In the early 1960s publication of the foreign trade yearbooks was discontinued, and summary foreign trade statistics began to be included in the general statistical yearbooks. Thus the currently published statistical yearbooks (*Anuario Estadístico de Cuba*) also contain selected statistics on sugar exports, including exports by destination (quantity and value) and some information (not current) on prices of sugar sold under fixed-price contracts. The yearbooks do not distinguish between sugar sales made to the free market (presumably payable in convertible currencies) and under bilateral arrangements (e.g., with centrally planned economies), which might be subject to barter arrangements and/or to preferential pricing.

## Problems with Sugar Statistics

Certain problems with Cuban sugar industry or sugar trade statistics have been identified in the literature.

#### DIFFERENCES IN DEFINITIONS

Comparisons of sugar production statistics in prerevolutionary and revolutionary Cuba cannot be made directly because of certain differences in definitions.

1. Statistics prior to 1959 fail to take into account the production of high-test molasses, an alternative to centrifugal sugar, developed in the 1930s in order to circumvent production restrictions on raw sugar. According to one estimate, inclusion of the raw sugar equivalent of high-test molasses would, on average, increase production figures during the 1950s by about 200,000 tons per annum, or by about 3–4 percent (Hagelberg 1979, 33). For certain years during the 1950s, production of high-test molasses was extremely significant. For example, in 1955 the equivalent of 910,000 tons of sugar was produced in the form of high-test molasses; inclusion of high-test molasses increases 1955 sugar production from 4,538,000 tons to 5,449,000 tons, or by 20 percent (Hagelberg 1974a, 133; 1974b, 434). In 1954 the equivalent of 525,000 Spanish long tons of sugar was manufactured in the form of high-test molasses (CERP 1965b, 503). Reportedly, high-test molasses have not been produced since 1960 (Hagelberg 1974a, 133), and no production data are reported in Cuban statistical yearbooks.

2. Pre-1959 statistics tend to understate production because they fail to take into account "clandestine" production (i.e., output beyond the official production quotas) for sales to the domestic market. It has been estimated that this so-called *azúcar de bibijagua* (ant sugar) amounted to between 500,000 and 600,000 tons during 1953–56; production has been estimated at 50,000–100,000 tons in 1953 and about 200,000 tons in 1955 (Cepero Bonilla 1963, 431–34).

3. Fodder sugar production (i.e., production for animal consumption) was not included in prerevolutionary sugar production statistics. Though

the quantities involved are small (e.g., 7,700 tons in 1956; 14,300 tons in 1959; and 27,600 tons in 1960), it is another instance of the problems in using available data for secular comparisons (Hagelberg 1974a, 133).

CALENDAR YEAR VERSUS *ZAFRA* DATA

For certain periods there are significant differences in production statistics reported by revolutionary Cuba in its own statistical yearbooks and those supplied to international organizations such as the ISO or the International Sugar Council. These differences, compounded by the veil of secrecy that surrounds Cuban economic statistics generally and the admission by Castro (in 1965) that Cuba had at times deliberately released false sugar statistics to mislead "enemies of the revolution," have given rise to doubts regarding the reliability of sugar statistics (Mesa-Lago 1969b, 53–54).

Hagelberg suggests that part of the discrepancies in the sugar production data reported directly by Cuba and those submitted to the ISO stem from confusion over whether the reporting is related to a calendar year or to a *zafra* and from methodological problems—primarily relating to the conversion from physical production to production on the basis of a standard polarization level. However, there are some differences (e.g., for 1964–66, a period during which Cuban production as reported to the ISO is higher than that given in statistical yearbooks by about 270,000 tons per annum) that he was unable to explain satisfactorily (Hagelberg 1974a, 55–57; 1974b, 435).

Prior to the revolution the sugar crop was typically harvested during the months of January to April, when sucrose concentration in sugarcane is highest (Morales Pita 1983, 8). During the 1950s, *zafras* lasted an average of 98.5 days, of which 85.8 days were "effective" production days (AAC 1961, 26–27). Because of organizational problems, labor force shortages, breakdowns in industrial plant resulting from maintenance problems, and so on, the beginning of the *zafras* has been brought forward to as early as mid November, and their end has been pushed back considerably: during 1981–84, for instance, the average length of the *zafras* was 153.5 days, of which 119.3 were effective production days (AEC 1984, 141). The 1985 and 1986 *zafras* were considerably shorter, averaging 136.0 days and 103.5 effective days (AEC 1986, 242), but still markedly longer than in the prerevolutionary period.

The moving forward of the start of the *zafras* means that production during a given sugar crop falls in two calendar years; as is shown in table 51, the difference between production on a *zafra* basis and on a calendar year basis can be significant: over 6 percent in 1972, 1981, and 1984. This gap was probably even more significant in the period around the giant 1970

*Appendix 1*

TABLE 51
COMMERCIAL RAW SUGAR PRODUCTION, *ZAFRA*
COMPARED TO CALENDAR YEAR, 1971–1987
(*in thousands of tons*)

|      | *Zafra*[a] | Calendar Year | Calendar/*Zafra* |
|------|---------|---------------|----------------|
| 1971 | 5,825.3 | 5,762.5 | −1.1 |
| 1972 | 4,250.1 | 4,540.5 | +6.8 |
| 1973 | 5,159.8 | 5,188.1 | +0.6 |
| 1974 | 5,815.2 | 5,700.6 | −2.0 |
| 1975 | 6,201.7 | 6,193.1 | −0.1 |
| 1976 | 6,044.9 | 5,917.6 | −2.1 |
| 1977 | 6,369.0 | 6,705.1 | +5.3 |
| 1978 | 7,216.6 | 7,427.1 | +2.9 |
| 1979 | 7,843.6 | 7,515.1 | −4.2 |
| 1980 | 6,517.5 | 6,554.4 | +0.6 |
| 1981 | 7,195.9 | 7,646.6 | +6.3 |
| 1982 | 8,031.3 | 7,777.6 | −3.2 |
| 1983 | 6,953.5 | 7,231.9 | +4.0 |
| 1984 | 8,026.7 | 7,513.5 | −6.4 |
| 1985 | 7,824.8 | 7,603.4 | −2.8 |
| 1986 | 7,087.9 | 7,203.8 | +1.6 |
| 1987 | 6,950.5 | 6,961.5 | +0.2 |

SOURCES: 1987—AEC 1987, 243, 254; 1985–86—AEC 1986, 242, 253; 1978–84—AEC 1984, 141, 153; 1973–77—AEC 1980, 90, 97; 1971–72—AEC 1977, 86, 93.

a. *Zafra* ending in the year indicated.

*zafra*—over 1 million tons, or about 12 percent of total production of roughly 8.5 million tons, were attained before the end of calendar year 1969 (Roca 1976, 25)—but data are not available to make a systematic comparison.

The differences between *zafra* and calendar year statistics give rise to considerable confusion in statistical reports, since generally it is not clear whether the data refer to one basis or the other. For example, in his speech to the Third Congress of the Cuban Communist party in February 1986, President Fidel Castro (1986, 51) stated that during the five-year period 1981–85 sugar output had grown significantly compared to the previous five-year period, "reaching stable production of about 8 million tons per annum." If Castro was referring to production on a *zafra* basis (table 51), production did exceed 8 million tons in two years (1982 and 1984); however, on a calendar year basis, peak production was just under 7.8 million tons (in 1982). Using either of the two concepts, production during 1981–85 averaged 7.5–7.6 million tons, presumably rounded up by Castro to 8 million.

It should also be noted that, because they take into account two crops, the calendar year data tend to smooth out sharp year-to-year fluctuations in output and present a more stable picture of performance. Whereas during 1981–85 the swing in output on a *zafra* basis is about 1 million tons (from about 7 million tons in 1983 to about 8 million tons in 1982 and 1984), on a calendar year basis it is only 0.6 million tons (from about 7.2 million tons in 1983 to about 7.8 million tons in 1982).

PHYSICAL VERSUS STANDARDIZED OUTPUT

For each *zafra*, Cuba releases two aggregate sugar output figures: one refers to actual commercial raw sugar produced (*azúcar crudo físico*) and the other to the volume of production converted to an internationally recognized polarization standard (i.e., raw value–equivalent testing 96 degrees polarization). Because the average polarization of Cuban sugar generally differs from the standard (it typically exceeds it), the conversion from commercial production to 96 degrees polarization production leads to a difference in production volume (an increase) of about 2 percent. Particularly in speeches, but also in other sources, production data are often reported without proper indication of whether they refer to commercial production or production standardized to 96 degrees polarization.

To make things more difficult, prior to the publication of the 1986 statistical yearbook (AEC 1986, 253), sugar production data available on a calendar year basis referred to commercial production, while export data, also available on a calendar year basis, referred to output standardized to 96 degrees polarization. Thus calendar year data for production and exports referred to different concepts and were not directly comparable. To be sure, one set of data could be converted to the other by using a factor (about 1.02 for most years) derived from comparing *zafra* statistics on a commercial and standardized 96 degrees polarization basis, but this would be only a rough approximation. The more precise way of converting would be via the polarization rate; however, since this rate varies from one sugar crop to another and calendar year data include production from two sugar harvests, conversion is problematic with the available information.

As was noted above, the *Anuario Estadístico de Cuba 1986* for the first time provides calendar year sugar production on both on a commercial and 96 degrees polarization basis. Included in this source are data on both bases for 1975 and 1980–86 (AEC 1986, 253); similar data for 1987 are reported in the subsequent yearbook (AEC 1987, 254). Other than for this nine-year period, the problem of not being able to relate exports and production data still remains.

## IMPORT STATISTICS

While official Cuban statistics on sugar exports currently available in the statistical yearbooks can be cross-checked with those published by the ISO, this cannot be done with data related to imports. In the 1980s, Cuba turned to the world market to purchase sugar in order to meet export commitments. For example, in mid 1980, it reportedly purchased sugar from Colombia for reexport to socialist countries. Cuba reportedly purchased sugar from Nicaragua in 1986—at preferential prices—produced by a Cuban-built mill (Serán manejadas 1986). Official Cuban statistics do not record such purchases, however, and neither do statistics of the ISO, although the latter do record Cuban sugar imports from Colombia (12,000 tons) and the Dominican Republic (73,000 tons) in 1982 (ISO 1982, 55).

According to the BNC (see chapter 9), Cuba bought significant amounts of sugar in the world market during 1984–87 for reexport, presumably to the Soviet Union: $101 million in 1984 (BNC 1985, 35); $106 million in 1985 (BNC 1987, 25); and $90 and $189 million, respectively, in 1986 and 1987 (BNC 1988b). These imports are not recorded in official Cuban trade statistics or in ISO statistics.

The *Anuario Estadístico de Cuba 1982* (AEC 1982, 341) for the first time reported Cuban imports under the broad category "sugar, sugar preparations, and honey." Data on the value of such imports are provided, but not on quantities imported. Since 1982, Cuba has reported the following value of imports of "sugar, sugar preparations, and honey" (AEC 1986, 439):

| | |
|---|---:|
| 1982 | 14,147,000 pesos |
| 1983 | 33,643,000 pesos |
| 1984 | 33,000 pesos |
| 1985 | 20,000 pesos |
| 1986 | 54,000 pesos |

These data do not track the value of imports from the world market reported by the BNC. Cuban official statistics report no imports of sugar, sugar preparations, and honey in 1987 (AEC 1987, 447).

## CONSUMPTION STATISTICS

Although Cuba does not publish statistics on domestic consumption of sugar, it does report them to the ISO and other international organizations. Questions have been raised by industry analysts regarding the peculiar behavior of Cuban sugar consumption statistics reported to the ISO since the mid 1960s, and some analysts have gone so far as to suggest that they were inflated to present a more favorable picture of domestic production (cited in Mesa-Lago 1969b, 54).

Hagelberg suggests that the odd behavior in consumption statistics may be related to the fact that internal consumption statistics reported by Cuba since the mid 1960s include not only consumption but also production losses (due to fire, handling, etcetera) as well as statistical adjustments (Hagelberg 1974b, 436).

# APPENDIX 2

Cuban Sugar Mill Complexes by Province, mid 1970s

| Code | Current Name | Former Name | Grinding Capacity (tons/day)[a] |
|---|---|---|---|
| PINAR DEL RÍO | | | |
| 102 | Harlem | Bahía Honda | 2,380 |
| 106 | Manuel Sanguily | Niágara | 1,475 |
| 107 | Pablo de la Torriente Brau | Orozco | 3,120 |
| 108 | Jose Martí | San Cristóbal | 3,570 |
| LA HABANA | | | |
| 101 | Abraham Lincoln | Andorra | 2,440 |
| 103 | Eduardo García Lavandero | Pilar | 3,060 |
| 105 | Augusto César Sandino | Merceditas | 1,980 |
| 109 | Orlando Nodarse | San Ramón | 2,495 |
| 201 | Amistad con los Pueblos | Amistad | 3,060 |
| 202 | Comandante Manuel Fajardo | Fajardo | 1,760 |
| 203 | Hector Molina Riano | Gómez Mena | 6,920 |
| 204 | Habana Libre | Habana | 1,700 |
| 205 | Camilo Cienfuegos | Hershey | 6,690 |
| 206 | Manuel Isla | Josefita | 1,870 |
| 207 | Gregorio Arlee Mañalich | Mercedita | 3,970 |
| 208 | Pablo Noriega | Occidente | 910 |
| 210 | Osvaldo Sánchez | Providencia | 2,950 |
| 211 | Rubén Martínez Villena | Rosario | 3,060 |
| 212 | Boris Luis Santa Coloma | San Antonio | 3,060 |
| 213 | Manuel Martínez Prieto | Toledo | 5,160 |
| MATANZAS | | | |
| 301 | México | Alava | 5,500 |
| 302 | Reynold García | Araujo | 2,440 |
| 303 | Australia | Australia | 2,325 |
| 304 | Granma | Carolina | 2,265 |
| 305 | Puerto Rico Libre | Conchita | 4,195 |

*241*

| Code | Current Name | Former Name | Grinding Capacity (tons/day)[a] |
|---|---|---|---|
| MATANZAS (continued) | | | |
| 306 | Cuba Libre | Cuba | 5,840 |
| 307 | Jaime López | Dolores | 1,645 |
| 308 | Humberto Alvarez | Dos Rosas | 1,815 |
| 310 | España Republicana | España | 6,465 |
| 311 | Esteban Hernández | Gipúzcoa | 2,950 |
| 312 | Fructuoso Rodríguez | Limones | 2,550 |
| 313 | Seis de Agosto | Mercedes | 4,310 |
| 314 | Jesús Rabí | Porfuerza | 2,835 |
| 315 | José Smith Comas | Progreso | 2,950 |
| 318 | Victoria de Yagüajay | Santa Amalia | 2,440 |
| 319 | René Fraga | Santa Rita | 2,265 |
| 320 | Juan Avila | Santo Domingo | 2,720 |
| 321 | Julio Reyes Cairo | Soledad | 2,720 |
| 322 | Sergio González | Tinguaro | 4,480 |
| 323 | Horacio Rodríguez | Triunfo | 1,760 |
| VILLA CLARA | | | |
| 401 | Heriberto Duquesne | Adela | 2,720 |
| 405 | Luis Arcos Bergnes | Carmita | 1,760 |
| 407 | Abel Santamaría | Constancia-E | 2,495 |
| 408 | Mariana Grajales | Corazón de Jesús | 2,095 |
| 411 | José María Pérez | Fe | 3,630 |
| 412 | Juan Pedro Carbó Serviá | Fidencia | 2,265 |
| 415 | Braulio Coroneaux | Macagua | 1,700 |
| 417 | 26 de Julio | María Antonia | 910 |
| 420 | Emilio Córdova | Nazábal | 2,835 |
| 423 | Osvaldo Herrera | Pastora | 2,495 |
| 426 | Perucho Figueredo | Purio | 2,265 |
| 427 | Quintín Banderas | Ramona | 3,855 |
| 428 | Marcelo Salado | Reforma | 2,550 |
| 429 | José R. Rimelque | Resolución | 1,815 |
| 430 | Antonio Finalet | Resulta | 2,890 |
| 432 | Chiquitico Fabregat | San Agustín R | 2,720 |
| 434 | Panchito Gómez Toro | San Isidro | 2,890 |
| 435 | Hermanos Ameijeiras | San José | 2,890 |
| 437 | Carlos Caraballo | Santa Catalina | 2,550 |
| 439 | El Vaquerito | Santa Lutgarda | 2,495 |
| 440 | Efraín Alfonso | Santa María | 2,440 |
| 441 | 10 de Octubre | Santa Rosa | 2,610 |
| 442 | Héctor Rodríguez | Santa Teresa | 3,400 |

| Code | Current Name | Former Name | Grinding Capacity (tons/day)[a] |
|---|---|---|---|
| VILLA CLARA (continued) | | | |
| 446 | Carlos Baliño | Ulacia | 2,265 |
| 447 | Unidad Proletaria | Unidad | 1,815 |
| 449 | George Washington | Washington | 3,335 |
| 450 | Benito Juárez | Zaza | 2,495 |
| CIENFUEGOS | | | |
| 403 | Mal Tiempo | Andreíta | 2,950 |
| 404 | Ciudad Caracas | Caracasa | 4,195 |
| 406 | Guillermo Moncada | Constancia-A | 3,970 |
| 409 | Antonio Sánchez | Covadonga | 3,515 |
| 413 | Espartaco | Hormiguero | 3,970 |
| 416 | 14 de Julio | Manuelita | 2,550 |
| 424 | Primero de Mayo | Perseverancia | 4,535 |
| 425 | Elpidio Gómez | Portugalete | 2,380 |
| 431 | Ramón Balboa | San Agustín L | 3,685 |
| 433 | Marta Abreu | San Francisco | 1,700 |
| 443 | Pepito Tey | Soledad | 2,550 |
| SANCTI SPÍRITUS | | | |
| 414 | Remberto Abad Aleman | La Vega | 1,645 |
| 418 | Obdulio Morales | Narcisa | 3,630 |
| 419 | Siete de Noviembre | Natividad | 1,985 |
| 421 | Aracelio Iglesias | Nela | 1,590 |
| 438 | Ramón Ponciano | Santa Isabel | 2,495 |
| 444 | F.N.T.A. | Trinidad | 2,38 0 |
| 445 | Melani o Hernández | Tuinicu´ | 4,535 |
| 448 | Simón B olívar | Victoria | 2,495 |
| 512 | Uruguay | Jatibonico | 5,100 |
| CIEGO DE AVILA | | | |
| 501 | Enrique José Varona | Adelaida | 4,310 |
| 503 | Orlando Go nzález | Algodones | 3,630 |
| 504 | Ecuador | Baraguá | 7,600 |
| 505 | Bolivia | Cunagua | 9,070 |
| 515 | Ciro Redondo | Morón | 11,340 |
| 517 | Patria o Muerte | Patria | 2,495 |
| 518 | Maximo Gómez | Punta Alegre | 5,610 |
| 522 | Venezuela | Stewart | 9,640 |
| 524 | Primero de Enero | Violeta | 8,280 |

| Code | Current Name | Former Name | Grinding Capacity (tons/day)[a] |
|---|---|---|---|
| **CAMAGÜEY** | | | |
| 502 | Ignacio Agramonte | Agramonte | 4,310 |
| 505 | Carlos M. de Céspedes | Céspedes | 4,365 |
| 508 | República Dominicana | Estrella | 4,875 |
| 509 | Argentina | Florida | 3,400 |
| 511 | Brasil | Jaronú | 13,610 |
| 513 | Sierra de Cubitas | Lugareño | 6,010 |
| 514 | Haití | Macareño | 3,685 |
| 516 | Alfredo Alvarez Mola | Najasa | 2,155 |
| 519 | Cándido González | Santa Marta | 4,765 |
| 520 | Noel Fernández | Senado | 4,875 |
| 521 | Siboney | Siboney | 1,930 |
| 523 | Panamá | Vertientes | 10,090 |
| **LAS TUNAS** | | | |
| 507 | Colombia | Elia | 5,330 |
| 510 | Amancio Rodríguez | Francisco | 7,485 |
| 610 | Jesús Menéndez | Chaparra | 7,995 |
| 611 | Antonio Guiteras | Delicias | 10,150 |
| 618 | Perú | Jobabo | 4,765 |
| 622 | Argelia Libre | Manatí | 9,185 |
| **HOLGUÍN** | | | |
| 602 | Loynaz Hechevarría | Alto Cedro | 3,120 |
| 604 | López Peña | Baguanes | 3,345 |
| 607 | Nicaragua | Boston | 7,430 |
| 608 | Cristino Naranjo | Cacocúm | 2,325 |
| 621 | Antonio Maceo | Maceo | 1,985 |
| 626 | Guatemala | Preston | 9,185 |
| 631 | Urbano Noris | San Germán | 7,995 |
| 635 | Rafael Freyre | Santa Lucía | 4,025 |
| 639 | Fernando de Diós | Tacajo | 3,460 |
| 640 | Frank País | Tánamo | 3,855 |
| **GRANMA** | | | |
| 609 | Luis E. Carracedo | Cape Cruz | 1,985 |
| 612 | Francisco Castro Ceruto | Dos Amigos | 2,040 |
| 615 | Bartolomé Masó | Estrada Palma | 3,060 |
| 616 | Juan Manuel Márquez | Isabel-B | 3,345 |
| 620 | Arquímedes Colina | Mabay | 2,270 |
| 624 | Roberto Ramírez | Niquero | 3,345 |
| 627 | José N. Figueredo | Río Cauto | 4,765 |

| Code | Current Name | Former Name | Grinding Capacity (tons/day)[a] |
|---|---|---|---|
| GRANMA (continued) | | | |
| 629 | La Demajagua | Salvador | 2,100 |
| 634 | Enidio Díaz Machado | Santa Regina | 2,380 |
| 637 | Ranulfo Leyva | Sofía | 1,930 |
| SANTIAGO DE CUBA | | | |
| 601 | Salvador Rosales | Algodonal | 1,815 |
| 603 | América Libre | América | 2,835 |
| 605 | Los Reynaldos | Baltony | 4,765 |
| 606 | Paquito Rosales | Borjita | 2,665 |
| 623 | Julio Antonio Mella | Miranda | 5,840 |
| 625 | Dos Ríos | Palma | 4,650 |
| 633 | Chile | Santa Ana | 2,720 |
| 641 | Rafael Reyes | Unión | 1,930 |
| GUANTÁNAMO | | | |
| 613 | Costa Rica | Ermita | 1,870 |
| 614 | Argeo Martínez | Esperanza | 2,380 |
| 617 | Honduras | Isabel-G | 1,700 |
| 619 | Paraguay | Las Cañas | 2,040 |
| 630 | Manuel Tames | San Antonio | 1,415 |
| 638 | El Salvador | Soledad | 2,380 |
| Total | | | 537,745 |

SOURCE: Los centrales, 1978.

a. Grinding capacity around 1970 from *Manual Azucarero* 1971. Capacity of each mill was essentially unchanged in the 1970s.

# APPENDIX 3

Cuban Sugar Refineries by Province, Mid 1970s

| Code | Current Name | Former Name | Refining Capacity (tons/day)[a] |
|---|---|---|---|
| **PINAR DEL RÍO** | | | |
| 108 | Jose Martí | Central San Cristóbal | 454 |
| **LA HABANA** | | | |
| 101 | Abraham Lincoln | Central Andorra | 272 |
| 205 | Camilo Cienfuegos | Central Hershey | 1,043 |
| 213 | Manuel Martínez Prieto | Central Toledo | 318 |
| **MATANZAS** | | | |
| 310 | España Republicana | Central España | 318 |
| 314 | Jesús Rabí | Central Porfuerza | 318 |
| 325 | Jose Antonio Echeverría | Arechabala | 454 |
| **VILLA CLARA** | | | |
| 427 | Quintín Banderas | Central Ramona | 295 |
| 432 | Chiquitico Fabregat | Central San Agustín | 227 |
| 449 | George Washington | Central Washington | 363 |
| **SANCTI SPÍRITUS** | | | |
| 438 | Ramón Ponciano | Central Santa Isabel | 286 |
| **CIEGO DE AVILA** | | | |
| 504 | Ecuador | Central Baraguá | 318 |
| **CAMAGÜEY** | | | |
| 502 | Ignacio Agramonte | Central Agramonte | 318 |
| 504 | Argentina | Central Florida | 272 |
| **HOLGUÍN** | | | |
| 640 | Frank País | Central Tánamo | 272 |

| Code | Current Name | Former Name | Refining Capacity (tons/day)[a] |
|---|---|---|---|
| GRANMA | | | |
| 620 | Arquímedes Colina | Central Mabay | 181 |
| | Total | | 5,709 |

SOURCE: *Manual Azucarero* 1971, 1134–69.

a. Refining capacity in 1958 from AAC 1958, 194. Capacity of each refinery was essentially unchanged in the 1960s and 1970s.

# APPENDIX 4

### Industrial Facilities Producing Sugar Derivatives, 1982
*(in tons/annum or hectoliters/annum)*

| Derivative/Plant | Capacity |
|---|---|
| **BAGASSE PULP AND PAPER** | |
| Cuba-9 | 900 dissolving pulp |
| | 7,200 newsprint |
| Capitán Guillermo Geilín | |
| (formerly Técnica Cubana) | 15,000 pulp |
| | 24,000 printing & writing paper |
| Sergio González | |
| (formerly Papelera Damují) | 12,000 pulp |
| | 21,000 cardboard |
| Capitán Roberto Rodríguez | |
| (formerly Pulpa Cuba) | 16,200 pulp[a] |
| | 27,000 white paper |
| Panchito Gómez Toro[b] | 60,000 pulp |
| | 60,000 printing & writing paper |
| **BAGASSE BOARDS** | |
| Ramón Balboa | |
| (formerly Pro-Cuba) | 22,500 particleboard |
| Manuel Fajardo | |
| (formerly Maderas Técnicas) | 13,500 particleboard |
| Amancio Rodríguez | |
| (formerly Primadera) | 12,000 fiberboard |
| Henetec (same name as before nationalization) | 3,000 particleboard |
| Camilo Cienfuegos | 36,000 particleboard |
| Primero de Enero | 36,000 particleboard |
| Jesús Menéndez | 36,000 particleboard |
| | 28,000 fine particleboard |
| **BAGACILLO** | |
| 18 plants | 80,000 predigested pith |

## Appendix 4

| Derivative/plant | Capacity |
|---|---|
| **ETHANOL AND RUM** | |
| Héctor Molina | 144,000 hl ethanol |
| Habana | 118,800 hl ethanol |
| José A. Echeverría | 228,000 hl ethanol |
| Jesús Rabí | 99,200 hl ethanol |
| Heriberto Duquesne | 91,200 hl ethanol |
| Melanio Hernández | 144,000 hl ethanol |
| Enrique Varona | 139,200 hl ethanol |
| Antonio Maceo | 57,600 hl ethanol |
| Arquímedes Colina | 87,600 hl ethanol |
| Amancio Rodríguez | 144,000 hl ethanol |
| Antonio Guiteras | 84,000 hl ethanol |
| Argeo Martínez | 48,000 hl ethanol |
| Santiago | 48,000 hl rum |
| Jorge Washington | 43,200 hl rum |
| Santa Cruz | 240,000 hl rum |
| **YEAST** | |
| Esteban Hernández | 12,000 torula |
| Perucho Figueredo | 12,000 torula |
| Antonio Sánchez | 12,000 torula |
| Simón Bolivar | 12,000 torula |
| Primero de Enero | 12,000 torula |
| Alfredo Pérez | 10,000 torula |
| Antonio Guiteras | 12,000 torula |
| Guatemala | 12,000 torula |
| Juan M. Márquez | 12,000 torula |
| Venezuela | 12,000 torula |
| Héroes de Bolivia | 2,000 baker's |
| San Antonio de los Baños | 3,600 baker's |
| Héctor Molina | 1,092 Saccharomyces |
| Melanio Hernández | 1,210 Saccharomyces |
| Jose A. Echeverría | 2,487 Saccharomyces |
| Enrique Varona | 1,267 Saccharomyces |
| Amancio Rodríguez | 1,176 Saccharomyces |
| **WAX** | |
| Jesús Menéndez | 115 refined wax |
| | 108 oil |
| | 41 resin |
| **DEXTRAN** | |
| España Republicana | 450 dextran |

SOURCE: Noa Silverio 1983, 129.
 a. Estimated.
 b. Adjacent to Uruguay sugar mill; came on line in 1986.

# APPENDIX 5

•

### Cuban Sugar Trade, 1954–1958
*(in metric tons)*

|  | 1954 | 1955 | 1956 | 1957 | 1958 |
|---|---|---|---|---|---|
| Albania | 0 | 0 | 0 | 0 | 0 |
| Algeria | 0 | 0 | 0 | 0 | 0 |
| Angola | 0 | 0 | 0 | 0 | 0 |
| Austria | 11,211 | 10,466 | 56,702 | 11,000 | 7,932 |
| Bahamas | 0 | 0 | 598 | 0 | 0 |
| Bahrein | 0 | 0 | 0 | 0 | 0 |
| Bangladesh | 0 | 0 | 0 | 0 | 0 |
| Belgium/Luxembourg | 30,002 | 5,854 | 15,811 | 9,822 | 17,063 |
| Bermuda | 0 | 1,376 | 1,073 | 1,351 | 242 |
| Bolivia | 0 | 0 | 0 | 1,070 | 0 |
| Bulgaria | 0 | 0 | 0 | 0 | 0 |
| Canada | 72,988 | 76,157 | 86,966 | 94,789 | 190,149 |
| Ceylon (Sri Lanka) | 23,548 | 65,553 | 29,886 | 8,369 | 37,716 |
| Chile | 61,947 | 65,094 | 39,821 | 41,675 | 4,235 |
| China (Mainland) | 0 | 0 | 0 | 0 | 50,082 |
| Colombia | 0 | 0 | 0 | 0 | 27,903 |
| Costa Rica | 0 | 0 | 9,706 | 0 | 0 |
| Czechoslovakia | 0 | 0 | 5,217 | 0 | 0 |
| Denmark | 0 | 0 | 0 | 0 | 0 |
| EEC | 0 | 0 | 0 | 0 | 0 |
| Ethiopia | 0 | 0 | 0 | 0 | 0 |
| Finland | 0 | 32,742 | 26,847 | 0 | 0 |
| France | 34,800 | 59,174 | 127,667 | 99,907 | 61,856 |
| East Germany | 0 | 0 | 23,111 | 6,910 | 0 |
| West Germany | 171,647 | 124,662 | 183,432 | 384,542 | 37,530 |
| Ghana | 0 | 0 | 0 | 0 | 0 |
| Greece | 28,516 | 49,685 | 41,097 | 29,678 | 60,042 |
| Guam | 0 | 0 | 73 | 131 | 0 |
| Guinea | 0 | 0 | 0 | 0 | 0 |
| Guinea Bissau | 0 | 0 | 0 | 0 | 0 |
| Honduras | 2,427 | 3,300 | 3,252 | 4,717 | 971 |
| Hong Kong | 19,686 | 20,310 | 0 | 0 | 7,912 |

|  | *1954* | *1955* | *1956* | *1957* | *1958* |
|---|---|---|---|---|---|
| Hungary | 0 | 0 | 19,287 | 0 | 11,234 |
| Iceland | 3,281 | 3,665 | 6,790 | 4,079 | 4,643 |
| India | 283,359 | 11,205 | 0 | 0 | 0 |
| Indonesia | 0 | 0 | 0 | 0 | 0 |
| Iran | 20,530 | 52,668 | 62,807 | 4,829 | 10,195 |
| Iraq | 0 | 0 | 0 | 7,610 | 18,029 |
| Ireland | 20,486 | 35,142 | 0 | 9,753 | 33,567 |
| Israel | 3,369 | 36,261 | 38,866 | 16,266 | 20,313 |
| Italy | 5,138 | 2,914 | 749 | 8,930 | 1,172 |
| Jamaica | 0 | 0 | 0 | 217 | 0 |
| Japan | 291,996 | 306,366 | 603,807 | 459,848 | 556,342 |
| Jordan | 0 | 0 | 0 | 5,435 | 0 |
| Kenya | 0 | 0 | 0 | 0 | 0 |
| Korea (North) | 0 | 0 | 0 | 0 | 0 |
| Korea (South) | 11,743 | 4,941 | 0 | 0 | 5,066 |
| Kuwait | 0 | 0 | 0 | 0 | 0 |
| Lebanon | 11,879 | 47,616 | 48,477 | 14,168 | 8,867 |
| Libya | 0 | 0 | 0 | 0 | 0 |
| Malaysia | 0 | 0 | 0 | 0 | 0 |
| Mali | 0 | 0 | 0 | 0 | 0 |
| Malta | 0 | 0 | 0 | 0 | 2,989 |
| Mexico | 0 | 0 | 50,712 | 0 | 0 |
| Mongolia | 0 | 0 | 0 | 0 | 0 |
| Morocco | 187,099 | 132,813 | 162,088 | 189,102 | 156,227 |
| Mozambique | 0 | 0 | 0 | 0 | 0 |
| Netherlands | 122,013 | 161,217 | 98,297 | 149,700 | 183,316 |
| Netherlands Antilles | 207 | 194 | 0 | 851 | 1,601 |
| New Zealand | 6,509 | 0 | 0 | 0 | 0 |
| Nicaragua | 0 | 0 | 0 | 0 | 0 |
| Norway | 0 | 0 | 3,353 | 0 | 0 |
| Oman | 0 | 0 | 0 | 0 | 0 |
| Pakistan | 0 | 10,421 | 45,599 | 32,039 | 0 |
| Panama | 0 | 0 | 0 | 0 | 0 |
| Peru | 0 | 0 | 0 | 0 | 0 |
| Poland | 0 | 0 | 0 | 0 | 0 |
| Portugal | 222 | 340 | 354 | 9,973 | 102 |
| Qatar | 0 | 0 | 0 | 0 | 0 |
| Romania | 0 | 0 | 0 | 0 | 0 |
| Saudi Arabia | 0 | 0 | 0 | 0 | 0 |
| Senegal | 0 | 0 | 0 | 0 | 0 |
| Sierra Leone | 0 | 0 | 0 | 0 | 0 |
| Singapore | 0 | 0 | 0 | 0 | 0 |
| Somalia | 0 | 0 | 0 | 0 | 0 |
| South Arabia, Fedn. | 0 | 0 | 0 | 0 | 0 |
| Southern Yemen | 0 | 0 | 0 | 0 | 0 |

|  | 1954 | 1955 | 1956 | 1957 | 1958 |
|---|---|---|---|---|---|
| Spain & territories | 10,700 | 31,809 | 0 | 30,145 | 68,593 |
| St. Pierre et Miquelon | 0 | 0 | 0 | 48 | 149 |
| Sudan | 0 | 0 | 0 | 0 | 0 |
| Suriname | 0 | 0 | 0 | 0 | 0 |
| Sweden | 11,874 | 48,962 | 77,148 | 15,856 | 34,194 |
| Switzerland | 24,107 | 16,521 | 18,706 | 7,709 | 16,054 |
| Tahiti | 0 | 0 | 172 | 333 | 200 |
| Tanzania | 0 | 0 | 0 | 0 | 0 |
| Thailand | 0 | 0 | 0 | 0 | 0 |
| Trinidad and Tobago | 0 | 0 | 0 | 0 | 0 |
| Tunisia | 0 | 0 | 0 | 3,098 | 5,618 |
| Turkey | 0 | 0 | 0 | 0 | 0 |
| U.A.R. (Egypt) | 0 | 0 | 0 | 0 | 0 |
| U.A.R. (Syria) | 13,015 | 20,162 | 38,128 | 21,165 | 38,366 |
| United Kingdom | 291,370 | 123,995 | 381,711 | 423,868 | 487,299 |
| United States | 2,410,040 | 2,574,083 | 2,812,744 | 2,753,456 | 3,241,374 |
| U.S.S.R. | 9,506 | 456,379 | 212,624 | 358,242 | 187,683 |
| Uganda | 0 | 0 | 0 | 0 | 0 |
| Uruguay | 7,140 | 0 | 46,345 | 32,787 | 0 |
| Venezuela | 22,060 | 1,694 | 194 | 0 | 8,331 |
| Vietnam, Cambodia, and Laos | 8,903 | 17,927 | 3,781 | 0 | 24,028 |
| Yemen Dem. Rep. | 0 | 0 | 0 | 0 | 0 |
| Yugoslavia | 0 | 29,011 | 9,242 | 21,513 | 2,407 |
| Zambia | 0 | 0 | 0 | 0 | 0 |
| Others | 2,880 | 3,416 | 0 | 0 | 0 |
| Total Exports | 4,236,198 | 4,644,095 | 5,393,240 | 5,274,981 | 5,631,592 |
| United States | 2,410,040 | 2,574,083 | 2,812,744 | 2,753,456 | 3,241,374 |
| Percent | 57 | 55 | 52 | 52 | 58 |
| Socialist countries | 9,506 | 485,390 | 269,481 | 386,665 | 251,406 |
| Percent | 0 | 10 | 5 | 7 | 4 |
| U.S.S.R. | 9,506 | 456,379 | 212,624 | 358,242 | 187,683 |
| Percent | 0 | 10 | 4 | 7 | 3 |
| Other countries | 1,816,652 | 1,584,622 | 2,311,015 | 2,134,860 | 2,138,812 |
| Percent | 43 | 34 | 43 | 40 | 38 |

CUBAN SUGAR TRADE, 1959–1963

|  | 1959 | 1960 | 1961 | 1962 | 1963 |
|---|---|---|---|---|---|
| Albania | 0 | 0 | 0 | 10,700 | 6,419 |
| Algeria | 0 | 0 | 0 | 0 | 5,389 |

## Appendix 5

|  | 1959 | 1960 | 1961 | 1962 | 1963 |
|---|---|---|---|---|---|
| Angola | 0 | 0 | 0 | 0 | 0 |
| Austria | 0 | 0 | 0 | 0 | 0 |
| Bahamas | 0 | 0 | 0 | 0 | 0 |
| Bahrein | 0 | 0 | 11,207 | 0 | 3,316 |
| Bangladesh | 0 | 0 | 0 | 0 | 0 |
| Belgium/Luxembourg | 49,178 | 6,531 | 6,819 | 18,622 | 20,386 |
| Bermuda | 645 | 519 | 0 | 0 | 0 |
| Bolivia | 0 | 0 | 0 | 0 | 0 |
| Bulgaria | 0 | 0 | 57,258 | 117,796 | 56,177 |
| Canada | 92,810 | 74,970 | 15,822 | 19,880 | 70,068 |
| Ceylon (Sri Lanka) | 10,343 | 0 | 104,033 | 0 | 0 |
| Chile | 3,584 | 5,591 | 169,952 | 80,867 | 4,585 |
| China (Mainland) | 0 | 476,537 | 1,032,136 | 937,893 | 500,928 |
| Colombia | 5,398 | 5,350 | 0 | 0 | 0 |
| Costa Rica | 0 | 0 | 0 | 0 | 0 |
| Czechoslovakia | 0 | 8,988 | 25,322 | 155,680 | 150,105 |
| Denmark | 0 | 0 | 0 | 0 | 0 |
| EEC | 0 | 0 | 0 | 0 | 0 |
| Ethiopia | 0 | 0 | 0 | 0 | 0 |
| Finland | 0 | 0 | 5,449 | 5,881 | 0 |
| France | 138,876 | 107,339 | 0 | 0 | 0 |
| East Germany | 0 | 61,867 | 111,910 | 179,343 | 244,490 |
| West Germany | 132,120 | 101,924 | 41,231 | 3,800 | 0 |
| Ghana | 0 | 0 | 0 | 0 | 0 |
| Greece | 33,549 | 45,703 | 45,920 | 49,658 | 15,483 |
| Guam | 0 | 0 | 0 | 0 | 0 |
| Guinea | 0 | 0 | 0 | 0 | 0 |
| Guinea Bissau | 0 | 0 | 0 | 0 | 0 |
| Honduras | 97 | 25 | 0 | 0 | 0 |
| Hong Kong | 10,157 | 544 | 0 | 0 | 0 |
| Hungary | 0 | 0 | 0 | 0 | 0 |
| Iceland | 4,497 | 3,541 | 5,230 | 749 | 0 |
| India | 0 | 0 | 0 | 0 | 0 |
| Indonesia | 0 | 0 | 0 | 0 | 0 |
| Iran | 9,509 | 19,207 | 61,340 | 0 | 10,431 |
| Iraq | 6,013 | 22,155 | 34,933 | 17,991 | 36,711 |
| Ireland | 3,105 | 23,374 | 0 | 0 | 0 |
| Israel | 22,428 | 0 | 0 | 0 | 0 |
| Italy | 9,679 | 551 | 0 | 2,167 | 157,904 |
| Jamaica | 0 | 0 | 0 | 0 | 0 |
| Japan | 349,323 | 204,559 | 423,256 | 431,482 | 160,771 |
| Jordan | 0 | 0 | 0 | 10,907 | 0 |
| Kenya | 0 | 0 | 0 | 0 | 0 |
| Korea (North) | 0 | 0 | 0 | 14,038 | 20,000 |
| Korea (South) | 15,743 | 0 | 32,491 | 0 | 0 |

## Appendix 5

|  | 1959 | 1960 | 1961 | 1962 | 1963 |
|---|---|---|---|---|---|
| Kuwait | 0 | 31,053 | 0 | 0 | 4,280 |
| Lebanon | 25,104 | 634 | 0 | 1,795 | 10,437 |
| Libya | 2,809 | 0 | 0 | 0 | 0 |
| Malaysia | 0 | 0 | 0 | 0 | 0 |
| Mali | 0 | 0 | 0 | 0 | 0 |
| Malta | 0 | 0 | 5,707 | 0 | 0 |
| Mexico | 0 | 0 | 0 | 0 | 0 |
| Mongolia | 0 | 0 | 0 | 0 | 0 |
| Morocco | 200,590 | 160,986 | 157,287 | 265,124 | 285,028 |
| Mozambique | 0 | 6,684 | 0 | 0 | 0 |
| Netherlands | 107,507 | 98,987 | 27,833 | 15,104 | 123,545 |
| Netherlands Antilles | 2,239 | 2,580 | 3,318 | 2,122 | 0 |
| New Zealand | 0 | 0 | 0 | 0 | 0 |
| Nicaragua | 0 | 0 | 0 | 0 | 0 |
| Norway | 0 | 0 | 32,132 | 36,138 | 22,636 |
| Oman | 0 | 0 | 0 | 0 | 1,124 |
| Pakistan | 0 | 0 | 38,204 | 0 | 0 |
| Panama | 0 | 0 | 0 | 0 | 0 |
| Peru | 0 | 0 | 0 | 0 | 0 |
| Poland | 0 | 143,990 | 261,927 | 151,285 | 103,895 |
| Portugal | 97 | 88 | 9,657 | 0 | 0 |
| Qatar | 0 | 0 | 0 | 0 | 4,494 |
| Romania | 0 | 0 | 0 | 0 | 0 |
| Saudi Arabia | 0 | 0 | 0 | 0 | 7,651 |
| Senegal | 0 | 0 | 0 | 0 | 0 |
| Sierra Leone | 0 | 0 | 0 | 0 | 0 |
| Singapore | 0 | 1,255 | 0 | 0 | 0 |
| Somalia | 0 | 0 | 0 | 0 | 0 |
| South Arabia, Fedn. | 0 | 0 | 0 | 0 | 15,340 |
| Southern Yemen | 0 | 0 | 0 | 0 | 0 |
| Spain & territories | 0 | 33,247 | 53,208 | 58,312 | 102,737 |
| St. Pierre et Miquelon | 131 | 0 | 0 | 0 | 0 |
| Sudan | 0 | 0 | 0 | 0 | 8,988 |
| Suriname | 0 | 0 | 0 | 0 | 0 |
| Sweden | 13,097 | 8,458 | 805 | 28,232 | 15,243 |
| Switzerland | 7,374 | 24,705 | 21,380 | 16,814 | 61,502 |
| Tahiti | 0 | 0 | 0 | 0 | 0 |
| Tanzania | 0 | 0 | 0 | 0 | 0 |
| Thailand | 0 | 0 | 19,028 | 0 | 0 |
| Trinidad and Tobago | 0 | 0 | 0 | 0 | 0 |
| Tunisia | 0 | 22,425 | 31,990 | 90,057 | 0 |
| Turkey | 0 | 0 | 0 | 0 | 0 |
| U.A.R. (Egypt) | 0 | 108,114 | 150,160 | 105,112 | 78,115 |
| U.A.R. (Syria) | 29,324 | 67,350 | 0 | 50,478 | 20,666 |
| United Kingdom | 358,102 | 173,368 | 79,382 | 76,143 | 173,698 |

|  | 1959 | 1960 | 1961 | 1962 | 1963 |
|---|---|---|---|---|---|
| United States | 2,937,216 | 1,948,574 | 0 | 0 | 0 |
| U.S.S.R. | 273,776 | 1,577,683 | 3,302,865 | 2,112,245 | 973,423 |
| Uganda | 0 | 0 | 0 | 0 | 0 |
| Uruguay | 0 | 0 | 0 | 0 | 20,467 |
| Venezuela | 64,967 | 0 | 0 | 0 | 0 |
| Vietnam, Cambodia, and Laos | 32,487 | 43,214 | 0 | 10,490 | 13,373 |
| Yemen Dem. Rep. | 0 | 0 | 0 | 0 | 0 |
| Yugoslavia | 0 | 11,843 | 33,869 | 54,002 | 10,700 |
| Zambia | 0 | 0 | 0 | 0 | 0 |
| Others | 873 | 544 | 500 | 33 | 0 |
| Total Exports | 4,952,747 | 5,635,057 | 6,413,561 | 5,130,940 | 3,520,505 |
| United States | 2,937,216 | 1,948,574 | 0 | 0 | 0 |
| Percent | 59 | 35 | 0 | 0 | 0 |
| Socialist countries | 273,776 | 2,280,908 | 4,825,287 | 3,732,982 | 2,066,137 |
| Percent | 6 | 40 | 75 | 73 | 59 |
| U.S.S.R. | 273,776 | 1,577,683 | 3,302,865 | 2,112,245 | 973,423 |
| Percent | 6 | 28 | 51 | 41 | 27 |
| Other countries | 1,741,755 | 1,405,575 | 1,588,274 | 1,397,958 | 1,454,368 |
| Percent | 35 | 25 | 25 | 27 | 41 |

CUBAN SUGAR TRADE, 1964–1968

|  | 1964 | 1965 | 1966 | 1967 | 1968 |
|---|---|---|---|---|---|
| Albania | 10,810 | 11,297 | 10,490 | 4,235 | 17,098 |
| Algeria | 37,696 | 18,291 | 618 | 42,713 | 43,494 |
| Angola | 0 | 0 | 0 | 0 | 0 |
| Austria | 0 | 0 | 0 | 0 | 0 |
| Bahamas | 0 | 0 | 0 | 0 | 0 |
| Bahrein | 0 | 4,780 | 0 | 5,176 | 0 |
| Bangladesh | 0 | 0 | 0 | 0 | 0 |
| Belgium/Luxembourg | 0 | 0 | 6,704 | 511 | 12,859 |
| Bermuda | 0 | 0 | 0 | 0 | 0 |
| Bolivia | 0 | 0 | 0 | 0 | 0 |
| Bulgaria | 87,248 | 157,692 | 158,051 | 194,671 | 186,431 |
| Canada | 3,268 | 68,614 | 69,378 | 66,175 | 46,739 |
| Ceylon (Sri Lanka) | 21,596 | 43,443 | 0 | 0 | 68,525 |
| Chile | 0 | 10,210 | 0 | 0 | 0 |
| China (Mainland) | 386,352 | 398,216 | 619,731 | 556,079 | 431,108 |
| Colombia | 0 | 0 | 0 | 0 | 0 |
| Costa Rica | 0 | 0 | 0 | 0 | 0 |

## Appendix 5

|  | 1964 | 1965 | 1966 | 1967 | 1968 |
|---|---|---|---|---|---|
| Czechoslovakia | 52,071 | 244,618 | 262,098 | 214,884 | 193,490 |
| Denmark | 0 | 0 | 0 | 0 | 0 |
| EEC | 0 | 0 | 0 | 0 | 0 |
| Ethiopia | 0 | 0 | 0 | 0 | 0 |
| Finland | 0 | 0 | 10,789 | 21,158 | 30,267 |
| France | 0 | 0 | 0 | 0 | 20,634 |
| East Germany | 81,054 | 169,878 | 207,192 | 249,623 | 243,656 |
| West Germany | 0 | 0 | 0 | 0 | 0 |
| Ghana | 0 | 0 | 0 | 0 | 0 |
| Greece | 0 | 0 | 0 | 0 | 34,169 |
| Guam | 0 | 0 | 0 | 0 | 0 |
| Guinea | 0 | 0 | 0 | 0 | 3,792 |
| Guinea Bissau | 0 | 0 | 0 | 0 | 0 |
| Honduras | 0 | 0 | 0 | 0 | 0 |
| Hong Kong | 0 | 0 | 0 | 0 | 0 |
| Hungary | 0 | 0 | 0 | 16,730 | 16,574 |
| Iceland | 0 | 0 | 0 | 0 | 0 |
| India | 0 | 0 | 0 | 0 | 0 |
| Indonesia | 0 | 0 | 0 | 0 | 0 |
| Iran | 31,446 | 73,446 | 10,336 | 71,327 | 10,664 |
| Iraq | 0 | 126,313 | 0 | 42,095 | 53,124 |
| Ireland | 0 | 0 | 0 | 0 | 0 |
| Israel | 0 | 9,138 | 0 | 0 | 0 |
| Italy | 149,455 | 52,533 | 45,399 | 58,890 | 0 |
| Jamaica | 0 | 0 | 0 | 0 | 0 |
| Japan | 345,582 | 415,215 | 359,961 | 542,127 | 555,422 |
| Jordan | 0 | 33,940 | 69 | 14 | 0 |
| Kenya | 0 | 0 | 0 | 0 | 0 |
| Korea (North) | 21,051 | 21,458 | 21,335 | 83,346 | 74,910 |
| Korea (South) | 0 | 0 | 0 | 0 | 0 |
| Kuwait | 10,417 | 0 | 0 | 16,115 | 0 |
| Lebanon | 10,591 | 10,459 | 329 | 753 | 0 |
| Libya | 0 | 0 | 0 | 23,417 | 0 |
| Malaysia | 0 | 0 | 0 | 118,989 | 0 |
| Mali | 0 | 10,546 | 0 | 0 | 0 |
| Malta | 0 | 0 | 0 | 0 | 5,482 |
| Mexico | 0 | 0 | 0 | 0 | 0 |
| Mongolia | 0 | 0 | 0 | 5,273 | 5,193 |
| Morocco | 323,259 | 182,209 | 181,327 | 152,768 | 85,635 |
| Mozambique | 0 | 0 | 0 | 0 | 0 |
| Netherlands | 10,387 | 31,005 | 22,294 | 71,318 | 58,520 |
| Netherlands Antilles | 0 | 0 | 0 | 0 | 0 |
| New Zealand | 0 | 0 | 0 | 0 | 0 |
| Nicaragua | 0 | 0 | 0 | 0 | 0 |
| Norway | 0 | 5,487 | 18,862 | 22,216 | 10,467 |

|  | 1964 | 1965 | 1966 | 1967 | 1968 |
|---|---|---|---|---|---|
| Oman | 0 | 0 | 0 | 0 | 0 |
| Pakistan | 0 | 0 | 0 | 0 | 0 |
| Panama | 0 | 0 | 0 | 0 | 0 |
| Peru | 0 | 0 | 0 | 0 | 0 |
| Poland | 32,148 | 0 | 52,843 | 22,327 | 20,713 |
| Portugal | 0 | 41,520 | 0 | 0 | 0 |
| Qatar | 0 | 0 | 0 | 0 | 0 |
| Romania | 0 | 0 | 0 | 0 | 53,552 |
| Saudi Arabia | 0 | 0 | 0 | 0 | 0 |
| Senegal | 0 | 0 | 0 | 0 | 0 |
| Sierra Leone | 0 | 0 | 0 | 0 | 0 |
| Singapore | 0 | 0 | 0 | 0 | 0 |
| Somalia | 11,477 | 0 | 0 | 0 | 0 |
| South Arabia, Fedn. | 0 | 0 | 0 | 0 | 0 |
| Southern Yemen | 0 | 0 | 0 | 0 | 0 |
| Spain & territories | 275,704 | 173,771 | 145,343 | 158,581 | 175,678 |
| St. Pierre et Miquelon | 0 | 0 | 0 | 0 | 0 |
| Sudan | 0 | 31,556 | 0 | 205 | 0 |
| Suriname | 0 | 0 | 0 | 0 | 0 |
| Sweden | 10,721 | 42,399 | 44,741 | 22,223 | 40,893 |
| Switzerland | 42,573 | 18,818 | 48,437 | 51,487 | 3,443 |
| Tahiti | 0 | 0 | 0 | 0 | 0 |
| Tanzania | 0 | 0 | 0 | 0 | 0 |
| Thailand | 0 | 0 | 0 | 0 | 0 |
| Trinidad and Tobago | 0 | 0 | 0 | 0 | 0 |
| Tunisia | 0 | 0 | 0 | 0 | 0 |
| Turkey | 0 | 0 | 0 | 0 | 0 |
| U.A.R. (Egypt) | 95,284 | 126,168 | 97,038 | 114,278 | 65,599 |
| U.A.R. (Syria) | 30,961 | 62,167 | 53,309 | 63,789 | 64,133 |
| United Kingdom | 94,144 | 113,237 | 61,646 | 70,290 | 20,065 |
| United States | 0 | 0 | 0 | 0 | 0 |
| U.S.S.R. | 1,936,798 | 2,456,144 | 1,814,930 | 2,473,305 | 1,831,727 |
| Uganda | 0 | 0 | 0 | 0 | 0 |
| Uruguay | 10,599 | 0 | 0 | 0 | 0 |
| Venezuela | 0 | 0 | 0 | 0 | 0 |
| Vietnam, Cambodia, and Laos | 10,542 | 65,997 | 13,077 | 45,510 | 49,777 |
| Yemen Dem. Rep. | 0 | 0 | 0 | 0 | 0 |
| Yugoslavia | 42,797 | 85,045 | 97,912 | 64,678 | 75,685 |
| Zambia | 0 | 0 | 0 | 10,727 | 0 |
| Others | 0 | 0 | 400 | 4,869 | 3,405 |
| Total Exports | 4,176,031 | 5,315,610 | 4,434,639 | 5,682,872 | 4,612,923 |
| United States | 0 | 0 | 0 | 0 | 0 |
| Percent | 0 | 0 | 0 | 0 | 0 |

|  | 1964 | 1965 | 1966 | 1967 | 1968 |
|---|---|---|---|---|---|
| Socialist countries | 2,650,329 | 3,544,348 | 3,244,582 | 3,885,151 | 3,150,137 |
| Percent | 63 | 66 | 73 | 68 | 68 |
| U.S.S.R. | 1,936,798 | 2,456,144 | 1,814,930 | 2,473,305 | 1,831,727 |
| Percent | 46 | 46 | 41 | 44 | 40 |
| Other countries | 1,525,702 | 1,771,262 | 1,190,057 | 1,797,721 | 1,462,786 |
| Percent | 37 | 33 | 27 | 32 | 32 |

## Cuban Sugar Trade, 1969–1973

|  | 1969 | 1970 | 1971 | 1972 | 1973 |
|---|---|---|---|---|---|
| Albania | 0 | 10,807 | 23,278 | 15,108 | 13,855 |
| Algeria | 41,832 | 37,691 | 24,619 | 25,417 | 5,974 |
| Angola | 0 | 0 | 0 | 0 | 0 |
| Austria | 0 | 0 | 0 | 0 | 0 |
| Bahamas | 0 | 0 | 0 | 0 | 0 |
| Bahrein | 0 | 0 | 0 | 0 | 0 |
| Bangladesh | 0 | 0 | 0 | 0 | 0 |
| Belgium/Luxembourg | 516 | 1,027 | 1,092 | 1,086 | 0 |
| Bermuda | 0 | 0 | 0 | 0 | 0 |
| Bolivia | 0 | 0 | 0 | 0 | 0 |
| Bulgaria | 205,308 | 231,170 | 210,655 | 154,257 | 212,634 |
| Canada | 79,900 | 65,411 | 73,367 | 31,125 | 46,681 |
| Ceylon (Sri Lanka) | 46,098 | 0 | 23,134 | 0 | 0 |
| Chile | 0 | 0 | 191,424 | 172,129 | 129,609 |
| China (Mainland) | 444,554 | 530,430 | 463,947 | 295,176 | 302,030 |
| Colombia | 0 | 0 | 0 | 0 | 0 |
| Costa Rica | 0 | 0 | 0 | 0 | 0 |
| Czechoslovakia | 224,356 | 226,605 | 189,638 | 151,132 | 163,018 |
| Denmark | 2,065 | 0 | 0 | 0 | 0 |
| EEC | 0 | 0 | 0 | 0 | 0 |
| Ethiopia | 0 | 0 | 0 | 0 | 0 |
| Finland | 0 | 0 | 11,936 | 16,005 | 26,399 |
| France | 0 | 0 | 7,721 | 0 | 0 |
| East Germany | 252,508 | 352,666 | 338,096 | 243,028 | 259,488 |
| West Germany | 0 | 1,027 | 2,622 | 525 | 0 |
| Ghana | 0 | 0 | 0 | 0 | 0 |
| Greece | 0 | 0 | 0 | 0 | 0 |
| Guam | 0 | 0 | 0 | 0 | 0 |
| Guinea | 0 | 0 | 0 | 0 | 0 |
| Guinea Bissau | 0 | 0 | 0 | 0 | 0 |
| Honduras | 0 | 0 | 0 | 0 | 11,157 |
| Hong Kong | 0 | 10,405 | 10,292 | 7,965 | 0 |
| Hungary | 16,663 | 16,304 | 59,396 | 38,069 | 52,422 |

## Appendix 5

|  | 1969 | 1970 | 1971 | 1972 | 1973 |
|---|---|---|---|---|---|
| Iceland | 0 | 0 | 0 | 0 | 0 |
| India | 0 | 0 | 0 | 0 | 0 |
| Indonesia | 0 | 0 | 0 | 0 | 0 |
| Iran | 0 | 0 | 25,458 | 51,845 | 0 |
| Iraq | 21,795 | 21,286 | 52,117 | 55,528 | 0 |
| Ireland | 0 | 0 | 0 | 0 | 0 |
| Israel | 0 | 0 | 0 | 0 | 0 |
| Italy | 0 | 0 | 0 | 0 | 0 |
| Jamaica | 0 | 0 | 0 | 0 | 0 |
| Japan | 1,017,689 | 1,220,941 | 912,234 | 909,381 | 984,558 |
| Jordan | 0 | 0 | 0 | 0 | 0 |
| Kenya | 0 | 0 | 46,095 | 27,278 | 37,739 |
| Korea (North) | 154,851 | 149,110 | 196,704 | 119,233 | 135,576 |
| Korea (South) | 0 | 0 | 0 | 0 | 0 |
| Kuwait | 0 | 0 | 0 | 0 | 0 |
| Lebanon | 0 | 9,915 | 44,878 | 0 | 9,322 |
| Libya | 0 | 10,832 | 0 | 0 | 0 |
| Malaysia | 104,938 | 214,536 | 140,551 | 87,691 | 29,223 |
| Mali | 0 | 0 | 0 | 0 | 0 |
| Malta | 0 | 2,283 | 2,283 | 2,108 | 0 |
| Mexico | 0 | 0 | 0 | 0 | 0 |
| Mongolia | 0 | 0 | 0 | 10,739 | 2,670 |
| Morocco | 175,760 | 106,035 | 165,312 | 55,204 | 61,757 |
| Mozambique | 0 | 0 | 0 | 0 | 0 |
| Netherlands | 0 | 2,074 | 787 | 551 | 11 |
| Netherlands Antilles | 0 | 0 | 0 | 0 | 0 |
| New Zealand | 0 | 0 | 0 | 0 | 13,282 |
| Nicaragua | 0 | 0 | 0 | 0 | 0 |
| Norway | 0 | 0 | 0 | 0 | 0 |
| Oman | 0 | 0 | 0 | 0 | 0 |
| Pakistan | 0 | 0 | 0 | 0 | 0 |
| Panama | 0 | 0 | 0 | 0 | 1,150 |
| Peru | 0 | 0 | 0 | 0 | 0 |
| Poland | 28,134 | 24,177 | 30,313 | 22,247 | 55,124 |
| Portugal | 0 | 0 | 0 | 0 | 0 |
| Qatar | 0 | 0 | 0 | 0 | 0 |
| Romania | 69,143 | 99,178 | 109,312 | 72,583 | 78,174 |
| Saudi Arabia | 0 | 0 | 0 | 0 | 0 |
| Senegal | 0 | 0 | 6,518 | 5,117 | 0 |
| Sierra Leone | 0 | 0 | 0 | 1,087 | 0 |
| Singapore | 36,679 | 47,467 | 37,560 | 0 | 14,280 |
| Somalia | 0 | 0 | 0 | 0 | 0 |
| South Arabia, Fedn. | 0 | 0 | 0 | 0 | 0 |
| Southern Yemen | 0 | 0 | 0 | 10,539 | 0 |
| Spain & territories | 181,577 | 143,401 | 81,881 | 97,702 | 103,522 |

260     *Appendix 5*

|  | *1969* | *1970* | *1971* | *1972* | *1973* |
|---|---|---|---|---|---|
| St. Pierre et Miquelon | 0 | 0 | 0 | 0 | 0 |
| Sudan | 0 | 14,229 | 36,535 | 24,835 | 0 |
| Suriname | 0 | 0 | 0 | 0 | 0 |
| Sweden | 10,177 | 60,323 | 47,307 | 64,561 | 56,308 |
| Switzerland | 516 | 1,334 | 2,607 | 550 | 2,282 |
| Tahiti | 0 | 0 | 0 | 0 | 0 |
| Tanzania | 0 | 0 | 0 | 0 | 0 |
| Thailand | 0 | 0 | 0 | 0 | 0 |
| Trinidad and Tobago | 0 | 0 | 0 | 0 | 0 |
| Tunisia | 0 | 0 | 0 | 0 | 0 |
| Turkey | 0 | 0 | 0 | 0 | 0 |
| U.A.R. (Egypt) | 68,720 | 31,689 | 42,590 | 21,342 | 5,172 |
| U.A.R. (Syria) | 87,217 | 97,959 | 115,995 | 101,147 | 106,754 |
| United Kingdom | 42,912 | 0 | 50,603 | 28,848 | 121,880 |
| United States | 0 | 0 | 0 | 0 | 0 |
| U.S.S.R. | 1,352,329 | 3,105,030 | 1,580,988 | 1,097,406 | 1,660,681 |
| Uganda | 0 | 0 | 0 | 0 | 0 |
| Uruguay | 0 | 0 | 0 | 0 | 0 |
| Venezuela | 0 | 0 | 0 | 0 | 5,193 |
| Vietnam, Cambodia, and Laos | 60,129 | 56,512 | 76,106 | 75,633 | 75,910 |
| Yemen Dem. Rep. | 0 | 0 | 0 | 0 | 0 |
| Yugoslavia | 67,360 | 0 | 72,300 | 43,478 | 11,804 |
| Zambia | 0 | 0 | 0 | 0 | 0 |
| Others | 5,091 | 4,432 | 2,609 | 1,901 | 1,738 |
| Total Exports | 4,798,817 | 6,906,286 | 5,510,860 | 4,139,556 | 4,797,377 |
| United States | 0 | 0 | 0 | 0 | 0 |
| Percent | 0 | 0 | 0 | 0 | 0 |
| Socialist countries | 2,815,206 | 4,745,477 | 3,274,627 | 2,262,456 | 2,947,476 |
| Percent | 59 | 69 | 59 | 55 | 61 |
| U.S.S.R. | 1,352,329 | 3,105,030 | 1,580,988 | 1,097,406 | 1,660,681 |
| Percent | 28 | 45 | 29 | 27 | 35 |
| Other countries | 1,983,611 | 2,160,809 | 2,236,233 | 1,877,100 | 1,849,901 |
| Percent | 41 | 31 | 41 | 45 | 39 |

CUBAN SUGAR TRADE, 1974–1978

|  | *1974* | *1975* | *1976* | *1977* | *1978* |
|---|---|---|---|---|---|
| Albania | 12,850 | 14,171 | 13,169 | 8,370 | 20,997 |
| Algeria | 7,182 | 46,495 | 35,191 | 51,145 | 175,633 |
| Angola | 0 | 0 | 31,881 | 51,063 | 68,059 |

## Appendix 5

|  | 1974 | 1975 | 1976 | 1977 | 1978 |
|---|---|---|---|---|---|
| Austria | 0 | 0 | 0 | 0 | 0 |
| Bahamas | 0 | 0 | 0 | 0 | 0 |
| Bahrein | 0 | 0 | 0 | 0 | 0 |
| Bangladesh | 0 | 0 | 0 | 0 | 0 |
| Belgium/Luxembourg | 0 | 0 | 0 | 0 | 0 |
| Bermuda | 0 | 0 | 0 | 0 | 0 |
| Bolivia | 0 | 0 | 0 | 0 | 0 |
| Bulgaria | 190,144 | 185,728 | 232,042 | 218,585 | 189,623 |
| Canada | 115,669 | 156,192 | 149,041 | 139,058 | 279,021 |
| Ceylon (Sri Lanka) | 0 | 0 | 0 | 0 | 0 |
| Chile | 0 | 0 | 0 | 0 | 0 |
| China (Mainland) | 358,670 | 182,877 | 254,315 | 228,087 | 533,853 |
| Colombia | 0 | 0 | 0 | 41,936 | 0 |
| Costa Rica | 0 | 0 | 0 | 0 | 0 |
| Czechoslovakia | 160,484 | 55,745 | 109,172 | 67,374 | 84,850 |
| Denmark | 0 | 21,089 | 21,739 | 0 | 0 |
| EEC | 0 | 0 | 0 | 0 | 0 |
| Ethiopia | 0 | 0 | 0 | 11,430 | 0 |
| Finland | 82,702 | 95,978 | 71,111 | 131,166 | 88,197 |
| France | 0 | 12,127 | 15,100 | 0 | 0 |
| East Germany | 276,003 | 169,195 | 194,868 | 228,940 | 200,717 |
| West Germany | 0 | 0 | 0 | 0 | 0 |
| Ghana | 0 | 0 | 0 | 0 | 0 |
| Greece | 0 | 0 | 0 | 0 | 0 |
| Guam | 0 | 0 | 0 | 0 | 0 |
| Guinea | 0 | 0 | 0 | 0 | 0 |
| Guinea Bissau | 0 | 0 | 0 | 0 | 0 |
| Honduras | 0 | 0 | 0 | 0 | 0 |
| Hong Kong | 0 | 0 | 13,332 | 12,035 | 0 |
| Hungary | 51,369 | 41,762 | 70,007 | 51,416 | 58,424 |
| Iceland | 0 | 0 | 0 | 0 | 0 |
| India | 0 | 0 | 0 | 0 | 0 |
| Indonesia | 0 | 0 | 0 | 140,991 | 105,159 |
| Iran | 0 | 0 | 0 | 0 | 0 |
| Iraq | 65,162 | 78,395 | 83,003 | 86,591 | 191,421 |
| Ireland | 0 | 0 | 10,581 | 0 | 0 |
| Israel | 0 | 0 | 0 | 0 | 0 |
| Italy | 0 | 0 | 0 | 0 | 0 |
| Jamaica | 0 | 4,468 | 0 | 0 | 11,102 |
| Japan | 1,151,981 | 338,825 | 149,941 | 183,452 | 530,096 |
| Jordan | 0 | 0 | 0 | 0 | 0 |
| Kenya | 0 | 0 | 0 | 0 | 0 |
| Korea (North) | 55,305 | 50,441 | 21,999 | 18,542 | 11,838 |
| Korea (South) | 0 | 0 | 0 | 0 | 0 |
| Kuwait | 0 | 0 | 0 | 0 | 0 |

## Appendix 5

|  | 1974 | 1975 | 1976 | 1977 | 1978 |
|---|---|---|---|---|---|
| Lebanon | 10,920 | 22,035 | 0 | 5,708 | 0 |
| Libya | 0 | 0 | 0 | 0 | 27,073 |
| Malaysia | 64,222 | 0 | 18,861 | 0 | 64,401 |
| Mali | 0 | 22,143 | 0 | 0 | 0 |
| Malta | 0 | 0 | 4,096 | 0 | 0 |
| Mexico | 0 | 0 | 0 | 0 | 0 |
| Mongolia | 2,702 | 2,698 | 2,083 | 2,283 | 4,678 |
| Morocco | 40,793 | 100,280 | 108,777 | 166,502 | 132,366 |
| Mozambique | 0 | 0 | 0 | 0 | 0 |
| Netherlands | 0 | 0 | 0 | 0 | 0 |
| Netherlands Antilles | 0 | 0 | 0 | 0 | 0 |
| New Zealand | 38,736 | 93,673 | 34,990 | 17,435 | 0 |
| Nicaragua | 0 | 0 | 0 | 0 | 0 |
| Norway | 0 | 0 | 0 | 0 | 0 |
| Oman | 0 | 0 | 0 | 0 | 0 |
| Pakistan | 0 | 0 | 0 | 0 | 0 |
| Panama | 0 | 0 | 0 | 0 | 0 |
| Peru | 0 | 0 | 0 | 0 | 0 |
| Poland | 28,278 | 43,100 | 16,642 | 31,099 | 60,209 |
| Portugal | 51,502 | 115,656 | 92,011 | 25,582 | 141,771 |
| Qatar | 0 | 0 | 0 | 0 | 0 |
| Romania | 77,953 | 11,224 | 39,303 | 25,868 | 0 |
| Saudi Arabia | 0 | 0 | 0 | 0 | 0 |
| Senegal | 0 | 31,831 | 46,175 | 0 | 0 |
| Sierra Leone | 0 | 0 | 0 | 0 | 0 |
| Singapore | 0 | 0 | 0 | 0 | 0 |
| Somalia | 0 | 0 | 0 | 0 | 0 |
| South Arabia, Fedn. | 0 | 0 | 0 | 0 | 0 |
| Southern Yemen | 0 | 0 | 0 | 0 | 0 |
| Spain & territories | 363,127 | 326,523 | 114,519 | 158,948 | 0 |
| St. Pierre et Miquelon | 0 | 0 | 0 | 0 | 0 |
| Sudan | 0 | 27,260 | 0 | 24,003 | 0 |
| Suriname | 0 | 0 | 1,098 | 3,972 | 2,654 |
| Sweden | 50,818 | 35,252 | 108,291 | 35,349 | 0 |
| Switzerland | 2,806 | 1,038 | 2,097 | 2,750 | 1,453 |
| Tahiti | 0 | 0 | 0 | 0 | 0 |
| Tanzania | 0 | 0 | 0 | 0 | 0 |
| Thailand | 0 | 0 | 0 | 0 | 0 |
| Trinidad and Tobago | 0 | 4,073 | 0 | 0 | 0 |
| Tunisia | 0 | 12,442 | 0 | 10,897 | 10,647 |
| Turkey | 11,925 | 22,828 | 0 | 0 | 0 |
| U.A.R. (Egypt) | 0 | 13,699 | 23,006 | 71,893 | 127,054 |
| U.A.R. (Syria) | 41,311 | 52,794 | 106,222 | 109,476 | 87,044 |
| United Kingdom | 70,951 | 16,671 | 138,756 | 0 | 0 |
| United States | 0 | 0 | 0 | 0 | 0 |

*Appendix 5*

|  | 1974 | 1975 | 1976 | 1977 | 1978 |
|---|---|---|---|---|---|
| U.S.S.R. | 1,974,761 | 3,186,724 | 3,035,566 | 3,790,424 | 3,936,133 |
| Uganda | 0 | 0 | 0 | 0 | 0 |
| Uruguay | 0 | 0 | 0 | 0 | 0 |
| Venezuela | 0 | 0 | 0 | 0 | 0 |
| Vietnam, Cambodia, and Laos | 78,018 | 86,918 | 124,538 | 67,680 | 82,468 |
| Yemen Dem. Rep. | 0 | 0 | 0 | 0 | 0 |
| Yugoslavia | 50,371 | 60,767 | 266,360 | 12,573 | 0 |
| Zambia | 0 | 0 | 0 | 0 | 0 |
| Others | 4,532 | 594 | 3,769 | 5,989 | 4,278 |
| Total Exports | 5,491,247 | 5,743,711 | 5,763,652 | 6,238,612 | 7,231,219 |
| United States | 0 | 0 | 0 | 0 | 0 |
| Percent | 0 | 0 | 0 | 0 | 0 |
| Socialist countries | 3,238,890 | 4,004,432 | 4,255,526 | 4,683,561 | 5,101,322 |
| Percent | 59 | 70 | 74 | 75 | 71 |
| U.S.S.R. | 1,974,761 | 3,186,724 | 3,035,566 | 3,790,424 | 3,936,133 |
| Percent | 36 | 55 | 53 | 61 | 54 |
| Other countries | 2,252,357 | 1,739,279 | 1,508,126 | 1,555,051 | 2,129,897 |
| Percent | 41 | 30 | 26 | 25 | 29 |

CUBAN SUGAR TRADE, 1979–1983

|  | 1979 | 1980 | 1981 | 1982 | 1983 |
|---|---|---|---|---|---|
| Albania | 24,649 | 17,069 | 12,143 | 15,946 | 15,698 |
| Algeria | 203,088 | 207,131 | 253,259 | 207,896 | 99,005 |
| Angola | 53,886 | 67,173 | 57,641 | 52,028 | 40,633 |
| Austria | 0 | 0 | 0 | 0 | 0 |
| Bahamas | 0 | 0 | 0 | 0 | 0 |
| Bahrein | 0 | 0 | 0 | 0 | 0 |
| Bangladesh | 0 | 0 | 0 | 0 | 0 |
| Belgium/Luxembourg | 0 | 0 | 0 | 0 | 0 |
| Bermuda | 0 | 0 | 0 | 0 | 0 |
| Bolivia | 0 | 0 | 0 | 0 | 0 |
| Bulgaria | 218,223 | 234,112 | 249,851 | 277,678 | 331,485 |
| Canada | 316,249 | 263,508 | 375,985 | 169,299 | 190,490 |
| Ceylon (Sri Lanka) | 0 | 0 | 0 | 0 | 0 |
| Chile | 0 | 0 | 0 | 0 | 0 |
| China (Mainland) | 485,625 | 512,095 | 573,246 | 915,311 | 771,717 |
| Colombia | 0 | 0 | 0 | 0 | 0 |
| Costa Rica | 0 | 0 | 0 | 0 | 0 |
| Czechoslovakia | 99,060 | 98,755 | 99,871 | 134,892 | 144,648 |

## Appendix 5

|  | 1979 | 1980 | 1981 | 1982 | 1983 |
|---|---|---|---|---|---|
| Denmark | 38,622 | 0 | 0 | 0 | 0 |
| EEC | 0 | 0 | 0 | 0 | 0 |
| Ethiopia | 0 | 0 | 0 | 0 | 0 |
| Finland | 102,162 | 78,124 | 173,261 | 38,816 | 64,870 |
| France | 0 | 0 | 0 | 0 | 0 |
| East Germany | 223,100 | 209,900 | 254,770 | 213,461 | 280,922 |
| West Germany | 0 | 0 | 0 | 0 | 0 |
| Ghana | 0 | 0 | 0 | 0 | 0 |
| Greece | 0 | 0 | 0 | 0 | 0 |
| Guam | 0 | 0 | 0 | 0 | 0 |
| Guinea | 0 | 0 | 0 | 0 | 0 |
| Guinea Bissau | 0 | 0 | 2,131 | 2,096 | 0 |
| Honduras | 0 | 0 | 0 | 0 | 0 |
| Hong Kong | 0 | 0 | 0 | 0 | 0 |
| Hungary | 72,414 | 34,152 | 76,216 | 72,903 | 0 |
| Iceland | 0 | 0 | 0 | 0 | 0 |
| India | 0 | 0 | 0 | 0 | 0 |
| Indonesia | 132,531 | 39,394 | 13,646 | 14,236 | 0 |
| Iran | 0 | 0 | 0 | 0 | 61,595 |
| Iraq | 248,484 | 277,840 | 178,184 | 133,783 | 158,217 |
| Ireland | 0 | 0 | 0 | 0 | 0 |
| Israel | 0 | 0 | 0 | 0 | 0 |
| Italy | 0 | 0 | 0 | 0 | 0 |
| Jamaica | 0 | 1,081 | 8,872 | 1,626 | 0 |
| Japan | 297,300 | 267,082 | 354,593 | 294,986 | 354,532 |
| Jordan | 0 | 0 | 0 | 0 | 0 |
| Kenya | 0 | 0 | 0 | 0 | 0 |
| Korea (North) | 21,621 | 10,897 | 27,559 | 17,079 | 22,511 |
| Korea (South) | 0 | 0 | 0 | 0 | 0 |
| Kuwait | 0 | 0 | 0 | 0 | 0 |
| Lebanon | 0 | 0 | 0 | 0 | 0 |
| Libya | 42,694 | 75,723 | 54,729 | 45,055 | 90,191 |
| Malaysia | 25,299 | 25,206 | 107,749 | 26,269 | 60,463 |
| Mali | 0 | 0 | 0 | 0 | 0 |
| Malta | 0 | 0 | 0 | 0 | 0 |
| Mexico | 0 | 401,122 | 138,126 | 139,702 | 62,732 |
| Mongolia | 4,658 | 4,720 | 4,697 | 4,701 | 4,699 |
| Morocco | 12,443 | 0 | 0 | 0 | 0 |
| Mozambique | 0 | 0 | 0 | 0 | 0 |
| Netherlands | 0 | 0 | 0 | 0 | 0 |
| Netherlands Antilles | 0 | 2,183 | 977 | 2,346 | 3,413 |
| New Zealand | 58,781 | 0 | 0 | 15,662 | 0 |
| Nicaragua | 0 | 10,830 | 0 | 0 | 0 |
| Norway | 0 | 0 | 0 | 0 | 0 |
| Oman | 0 | 0 | 0 | 0 | 0 |

## Appendix 5

|  | 1979 | 1980 | 1981 | 1982 | 1983 |
|---|---|---|---|---|---|
| Pakistan | 0 | 0 | 0 | 0 | 0 |
| Panama | 0 | 0 | 0 | 0 | 0 |
| Peru | 0 | 0 | 0 | 0 | 25,037 |
| Poland | 63,660 | 63,128 | 70,154 | 0 | 0 |
| Portugal | 116,613 | 131,377 | 155,405 | 70,814 | 15,086 |
| Qatar | 0 | 0 | 0 | 0 | 0 |
| Romania | 39,017 | 46,754 | 138,820 | 89,663 | 221,454 |
| Saudi Arabia | 0 | 0 | 0 | 0 | 0 |
| Senegal | 0 | 0 | 27,560 | 0 | 0 |
| Sierra Leone | 0 | 0 | 0 | 0 | 0 |
| Singapore | 12,611 | 12,611 | 0 | 0 | 0 |
| Somalia | 0 | 0 | 0 | 0 | 0 |
| South Arabia, Fedn. | 0 | 0 | 0 | 0 | 0 |
| Southern Yemen | 0 | 0 | 0 | 0 | 0 |
| Spain & territories | 79,807 | 0 | 22,746 | 21,588 | 0 |
| St. Pierre et Miquelon | 0 | 0 | 0 | 0 | 0 |
| Sudan | 0 | 0 | 0 | 0 | 0 |
| Suriname | 0 | 0 | 1,080 | 4,558 | 3,307 |
| Sweden | 0 | 0 | 24,647 | 0 | 5,196 |
| Switzerland | 2,870 | 3,640 | 3,072 | 3,089 | 2,232 |
| Tahiti | 0 | 0 | 0 | 0 | 0 |
| Tanzania | 0 | 11,383 | 0 | 0 | 0 |
| Thailand | 0 | 0 | 0 | 0 | 0 |
| Trinidad and Tobago | 0 | 0 | 0 | 0 | 0 |
| Tunisia | 35,963 | 32,904 | 14,354 | 0 | 12,114 |
| Turkey | 0 | 0 | 0 | 0 | 0 |
| U.A.R. (Egypt) | 111,320 | 138,088 | 162,415 | 190,269 | 230,779 |
| U.A.R. (Syria) | 140,779 | 133,999 | 108,714 | 109,274 | 109,323 |
| United Kingdom | 12,584 | 0 | 0 | 0 | 0 |
| United States | 0 | 0 | 0 | 0 | 0 |
| U.S.S.R. | 3,842,211 | 2,726,339 | 3,204,475 | 4,425,519 | 3,314,985 |
| Uganda | 0 | 1,084 | 0 | 0 | 0 |
| Uruguay | 0 | 0 | 0 | 0 | 0 |
| Venezuela | 0 | 0 | 0 | 0 | 0 |
| Vietnam, Cambodia, and Laos | 111,498 | 47,264 | 104,239 | 24,155 | 77,663 |
| Yemen Dem. Rep. | 10,839 | 0 | 0 | 0 | 2,096 |
| Yugoslavia | 0 | 0 | 10,389 | 0 | 9,397 |
| Zambia | 0 | 0 | 0 | 0 | 0 |
| Others | 8,748 | 4,386 | 6,869 | 8,583 | 5,603 |
| Total Exports | 7,269,409 | 6,191,054 | 7,072,445 | 7,743,283 | 6,792,093 |
| United States | 0 | 0 | 0 | 0 | 0 |
| Percent | 0 | 0 | 0 | 0 | 0 |

|  | 1979 | 1980 | 1981 | 1982 | 1983 |
|---|---|---|---|---|---|
| Socialist countries | 5,094,238 | 3,957,921 | 4,722,191 | 6,167,153 | 5,117,516 |
| Percent | 70 | 64 | 67 | 80 | 75 |
| U.S.S.R. | 3,842,211 | 2,726,339 | 3,204,475 | 4,425,519 | 3,314,985 |
| Percent | 53 | 44 | 45 | 57 | 49 |
| Other countries | 2,175,171 | 2,233,133 | 2,350,254 | 1,576,130 | 1,674,577 |
| Percent | 30 | 36 | 33 | 20 | 25 |

CUBAN SUGAR TRADE, 1984–1987

|  | 1984 | 1985 | 1986 | 1987 |
|---|---|---|---|---|
| Albania | 14,673 | 21,981 | 22,154 | 23,501 |
| Algeria | 40,935 | 80,666 | 98,767 | 33,677 |
| Angola | 45,648 | 51,029 | 57,991 | 32,421 |
| Austria | 0 | 0 | 0 | 0 |
| Bahamas | 0 | 0 | 0 | 0 |
| Bahrein | 0 | 0 | 0 | 0 |
| Bangladesh | 0 | 0 | 12,349 | 0 |
| Belgium/Luxembourg | 0 | 0 | 0 | 0 |
| Bermuda | 0 | 0 | 0 | 0 |
| Bolivia | 0 | 0 | 0 | 0 |
| Bulgaria | 360,107 | 399,531 | 302,838 | 304,699 |
| Canada | 241,070 | 152,279 | 168,025 | 87,011 |
| Ceylon (Sri Lanka) | 0 | 13,195 | 12,999 | 0 |
| Chile | 0 | 0 | 0 | 0 |
| China (Mainland) | 705,054 | 680,134 | 307,241 | 611,827 |
| Colombia | 0 | 0 | 0 | 0 |
| Costa Rica | 0 | 0 | 0 | 0 |
| Czechoslovakia | 226,489 | 133,678 | 105,803 | 128,509 |
| Denmark | 0 | 0 | 0 | 0 |
| EEC | 27,050 | 6,995 | 12,438 | 0 |
| Ethiopia | 4,809 | 0 | 0 | 0 |
| Finland | 39,340 | 75,508 | 61,744 | 56,689 |
| France | 0 | 0 | 0 | 0 |
| East Germany | 278,773 | 277,152 | 271,079 | 283,510 |
| West Germany | 0 | 0 | 0 | 0 |
| Ghana | 0 | 0 | 12,388 | 13,032 |
| Greece | 0 | 0 | 0 | 0 |
| Guam | 0 | 0 | 0 | 0 |
| Guinea | 0 | 0 | 0 | 0 |
| Guinea Bissau | 0 | 0 | 1,083 | 0 |
| Honduras | 0 | 0 | 0 | 0 |
| Hong Kong | 0 | 0 | 0 | 0 |
| Hungary | 0 | 0 | 0 | 0 |

*Appendix 5*

|  | 1984 | 1985 | 1986 | 1987 |
|---|---|---|---|---|
| Iceland | 0 | 0 | 0 | 0 |
| India | 40,999 | 108,498 | 0 | 122,799 |
| Indonesia | 0 | 0 | 0 | 26,434 |
| Iran | 0 | 0 | 0 | 0 |
| Iraq | 112,719 | 103,154 | 55,318 | 26,322 |
| Ireland | 0 | 0 | 0 | 0 |
| Israel | 0 | 0 | 0 | 0 |
| Italy | 0 | 0 | 0 | 0 |
| Jamaica | 0 | 0 | 0 | 0 |
| Japan | 231,087 | 511,375 | 534,487 | 222,931 |
| Jordan | 0 | 0 | 0 | 0 |
| Kenya | 0 | 0 | 0 | 0 |
| Korea (North) | 21,262 | 24,072 | 19,582 | 36,762 |
| Korea (South) | 0 | 0 | 0 | 0 |
| Kuwait | 0 | 0 | 0 | 0 |
| Lebanon | 0 | 0 | 0 | 0 |
| Libya | 44,345 | 113,156 | 57,819 | 23,232 |
| Malaysia | 39,269 | 52,180 | 56,311 | 0 |
| Mali | 0 | 0 | 0 | 0 |
| Malta | 0 | 0 | 0 | 0 |
| Mexico | 52,702 | 0 | 0 | 0 |
| Mongolia | 0 | 4,717 | 4,729 | 0 |
| Morocco | 0 | 0 | 0 | 0 |
| Mozambique | 0 | 0 | 0 | 0 |
| Netherlands | 0 | 0 | 0 | 0 |
| Netherlands Antilles | 974 | 1,083 | 0 | 0 |
| New Zealand | 44,044 | 0 | 0 | 0 |
| Nicaragua | 0 | 0 | 0 | 0 |
| Norway | 0 | 0 | 0 | 0 |
| Oman | 0 | 0 | 0 | 0 |
| Pakistan | 0 | 0 | 28,458 | 0 |
| Panama | 0 | 0 | 0 | 0 |
| Peru | 54,411 | 0 | 40,859 | 12,354 |
| Poland | 0 | 134,350 | 104,786 | 54,029 |
| Portugal | 84,974 | 0 | 0 | 0 |
| Qatar | 0 | 0 | 0 | 0 |
| Romania | 272,088 | 62,516 | 56,385 | 228,009 |
| Saudi Arabia | 0 | 0 | 0 | 0 |
| Senegal | 20,554 | 0 | 0 | 0 |
| Sierra Leone | 0 | 0 | 0 | 0 |
| Singapore | 0 | 0 | 0 | 0 |
| Somalia | 0 | 0 | 0 | 0 |
| South Arabia, Fedn. | 0 | 0 | 0 | 0 |
| Southern Yemen | 0 | 0 | 0 | 0 |
| Spain & territories | 0 | 0 | 0 | 0 |

## Appendix 5

|  | 1984 | 1985 | 1986 | 1987 |
|---|---|---|---|---|
| St. Pierre et Miquelon | 0 | 0 | 0 | 0 |
| Sudan | 0 | 0 | 0 | 0 |
| Suriname | 0 | 0 | 0 | 0 |
| Sweden | 0 | 12,761 | 25,129 | 25,130 |
| Switzerland | 2,934 | 3,013 | 3,257 | 3,023 |
| Tahiti | 0 | 0 | 0 | 0 |
| Tanzania | 0 | 0 | 0 | 0 |
| Thailand | 0 | 0 | 0 | 0 |
| Trinidad and Tobago | 0 | 0 | 0 | 0 |
| Tunisia | 26,910 | 76,112 | 37,563 | 37,833 |
| Turkey | 0 | 0 | 0 | 0 |
| U.A.R. (Egypt) | 137,911 | 181,676 | 138,569 | 76,922 |
| U.A.R. (Syria) | 132,703 | 62,989 | 50,775 | 76,740 |
| United Kingdom | 0 | 0 | 0 | 0 |
| United States | 0 | 0 | 0 | 0 |
| U.S.S.R. | 3,649,996 | 3,709,272 | 4,019,793 | 3,863,158 |
| Uganda | 0 | 0 | 5,416 | 23,628 |
| Uruguay | 0 | 0 | 0 | 0 |
| Venezuela | 0 | 123,094 | 0 | 17,817 |
| Vietnam, Cambodia, and Laos | 39,082 | 3,137 | 13,741 | 27,069 |
| Yemen Dem. Rep. | 0 | 0 | 0 | 0 |
| Yugoslavia | 20,878 | 0 | 0 | 0 |
| Zambia | 0 | 0 | 0 | 0 |
| Others | 2,710 | 2,705 | 2,712 | 3,067 |
| Total Exports | 7,016,500 | 7,182,008 | 6,702,588 | 6,482,135 |
| United States | 0 | 0 | 0 | 0 |
| Percent | 0 | 0 | 0 | 0 |
| Socialist countries | 5,549,320 | 5,447,403 | 5,214,390 | 5,534,004 |
| Percent | 79 | 76 | 78 | 85 |
| U.S.S.R. | 3,649,996 | 3,709,272 | 4,019,793 | 3,863,158 |
| Percent | 52 | 52 | 60 | 60 |
| Other countries | 1,467,180 | 1,734,605 | 1,488,198 | 948,131 |
| Percent | 21 | 24 | 21 | 15 |

SOURCE: ISO.

# APPENDIX 6

Domestic Production, Imports, and Consumption
of Selected food Products
*(in thousands of tons)*

|      | Production | Imports | Apparent Consumption | Imports/ Consumption (%) |
|------|------------|---------|----------------------|--------------------------|
| RICE |            |         |                      |                          |
| 1961 | 213        | 187     | 400                  | 47                       |
| 1962 | 230        | 195     | 425                  | 46                       |
| 1963 | 140        | 190     | 330                  | 58                       |
| 1964 | 123        | 285     | 408                  | 70                       |
| 1965 | 55         | 282     | 337                  | 84                       |
| 1966 | 68         | 146     | 214                  | 68                       |
| 1967 | 93         | 157     | 250                  | 63                       |
| 1968 | 100        | 177     | 277                  | 64                       |
| 1969 | 205        | 186     | 391                  | 48                       |
| 1970 | 326        | 199     | 525                  | 38                       |
| 1971 | 330        | 280     | 610                  | 46                       |
| 1972 | 350        | 256     | 606                  | 42                       |
| 1973 | 375        | 201     | 576                  | 35                       |
| 1974 | 400        | 276     | 676                  | 41                       |
| 1975 | 417        | 216     | 633                  | 34                       |
| 1976 | 451        | 179     | 630                  | 28                       |
| 1977 | 420        | 144     | 564                  | 26                       |
| 1978 | 351        | 171     | 522                  | 33                       |
| 1979 | 425        | 161     | 586                  | 27                       |
| 1980 | 478        | 200     | 678                  | 29                       |
| 1981 | 461        | 199     | 660                  | 30                       |
| 1982 | 520        | 201     | 721                  | 28                       |
| 1983 | 518        | 207     | 725                  | 29                       |
| 1984 | 555        | 184     | 739                  | 25                       |
| 1985 | 524        | 242     | 766                  | 32                       |
| 1986 | 576        | 189     | 765                  | 25                       |
| 1987 | 466        | 200     | 666                  | 30                       |

## Appendix 6

|  | Production | Imports | Apparent Consumption | Imports/ Consumption (%) |
|---|---|---|---|---|
| BEANS | | | | |
| 1962 | 34 | 39 | 73 | 53 |
| 1963 | 30 | 64 | 94 | 68 |
| 1964 | 27 | 58 | 85 | 68 |
| 1965 | 25 | 62 | 87 | 71 |
| 1966 | 23 | 69 | 92 | 75 |
| 1967 | 22 | 76 | 98 | 78 |
| 1968 | 22 | 72 | 94 | 77 |
| 1969 | 23 | 81 | 104 | 78 |
| 1970 | 22 | 87 | 109 | 80 |
| 1971 | 23 | 83 | 106 | 78 |
| 1972 | 23 | 90 | 113 | 80 |
| 1973 | 24 | 89 | 113 | 79 |
| 1974 | 24 | 110 | 134 | 82 |
| 1975 | 24 | 87 | 111 | 78 |
| 1976 | 24 | 106 | 130 | 82 |
| 1977 | 24 | 100 | 124 | 81 |
| 1978 | 25 | 106 | 131 | 81 |
| 1979 | 26 | 87 | 113 | 77 |
| 1980 | 26 | 65 | 91 | 71 |
| 1981 | 26 | 102 | 128 | 80 |
| 1982 | 27 | 119 | 146 | 82 |
| 1983 | 27 | 107 | 134 | 80 |
| 1984 | 27 | 125 | 152 | 82 |
| 1985 | 27 | 128 | 155 | 83 |
| 1986 | 28 | 94 | 122 | 77 |
| 1987 | 28 | 72 | 100 | 72 |
| CORN | | | | |
| 1961 | 160 | 43 | 203 | 21 |
| 1962 | 152 | 103 | 255 | 40 |
| 1963 | 140 | 86 | 226 | 38 |
| 1964 | 129 | 232 | 361 | 64 |
| 1965 | 117 | 174 | 291 | 60 |
| 1966 | 127 | 180 | 307 | 59 |
| 1967 | 120 | 169 | 289 | 59 |
| 1968 | 115 | 160 | 275 | 58 |
| 1969 | 115 | 112 | 227 | 49 |
| 1970 | 115 | 170 | 285 | 60 |
| 1971 | 115 | 153 | 268 | 57 |
| 1972 | 120 | 172 | 292 | 59 |
| 1973 | 125 | 260 | 385 | 68 |
| 1974 | 125 | 301 | 426 | 71 |

## Appendix 6

| | | | | |
|---|---|---|---|---|
| 1975 | 125 | 376 | 501 | 75 |
| 1976 | 94 | 436 | 530 | 82 |
| 1977 | 94 | 212 | 306 | 69 |
| 1978 | 95 | 481 | 576 | 84 |
| 1979 | 95 | 350 | 445 | 79 |
| 1980 | 95 | 506 | 601 | 84 |
| 1981 | 95 | 524 | 619 | 85 |
| 1982 | 96 | 368 | 464 | 79 |
| 1983 | 96 | 402 | 498 | 81 |
| 1984 | 95 | 423 | 518 | 82 |
| 1985 | 95 | 409 | 504 | 81 |
| 1986 | 95 | 449 | 544 | 83 |
| 1987 | 95 | 430 | 525 | 82 |

| | Production | Imports Dry Milk | Imports Condensed | Apparent Consumption | Imports/ Consumption (%) |
|---|---|---|---|---|---|
| **MILK** | | | | | |
| 1965 | 462 | 159 | 126 | 747 | 38 |
| 1966 | 465 | 136 | 94 | 695 | 33 |
| 1967 | 580 | 203 | 109 | 892 | 35 |
| 1968 | 590 | 346 | 105 | 1,041 | 43 |
| 1969 | 520 | 255 | 99 | 874 | 41 |
| 1970 | 475 | 487 | 98 | 1,060 | 55 |
| 1971 | 505 | 434 | 110 | 1,049 | 52 |
| 1972 | 520 | 324 | 109 | 953 | 45 |
| 1973 | 530 | 404 | 117 | 1,051 | 50 |
| 1974 | 560 | 374 | 105 | 1,039 | 46 |
| 1975 | 612 | 388 | 97 | 1,097 | 44 |
| 1976 | 1,040 | 431 | 108 | 1,579 | 34 |
| 1977 | 1,080 | 421 | 97 | 1,598 | 32 |
| 1978 | 1,150 | 239 | 118 | 1,507 | 24 |
| 1979 | 1,180 | 308 | 123 | 1,611 | 27 |
| 1980 | 1,188 | 306 | 124 | 1,618 | 27 |
| 1981 | 1,180 | 329 | 129 | 1,638 | 28 |
| 1982 | 1,091 | 230 | 122 | 1,443 | 24 |
| 1983 | 1,109 | 250 | 117 | 1,476 | 25 |
| 1984 | 1,100 | 268 | 117 | 1,485 | 26 |
| 1985 | 1,100 | 308 | 114 | 1,509 | 27 |
| 1986 | 1,100 | 286 | 123 | 1,509 | 27 |
| 1987 | 1,128 | 291 | 127 | 1,564 | 27 |

|  | Production | Imports | Apparent Consumption | Imports/ Consumption (%) |
|---|---|---|---|---|
| **POULTRY** | | | | |
| 1974 | 34 | 14 | 48 | 29 |
| 1975 | 36 | 14 | 50 | 28 |
| 1976 | 70 | 10 | 80 | 13 |
| 1977 | 75 | 15 | 90 | 17 |
| 1978 | 67 | 20 | 87 | 23 |
| 1979 | 64 | 20[b] | 84[b] | 24[b] |
| 1980 | 73 | 20 | 93 | 22 |
| 1981 | 82 | 22 | 104 | 21 |
| 1982 | 85 | 23 | 108 | 21 |
| 1983 | 90 | 21 | 111 | 19 |
| 1984 | 107 | 18 | 125 | 14 |
| 1985 | 113 | 25 | 138 | 18 |
| 1986 | 95 | 20 | 115 | 17 |
| 1987 | 91 | 20 | 111 | 18 |

|  | Production Beef & Veal | Mutton | Pork | Imports[c] | Apparent Consumption | Imports/ Consumption (%) |
|---|---|---|---|---|---|---|
| **MEAT** | | | | | | |
| 1965 | 195[b] | 0[b] | 50[b] | 6 | 251[b] | 2[b] |
| 1966 | 195 | 0 | 50 | 18 | 263 | 7 |
| 1967 | 195 | 0 | 50 | 21 | 266 | 8 |
| 1968 | 195 | 0 | 50 | 20 | 265 | 8 |
| 1969 | 195 | 0 | 50 | 20 | 265 | 8 |
| 1970 | 181 | 1 | 39 | 22 | 243 | 9 |
| 1971 | 184 | 1 | 38 | 24 | 247 | 10 |
| 1972 | 186 | 1 | 38 | 26 | 251 | 10 |
| 1973 | 189 | 1 | 38 | 34 | 262 | 13 |
| 1974 | 190 | 1 | 38 | 44 | 273 | 16 |
| 1975 | 187 | 1 | 39 | 33 | 260 | 13 |
| 1976 | 138 | 1 | 55 | 29 | 223 | 13 |
| 1977 | 140 | 1 | 60 | 25 | 226 | 11 |
| 1978 | 143 | 1 | 62 | 29 | 235 | 12 |
| 1979 | 145 | 1 | 61 | 31 | 238 | 13 |
| 1980 | 147 | 1 | 58 | 35 | 241 | 15 |
| 1981 | 152 | 1 | 68 | 36 | 257 | 14 |

|      | Production |        |      |          | Apparent    | Imports/        |
|      | Beef & Veal | Mutton | Pork | Imports[c] | Consumption | Consumption (%) |
| ---- | ---- | --- | --- | --- | --- | --- |
| 1982 | 150 | 1 | 70 | 50 | 271 | 19 |
| 1983 | 151 | 1 | 72 | 43 | 267 | 16 |
| 1984 | 151 | 1 | 86 | 44 | 282 | 16 |
| 1985 | 150 | 1 | 95 | 41 | 287 | 14 |
| 1986 | 148 | 1 | 94 | 33 | 276 | 12 |
| 1987 | 140 | 1 | 95 | 36 | 272 | 13 |

SOURCES: Production—FAO *Production Yearbook,* various years. Imports—FAO *Trade Yearbook,* various years. Canned meat imports—AEC, various years. Apparent consumption—production plus imports.

a. Whole milk equivalents.
b. Estimated.
c. Canned meats.

# REFERENCES

•

*All journals are published in the United States or Cuba, unless otherwise indicated.*

Abascal López, Jesús. 1985. "El dulce símbolo de la amistad." *Cuba Internacional* (November): 42–47.
Acosta, José. 1972. "La estructura agraria y el sector agropecuario al triunfo de la revolución," *Economía y Desarrollo* 9 (January–February): 50–83.
"Acuerdan Cuba y México, en Santo Domingo, cooperación en la producción azucarera." 1975. *Granma* (28 April): 7.
"Adopta el Comité Ejecutivo del CAME medidas para establecer los precios en contratos comerciales." 1975. *Granma* (24 January): 8.
*Africa Contemporary Record* (ACR). 1968–86. New York: Africana Publishing Company of Holmes & Meier Publishers. Annual.
Aguirre, Severo. 1961. "El primer aniversario de las cooperativas cañeras." *Cuba Socialista* 1, no. 3 (November): 17–27.
Albuerne, Pedro. 1974. "Sistema de análisis y pronóstico de costos en la industria azucarera." *Economía y Desarrollo* 21 (January–February): 114–23.
Alfonso, Isabel, and Roberto González. 1981. "Comportamiento de un grupo de variedades de caña de azúcar ante la roya *puccinia melanocephala* Sydow." *Ciencias de la Agricultura* 8: 3–8.
Alienes Urosa, Julián. 1950. *Características fundamentales de la economía cubana.* Havana: Banco Nacional de Cuba.
Allen, Mark. 1977. "The Bulgarian Economy in the 1970s." In U.S. Congress, Joint Economic Committee. *East European Economies Post-Helsinki*, 649–97. Washington, D.C.: GPO.
Almazán del Olmo, Oscar. 1988. "Los derivados de la caña de azúcar: Actualidades y perspectivas en Cuba." *Cuba Socialista* 31 (January–February): 51–71.
Alonso, Hugo. 1977. "La mecanización cañera." *Panorama Económico Latinoamericano* 1, no. 26 (4 July): 16–19.
Alvarez, José. 1978. "Politics vs. Economics in International Trade: The Case of Cuba-U.S. Relations." Staff Paper No. 73. Food and Resource Economics Department, Institute of Food and Agricultural Sciences, University of Florida, Gainesville.

Alvarez Díaz, José, Alberto Arredondo, Raúl M. Shelton, and José Vizcaíno. 1964. *Cuba: Geopolítica y pensamiento económico.* Miami: Duplex Paper Products.

Alvarez Quiñones, Roberto. 1977. "Cuba no acepta cualquier convenio azucarero." *Panorama Económico Latinoamericano* 1, no. 26 (4 July): 1–7.

Alvarez Rosell, Silvia, and Gil Cruz Lemus. 1981. "Automatización para producir azúcar." *Juventud Técnica* 168 (October): 28–29.

*Anuario Azucarero de Cuba* (AAC). 1937–62? Havana: Cuba Económica y Financiera. Annual. Volume for 1961, and presumed volume for 1962, published by Ministerio del Comercio Exterior.

*Anuario Estadístico de Cuba* (AEC). 1972–87. Havana: Comité Estatal de Estadísticas. Annual. Early volumes published by the Junta Central de Planificación.

Arellano, George R. 1959. "Cuban Bagasse Products, S.A." *Cubaquímica* 29: 16–21.

de Armas, Mara, Armando Hechavarría, and Redel Hernández. 1983. "Análisis de la productividad horaria de la cosechadora KTP-1 en caña verde en función del rendimiento agrícola." *ATAC* 42, no. 4–5–6: 10–15.

de Armas, Mara, and Sergio Ortiz Linares. 1986. "La incidencia del rendimiento agrícola en la eficiencia de limpieza y las pérdidas de la KTP-1 cosechando en verde." *CubaAzúcar* (January–March): 13–16.

de Armas Casanova, Carlos M., and Paulino López Guzmán. 1978. "Suministro de bagazo a las fábricas de derivados y eficiencia térmica de las fábricas de azúcar." *CubaAzúcar* (April–June): 42–49.

Arrascaeta Recano, Abilio, Danilo Clerch Abreu, and Teresa Llanes Ortega. 1982. "Perspectiva del secado de bagazo como sistema." *CubaAzúcar* (July–September): 42–48.

Arredondo, Alberto. 1969. *Reforma agraria: La experiencia cubana.* San Juan, P.R.: Editorial San Juan.

"Assembly Line Production of KTP-2 Cane Harvesters Begins." 1987. *Cuba Economic News* 23, no. 153 (January–February): 19.

"Aumentará en el país la producción de cera refinada con la instalación de una nueva planta en las Tunas." 1986. *Granma* (24 October): 3.

Avilés, Ileana. 1985. "Agroindustria azucarera." *Colaboración* 7, no. 25 (October–December): 34–35.

"Ayuda internacional." 1985. *Colaboración* 7, no. 25 (October–December): 29–31.

Banco Nacional de Cuba (BNC). 1975. *Development and Prospects of the Cuban Economy.* Havana (September).

Banco Nacional de Cuba (BNC). 1982. *Economic Report.* Havana (August).

Banco Nacional de Cuba (BNC). 1985. *Economic Report.* Havana (February).

Banco Nacional de Cuba (BNC). 1987. *Economic Report.* Havana (May).

Banco Nacional de Cuba (BNC). 1988a. *Información estadística seleccionada de la economía cubana.* Havana (June).
Banco Nacional de Cuba (BNC). 1988b. *Informe económico.* Havana (June).
Barreda Sánchez, Nicanor. 1982. "Mecanización de la caña: Marcha de gigantes." *CubaAzúcar* (January–March): 41–45.
Benítez, José A. 1970. "Biografía de una industria." *Casa de las Américas* 11, no. 62 (September–October): 26–43.
Benítez, José A. 1977. *Las Antillas: Colonización, azúcar e imperialismo.* Havana: Casa de las Américas.
Benjamin, Medea, Joseph Collins, and Michael Scott. 1984. *No Free Lunch.* San Francisco: Institute for Food and Development Policy.
Betancourt, Armando F. 1970. "La mecanización de la cosecha y sus efectos en la calidad de la caña (Cuba: 1964–68)." *CubaAzúcar* (July–September): 2–22.
Bianchi, Andrés. 1964. "Agriculture." In *Cuba: The Economic and Social Revolution,* ed. Dudley Seers, 63–157. Chapel Hill: University of North Carolina Press.
Bianchi Ross, Ciro. 1985. "Al servicio del hombre." *Cuba Internacional* 17, no. 192 (November): 38–41.
Blanco Díaz, Elena. 1986. "En torno a la manipulación y transportación internacional de azúcar." *ATAC* 45, no. 5 (September–October): 50–54.
Blume, Helmut. 1987. "Cuban Cane Sugar Production." *Lateinamerika Studien* (Nuremberg, W. Germany) 23: 125–37.
*Boletín Estadístico de Cuba* (BEC). 1964–71. Havana: Junta Central de Planificación.
Boorstein, Edward. 1968. *The Economic Transformation of Cuba.* New York: Monthly Review Press.
Borrego Díaz, Orlando. 1965. "Problemas que plantea a la industria una zafra de 10 millones de toneladas de azúcar." *Cuba Socialista* 5, no. 44 (April): 10–30.
Borrego Díaz, Orlando. 1966. "La tarea económica: El problema fundamental." *Cuba Socialista* 6, no. 62 (October): 161–74.
Borroto Román, Noel, and Fernando Peñabaz Sánchez. 1980. "El precio del azúcar en las condiciones actuales del mercado capitalista," *Cuestiones de la Economía Planificada* 3, no. 6 (November–December): 66–92.
Boti, Regino. 1961. "El plan de desarrollo económico de 1962." *Cuba Socialista* 1, no. 4 (December): 19–32.
"Brasilia." 1985. *Direct from Cuba* 349 (16–30 June): 8–9.
Brezinski, Horst. 1986. "Economic Relations between European and the Less-Developed CMEA Countries." In U.S. Congress, Joint Economic Committee, *East European Economies: Slow Growth in the 1980s,* 302–28. Washington, D.C.: GPO.

Bronshtein, M. 1986. "Toward a Conception of the Economic Mechanism of the AIC." *Problems of Economics* 29, no. 8 (December): 73–87.

Brown, James G. 1987. *The International Sugar Industry: Developments and Prospects*. Commodity Working Paper 18. Washington, D.C.: World Bank.

Brundenius, Claes. 1984. *Revolutionary Cuba: The Challenge of Growth with Equity*. Boulder: Westview.

Brundenius, Claes. 1987. "Development and Prospects of Capital Goods Production in Revolutionary Cuba." *World Development* 15, no. 1 (January): 95–112.

Brundenius, Claes, and Andrew Zimbalist. 1985a. "Recent Studies on Cuban Economic Growth: A Review." *Comparative Economic Studies* 27, no. 1 (Spring): 21–45.

Brundenius, Claes, and Andrew Zimbalist. 1985b. "Cuban Economic Growth One More Time: A Response to Imbroglios." *Comparative Economic Studies* 27, no. 4 (Fall): 115–131.

Brunner, Heinrich. 1977. *Cuban Sugar Policy from 1963 to 1970*. Pittsburgh, Pa.: University of Pittsburgh Press.

Burmistrov, Vladimir. 1982. "The First Soviet-Cuban Long-Term Trade Agreement 1976–80): Its Results." *Foreign Trade* (Moscow) 1 (January): 7–11.

Caballero Almeida, Gilberto. 1978. "Nuevos éxitos con el bagazo de caña." *Panorama Económico Latinoamericano* 1, no. 52 (2 January) 21–23.

Cabrisas Ruiz, Ricardo. 1984. "El mercado internacional azucarero. Situación actual." *Cuba Socialista* 10 (March–May): 57–91.

Cámara de Comercio de la República de Cuba. 1980. *Directorio de exportadores cubanos*. Havana.

Cámara de Comercio de la República de Cuba. 1984. *Empresas cubanas relacionadas con el comercio exterior*. Havana.

Carciofi, Ricardo. 1983. "Cuba in the Seventies." In *Revolutionary Socialist Development in the Third World,* ed. Gordon White et. al., 193–233. Lexington: University of Kentucky Press.

Cardet, Ernesto. 1979. "Influencia de la calidad de la caña y del tipo de azúcar sobre el recobrado." *ATAC* 38, no. 2 (March–April): 14–19.

Carriba, Víctor M. 1981. "Cuban-Ethiopian Cooperation Expands." *Granma Weekly Review* (30 August): 8.

Carriba, Victor M. 1983. "Cuba-Benin: Colaboración en ascenso." *Colaboración* 5, no. 15 (April–June): 21.

Castell, Raquel. 1986. "Azúcar: Caña vs. remolacha." *Panorama Económico Latinoamericano* 295 (May): 16–19.

Castro, Fidel. 1965. "Discurso en el batey del Central Antonio Guiteras con motivo de haberse alcanzado la meta de 6 millones de toneladas de azúcar, el 7 de junio de 1965," *Verde Olivo* (20 June): 10–18, 58–63.

Castro, Fidel. 1970. "Speech on the Progress of the 1970 Sugar Harvest, on May 20, 1970." *Granma Weekly Review* (31 May): 7–12.
Castro, Fidel. 1973. "Comparecencia sobre convenios económicos suscritos con la Unión Soviética en diciembre de 1972." *Granma* (3 January): 2–3.
Castro, Fidel. 1975. "Informe del Comité Central del PCC al I Congreso—Punto II: El desarrollo económico." *Economía y Desarrollo* 36 (July–August): 12–63.
Castro, Fidel. 1976. "Discurso en el XVI aniversario de los Comités de Defensa de la Revolución, el 28 de septiembre de 1976." *Granma* (30 September): 2–4.
Castro, Fidel. 1977. "Speech at rally in Caxito, Angola, on March 24, 1977." *Granma Weekly Review* (3 April): 3.
Castro, Fidel. 1979. "Discurso en la clausura del II período de sesiones de 1979 de la Asamblea Nacional del Poder Popular, el 27 de diciembre de 1979." Mimeographed.
Castro, Fidel. 1980a. "Discurso en el acto de clausura del XVI Congreso del Sindicato Azucarero, el 30 de octubre de 1980." *Granma* (1 November): 2–4.
Castro, Fidel. 1980b. "Informe Central al II Congreso del Partido Comunista de Cuba." *Bohemia* 72, no. 52 (26 December): 34–67.
Castro, Fidel. 1981. "Discurso en el acto de clausura del II Congreso de los CDR, el 24 de octubre de 1981." *Granma* (26 October): 2–5.
Castro, Fidel. 1983. *The World Economic and Social Crisis*. Havana: Publishing Office of the Council of State.
Castro, Fidel. 1984. "Discurso en la clausura del Primer Forum Nacional de Energía." *Bohemia* 76, no. 50 (14 December): 50–63.
Castro, Fidel. 1985a. *Nuestra lucha es la de América Latina y el Tercer Mundo*. Havana. Interview with the Mexican newspaper *El Día* on 8 June 1985.
Castro, Fidel. 1985b. "Speech at the Inauguration Ceremony for the 'Victoria de Julio' Sugar Mill in Nicaragua, on January 11, 1985." In *War and Crisis in the Americas: Fidel Castro Speeches, 1984–85*, 82–107. New York: Pathfinder Press.
Castro, Fidel. 1986. "Informe Central al III Congreso del Partido Comunista de Cuba." *Bohemia* 78, no. 7 (14 February) 51–83.
Castro, Miriam. 1984. "Algo mas que amigos." *Prisma Latinoamericano* 10, no. 145 (September): 22–23.
"Castro, the 'Non-Smoker' Fudges Policy Confusion as Cuba's Economy Drifts and Drifts." 1986. *Latin American Times* 7, no. 8: 38–44.
"Los centrales azucareros en la nueva división político-administrativa." 1978. *ATAC* 37, no. 3 (May–June): 35–37.
Centro de Investigaciones de la Caña. 1972. "Efectos de la quema de los

campos en la producción de azúcar." *Economía y Desarrollo* 10 (March–April): 92–118.
Centro de Investigaciones de la Caña. 1973. "Introducción en Cuba del sistema australiano de corte." *Economía y Desarrollo* 15 (January–February): 48–71.
Cepero Bonilla, Raúl. 1960. *El convenio cubano-soviético.* Havana: Editorial Echevarría.
Cepero Bonilla, Raúl. 1962. "La conferencia azucarera de Ginebra." *Cuba Socialista* 2, no. 7 (March): 47–62.
Cepero Bonilla, Raúl. 1963. *Obras históricas.* Havana: Instituto de Historia.
Cernic, Barbara. 1985. *Sugar: International Control of Production and Trade.* Ljubljana, Yugoslavia: Research Centre for Cooperation with Developing Countries.
Chantez Oliva, Sara, and José M. Fernández Llorens. 1985. "El fenómeno económico del intensivismo en las zafras azucareras de la década de 1940," *Islas* 80 (April): 3–8.
Charadán López, Fernando. 1982. *La industria azucarera en Cuba.* Havana: Editorial de Ciencias Sociales.
Chilcote, Ronald H. 1986. *Cuba 1953–1978: A Bibliographical Guide to the Literature.* 2 vols. White Plains, N.Y.: Kraus International Publications.
Chinea, Antonio, and Eida Rodríguez. 1982. "Las enfermedades de la caña de azúcar en Cuba durante los últimos 30 años." *ATAC* 41, no. 3 (May–June): 9–21.
Clemens, Harrie, and Jan P. de Groot. 1988. "Agrarian Labor Market and Technology Under Different Regimes: A Comparison of Cuba and the Dominican Republic." *Latin American Perspectives* 15, no. 4 (Fall): 6–36.
"Colaboración en América y el Caribe." 1983. *Colaboración* 5, no. 17 (October–December): 11–13.
Collar Fraguela, Juan. 1977. "En defensa de nuestros recursos naturales: VI Reunión de Geplacea." *CubaAzúcar* (April–June): 28–42.
"La comercialización del azúcar en Cuba." 1984. *CubaAzúcar* (July–September): 43–46.
*Comercio Exterior.* 1902–64. Havana: Dirección General de Estadística, Ministerio de Hacienda. Annual, but not published in some years. Beginning with 1959, published by Dirección de Estadística, Junta Central de Planificación.
Comité Estatal de Estadísticas. Oficina Nacional del Censo. 1984. *Censo de población y vivienda, 1981.* Vol. 16, *República de Cuba.* Havana.
"Comunicado conjunto Cubano-Soviético sobre la estancia del Primer Ministro de la República de Cuba, Fidel Castro, en la Union Soviética." 1964. *Cuba Socialista* 4, no. 30 (February): 157–165.

"Comparecencia de Diocles Torralbas en información pública." 1981. *Granma* (4 December): 2.
Contreras, Rafael. 1982. "Cuba: Un mayor impulso al azúcar." *ATAC* 41, no. 1 (January–February): 19–20.
"Convenio azucarero: Contrarrestar la erosión del precio." 1977. *Panorama Económico Latinoamericano* 1, no. 19 (16 May): 11–14.
"Convenio de intercambio comercial y de pagos entre la República de Cuba y la Unión de Repúblicas Socialistas Soviéticas." 1960. *Gaceta Oficial* (8 March): 5737–39.
Cordovés Herrera, Marianela. 1979. "El transporte: Etapa agroindustrial del proceso azucarero cañero." *CubaAzúcar* (January–March): 9–11.
"Cuba-Brasil." 1985. *Direct from Cuba* (16–30 June): 21–2.
"Cuba-Burundi." 1981. *Colaboración* 3, no. 8 (July–September): 40–41.
"Cuba-Burundi." 1983. *Colaboración* 5, no. 17 (October–December): 40.
"Cuba económica." 1971. *Economía y Desarrollo* 5 (January–March): 176–84.
"Cuba-Ghana." 1983. *Colaboración* 5, no. 16 (July–September): 41.
"Cuba-Nicaragua." 1982. *Colaboración* 4, no. 12 (July–September): 40.
Cuban Economic Research Project (CERP). 1965a. *Cuba: Agriculture and Planning*. Coral Gables, Fla.: University of Miami Press.
Cuban Economic Research Project (CERP). 1965b. *A Study on Cuba*. Coral Gables, Fla.: University of Miami Press.
Cuban Economic Research Project (CERP). 1965c. *Stages and Problems of Industrial Development in Cuba*. Coral Gables, Fla.: University of Miami Press.
"Cuban Sugar Factory Pact Signed." 1985. *Ghanaian Times* (21 October) in *Joint Publications Research Service-Sub-Saharan Africa* (25 November): 26.
de la Cuesta, Leonel. 1974. *Constituciones cubanas*. Miami: Editorial Exilio.
Danilo Rodríguez, Héctor. 1977. "Cuba: Impacto de un proyecto azucarero." *Panorama Económico Latinoamericano* 1, no. 43 (31 October): 1–6.
Danilo Rodríguez, Héctor. 1978. "Cuba y los convenios azucareros." *Panorama Económico Latinoamericano* 2, no. 103 (25 December): 7–14.
Danilo Rodríguez, Héctor. 1982. "Cuba: Development and Building of New Sugar Mills." In *Cuban Sugar Industry at a Glance,* special issue of *World Sugar Journal,* 18–20.
David Posada, Eduardo. 1976. "Quince años de revolución en la producción azucarera." *CubaAzúcar* (January–March): 17-25.
David Posada, Eduardo. 1979. "El bagazo y la economía del combustible." *ATAC* 39, no. 3 (May–June): 11–13.
David Posada, Eduardo. 1981. "Caña, azúcar y alcohol." *ATAC* 40, no. 1 (January–February): 4–7.
David Posada, Eduardo. 1983. "Sugar Production in Cuba." *Sugar y Azúcar* 78, no. 2 (February): 100–08.

Departamento de Investigaciones Tecnológicas. 1972. "Comportamiento industrial de la caña quemada." *CubaAzúcar* (April–June): 33–41.

*Desarrollo económico y social de cuba durante el período 1958–1980.* 1981. Havana.

"Despegue hacia el desarrollo." 1983. *Colaboración* 5, no. 15 (May–June): 15–16.

Díaz Hernández, Lourdes, and Ramón Alvarez Portal. 1981. "Los rendimientos de las combinadas cañeras." *ATAC* 40, no. 1 (January–February): 47–65.

Díaz Sosa, Juana. 1981. "Efectos económicos de la levadura torula en la alimentación ganadera." *Economía y Desarrollo* 61 (March–April): 30–39.

Díaz-Vázquez, Julio A. 1980. "La integración económica socialista en el desarrollo de Cuba." *Economía y Desarrollo* 56 (March–April): 140–65.

Díaz-Vázquez, Julio A. 1981. "Cuba: Integración económica socialista y especialización de la producción." *Economía y Desarrollo* 63 (July–August): 132–65.

Díaz-Vázquez, Julio A. 1982. "Cuba: Colaboración económica y científico-técnica con países en vías de desarrollo de Africa, Asia y América Latina." *Economía y Desarrollo* 68 (May–June): 26–43.

Díaz-Vázquez, Julio A. 1985. *Cuba y el CAME.* Havana: Editorial de Ciencias Sociales.

Díaz-Vázquez, Julio A. 1986. "La producción de azúcar, cítricos y niquel en el desarrollo perspectivo de la economía cubana." *Economía y Desarrollo* 91 (March–April): 10–19.

Domínguez, Jorge I. 1971. "Sectoral Clashes in Cuban Politics and Development." *Latin American Research Review* 6, no. 3 (Fall): 61–87.

Domínguez, Jorge I. 1978. *Cuba: Order and Revolution.* Cambridge, Mass.: Harvard University Press, Belknap Press.

Domínguez, Jorge I. 1989. *To Make a World Safe for Revolution.* Cambridge, Mass.: Harvard University Press.

Domínguez, Lázaro. 1986. "Las brigadas permanentes e integrales: Nuevas formas de organización." *Cuba Socialista* 32 (July–August): 45–71.

Domínguez, Miguel, Manuel Fonseca, Achilbay Abdukadirov, and Ridel Ramírez. 1979. "La compactación del suelo en la cosecha de caña mecanizada." *ATAC* 38, no. 3 (May–June): 57–64.

Eckstein, Susan. 1980. "Capitalist Constraints on Cuban Socialist Development." *Comparative Politics* 12, no. 3: 253–74.

Eckstein, Susan. 1981. "The Socialist Transformation of Cuban Agriculture: Domestic and International Constraints." *Social Problems* 29, no. 2 (December): 178–96.

Economic Commission for Latin America (ECLA). 1978–82. *Economic Survey of Latin America.* New York: United Nations.

Economic Commission for Latin America (ECLA). 1983. *Cuba: Notas para*

*el Estudio Económico de América Latina 1983*. Santiago, Chile: United Nations.
Economic Commission for Latin America and the Caribbean (ECLAC). 1986. *Estudio económico de América Latina 1985: Cuba*, LC/L.390/Add.18. Santiago, Chile: United Nations.
Economic Commission for Latin America and the Caribbean (ECLAC). 1988. *Estudio económico de América Latina 1987: Cuba*, LC/L.463/Add.20. Santiago, Chile: United Nations.
Edquist, Charles 1983. "Mechanization of Sugarcane Harvesting in Cuba." *Cuban Studies/Estudios Cubanos* 13, no. 2 (Summer): 41–64.
Edquist, Charles 1985. *Capitalism, Socialism and Technology: A Comparative Study of Cuba and Jamaica*. London: Zed Books Ltd.
"El desarrollo de la mecanización de la caña de azúcar en Cuba." *ATAC* 35, no. 6 (November–December): 5–25.
"El desarrollo industrial de Cuba." 1966a. *Cuba Socialista* 6, no. 56 (April): 128–83.
"El desarrollo industrial de Cuba." 1966b. *Cuba Socialista* 6, no. 57 (May): 94–127.
Ely, Roland T. 1963. *Cuando reinaba su majestad el azúcar*. Buenos Aires: Editora Sud Americana.
"En el décimo aniversario del 26 de julio" 1963. *Cuba Socialista* 3, no. 23 (July): 1–10.
"Entrevístanse en México el President Luis Echeverría y el Ministro de Industria Básica de Cuba Antonio Esquivel." 1974. *Granma* (11 December): 1.
Escobar Casas, Reynaldo. 1978. "Cañaveral." *Cuba Internacional* (August/September): 66–70.
Estevez Martir, Manuel, and María E. González del Foyo. 1987. "Algunos de los problemas que influyen en la rentabilidad del C.A.I. 'Julio Antonio Mella' de la provincia de Santiago de Cuba." *Economía y Desarrollo* 99 (July–August): 44–51.
"Estrecharán Cuba y Jamaica lazos de cooperación en las ramas económicas." 1975. *Granma* (17 July): 8.
Evenson, Robert. 1976. "International Transmission of Technology in the Production of Sugarcane." *Journal of Development Studies* 12: 2 (January): 208–31.
"Experiencia y calidad." 1984. *Colaboración* 6, no. 21 (October–December): 41–42.
Felipe, Edith. 1985. "Cuba y la colaboración económica con el mundo subdesarrollado." *Temas de Economía Mundial* 15: 81–106.
Fernández, Wilfredo. 1975. "Aprueban Cuba y México protocolo azucarero." *Granma* (12 June): 6.
Fernández Arner, Agustín, and Lillian Plá García. 1982. "El comercio exte-

rior y la construcción del socialismo en Cuba." *Economía y Desarrollo* 90 (January–February): 35–49.

Fernández Colino, M. 1977a. "Conferencia de la ONU para negociar nuevo convenio internacional azucarero." *ATAC* 36, no. 3 (May–June): 20–23.

Fernández Colino, M. 1977b. "Fracasan negociaciones para convenio azucarero mundial debido a posición inflexible de los países importadores." *ATAC* 36, no. 4 (July–August): 16–17.

Fernández Font, Marcelo. 1986. *Cuba y la economía azucarera mundial*. Havana: Instituto Superior de Relaciones Internacionales Raúl Roa García.

Fernández Font, Marcelo. 1988. "Los edulcorantes sustitutos del azúcar," *Cuba Economía Planificada* 3, no. 3 (July–September): 46–78.

Fernández Martín, Raquel, Marili Martín García, and Eugenio Rodríguez Pérez. 1984. "Cálculo del costo de producción del azúcar crudo: Su perfeccionamiento." *ATAC* 43, no. 5 (September–October): 23–30.

Ferrán, Juan. 1972. "Las micro-inversiones y la productividad en la industria azucarera." *Economía y Desarrollo* 14 (November–December): 114–28.

Ferrer, Mario. 1981. "Cuba: Principal abastecedor azucarero del CAME." *Granma* (13 August): 2.

Feuer, Carl Henry. 1987. "The Performance of the Cuban Sugar Industry, 1981–85." *World Development* 15, no. 1 (January): 67–81.

Figueras, Miguel A. 1985a. "Consideraciones sobre la producción de maquinarias en Cuba." *Revista Cubana de Ciencias Sociales* 7: 105–32.

Figueras, Miguel A. 1985b. *Producción de maquinarias y equipos en Cuba*. Havana: Editorial Científico-Técnica.

Fonseca, Jorge. 1982. "La caldera Reto: Un logro de la colaboración Cuba-URSS." *Colaboración* 5, no. 12 (July–September): 5.

Food and Agriculture Organization (FAO). 1947–86. *FAO Production Yearbook*. Rome. Annual.

Food and Agriculture Organization (FAO). 1947–86. *FAO Trade Yearbook*. Rome. Annual.

Food and Agriculture Organization (FAO). 1961. *The World Sugar Economy in Figures*. Rome.

Forster, Nancy. 1982. "Cuban Agricultural Productivity: A Comparison of State and Private Farm Sectors." *Cuban Studies/Estudios Cubanos* 11, no. 2–12, no. 1 (July 1981–January 1982): 105–25.

Fowler, Elizabeth. 1974. "Russian Actions in Sugar Emerge." *New York Times* (29 November): 63–64.

Friedman, Paul, and Abilio Arrascaeta. 1984. "¿Por qué secar el bagazo?" *CubaAzúcar* (July–September): 27–36.

Fry, James. 1985. *Sugar: Aspects of a Complex Commodity Market*. Commodities and Exports Projects Division, Division Working Paper 1985–1. Washington, D.C.: World Bank.

Fry, James. 1988. "Cuba's Sugar Statistics: How Reliable are They?" *Cuba Business* (London) 2, no. 2 (April): 8–10.

Gálvez Taupier, Luis O. 1987. *La diversificación de la caña de azúcar,* ID/WG.471/2(SPEC). Vienna: United National Industial Development Organization.
Gálvez Taupier, Luis O., and Herly Noa Silverio 1985. "Importancia económica de los derivados de la caña de azúcar." *El Economista* 1, no. 1 (December): 113–26.
García, José R., and Nildemia Pérez. 1988. "Del bagazo al papel periódico." *Juventud Técnica* 246 (1988): 18–23.
García Giraldino, Iliana. 1983. "Salto al futuro: Mecanización cañera de Cuba." *CubaAzúcar* (January–February): 9–14.
García López, Francisco, and José A. Clark. 1969. "Combinaciones de evaporación de alta eficiencia y producción de bagazo y energía eléctrica." *CubaAzúcar* (October–December): 17–31.
García López, José, Orlando Quiñones, and Manuel Paneque. 1977. "Influencia de la mecanización de la cosecha en la fabricación de azúcar crudo." *ATAC* 35, no. 2 (March–April): 39–43.
García Marrero, Agustín, and Antonio Morales Pita. 1987. "El desarrollo de los complejos agroindustriales azucareros en las condiciones de la República de Cuba." *Economía y Desarrollo* 96 (January–February): 60–79.
Gatria, José. 1959. "El complejo industrial azucarero cubano." *Humanismo* 8, nos. 55–56 (May–August): 103–14.
Ghai, Dharam, Cristóbal Kay, and Peter Peek. 1988. *Labour and Development in Rural Cuba.* London: Macmillan.
Gispert, Lucy. 1980. "Perfiles de la caña de azúcar." *Juventud Técnica* (March): 60–65.
Gispert, Lucy. 1981. "¿Por qué las variedades?" *Juventud Técnica* (July): 19–21.
Goldman, Marshall I. 1967. *Soviet Foreign Aid.* New York: Frederick A. Praeger.
Gómez, Marlene. 1986a. "Cubanos en Lao." *Colaboración* 8: 26 (January–March): 26–29.
Gómez, Marlene. 1986b. "Una entrevista singular." *Colaboración* 10: 28 (June–September): 2–3.
González Carrillo, Severiano. 1982. "Evaluaciones de las materias extrañas en la economía agroindustrial azucarera." *ATAC* 41: 1 (January–February): 10–18.
González Cofiño, Roberto. 1976. "Comercio exterior de Cuba." In *Política económica en Centro y Periferia,* ed. Carlos F. Díaz-Alejandro, Simón Teitel and Victor E. Tokman, 649–709. Mexico City: Fondo de Cultura Económica.
González Eguiluz, Víctor, and Juan J. García Núñez. 1977. "Influencia de las materias extrañas de la caña en el recobrado." *ATAC* 36, no. 1 (January/February): 11–21.

González Fontes, Ramón, and Miguel Ramírez Reyes. 1984. "La estructura organizativa de la dirección en las brigadas integrales de producción de caña de azúcar." *Economía y Desarrollo* 83 (November–December): 61–66.

González Jordán, Roberto. 1986. *Ahorro de energía en Cuba.* Havana: Editorial Científico-Técnica.

González Maicas, Zoila. 1964. "La matriz de insumo-producto: un nuevo instrumento de planificación industrial." *Nuestra Industria. Revista Económica* 2, no. 8 (August): 64–75.

González Maicas, Zoila, and Julio A. Díaz-Vázquez. 1988. "Los convenios de especialización agrícola de Cuba con los países miembros del CAME," *Economía y Desarrollo* 88, no. 3 (May–June): 146–55.

Gorbachev, B. 1973. "Cuba and Socialist Integration." *Socialism Theory and Practice* (Moscow) 5 (December): 82–94.

Gouré, Leon, and Julian Weinkle. 1972. "Cuba's New Dependency." *Problems of Communism* 21, no. 2 (March–April): 68–79.

Gouré, Leon, and Morris Rothenberg. 1975. *Soviet Penetration of Latin America.* Coral Gables, Fla.: University of Miami Press.

Grant, María. 1982. "Cuba: Machine Industry." *Direct from Cuba* 294 (30 November): 9.

"Greater Availability of Refined Sugar." 1981. *Direct from Cuba* 260 (30 June): 10–11.

Grissa, Abdessatar. 1976. *Structure of the International Sugar Market.* Paris: Organization for Economic Cooperation and Development.

Grupo Cubano de Estudios Económicos. 1963. *Un estudio sobre Cuba.* Coral Gables, Fla.: University of Miami Press.

"Grupo de Países Latinoamericanos y del Caribe Exportadores de Azúcar." 1987. *Economía y Desarrollo* 100 (September–October): 178–83.

Guevara, Ernesto. 1960. "Political Sovereignty and Economic Independence." In *Che: Selected Works of Ernesto Guevara,* ed. Rolando E. Bonachea and Nelson P. Valdés, 214–29. Cambridge, Mass.: MIT Press, 1969.

Guevara, Ernesto. 1961a. "Discurso en la Conferencia del Consejo Interamericano Económico y Social de la OEA." In Ernesto Guevara, *Obra Revolucionaria,* 423–41. Mexico City: Ediciones Era, 1971.

Guevara, Ernesto. 1961b. "La industrialización de Cuba." In Universidad Popular, *Economía y Planificación,* 15–65. Havana.

Guevara, Ernesto. 1964. "Cuba: Su economía, su comercio exterior, su significado en el mundo actual." In Ernesto Guevara, *Obra Revolucionaria,* 616–26. Mexico City: Ediciones Era, 1971.

Gutelman, Michel. 1970. *La agricultura socializada en Cuba.* Mexico City: Ediciones Era.

Gutiérrez, P. L., Israel Cepero, and Caridad Agüero. 1976. "Investigaciones

para obtener pulpa de alto rendimiento para la producción de papel periódico." *ATAC* 35, no. 1 (January–February): 21–34.
Hagelberg, G. B. 1974a. *The Caribbean Sugar Industries: Constraints and Opportunities.* New Haven, Conn.: Antilles Research Program, Yale University.
Hagelberg, G. B. 1974b. "Some Problems of Sugar Statistics, with Special Reference to Cuba." *Zeitschrift fur die Zuckerindustrie* 24, no. 8 (August): 433–37.
Hagelberg, G. B. 1977. "International Sugar Agreements, 1864–1977." In *F.O. Licht's International Sugar Report,* 5–10. Ratzburg.
Hagelberg, G. B. 1979. "Cuba's Sugar Policy." In *Revolutionary Cuba in the World Arena,* ed. Martin Weinstein, 31–50. Philadelphia: Institute for the Study of Human Issues.
Hagelberg, G. B. 1985. "Sugar in the Caribbean: Turning Sunshine into Money." In *Caribbean Contours,* ed. Sideny W. Mintz and Sally Price, 85–126. Baltimore: Johns Hopkins University Press.
Harbron, John D. 1959. "Cuba's Bagasse Success." *Pulp and Paper International* 1, no. 2 (February): 38–42.
Harris, Simon. 1987. "Current Issues in the World Sugar Economy." *Food Policy* 12, no. 2 (May): 127–145.
Hernández, María Teresa, Guillermo Moya Castro, and Humberto Cuellar Fariñas. 1985. "Estimación de pérdidas de azúcar por atraso de la caña." *ATAC* 44, no. 3 (May–June): 12–17.
Hernández, Raúl. 1974. "Estudios sobre economías de escala en ingenios de crudos." *Economía y Desarrollo* 23 (May–June): 94–111.
Hernández Serrano, Luis. 1979. "Cuba-9: Proyecto único de su género en el mundo." *Juventud Rebelde* (8 January): 2.
Herrera, Raúl. 1965. "Problemas que plantea a la agricultura una zafra de 10 millones de toneladas." *Cuba Socialista* 5, no. 43 (March): 1–23.
Herrera Machado, Juan. 1986. "Principales objetivos de la estrategia general del desarrollo azucarero." *ATAC* 45, no. 4 (July–August): 8–15.
Heston, Thomas J. 1987. *Sweet Subsidy: The Economic and Diplomatic Effects of the U.S. Sugar Acts, 1934–74.* New York: Garland Publishers.
Hidalgo, Alcibíades. 1978. "Relations between Ethiopia and Cuba Steadily Grow." *Granma Weekly Review* (22 October): 9.
Hoff, Frederic, and Max Lawrence. 1985. *Implications of World Sugar Markets, Policies and Production Costs for U.S. Sugar.* Agricultural Economic Report no. 543, Economic Research Service, U.S. Department of Agriculture. Washington, D.C.: GPO.
Ibáñez López, Juan. 1983. "Cuba en la división internacional socialista del trabajo," *Verde Olivo* 24, no. 19 (12 May): 36–38.
*Industria azucarera y sus derivados.* 1903–31. Havana: Sección de Estadística, Secretaría de Hacienda.

Instituto Nacional de Reforma Agraria (INRA). 1976. "El desarrollo de la mecanización de la caña de azúcar en Cuba." *ATAC* 35, no. 6 (November–December): 5–25.

International Bank for Reconstruction and Development (IBRD). *See* World Bank.

*International Financial Statistics* (IFS). Monthly.

"The International Sugar Agreement of 1968." 1968. *Monthly Bulletin of Agricultural Economics and Statistics* 17: 12 (December): 9–14.

International Sugar Council. 1963. *The World Sugar Economy: Structure and Policies.* London.

International Sugar Organization (ISO). 1949–88. *Sugar Year Book.* London. Annual.

International Sugar Organization (ISO). 1982. *The World Sugar Economy: Structure and Policies.* Vol. 1, *National Sugar Economies and Policies: Central and South America.* London: ISO.

Ivanovich Serazhim, Vitaly, and Alfredo Díaz Romero. 1985. "El complejo agroindustrial como forma del proceso de socialización de la producción." *Economía y Desarrollo* 89 (November–December): 64–75.

Junta Central de Planificación. 1975. *Censo de población y viviendas 1970.* Havana: Editorial Orbe.

Junta Nacional de Planificación. 1960. *Estudio de producción y consumo de energía eléctrica y uso de combustible en los centrales azucareros.* Havana.

Jurasek, Prokop. 1987. "Grado comparativo del autoabastecimiento de los países miembros del CAME en productos agropecuarios." *Economía y Desarrrollo* 97 (March–April): 74–91.

Kalecki, Michal. 1960. "Hypothetical Outline of the Five-Year Plan 1961–5 for the Cuban Economy." In Michal Kalecki, *Essays on Developing Economies,* 155–97. London: Harvester Press, 1976.

Karol, K. S. 1970. *Guerrillas in Power.* New York: Hill & Wang.

Kendrick, John W. 1972. *Economic Accounts and Their Uses.* New York: McGraw Hill.

Kohn, Martin J., and Nicholas R. Lang. 1977. "The Intra-CMEA Foreign Trade System: Major Price Changes, Little Reform." In U.S. Congress, Joint Economic Committee. *East European Economies Post-Helsinki,* 135–51. Washington, D.C.: GPO.

Lamb, David. 1978. "Angola Moving to End Isolation from the West and Dependency on Cuba." *Los Angeles Times* (3 December): 6–7.

Landell Mills Commodities Studies. 1985. *World Sugar Trade and U.S. Sugar Policy.* Report prepared for the Congressional Research Service, U.S. Congress. Washington, D.C.

La Serna, Nelson, and Ofelia Carvajal. 1983. "Investigación y desarrollo de productos aglomerados a partir del bagazo." *Sobre los Derivados de la Caña de Azúcar* 17, no. 1 (January–April): 21–26.

Lazo, Raúl. 1975. "Suscriben Cuba y la URSS protocolo para el desarrollo azucarero cubano." *ATAC* 34, no. 6 (November–December): 38–39.

Lazo, Raúl. 1982. "Cuba y el mercado azucarero mundial." *Bohemia* 74, no. 29 (16 July): 28–31.

Lazo, Raúl. 1983. "Se ofertan 460 años de experiencia." *Bohemia* 75, no. 19 (13 May): 32–33.

Lazo, Raúl. 1984. "¿Por qué no se firmó el nuevo convenio?" *Bohemia* 76, no. 32 (10 August): 46–49.

Lazo, Raúl. 1985a. "Invertir los términos." *Bohemia* 77, no. 6 (8 February): 44–46.

Lazo, Raúl. 1985b. "El viejo y las cañas." *Bohemia* 77, no. 11 (15 March): 57–59.

Lazo, Raúl. 1985c. "Desde un piñón hasta un tandem." *Bohemia* 77, no. 44 (29 November): 26–31.

Lazo, Raúl. 1987. "Del azúcar al mañana." *Bohemia* 79, no. 38 (19 September): 48–56.

Lechuga, Lillian. 1972. "Caña sobre rieles." *Bohemia* 64, no. 11 (17 March): 12–17.

Lechuga, Lillian. 1982. "Los siete pioneros." *Colaboración* 4, no. 12 (July–September): 38–39.

Lehmann, David. 1985. "Smallholding Agriculture in Revolutionary Cuba: A Case of Under-Exploitation?" *Development and Change* 16, no. 2 (April): 251–70.

LeoGrande, William M. 1979. "Cuban Dependency: A Comparison of Pre-Revolutionary and Post-Revolutionary International Economic Relations." *Cuban Studies/Estudios Cubanos* 9, no. 2 (July): 1–28.

Le Riverend, Julio. 1974. *Historia económica de Cuba*. Havana: Editorial Pueblo y Revolución.

Levi, Rozita. 1979. "Cuba and the Nonaligned Movement." In *Cuba in the World*, ed. Cole Blasier and Carmelo Mesa-Lago, 147–51. Pittsburgh, Pa.: University of Pittsburgh Press.

*Lineamientos económicos y sociales para el quinquenio 1981–1985*. 1981. Havana: Editora Política.

*Lineamientos económicos y sociales para el quinquenio (1986–1990)*. 1986. Havana: Editora Política.

Llovio-Menéndez, José Luis. 1988. *Insider: My Secret Life as a Revolutionary in Cuba*. New York: Bantam Books.

Lodos, Jorge. 1977. "El objetivo: Mas azúcar con menos área, con la mayor eficiencia." *ATAC* 36, no. 2 (March–April): 13–17.

López Guzmán, Paulino. 1982. "Bagazo: Recurso fibroso para el desarrollo de la industria de celulosa y papel en Cuba." *Sobre los Derivados de la Caña de Azúcar* 17, no. 1 (January–April): 12–20.

López Guzmán, Paulino. 1983. "Pulpa de alto rendimiento de bagazo: Posibilidades y perspectivas." *CubaAzúcar* (July–September): 42–45.
López Guzmán, Paulino, and Carlos M. de Armas Casanova. 1979. "La industria de la caña de azúcar en el marco de la crisis energética." *Sobre los Derivados de la Caña de Azúcar* 13, no. 1–3: 14–23.
López Guzmán, Paulino, and Carlos M. de Armas Casanova. 1980. "La potencialidad de la caña de azúcar como recurso energético renovable." Organización Latinoamericana de Energía, *Boletin Energético* 17 (October–December): 50–67.
López Rivera, Armando. 1977. "Nueva vida." *Verde Olivo* 18, no. 8: 18–21.
López Segrera, Francisco. 1981 (orig. publ. 1972). *Cuba: Capitalismo dependiente y subdesarrollo (1510–1959)*. Havana: Editorial de Ciencias Sociales.
Luzón, José Luis. 1987. *Economía, población y territorio en Cuba (1899–1983)*. Madrid: Ediciones de Cultura Hispánica.
MacDonald, Scott B., and F. Joseph Demetrius. 1986. "The Caribbean Sugar Crisis: Consequences and Challenges." *Journal of Interamerican Studies and World Affairs* 28, no. 1 (Spring): 35–58.
MacEwan, Arthur. 1981. *Revolution and Economic Development in Cuba*. New York: St. Martin's Press.
Madhavan, Vimal. 1987. "Fiji Shares Sugar-Cane Research." *Cooperation South* 2: 5–6.
Mahler, Vincent A. 1984. "The Political Economy of North-South Commodity Bargaining: the Case of the ISA." *International Organization* 38, no. 4 (Autumn): 709–31.
*Manual azucarero de Cuba*. 1971. Havana: Ediciones de Ciencia y Técnica.
Marer, Paul. 1972. *Postwar Pricing and Price Patterns in Socialist Foreign Trade (1946–1971)*. Bloomington: International Development Research Center, Indiana University.
Marrero, Leví. 1972– . *Cuba: Economía y sociedad*. 13 vols. to date. San Juan: Editorial San Juan and Madrid: Editorial Playor.
Marrese, Michael, and Jan Vanous. 1983a. *Soviet Subsidization of Trade with Eastern Europe*. Berkeley: Institute of International Studies, University of California.
Marrese, Michael, and Jan Vanous. 1983b. "Unconventional Gains from Trade." *Journal of Comparative Economics* 3, no. 4 (December): 382–99.
Marsán, Gloria. 1977. "Las fábricas de levadura torula." *Bohemia* 69, no. 19 (13 May): 16–23.
Martí, Agenor. 1974. "De brillante porvenir." *Cuba Internacional* (June): 16–21.
Martín Oria, José Roberto, Guillermo Gálvez Rodríguez, Roberto de Armas Urquiza, Raúl Espinosa Olivera, Rafael Vigoa Hernández, and Alcides

León Méndez. 1987. *La caña de azúcar en Cuba.* Havana: Editorial Científico-Técnica.
Martínez, Caridad. 1984. "Cuba-México: Dos décadas de fecunda labor." *Colaboración* 6, no. 21 (October–December): 20–26.
Martínez, Ramón. 1983a. "Alto grado de amistad y cooperación." *Colaboración* 5, no. 14 (January–March): 11–12.
Martínez, Ramón. 1983b. "Colaboración azucarera cubana." *Verde Olivo* 24, no. 51 (22 December): 13.
Martínez, Tomás. 1967. "Nuevas metas en el desarrollo de la industria azucarera cubana." *CubaAzúcar* (May–June): 2–17.
Martínez-Alier, Juan. 1973. "The Cuban Sugar Planters, 1934–1960." *Oxford Agrarian Studies* 2, no. 1: 3–31.
Martínez Salsamendi, Carlos. 1984. "El papel de Cuba en el tercer mundo: América Central, el Caribe y Africa." In *Cuba y Estados Unidos: Un debate para la convivencia,* ed. Juan Gabriel Tokatlian, 127–98. Buenos Aires: Grupo Impresor Latinoamericano.
"Medidas que permiten ahorrar combustible en los centrales." 1970. *Granma* (13 May): 5.
Menéndez Cruz, Alfredo. 1961. "Balance de la zafra de 1961: Primera zafra del pueblo." *Cuba Socialista* 1, no. 1 (September): 34–46.
Menéndez Cruz, Alfredo. 1962a. "Problemas de la industria azucarera." *Cuba Socialista* 2, no. 12 (August): 1–17.
Menéndez Cruz, Alfredo. 1962b. "La transformación de las cooperativas cañeras en granjas cañeras." *Cuba Socialista* 2, no. 14 (October): 31–43.
Menéndez Cruz, Alfredo. 1963. "Algunas experiencias de la zafra de 1963." *Cuba Socialista* 3, no. 23 (July): 11–28.
Menéndez Cruz, Alfredo. 1964. "Los costos y el análisis económico en la industria azucarera." *Nuestra Industria. Revista Económica* 2, no. 6 (April): 3–9.
Mesa-Lago, Carmelo. 1969a. "Availability and Reliability of Statistics in Socialist Cuba." Part 1. *Latin American Research Review* 4, no. 1 (Winter): 53–91.
Mesa-Lago, Carmelo. 1969b. "Availability and Reliability of Statistics in Socialist Cuba." Part 2. *Latin American Research Review* 4, no. 2 (Summer): 47–81.
Mesa-Lago, Carmelo. 1969c. "Economic Significance of Unpaid Labor in Socialist Cuba." *Industrial and Labor Relations Review* 22, no. 3 (April): 339–357.
Mesa-Lago, Carmelo. 1970. "Ideological Radicalization and Economic Policy in Cuba." *Studies in Comparative International Development* 5, no. 10: 203–16.
Mesa-Lago, Carmelo. 1971. "Economic Policies and Growth." In *Revolu-*

*tionary Change in Cuba,* ed. Carmelo Mesa-Lago, 277–338. Pittsburgh, Pa.: University of Pittsburgh Press.

Mesa-Lago, Carmelo. 1972. *The Labor Force, Employment, Unemployment and Underemployment in Cuba: 1899–1970.* Beverly Hills, Calif.: Sage Publications.

Mesa-Lago, Carmelo. 1976. "Farm Payments in Socialist Cuba." *Studies in Comparative Communism* 9, no. 3 (Autumn): 275–84.

Mesa-Lago, Carmelo. 1978. *Cuba in the 1970s: Pragmatism and Institutionalization.* Rev. ed. Albuquerque: University of New Mexico Press.

Mesa-Lago, Carmelo. 1979. "Cuban Statistics Revisited." *Cuban Studies/Estudios Cubanos* 9, no. 2 (July): 59–62.

Mesa-Lago, Carmelo. 1981. *The Economy of Socialist Cuba: A Two Decade Appraisal.* Albuquerque: University of New Mexico Press.

Mesa-Lago, Carmelo. 1982. "The Economy: Caution, Frugality and Resilient Ideology." In *Cuba: Internal and International Affairs,* ed. Jorge I. Domínguez, 113–66. Beverly Hills, Calif.: Sage Publications.

Mesa-Lago, Carmelo. 1986. "Cuba's Centrally Planned Economy: An Equity Trade-off for Growth." In *Latin American Political Economy: Financial Crisis and Political Change,* ed. Jonathan Hartley and Samuel A. Morley, 292–318. Boulder, Colo.: Westview.

Mesa-Lago, Carmelo, and Fernando Gil. 1989. "Soviet Economic Relations with Cuba." In *The USSR and Latin America in the 1980s,* ed. Eusebio Mujal-León, 183–232. Boston: Unwin Hyman.

Mesa-Lago, Carmelo, and Jorge Pérez-López. 1985a. *Study of Cuba's Material Product System, Its Conversion to the System of National Accounts, and Estimation of Gross Domestic Product per Capita and Growth Rates.* Staff Working Paper no. 770. Washington, D.C.: World Bank.

Mesa-Lago, Carmelo, and Jorge Pérez-López. 1985b. "Estimating Cuban Gross Domestic Product per Capita in Dollars Using Physical Indicators." *Social Indicators Research* 16: 275–300.

Mesa-Lago, Carmelo, and Jorge Pérez-López. 1985c. "Imbroglios on the Cuban Economy: A Reply to Brundenius and Zimbalist." *Comparative Economic Studies* 27, no. 1 (Spring): 47–83.

Mesa-Lago, Carmelo, and Jorge Pérez-López. 1985d. "The Endless Cuban Economy Saga: A Terminal Rebuttal." *Comparative Economic Studies* 27, no. 4 (Winter): 67–82.

Milián, Arnaldo. 1977. "Discurso en la sesión de clausura del II Congreso del Sindicato de Trabajadores Azucareros Agrícolas, el 19 de agosto de 1977." *Granma* (24 August): 2.

Miller, Julie Ann. 1986a. "For Cuba, the Key is Bioresearch." *Chemical Week* 138, no. 19 (7 May): 71–73.

Miller, Julie Ann. 1986b. "Sweeter Prospects for Cuban Sugar Cane." *New Scientist* 110, no. 1502 (3 April): 24.

Mina, Gianni. 1988. *Habla Fidel*. Madrid: Mondadori España.
"Minrex Reshuffle to Please Soviets." 1986. *Caribbean Report* (2 October): 2.
Miranda Torres, Rubén, and José A. Rodríguez Valdés. 1984. "La determinación del tipo de cambio a utilizar en la evaluación de inversiones." *Economía y Desarrollo* 80 (May–June): 116–51.
Molina, Gabriel. 1977. "In 10 Years, Tricontinental Bulk Sugar Shipping Terminal Saves Enough Foreign Exchange to Pay for 2 Terminals Just Like It." *Granma Weekly Review* (13 February): 5.
del Monte, Armelio. 1981. "La integración agroindustrial azucarera." *Cuestiones de la Economía Planificada* 8 (March–April): 71–95.
del Monte, Armelio. 1983. "La colaboración económica cubano-soviética en la esfera de la producción azucarera." *ATAC* 41, nos. 4–6: 16–23.
Montero, Isabel. 1981. "Cuba: Industrial Development Project." *Direct from Cuba* 258 (30 May): 22–24.
Morales, Pedro. 1985. "A la altura de los tiempos." *Cuba Internacional* 17, no. 190 (September): 18–21.
Morales, René. 1967. "Los embarques de azúcar a granel." *Teoría y Práctica* 33 (February): 59–62.
Morales Pita, Antonio E. 1983. "La programación óptima del período de zafra." *CubaAzúcar* (October–December): 7–13. (Also published in *Economía y Desarrollo* 79 [March–April 1984]: 143–56.)
Morales Rodríguez, Eliodoro, and Enrique Rodríguez Corominas. 1986. "La duración de la zafra y su efecto en la eficiencia agroindustrial." *Economía y Desarrollo* 91 (March–April): 96–101.
Moreno, Isabel. 1981. "Cuba: Industrial Development Project." *Direct from Cuba* 258 (30 May): 22–24.
Moreno Fraginals, Manuel. 1970. "Desgarramiento azucarero e integración nacional." *Casa de las Américas* 11, no. 62 (September–October): 6–22.
Moreno Fraginals, Manuel. 1978. *El ingenio*, 3 vols. Havana: Editorial de Ciencias Sociales.
"Muy valiosa y útil ha sido la experiencia de esta gran obra." 1985. *Granma* (6 February): 4.
Navarrete, Hilda. 1980. "Cuba: Las maravillas del bagazo." *Panorama Económico Latinoamericano* 6, no. 156 (6 July): 1–3.
Navarrete, Hilda. 1983a. "Azúcar: Balance y perspectivas." *Panorama Económico Latinoamericano* 7, no. 236 (14 November): 1–4.
Navarrete, Hilda. 1983b. "Cuba ante el nuevo convenio azucarero." *Panorama Económico Latinoamericano* 7, no. 226 (12 June): 6–10.
Nazario, Olga. 1986. "Brazil's Rapprochement with Cuba: The Process and Prospects." *Journal of Interamerican Studies and World Affairs* 28, no. 3 (Fall): 67–86.
Noa Silverio, Herly. 1978. "Aspectos económicos de la industrialización del bagazo." *ATAC* 37, no. 3 (May–June): 16–26.

Noa Silverio, Herly. 1983. "The Development of By-Products from Sugar Cane in Cuba." *Sugar y Azúcar* 78, no. 2 (February): 126–30.

Nocedo de León, Iris. 1988. "Perspectivas de la cooperación en la industria azucarera latinoamericana," *Cuba Economía Planificada* 3, no. 4 (October–December): 49–77.

Nolff, Max. 1963. "El desarrollo industrial de Cuba." *Panorama Económico* (Santiago, Chile) 17, no. 240 (November): 183–88.

Nolff, Max. 1964a. "El desarrollo industrial de Cuba." *Panorama Económico* (Santiago, Chile) 17, no. 241 (May): 32–35.

Nolff, Max. 1964b. "Industry." In *Cuba: The Economic and Social Revolution*, ed. Dudley Seers, 281–337. Chapel Hill: University of North Carolina Press.

Norniella, José M. 1985. "Las reuniones abiertas ayudaron mucho en el trabajo del partido y en la obtención de mejores resultados económicos." *Granma* (14 March): 2.

"Ochocientas combinadas cañeras en 1988." 1987. *Cuba Internacional* 19, no. 215 (November): 10.

Ojeda Fagundo, Aurelio, and Héctor F. Fiandor Rosario. 1988. 'Estudio de la influencia de algunos factores en la producción cañera," *Cuba Economía Planificada* 3, no. 2 (April–June): 178–95.

Olema, Daura. 1980. "La caña de azúcar: Materia prima del futuro." *Verde Olivo* 34: 40–3.

Oramas, Joaquín. 1981. "La fábrica de calderas de Sagua la Grande nace con el sello importante de la calidad." *Granma* (23 July): 2.

Oramas, Joaquín. 1984. "Los sobreconsumos del combustible diesel, una situación que urge resolver." *Granma* (21 June): 1.

Oramas, Lino. 1986. "Cuba puede y debe expandir su producción." *Granma* (20 October): 7.

"Otra batalla en Las Guásimas." 1979. *Cuba Internacional* (February): 20–1.

Packenham, Robert A. 1986. "Capitalist Dependency and Socialist Dependency: The Case of Cuba." *Journal of Interamerican Studies and World Affairs* 28, no. 1 (Spring): 59–92.

Pagés, Raisa. 1984. "El Gicabú, patente industrial cubana para adaptar la cachaza al consumo animal." *Granma* (6 February): 5.

Pagés, Raisa. 1985. "Inauguran plataforma de procesar Gicabú en La Habana." *Granma* (22 March): 1.

Pagés, Raisa. 1986. "El bagacillo." *Granma* (8 March): 2.

Palezuelos, Raúl. 1979a. "El caso KTP: Vestirse despacio." *Bohemia* 71, no. 46 (16 November): 16–21.

Palezuelos, Raúl. 1979b. "Una tradición industrial donde no la había." *Bohemia* 71, no. 32 (10 August): 16–23.

Paneque Brizuelas, Antonio. 1983. "Cuba Builds Sugar Mill in Nicaragua." *Granma Weekly Review* (2 April): 12.

Paneque Brizuelas, Antonio. 1976. "Mechanization of Sugarcane Harvesting in Cuba." *Granma Weekly Review* (4 April): 7.

"Papel, celulosa y energía en Iberoamérica." 1955. *Revista del Banco Nacional de Cuba* 1, no. 11 (November): 501–14.

Penkina, Svetlana. 1979. "Cuba y la división socialista internacional del trabajo." *América Latina* (Moscow) 4: 18–34.

Peralta, Urioste, Guillermo Frías, and Anatoli Gasparov. 1979. "La operación de las combinadas para la cosecha de caña." *ATAC* 38, no. 2 (March–April): 42–48.

Peraza Chapeau, José. 1984. *El CAME y la integración económica socialista.* Havana: Editorial de Ciencias Sociales.

Pereira, Manuel. 1975. "Al bagazo, mucho caso." *Cuba Internacional* (June): 32–35.

Pérez, Humberto. 1978. "Discurso en el acto de clausura del seminario nacional preparativo para la elaboración de los estudios de la estrategia del desarrollo perspectivo económico y social hasta el año 2000, el 16 de octubre de 1978." *Granma* (18 October): 2.

Pérez, Humberto. 1982. "La Plataforma programática y el desarrollo económico de Cuba." *Cuba Socialista* 2, no. 2 (June): 3–42.

Pérez, Louis A. 1978. "'La Chambelona': Political Protest, Sugar, and Social Banditry in Cuba, 1914–1917." *Journal of Inter-American Economic Affairs* 31, no. 4 (Spring): 3–27.

Pérez, Louis A. 1980. "Class, Property, and Sugar: Conflict and Contradiction in Cuban Separatism, 1895–1898." *Journal of Inter-American Economic Affairs* 34, no. 1 (Summer): 3–26.

Pérez, Louis A. 1983. "Toward Dependency and Revolution: The Political Economy of Cuba between Wars, 1878–1895." *Latin American Research Review* 18, no. 1: 127–42.

Pérez, Silvia N. 1984. "La participación de Cuba en la comunidad socialista y su ejemplo para el tercer mundo." In *Cuba y Estados Unidos: Un debate para la convivencia,* ed. Juan Gabriel Tokatlian, 111–26. Buenos Aires: Grupo Impresor Latinoamericano.

Pérez Alcina, Nimedia. 1988. "Del bagazo de caña al papel periódico." *CubaAzúcar* (July–September): 20–24.

Pérez Alcina, Nimedia. 1987. "La industria cubana de tableros." *CubaAzúcar* (April–June): 46–8.

Pérez Betancourt, Roberto. 1984. "Tiempo que alegra el corazón." *Bohemia* 76, no. 23 (8 June): 28–31.

Pérez-Cisneros, Enrique. 1957. *Cuba y el mercado azucarero mundial.* Havana: Impresores Ucar, García.

Pérez-López, Jorge F. 1977. "An Index of Cuban Industrial Output, 1930–58." In *Quantitative Latin American Studies: Methods and Findings,* ed. James W. Wilkie and Kenneth Ruddle, Supplement 6 of *Statistical Ab-*

stract of Latin America, 37–72. Los Angeles: UCLA Latin American Center.
Pérez-López, Jorge F. 1979. "Sugar and Petroleum in Cuban-Soviet Terms of Trade." In *Cuba in the World,* ed. Cole Blasier and Carmelo Mesa-Lago, 273–96. Pittsburgh, Pa.: University of Pittsburgh Press.
Pérez-López, Jorge F. 1981. "Energy Production, Imports and Consumption in Revolutionary Cuba." *Latin American Research Review* 16, no. 3: 111–37.
Pérez-López, Jorge F. 1986. "Cuba as an Oil Trader." *Caribbean Review* 15, no. 2 (Spring): 26–29, 43–44.
Pérez-López, Jorge F. 1987. "Cuban Oil Reexports: Significance and Prospects." *Energy Journal* 8, no. 1: 1–16.
Pérez-López, Jorge F. 1988. "Cuban-Soviet Sugar Trade: Price and Subsidy Issues." *Bulletin of Latin American Research* 7, no. 1: 123–47.
Pérez-López, Jorge F. 1989. "Sugar and Structural Change in the Cuban Economy." *World Development* 17, no. 10 (October): 1627–46.
Pérez-López, Jorge F., and Rene Pérez-López. 1980. *A Calendar of Cuban Bilateral Agreements 1959–1976.* Pittsburgh, Pa.: University Center for International Studies, University of Pittsburgh.
Pérez Rojas, Niurka. 1987. "Algunas manifestaciones ideológicas sobre la cooperativización en complejos agroindustriales azucareros." *Economía y Desarrollo* 96 (January–February): 100–09.
Pérez Viera, Julio Cesar, and Andrés Castellanos. 1988. "Ya produce la primera fábrica cubana de furfural." *Granma* (18 July): 2.
Pernas, Manuel M. 1965. "Bagazo: Línea potencial de desarrollo y problemas." *Nuestra Industria. Revista Económica* 12 (April): 64–82.
Petushkov, Ivan. 1975. "Desarrollo integral de la industria azúcarera de Cuba." *America Latina* (Moscow) 1: 29–44.
Pflaum, Irving P. 1960. "Aspects of the Cuban Economy: The Sugar Industry." *American Universities Field Staff Reports Service* (Mexico and Caribbean Area Series) 5, no. 8 (August): 1–12.
Pickett, James, and Robert Robson. 1986. *Manual on the Choice of Industrial Technique in Developing Countries.* Paris: Organization for Economic Cooperation and Development.
Pino-Santos, Oscar. 1975. *El asalto a Cuba por la oligarquía financiera yanki.* Havana: Editorial Orbe.
Pino-Santos, Oscar. 1984. *Cuba: Historia y economía.* Havana, Editorial de Ciencias Sociales. Contains revised version of *El asalto a Cuba por la oligarquía financiera yanki.*
Pino-Santos, Oscar, and Osvaldo Martínez. 1979. *Relaciones económicas de Cuba con los países miembros del Consejo de Asistencia Mútua Económica (CAME),* E/CEPAL/PROY.4/R.6. Santiago, Chile: Economic Commission for Latin America.

"Planta mecánica." 1963. *Nuestra Industria. Revista Económica* 3, no. 6 (June): 30–34.
Pollitt, Brian H. 1973. "Employment Plans, Performance and Future Prospects in Cuba." In *Third World Employment,* ed. Richard Jolly, Emmanual de Kadt, Hans Singer, and Fiona Wilson, 248–65. Harmandsworth, England: Penguin.
Pollitt, Brian H. 1982a. "Transformación de la agricultura cañera de Cuba: 1959–1980." *Areíto* 8, no. 30: 13–17.
Pollitt, Brian H. 1982b. "The Transition to Socialist Agriculture in Cuba: Some Salient Features." Institute of Development Studies, University of Sussex, *Bulletin* 13, no. 4 (September): 12–22.
Pollitt, Brian H. 1984. "The Cuban Sugar Economy and the Great Depression." *Bulletin of Latin American Research* 3, no. 2: 3–28.
Pollitt, Brian H. 1986. "Sugar, 'Dependency' and the Cuban Revolution." *Development and Change* 17: 195–230.
Pozo, Alberto. 1970. "¿Por qué la quema de cañas?" *Bohemia* 62, no. 50 (11 December): 28–34.
*Proyecto de directivas para el desarrollo económico y social en el quinquenio 1976–80.* 1975. Havana.
Quesada González, Ramón. 1969. "Consumo de energía térmica en la producción de azúcar cruda." *CubaAzúcar* (July–September): 2–8.
Radell, Willard W. 1983. "Cuban-Soviet Sugar Trade, 1960–76: How Great Was the Subsidy." *Journal of Developing Areas* 17, no. 3 (April): 365–82.
Radell, Willard W. 1987. "Comparative Performance of Large Cuban Factories in the 1984 'Zafra.'" *Cuban Studies* 17: 141–55.
Ramírez Cruz, José. 1984. "El sector cooperativo en la agricultura cubana." *Cuba Socialista* 11 (July–August): 1–24.
Ramos, Mercedes. 1982. "Cuba: Un combinado azucarero industrial." *Panorama Económico Latinoamericano* 6, no. 201 (23 May): 1–4.
Recarte, Alberto. 1980. *Cuba: Economía y poder (1959–1980).* Madrid: Alianza Editorial.
"Recibe Fidel a delegación de Nicaragua." 1981. *Cuba Internacional* (May): 5.
Reed, Steven L. 1979. "Participation in Multinational Organizations and Programs." In *Cuba in the World,* ed. Cole Blasier and Carmelo Mesa-Lago, 297–312. Pittsburgh, Pa.: University of Pittsburgh Press.
Regalado, Antero. 1965. "Los pequeños agricultores y el plan azucarero para 1970." *Cuba Socialista* 5, no. 48 (August): 36–50.
*La revolución de octubre y la revolución cubana.* 1987. Havana: Editora Política.
Risquet Valdés, Jorge. 1963. "Los batallones rojos, valiosa experiencia de la zafra en la provincia de Oriente." *Cuba Socialista* 3, no. 19 (March): 126–34.
Risquet Valdés, Jorge. 1964. "Algunas experiencias de las brigadas de corte

y alza mecanizada de la caña en Oriente." *Cuba Socialista* 4, no. 34 (June): 65–83.

Ritter, Archibald R. M. 1974. *The Economic Development of Revolutionary Cuba: Strategy and Performance.* New York: Praeger Publishers.

Rivero, Miguel. 1981. "Cuba-Tanzania: Una cooperación fructífera." *Colaboración* 3, no. 8 (July–September): 26–29.

Rivero, Raúl. 1976. "El convenio entre Cuba y la URSS continúa, por su espíritu, la línea trazada en la declaración firmada hace 3 años por Brezhnev y Fidel, dijo Carlos Rafael." *Granma* (15 April): 8.

Rizo Alvarez, Julián. 1981. "La zafra 1980–81: Nueva calidad en el proceso cañero azucarero." *Cuba Socialista* 1, no. 1 (December): 34–55.

Roca, Sergio G. 1976. *Cuban Economic Policy and Ideology: The Ten Million Ton Harvest.* Beverly Hills: Sage Publications.

Roca, Sergio G. 1988. "Cuba's International Economic Relations in the Late 1980s." In *Socialist Cuba: Past Interpretations and Future Challenges,* ed. Sergio G. Roca, 101–21. Boulder, Colo.: Westview.

Roca, Sergio G., and Roberto E. Hernández. 1972. "Structural Economic Problems." In *Cuba, Castro and Revolution,* ed. Jaime Suchlicki, 67–93. Coral Gables, Fla.: University of Miami Press.

Rodríguez, Andrés. 1973. "Un tablero de ajedrez." *Bohemia* 65, no. 13 (30 March): 18–23.

Rodríguez, Andrés. 1976a. "Mecanización cañera y socialismo." *Bohemia* 68, no. 47 (16 November): 12–17.

Rodríguez, Andrés. 1976b. "Un proyecto prometedor." *Bohemia* 68, no. 44 (29 October): 14–19.

Rodríguez, Andrés 1979. "ATAC: Una herramienta técnica del sector azucarero." *Bohemia* 71, no. 40 (5 October): 16–23.

Rodríguez, Andrés. 1980a. "Hecho en Cuba." *Bohemia* 72, no. 5 (1 February): 16–23.

Rodríguez, Andrés. 1980b. "Las Tunas: ¿qué sucede?" *Bohemia* 72, no. 26 (27 June): 16–23.

Rodríguez, Andrés. 1982a. "Sacarosa, formula potente." *Bohemia* 74, no. 28 (9 July): 28–31.

Rodríguez, Andrés. 1982b. "Tremendas posibilidades." *Bohemia* 74, no. 15 (9 April): 12–13.

Rodríguez, Andrés. 1983. "Visión de los derivados." *CubaAzúcar* (February): 4–8.

Rodríguez, Carlos Rafael. 1963. "Cuatro años de reforma agraria," *Cuba Socialista* 3, no. 21 (May): 1–30.

Rodríguez, Javier. 1983. "Cuando de azúcar se trata." *Cuba Internacional* (December): 42–44.

Rodríguez, José Luis. 1981. "La economía de Cuba socialista." *Economía y Desarrollo* 61 (March—April): 112–48.

Rodríguez, José Luis. 1982. "La economía cubana entre 1976 y 1980: Resulta-

dos y perspectivas." *Economía y Desarrollo* 66 (January–February): 108–49.
Rodríguez, José Luis. 1984a. "El desarrollo económico de Cuba y sus perspectivas para el futuro." In *Cuba y Estados Unidos: Un debate para la convivencia,* ed. Juan Gabriel Tokatlian, 201–47. Buenos Aires: Grupo Impresor Latinoamericano.
Rodríguez, José Luis. 1984b. *Dos ensayos sobre la economía cubana.* Havana: Editorial de Ciencias Sociales.
Rodríguez, José Luis. 1985. "Un enfoque burgués del sector externo de la economía cubana." *Cuba Socialista* 5, no. 1 (March–April): 78–104.
Rodríguez, José Luis. 1986. "Las relaciones económicas Cuba-URSS: 1960–1985." *Temas de Economía Mundial* 17: 9–33.
Rodríguez, Magali, and Raúl Gutiérrez. 1978. "Estudio sobre la calidad del bagazo." *ATAC* 37, no. 1 (January–February): 20–26.
Rodríguez Córdova, Roberto. 1986. "Los complejos agroindustriales en los países socialistas." *Economía y Desarrollo* 95 (November–December): 198–209.
Rodríguez Corominas, Enrique, and Guenadyi Likichev. 1984. "Una clasificación de los factores que influyen sobre la eficiencia de la producción azucarera." *Economía y Desarrollo* 79 (March–April): 213–29.
Rodríguez Pérez, Osvaldo. 1982. "Logros del sector azucarero en los últimos años," *Verde Olivo* 23, no. 46 (18 November): 54–55.
Rojas Aguilera, Alexis. 1985. "Cumplió plan quinquenal la fábrica de combinadas cañeras KTP de Holguín." *Granma* (18 December): 3.
Rojas Aguilera, Alexis. 1988. "Cortó un millón de arrobas de caña la KTP-3," *Granma* (9 July): 1.
Rojas Requena, Iliana, Mariana Ravenet Ramírez, and Jorge Hernández Ramírez. 1985. *Sociología y desarrollo rural en Cuba.* Havana: Editorial de Ciencias Sociales.
Romero Revuelta, Juan. 1985. "Estudio preliminar de obtención de concentrados proteicos a partir de las hojas y cogollos de la caña de azúcar." *ATAC* 44, no. 2 (March–April): 44–47.
Ruiz, Angel Ramón. 1952. *Una estrategia de fomento de largo alcance.* Havana: Turull.
Ruiz, Angel Ramón. 1959. "Desarrollo de subproductos en la industria azucarera de Cuba." *Cubaquímica* 29: 24–27.
Ruiz Portal, Antonio. 1980. "Azúcar: Brazos mecánicos." *Panorama Económico Latinoamericano* 4, no. 167 (21 December): 19–21.
Salomón Llanes, Roberto. 1977a. "El nuevo Convenio Internacional Azucarero acordado será un eficaz regulador de mercados." *ATAC* 36, no. 6 (November–December): 43–45.
Salomón Llanes, Roberto. 1977b. "Se efectúa en La Habana la VI Reunión de GEPLACEA." *ATAC* 36, no. 2 (March–April): 4–12.
Salomón Llanes, Roberto. 1978. "El mayor y mas moderno sistema de

exportación de azúcar del mundo." *ATAC* 37, no. 1 (January–February): 12–19.
Salomón Llanes, Roberto. 1984. "Cuba estará a la vanguardia de las investigaciones de la caña de azúcar." *Bohemia* 76, no. 31 (3 August): 28–31.
Salomón Llanes, Roberto. 1985a. "La hora de las máquinas." *Bohemia* 77, no. 35 (30 August): 31–33.
Salomón Llanes, Roberto. 1985b. "El transporte azucarero: Eslabón vital de la zafra." *Verde Olivo* 25, no. 4 (24 January): 24–25.
Salomón Llanes, Roberto. 1986a. "Una materia prima de grandes perspectivas." *Bohemia* 78, no. 41 (10 October): 78–9.
Salomón Llanes, Roberto. 1986b. "El rey de los derivados." *Bohemia* 78, no. 46 (14 November): 55–6.
Salomón Llanes, Roberto. 1986c. "La mano hermana." *Colaboración* 10, no. 28 (June–September): 31–32.
Salomón Llanes, Roberto. 1986d. "Dos etapas y un solo fin." *Bohemia* 78, no. 39 (26 September): 8–9.
Sánchez, Pedro A., and Grant M. Scobie. 1986. *Cuba and the CGIAR Centers*. Study Paper no. 14. Washington, D.C.: World Bank for the Consultative Group on International Agricultural Research.
Sánchez del Toro, Luis. 1985. "Refinando azúcar para crecer." *Bohemia* 77, no. 46 (15 November): 35.
Sánchez García-Calzadilla, María. 1982. "La participación de Cuba en la integración socialista." *Revista Estadística* 5, no. 9 (December): 59–87.
Santana Palenzuela, Otto, and Marianela Cordovés Herrera. 1988. "Evaluación económica del secado y compactación de residuos cañeros para su exportación." *CubaAzúcar* (July–September): 3–7.
Santos, Angel, and Ciro Castro. 1970. "Análisis de los rendimientos en azúcar del Central Ecuador." *Economía y Desarrollo* 3 (July–September): 77–119.
Savall, José R. 1984. "Sugar Project." *Direct from Cuba* 320 (1 March): 14–16.
Scott, Rebecca J. 1985a. "Class Relations in Sugar and Political Mobilization in Cuba, 1868–1899." *Cuban Studies/Estudios Cubanos* 15, no. 1 (Winter): 15–28.
Scott, Rebecca J. 1985b. *Slave Emancipation in Cuba*. Princeton: Princeton University Press.
"Serán manejadas por cubanos las máquinas cosechadoras en un ingenio de Nicaragua." 1986. *Diario las Américas* (9 January): 6A.
Silva León, Arnaldo. 1975. *Cuba y el mercado internacional azucarero*. Havana: Editorial de Ciencias Sociales.
Simón, Mary. 1987. "Trata Zaire cooperación con Cuba para impulsar industria azucarera." *Granma* (19 October): 7.
Smith, Ian. 1981a. "GATT: EEC Sugar Export Refunds Disputes." *Journal of World Trade Law* 15, no. 6 (November–December): 534–43.

Smith, Ian. 1981b. "EEC Sugar Policy in an International Context." *Journal of World Trade Law* 15, no. 2 (March–April): 95–110.
Smith, Ian. 1983. "Prospects for a New International Sugar Agreement." *Journal of World Trade Law* 17, no. 4 (July–August): 308–24.
Smith, Ian. 1985. "UNCTAD: Failure of the UN Sugar Conference." *Journal of World Trade Law* 19, no. 3 (May–June): 296–301.
Smith, John T. 1984. "Sugar Dependency in Cuba: Capitalism versus Socialism." In *The Gap Between the Rich and the Poor,* ed. Mitchell A. Seligson, 366–78. Boulder: Westview.
Suárez Guerra, Marcio. 1983. "Perfeccionamiento de la contabilidad de los gastos de producción y cálculo del costo de la caña de azúcar." *Economía y Desarrollo* 73 (March–April): 182–215.
"The Sugar Economy of the COMECON Countries." 1974. *F.O. Licht's International Sugar Report* (December, special issue).
"Sugar Industry Saved More Than 13 Million Gallons of Oil." 1981. *Juventud Rebelde* (24 September): 1. In Foreign Broadcast Information Service, *Latin America Report* (6 November): 39–40.
Swerling, Boris. 1951. "Domestic Control of an Export Industry: Cuban Sugar." *Journal of Farm Economics* 33, no. 3 (August): 346–56.
Tabío York, Horacio. 1982. "La primera acción conjunta ante el Acuerdo General de Aranceles Aduaneros y Comercio." *Cuadernos Económicos Trimestrales* 4 (November): 212–28.
Tan, C. Suan. 1986. *Cuba-USSR Sugar Trade.* Washington, D.C.: Commodity Studies and Projections Division, Economic Analysis and Projections Department, World Bank.
"Texto del convenio a largo plazo sobre suministros de azúcar a la URSS por parte de la República de Cuba." 1964. *Cuba Socialista* 4, no. 30 (February): 165–66.
Tijonov, V. 1981. "Esencia del complejo agroindustrial." *Cuestiones de la Economía Planificada* 8 (March–April): 32–49.
Torralbas González, Diocles. 1983. "The Development and Prospects for Cuban Sugar Production." *Sugar y Azúcar* 78, no. 2 (February): 95–97.
Torras, Jacinto. 1977 (orig. publ. 1953). "El Convenio Internacional Azucarero de 1953." *ATAC* 36, no. 3 (May–June): 35–39.
Torres Pérez, Miguel and Raúl Carballosa Torres. 1985. "Análisis crítico de algunos planteamientos de la cubanología burguesa sobre la economía cubana." *Economía y Desarrollo* 89 (November–December): 200–15.
Torres Ramírez, Blanca. 1971. *Las relaciones cubano-soviéticas (1959–1968).* Mexico City: El Colegio de México.
Tsadik, Tesfaye W. 1982. "The International Sugar Market: Self-sufficiency or Free Trade," *Journal of World Trade Law* 16, no. 2 (March–April): 133–51.
Turits, Richard. 1987. "Trade, Debt, and the Cuban Economy." *World Development* 15, no. 1 (January): 163–80.

Turu, Danielle. 1981. "En torno a los costos de producción azucarera en Cuba a mediados del siglo XIX." *Cuban Studies/Estudios Cubanos* 11, no. 1 (January): 65–86.

United Nations. 1953. *United Nations Sugar Conference 1953: Summary of Proceedings.* New York: United Nations.

United Nations Conference on Trade and Development (UNCTAD). 1982. *Marketing and Processing of Sugar: Areas for International Cooperation,* TD/B/C.1/PSC/20. Geneva.

United Nations Conference on Trade and Development (UNCTAD). 1985. *Handbook of International Trade and Development Statistics: 1985 Annual Supplement.* New York: United Nations.

United Nations Conference on Trade and Development (UNCTAD). 1987a. *International Sugar Agreement, 1987,* TD/Sugar.11/5. Geneva.

United Nations Conference on Trade and Development (UNCTAD). 1987b. *UNCTAD Commodity Yearbook 1987.* Geneva.

United Nations Industrial Development Organization (UNIDO). 1986. *Cuba.* Industrial Development Review Series, UNIDO/IS.615. New York: United Nations.

United States Cuban Sugar Council. 1948. *Sugar Facts and Figures.* New York.

U.S. Bureau of the Census. *Statistical Abstract of the United States.* Washington, D.C. Annual.

U.S. Central Intelligence Agency. 1975. *Cuban Foreign Trade.* ER75-69. Washington, D.C. (December).

U.S. Central Intelligence Agency. 1976. *The Cuban Economy: A Statistical Review, 1968-76.* ER76-10708. Washington, D.C. (December).

U.S. Central Intelligence Agency. 1981. *The Cuban Economy: A Statistical Review.* ER81-10052. Washington, D.C. (March).

U.S. Central Intelligence Agency. 1984. *The Cuban Economy: A Statistical Review.* ALA84-10052. Washington, D.C. (June).

U.S. Congress. House Committee on Agriculture. 1962. *History and Operations of the U.S. Sugar Program.* Washington, D.C.: GPO.

U.S. Department of Commerce. 1956. *Investment in Cuba.* Washington, D.C.: GPO.

U.S. Federal Energy Administration. National Energy Information Center. 1977. *Energy Interrelationships.* Washington, D.C.: U.S. GPO.

Valdés, María Teresa. 1983. "Notas acerca de la evolución del mercado azucarero internacional en los últimos años." *Temas de Economía Mundial* 5: 83–100.

Valdés, María Teresa. 1984. "La evolución de la producción azucarera en Cuba y su papel en las relaciones económicas externas." *Temas de Economía Mundial* 10: 117–49.

Valdés, Nelson P. 1970. "La diplomacia del azúcar: Estados Unidos y Cuba." *Aportes* 18 (October): 99–119.

Varela Pérez, Juan. 1978. "Consolida sus bases y se define la política energética en la industria azucarera." *Granma* (15 November): 3.

Varela Pérez, Juan. 1981a. "Ejecutarán en este quinquenio un programa que prevé la restauración de todas las refinerías de azúcar." *Granma* (22 January): 4.

Varela Pérez, Juan. 1981b. "Incorporan en este quinquenio 190 locomotoras soviéticas para el transporte azucarero." *Granma* (11 June): 3.

Varela Pérez, Juan. 1983. "The Cuban Sugar Industry Takes Off." *Granma Weekly Review* (17 July, special supplement): 3–5.

Varela Pérez, Juan. 1984a. "La batalla del petróleo está ganada, pero queda mucho por ahorrar en otras labores de la zafra," *Granma* (22 December): 1.

Varela Pérez, Juan. 1984b. "Un símbolo de los tiempos que vive nuestra patria." *Granma* (3 January): 1, no. 5.

Varela Pérez, Juan. 1984c. "Todavía el arrobaje por máquina-parque no llega a los valores planificados." *Granma* (9 January): 1.

Varela Pérez, Juan. 1984d. "Rebasar las 8,900 arrobas por máquina-parque es el objetivo de los operadores de combinadas." *Granma* (11 October): 3.

Varela Pérez, Juan. 1985a. "Erradicado el gasto de petróleo en azúcar crudo, pero continua alto en refino." *Granma* (17 October): 1.

Varela Pérez, Juan. 1985b. "Nicaragua: Cooperación azucarera cubana." *Panorama Económico Latinoamericano* 9, no. 265 (February): 6–8.

Varela Pérez, Juan. 1985c. "Complejo azucarero Victoria de Julio: Hermoso símbolo de amistad Cuba-Nicaragua." *Granma* (6 February): 4–5.

Varela Pérez, Juan. 1985d. "Sí, hacen falta los 8 recogedores de caña por cada combinada." *Granma* (18 December): 1, 3.

Varela Pérez, Juan. 1985e. "Alcanzará el corte mecanizado en la próxima zafra el 66 por ciento." *Granma* (12 October): 1–2.

Varela Pérez, Juan. 1985f. "José es un operador de combinadas que sabe cuanto gasta, pero ¿y los demás?" *Granma* (21 February): 1.

Varela Pérez, Juan. 1986a. "Probarán en abril próximo nuevo central en Las Tunas." *Granma* (28 January): 3.

Varela Pérez, Juan. 1986b. "Vuelven las brigadas de recogedores de caña." *Granma* (31 October): 1.

Varela Pérez, Juan. 1986c. "Temprano alerta sobre la recogida de caña." *Granma* (20 November): 1.

Varela Pérez, Juan. 1986d. "Montan sistema para embarque de azúcar a granel en 9 centrales." *Granma* (18 September): 1.

Varela Pérez, Juan. 1986e. "Un llamado a la reflexión." *Granma* (2 October): 3.

Varela Pérez, Juan. 1986f. "Sólo estamos en el comienzo de un renacer en las producciones derivadas de la caña de azúcar." *Granma* (23 September): 1.

Varela Pérez, Juan. 1987. "Operan los 10 sistemas a granel que se montaron para esta zafra." *Granma* (8 April): 1.
Varela Pérez, Juan. 1988. "Indispensable encauzar el trabajo de zafra sobre criterios comunes." *Granma* (7 March): 3.
Varela Rojas, Ricardo. 1984. "Una potencia en derivados de la caña." *Bohemia* 76, no. 25 (22 June): 32–34.
Vázquez, José. 1968. "¿Cuánto petróleo puede ahorrarse en la industria azucarera?" *Granma* (16 February): 3.
Vázquez, José. 1974. "5 Preguntas de zafra." *Cuba Internacional* (June): 44–47.
Vázquez, José. 1975. "En la III reunión de Lima se alcanzaron logros importantes, como la constitución de la base del grupo y la definición de sus objetivos." *ATAC* 34, no. 6 (November–December): 4–8.
Vázquez, José. 1977a. "Cuba contará en el futuro con una gran industria azucarera, con una potente y diversificada industria de los derivados." *ATAC* 36, no. 4 (July–August): 4–8.
Vázquez, José. 1977b. "Estará en producción en 1977 y a plena capacidad en 1980 la fábrica de combinadas de Holguín." *ATAC* 36, no. 1 (January–February): 5–10.
Vázquez, José. 1978a. "El desarrollo de la mecanización en las distintas fases de la agricultura cañera es hoy una tarea fundamental." *ATAC* 37, no. 6 (November–December): 4–12.
Vázquez, José. 1978b. "Entrarán en producción en 1980 los 4 nuevos centrales cubanos." *ATAC* 37, no. 2 (March–April): 4–10.
Vázquez, José. 1979a. "La nueva combinada cubana KTP-2 pasa con éxito las pruebas de explotación." *ATAC* 38, no. 3 (May–June): 4–10.
Vázquez, José. 1979b. "Para estudiar el azúcar." *Cuba Internacional* (July): 32–35.
Vázquez, José. 1980. "Los importantes derivados." *Cuba Internacional* (June): 13–14.
Vázquez, José 1981. "Desarrollo azucarero." *Cuba Internacional* (July): 38–43.
Vidal Valdés, Margarita. 1985. "Consideraciones generales sobre la pulpa de bagazo, sus usos finales y posibilidades de exportación." *El Economista* 1, no. 1 (December): 137–43.
Villa Montes, Roberto. 1983. "Hazañas de titanes: La base mecánica de la industria azucarera de Cuba." *CubaAzúcar* (February): 21–26.
Vladimirov, V. A. 1974. "Soviet Equipment Gives Trouble-Free Service in the Tropics." *Soviet Export* (Moscow) 17, no. 4: 21–27.
*Vneshniaia Torgovlia* (Foreign Trade). Moscow. Annual.
Volkov, Serguei. 1977. "Acerca de la elección de la estructura económica nacional: La experiencia de Cuba." *América Latina* (Moscow) 2: 55–72.
Wasserman, Ursula. 1977. "International Sugar Agreement, 1977." *Journal of World Trade Law* 12, no. 1 (January–February): 83–85.
Willetts, Peter. 1981. *The Non-Aligned in Havana*. New York: St. Martin's Press.

World Bank. 1951. *Report on Cuba*. Washington, D.C.: World Bank.
World Bank. 1980. *Alcohol Production from Biomass in the Developing Countries*. Washington, D.C.: World Bank.
Yañez González, Eugenio. 1981. "Desarrollo económico e integración agroindustrial." *Cuestiones de la Economía Planificada* 8 (March–April): 51–70.
Zimbalist, Andrew. 1982. "Soviet Aid, U.S. Blockade, and the Cuban Economy." *ACES Bulletin* 24, no. 4 (Winter): 137–46.
Zimbalist, Andrew. 1988. "Cuba's External Economy: Reflections on Export Dependence, Soviet Aid, and Foreign Debt." *Comparative Economic Studies* 30, no. 2 (Summer): 21–46.
Zimbalist, Andrew, and Susan Eckstein. 1987. "Patterns of Cuban Development: The First Twenty-Five Years." *World Development* 15, no. 1 (January): 5–22.

# Index

Accounting systems, 114, 201
Acoustical tiles, 103
Afro-Malagasy Sugar Agreement, 183
Agrarian Reform Law (1959), 9; Second (1963), 10
Agro-industrial complexes, 15, 72, 191–92
Albania, 138, 184
Alcohol, 106–08
Amancio Rodríguez mill, 106
American-owned property, 10, 111
Angola, 154, 192, 193
Antonio Guiteras mill, 109
Area under cultivation, 204–06
Argelia Libre mill, 99
Argentina, 211
Australia, 65, 66, 102, 118, 177, 185, 186
Austria, 104, 108

*Bagacill. See* Cattle feed
Bagasse, 78–82, 83–84, 101, 103–06
Balance of payments, 206
Banco Cubano del Comercio Exterior (Cuban Foreign Trade Bank), 7
Banco de Desarrollo Económico y Social (Economic and Social Development Bank), 7
Banco de Fomento Agrícola e Industrial de Cuba (Agricultural and Industrial Development Bank), 7
Banco Nacional de Cuba (BNC), 7, 153–54, 161, 162, 199, 226
Batista, Fulgencio, 9
Beans, 204, 208
Belgium, 173, 176
Benin, 192, 195–96
Bilateral arrangements, 122

*Blanco directo,* 98, 99
BNC. *See* Banco Nacional de Cuba
Bolivia, 211
Boti, Regino, 199
Brazil, 101–03, 118, 160, 161, 177, 185, 186, 211
Brussels Conference (1929), 173, 218
Brussels Convention (1902), 173
Bulgaria, 14, 18, 136, 138, 143, 146, 147
Bulk shipping, 90–91, 113, 116
Burnt fields system, 67, 72
Burundi, 192, 196
By-products, 100–01

Cabrisas Ruiz, Ricardo, 186
*Cachaza. See* Filter mud
Camagüey province, 58, 106, 116
Camilo Cienfuegos plant, 105
Canada, 93, 96, 105, 152, 154, 167, 168, 214
Cane cutters, 59–61
*Carburante nacional,* 107
Cardboard, 103–04
Castro, Fidel, 11, 17, 82, 86, 159, 171, 172, 210–11, 225–26
Cattle feed, 101, 106, 108–09, 109
Center for the Development of Agricultural Machinery (Centro de Desarrollo de la Maquinaria Agrícola), 65
Central Intelligence Agency (CIA), 164, 165, 167–68
Central Planning Board (Junta Central de Planificación [JUCEPLAN]), 12
Centralization. *See* Nationalization
*Centros de acopio,* 67, 71, 101
Cepero Bonilla, Raul, 138, 180, 182

*307*

Chadbourne Agreement (1931), 6, 173, 176–77
Chaparra (Jesús Menéndez) mill, 109
China, 177. *See also* People's Republic of China
CIA. *See* Central Intelligence Agency
Cienfuegos: bulk shipping terminal at, 90–91, 116; refinery at, 96, 97
CMEA. *See* Council for Mutual Economic Assistance
Coffee, 5
Colombia, 192
*Colonos,* 57, 58, 66
Combines, 63–65, 69. *See also* Mechanical harvesters
Commission on Economic and Scientific-Technical Cooperation (Comisión de Colaboración Económica y Científico Técnica), 190
Commonwealth Sugar Agreement, 122, 183
Complete circulation (*circulación completa*), 202
Congo, 192, 196
Consolidated Sugar Industry Enterprise of the Ministry of Industries, 114
Cooperatives, 9, 10, 11, 58
Corn, 5, 204, 208
Corporación de Fomento de Hipotecas Aseguradas (Mortgage Insurance Development Corporation), 7
Council for Mutual Economic Assistance (CMEA), 14–15, 144, 150, 158, 184, 207–08, 221, 225. *See also specific countries*
Cuba–9 plant, 105
Cuba–10 plant, 109
Cuban Institute for Research on Sugarcane Derivatives. *See* Instituto Cubano de Investigaciones de los Derivados de la Caña de Azúcar
"Cubanization," 8
Czechoslovakia, 136, 138, 143, 146, 147, 176

*Danza de los millones,* 174
DATAZUCAR. *See* Empresa de Procesamiento de Datos de la Industria Azucarera
Delicias (Antonio Guiteras) mill, 109
Dextran, 109–10
Diez de Octubre complex, 72
Distilleries, 107
Diversification, 5–8, 10–12, 199, 213
Domestic consumption, 18, 97–98, 122
Dominican Republic, 118, 177, 214

East Germany, 14, 18, 138, 143, 146, 147
Eastern Europe, 93. *See also specific countries*
ECLA, 145, 146
Economic boom, 4–5, 7
Economic Management and Planning System (Sistema de Dirección y Planificación de la Económica), 11, 115
*Economic Survey of Latin America 1980,* 145
Ecuador, 96
EDA. *See* Empresa de Automatización Industrial
EEC. *See* European Economic Community
Egypt, 154
Eisenhower, Dwight D., 134
Electricity, 83, 94, 204
EMCI. *See* Empresa de Construcción y Montaje
Empresa de Automatización Industrial (EDA), 191
Empresa de Construcción y Montaje (EMCI), 191
Empresa de Procesamiento de Datos de la Industria Azucarera (DATAZUCAR), 191
Empresa Importadora y Exportadora de Plantas Alimentarias (IMEXPAL), 194
Energy production. *See* Bagasse
Enterprise exit (*a salida de empresa*), 202
España Republicana mill, 96, 110
Ethanol, 101–03, 102, 107, 108
Ethiopia, 192, 194

European Economic Community (EEC), 122, 166, 167, 183, 185, 186, 214, 216
European sugar industry, 5, 7, 11
Exchange rates, 164
Export concentration indexes, 211–12
Export quotas. *See* Quotas
Exports, percentages of, 154–56

Fernández Font, Marcelo, 17, 117, 185
Fiji, 118
Filter mud, 109
Financiera Nacional de Cuba (National Finance Corporation), 7
Finland, 105
Fondo de Seguro de Crédito (Credit Insurance Fund), 7
Food and Agriculture Organization, 204
Food crops, 11; import of, 204, 206–10; and self-sufficiency, 207–08
Foreign debt, 225, 226
Foreign policy, 190
France, 93, 97, 108, 118, 152, 173, 177
Free market, 180, 184, 185, 222; definition of, 179
Freight costs, 147–49
Fuelwood, 78, 82, 83, 84
Furfural, 106

GAPLACEA. *See* Latin American and Caribbean Sugar Exporters Group
Gasohol, 107
GATT. *See* General Agreement on Tariffs and Trade
GDP. *See* Gross domestic product
General Agreement on Tariffs and Trade (GATT), 185
General Agreement on the Integral Development of Sugar Production (CMEA Sugar Program), 14
German Democratic Republic. *See* East Germany
Germany, 176. *See also* East Germany; West Germany
Ghana, 192, 196
*Gicabú*, 109

Global social product (GSP), 200, 201, 202–03, 227
GNP. *See* Gross national product
Gorbachev, Mikhail, 150
Great Depression, 6, 132, 177
Grinding capacity, 76, 114
Gross domestic product (GDP), 200, 203, 227
Gross national product (GNP), 8, 200, 201, 203
Group of 77 (G–77), 187
GSP. *See* Global social product
Guayabal bulk shipping terminal, 90
Guevara, Ernesto (Che), 12, 63, 163
Guinea-Bissau, 192
Guyana, 192, 196
GVO, 202

Haiti, 177
Hard currency, 125, 156, 226
Harvesting: by manual labor, 57–58, 63, 67, 69, 70–71, 72; by professional cane cutters, 59–61; by voluntary labor, 59, 60, 61, 116; *See also* Mechanical harvesters
Hawaii, 134
Herrera Machado, Juan, 15–16
Hungary, 136, 138, 143, 176

ICIDCA. *See* Instituto Cubano Investigaciones de los Derivados de la Caña de Azúcar
ICINAZ. *See* Instituto Cubano de Investigaciones Azucareras
IMEXPAL. *See* Empresa Importadora y Exportadora de Plantas Alimentarias
Immigrant laborers, 5
Import Tariff (Arancel de Aduana) of 1927, 5, 6
Imports, 58, 116, 161–62, 204, 206–10. *See also* Oil
India, 118, 177
Indonesia, 176
Industrial yields, 15, 71–72, 76
Industrialization. *See* Diversification
Input-output matrices, 114

Instituto Cubano de Investigaciones Azucareras (ICINAZ), 101, 191
Instituto Cubano de Investigaciones Tecnológicas (Cuban Institute for Technological Research), 7
Instituto Cubano de Investigaciones de los Derivados de la Caña de Azúcar (ICIDCA), 92, 99, 191
Instituto de Proyectos Azucareros (IPROYAZ), 191, 192
International Bank for Reconstruction and Development, 111
International Sugar Agreements (ISA): (1937), 173, 177, 179; (1953), 173, 180–81; (1958), 181; (1968), 183–84, 221–22; (1977), 117, 184–86
International Sugar Committee, 132
International Sugar Organization (ISO), 127
Investments, 9–10, 203–04
IPROYAZ. See Instituto de Proyectos Azucareros
Iraq, 154
ISA. See International Sugar Agreements
ISO. See International Sugar Organization

Jamaica, 192, 196–97
Japan, 93, 152, 153, 167, 168, 214
Jaronú (Brasil) mill, 109
Jesús Menéndez plant, 109
Jones-Costigan Act. See Sugar Act (1934)
JUCEPLAN. See Central Planning Board (Junta Central de Planificación)
Juraguá nuclear power plant, 204

Korean War, 135, 173–74, 179

La Habana province, 105
Labor, 5, 74; laws pertaining to, 57–58; manual, 57–58, 63, 67, 69, 70–71, 72; productivity of, 62; shortages of, 13, 59, 76–77; voluntary, 59, 60, 61, 116

Landell Mills Commodities Studies, 111, 117–18
Land redistribution, 9, 10
Laos, 192, 197
Las Tunas province, 76–77, 106
Las Villas province, 58
Latin American and Caribbean Sugar Exporters Group (Grupo de Países Latinoamericanos y del Caribe Exportadores de Azúcar [GAPLACEA]), 117, 187, 188
Law-Decree on Industrial Stimulation (1953), 8
League of Nations, 176
Libya, 154
Lomé Agreement, 122
Louisiana, 113
Luxembourg, 176

Machado government, 6
*Macheteros,* 69
Macroeconomic data, 199, 201–03
Madagascar, 192, 197
Manual labor, 57–58, 63, 67, 69, 70–71, 72
Market economies, 167–68, 171–72, 214, 225. *See also specific countries*
Market socialism, 10
Matanzas bulk shipping terminal, 90
Material Product System, 201
Mauritania, 192
Meat, 5, 208, 210
Mechanical harvesters, 13, 56, 58, 59; and cutting and loading, 67, 69; and extraneous matter, 69–71; and oil consumption, 86; and productivity, 72–74; and Soviet collaboration, 63–66, 162; workers' opposition to, 57
Mexico, 96, 104, 192, 195, 211
MFN. See Most-favored-nation
*Miel protéica,* 109
Milk, 208
Mills, 99, 103, 105, 106, 109; American-owned, 111; and bagasse consumption, 78–82, 83; dismantling of, 12; grinding capacity of, 76, 114; modernization of, 14, 15; and oil

consumption, 84, 85–86; state control of, 9, 10
MINAZ, 111, 193
Minimum price indexation, 144–51, 166, 167
Ministry of Finance, 115
Ministry of Industrial Development (Ministerio de Desarrollo Industrial), 190
Molasses, 101, 106–09
Mongolia, 208
Monoculture, 11, 200
Morocco, 152
Most-favored-nation (MFN), 129
Mozambique, 192, 194

NAM. *See* Non-Aligned Movement
National Economic Council (Consejo Nacional de Economía), 58 Nationalization, 6, 9–11
Natural gas, 87
Netherlands, 93, 104, 173, 176
New International Economic Order (NIEO), 159, 160, 187
Newsprint. *See* Paper products
Nicaragua, 104, 161, 191–93, 214
Nickel, 204, 214
NIEO. *See* New International Economic Order
Nigeria, 192
Non-Aligned Movement (NAM), 187–88
North Korea, 143, 184

Oil, 78, 107; and bagasse, 82, 84, 103; domestic production of, 79; embargo of (1973), 108; and mills, 83–86; and refineries, 86–87, 99; Soviet imports of, 145, 150, 162; Soviet, reexport of, 213–14, 227
Opportunity costs, 163, 164, 165, 166, 167, 168, 214
Oriente province, 58
Orlando Nodarse mill, 99

Pablo Noriega mill, 105
Panama, 192, 197

Panchito Gómez Toro mill, 106; paper plant at, 103, 104
Paper products, 83, 103–05
Particleboard, 103, 105–06
People's Republic of China (PRC), 18, 19, 138; and preferential prices, 139, 143, 146, 184; prerevolutionary sales to, 136; and reexports, 221–22, 223, 224; and world market prices, 147
Permanent production brigades (brigadas permanentes de producción), 61
Peru, 176, 211
Philippines, 118, 133–34, 134, 160, 214
Poland, 136, 138, 176
Portugal, 177
PRC. *See* People's Republic of China
Preferential markets, 122; and the Soviet Union, 125, 127, 138, 139, 142, 145; and the United States, 127, 129, 132–35, 137, 139
Preferential prices: and the Soviet Union, 157, 158–60, 161; and the United States, 166, 167, 214, 217; and world market prices, 224, 225
Preston (Guatamala) mill, 103
Prices. *See* Minimum price indexation; Preferential prices; World market prices
Production: and cooperatives, 9, 10; cost of, compared to other sugar-producing countries, 117–20; cost of, prerevolutionary, 111–13; cost of, revolutionary, 113–17; decline of, 12; effect on other agricultural products of, 163; expansion of, 16–17; and export quota level, 182–83; and failure to meet projections, 15; investment in, 203–04; process of, 78; restrictions on, 174–76, 177; during wartime, 179
Prospective Plan for the Sugar Industry (1965–70), 13
Puerto Rico, 134

Quotas, 6, 9, 93, 132–35, 138, 176–77, 180–83, 186

Railroads, 87–88, 89–90, 90
Rationing, 97, 207
Raw-to-refined ratio, 95–96
Recession, 228
Reciprocity Agreement (1902), 4, 6, 129
Rectification Process, 11
Reexports, 161, 217–18, 220–24, 227
Refineries, 92–93, 96–97, 99; and oil consumption, 86–87; operating days per year of, 94–95
Refining capacity, 92–94, 96, 97
Research and development, 99–100
Rice, 204, 208
Risquet Valdés, Jorge, 64
Rodríguez, Carlos Rafael, 145, 225
Romania, 136, 138, 143
*Roya* (cane rust), 14
Rum, 107

Salaries and wages, 6, 57, 61–62, 75, 118, 119
Sancti Spíritus province, 103
Santiago de Cuba refinery, 96, 97
60 Aniversario de la Revolución de Octubre plant, 64
Skilled workers, 76–77
Smoot-Hawley Tariff Act (1930), 6, 132
*Sobre los Derivados de la Caña de Azúcar*, 99
Socialist countries, 17–19. *See also* Council for Mutual Economic Assistance; Soviet Union; *specific countries*
Somalia, 191–92, 197
South Africa, 118, 177
Soviet economic assistance. *See* Subsidies
Soviet Union, 17–18, 19, 93, 134, 208; below-market price sales to, 138; collaboration with on harvesting machinery, 63–66; and contract prices for other socialist countries, 146–47; disadvantage of trade with, 161–62; domestic sugar production of, 159; and freight costs, 147–49; imports from, 161–62; and International Sugar Agreements, 177, 181, 182, 186; long-term commercial agreement (1976–80) with, 145–46; and oil, 84, 145, 150, 162, 213–14, 227; and other sugar producing countries, 160–61; and preferential market, 122, 125, 127, 139, 142, 145; and preferential prices, 14, 157, 158–60, 161; prerevolutionary sales to, 135–37; and reexports, 218, 220–24; and subsidies, 214, 217–17, 227, 228; trade agreements with, 137–38, 142–44, 149, 157, 158
Spain, 3, 153, 167, 168, 214
Sri Lanka, 192, 197
St. Kitts, 118
State Committee on Economic Cooperation (Comité Estatal de Colaboración Económica), 190, 195
Subsidies, 158, 159, 163–65, 166–67; effect on trade statistics of, 214, 216–17; and market economies, 167–68, 171–72; and the United States, 134–35, 163, 165, 172
Suez crisis, 181
Sugar Act: (1934), 6, 132–33; (1937), 133; (1948), 135–39; amendments to, 134
Suriname, 211
System of National Accounts, 201

Tanzania, 192, 198
Tarafa Act (1927), 5, 176
Tariffs, 93, 129, 132
Taxes, 133
TECNOAZUCAR, 190–91, 192
Thailand, 118
Third World, 189–90. *See also specific countries*
*Tiempo muerto*, 58
Torralbas González, Diocles, 56
Torras, Jacinto, 180
Trade agreements: with the Soviet Union, 137–38, 142–44, 157, 158; and the world market, 152, 153–54
Trade unions, 57

Truck transportation, 88–89
Truslow Mission, 111, 113, 115, 116

UEMPROMEC. *See* Union de Empresas de Producción Mecánica
Uganda, 192, 198
Unconventional gains from trade, 158
UNCTAD. *See* United Nations Conference on Trade and Development
UNDP. *See* United Nations Development Program
Unemployment, 9, 11, 58
UNIDO. *See* United Nations Development Organization
Union de Empresas de Producción Mecánica (UEMPROMEC), 191
United Kingdom, 93, 152, 173
United Nations: Conference on Trade and Development (UNCTAD) of, 187, 211, 218; Development Program (UNDP) of, 105, 109; Food and Agriculture Organization of, 204; Group of 77 of, 187; Industrial Development Organization (UNIDO) of, 105, 226–27; Statistical Office of, 121; World Food Program of, 208
United States: dependence on, 3, 4, 7, 9; imports from, 58, 116; and International Sugar Agreements, 177, 180, 181–82, 183; and preferential market, 125, 127, 129, 132–35, 137, 139; and preferential prices, 214, 217; and quota regime (1934–1960), 6, 9, 93, 132–35, 138; and subsidies, 134–35, 163, 165, 172
United States Sugar Progam, 122

Uruguay, 211
Uruguay mill, 103

Venezuela, 211
Verdeja Act of May 1926, 174
Vietnam, 143, 184, 192, 198, 208
Virgin Islands, 134
Voluntary labor, 59, 60, 61, 116

Wax, 109
West Germany, 65, 93, 105, 152
Wheat, 207, 210
Workers' consumer cooperatives, 58
World Bank. *See* International Bank for Reconstruction and Development
World market prices, 100, 143, 158, 214; effect on economic performance of, 224, 225–28; fluctuations in, 124–25, 144, 145, 157, 161, 174, 183, 184; and high production, 5, 11, 132; and opportunity costs, 164, 165; and the People's Republic of China, 147; and production costs, 6, 116–17; and reexports, 217–18, 220, 221, 223–24; and the Soviet Union, 137–38, 139, 146, 149, 164–65; and trade agreements in the world market, 152, 153–54; and U.S. quotas, 135
World War I, 5, 132
World War II, 7, 107, 135, 173–74, 179

Yeast, 108–09
Yields, 14, 16; industrial, 15, 71–72, 76; *See also* Production
Youth Labor Army (Ejército Juvenil del Trabajo), 61
Yugoslavia, 136, 176, 184

Zaire, 192

# Pitt Latin American Series
*Cole Blasier,* Editor

ARGENTINA

Argentina Between the Great Powers, 1936–1946
*Guido di Tella and Cameron Watt,* Editors

Argentina in the Twentieth Century
*David Rock,* Editor

Argentina: Political Culture and Instability
*Susan Calvert and Peter Calvert*

Discreet Partners: Argentina and the USSR Since 1917
*Aldo César Vacs*

Juan Perón and the Reshaping of Argentina
*Frederick C. Turner and José Enrique Miguens,* Editors

The Life, Music, and Times of Carlos Gardel
*Simon Collier*

The Political Economy of Argentina, 1946–1983
*Guido di Tella and Rudiger Dornbusch,* Editors

BRAZIL

External Constraints on Economic Policy in Brazil, 1899–1930
*Winston Fritsch*

The Film Industry in Brazil: Culture and the State
*Randal Johnson*

The Manipulation of Consent: The State and Working-Class Consciousness in Brazil
*Youssef Cohen*

The Politics of Social Security in Brazil
*James M. Malloy*

Urban Politics in Brazil: The Rise of Populism, 1925–1945
*Michael L. Conniff*

COLOMBIA

Gaitán of Colombia: A Political Biography
Richard E. Sharpless

Roads to Reason: Transportation, Administration, and Rationality in Colombia
Richard E. Hartwig

CUBA

Cuba Between Empires, 1978–1902
Louis A. Pérez, Jr.

Cuba in the World
Cole Blasier and Carmelo Mesa-Lago, Editors

Cuba Under the Platt Amendment
Louis A. Pérez, Jr.

Cuban Studies, Vols. 16–20
Carmelo Mesa-Lago, Editor

The Economics of Cuban Sugar
Jorge F. Pérez-López

Intervention, Revolution, and Politics in Cuba, 1913–1921
Louis A. Pérez, Jr.

Lords of the Mountain: Social Banditry and Peasant Protest in Cuba, 1878–1918
Louis A. Pérez, Jr.

Revolutionary Change in Cuba
Carmelo Mesa-Lago, Editor

The United States and Cuba: Hegemony and Dependent Development, 1880–1934
Jules Robert Benjamin

MEXICO

The Expulsion of Mexico's Spaniards, 1821–1836
Harold Dana Sims

The Mexican Republic: The First Decade, 1823–1832
Stanley C. Green

Mexico Through Russian Eyes, 1806–1940
William Harrison Richardson

Oil and Mexican Foreign Policy
George W. Grayson

The Politics of Mexican Oil
George W. Grayson

Voices, Visions, and a New Reality: Mexican Fiction Since 1970
J. Ann Duncan

US POLICIES

The Hovering Giant: U.S. Responses to Revolutionary Change in Latin America
*Cole Blasier*

Illusions of Conflict: Anglo-American Diplomacy Toward Latin America
*Joseph Smith*

The United States and Cuba: Hegemony and Dependent Development, 1880–1934
*Jules Robert Benjamin*

The United States and Latin America in the 1980s: Contending Perspectives on a Decade of Crisis
*Kevin J. Middlebrook and Carlos Rico, Editors*

USSR POLICIES

Discreet Partners: Argentina and the USSR Since 1917
*Aldo César Vacs*

The Giant's Rival: The USSR and Latin America
*Cole Blasier*

Mexico Through Russian Eyes, 1806–1940
*William Harrison Richardson*

OTHER NATIONAL STUDIES

Beyond the Revolution: Bolivia Since 1952
*James M. Malloy and Richard S. Thorn, Editors*

Black Labor on a White Canal: Panama, 1904–1981
*Michael L. Conniff*

The Catholic Church and Politics in Nicaragua and Costa Rica
*Philip J. Williams*

The Origins of the Peruvian Labor Movement, 1883–1919
*Peter Blanchard*

The Overthrow of Allende and the Politics of Chile, 1964–1976
*Paul E. Sigmund*

Panajachel: A Guatemalan Town in Thirty-Year Perspective
*Robert E. Hinshaw*

Peru and the International Monetary Fund
*Thomas Scheetz*

Primary Medical Care in Chile: Accessibility Under Military Rule
*Joseph L. Scarpaci*

Rebirth of the Paraguayan Republic: The First Colorado Era, 1878–1904
*Harris G. Warren*

Restructuring Domination: Industrialists and the State in Ecuador
*Catherine M. Conaghan*

A Revolution Aborted: The Lessons of Grenada
*Jorge Heine, Editor*

SOCIAL SECURITY

Ascent to Bankruptcy: Financing Social Security in Latin America
*Carmelo Mesa-Lago*

The Politics of Social Security in Brazil
*James M. Malloy*

Social Security in Latin America: Pressure Groups, Stratification, and Inequality
*Carmelo Mesa-Lago*

OTHER STUDIES

Adventures and Proletarians: The Story of Migrants in Latin America
*Magnus Mörner, with the collaboration of Harold Sims*

Authoritarianism and Coporatism in Latin America
*James M. Malloy, Editor*

Authoritarians and Democrats: Regime Transition in Latin America
*James M. Malloy and Mitchell A. Seligson, Editors*

The Catholic Church and Politics in Nicaragua and Costa Rica
*Philip J. Williams*

Female and Male in Latin America: Essays
*Ann Pescatello, Editor*

Latin American Debt and the Adjustment Crisis
*Rosemary Thorp and Laurence Whitehead, Editors*

Public Policy in Latin America: A Comparative Survey
*John W. Sloan*

Selected Latin American One-Act Plays
*Francesca Collecchia and Julia Matas, Editors and Translators*

The Social Documentary in Latin America
*Julianne Burton, Editor*

The State and Capital Accumulation in Latin America. Vol. 1: Brazil, Chile, Mexico. Vol. 2: Argentina, Bolivia, Colombia, Ecuador, Peru, Uruguay, Venezuela
*Christian Anglade and Carlos Fortin, Editors*

Transnational Corporations and the Latin American Automobile Industry
*Rhys Jenkins*